W9-BWN-139

The Vendée

The Vendée

By CHARLES TILLY

HARVARD UNIVERSITY PRESS

Cambridge, Massachusetts, and London, England

Library of Congress Catalog Card Number 75-35483

ISBN 0-674-93300-1 (cloth)
ISBN 0-674-93302-8 (paper)

Printed in the United States of America

TO PITIRIM ALEXANDROVICH SOROKIN
MASTER SOCIOLOGIST

Preface

The Vendée was one of Europe's last great rural rebellions. There would be more: the Spanish insurrections which persisted into the twentieth century, the peasant movements which arose during the Russian Revolution, rural France's own massive resistance to Louis Napoleon's 1851 *coup d'état*, still others elsewhere. Nevertheless, the lineage of the Vendée was already declining in 1793. The family had been great. Among the ancestral portraits in the dark hall of rural rebellion, a curious visitor would find France's Jacquerie of 1358, England's Peasant Revolt of 1381, Bohemia's Hussite and Taborite rebellions in the 1420s, Germany's Peasant War of 1525. Although these ancients are recognizably of the lineage, details of the costume often give them an unfamiliar air; millenarian visions, egalitarian preaching, demands for freedom were paradoxically more characteristic of medieval than of modern rebellions.

The family resemblance to the Vendée would become more apparent as our imaginary visitor strolled by the great cluster of seventeenth-century canvases. In the French branch alone he would notice the Nu-Pieds, the Croquants, the Bonnets Rouges. There he would see many of the striking features of the Vendée's 1793 rebellion: its anti-bourgeois, anti-capitalist, anti-state animus, its mobilization of whole communities as communities, its reliance on nobles, priests, and professionals for almost all links and almost all leadership above the level of the single community. The Vendée came late, but did not lack a pedigree.

The apparent nineteenth-century dwindling of the rural rebellion was actually an intercontinental migration. As the rural rebellion disappeared in Europe, it swelled in Asia and Latin America. Nor was that simple coincidence. For the rural rebellion traced the rise of national states, markets, and bourgeois property. By the nineteenth century, national states, markets, and bourgeois property had triumphed over the privileges and liberties of rural communities in most of Europe. The European village's capacity to resist had collapsed. The same is true of most of North America. But in the rest of the world statemaking and the expansion of capitalism were proceeding apace. Where they encountered well-established rural communities and infringed the existing rights of those communities, rebellion ensued.

Not that all rural rebellions are alike. One of the most important lessons of recent research in rural history is that the grievances which lead to revolt are both concrete and variable. In contrast with an older picture of rural rebellions as unfocused reactions to hardship or to rapid social change, the last two decades' work on the subject has revealed a general pattern of response to specific violations of well-established rights. In Europe, and very likely in the rest of the world, new and intensified taxation has been the single most important stimulus to rural rebellion on a scale larger than the individual village. Tax rebellions have an important lesson to teach. On the surface, they seem like direct, uncomplicated reactions to misery. New taxes, one might think, are simply the last straw. On closer examination, however, rebellions turn out to focus on taxes which violate existing local rights and which threaten the rural community's ability to carry on its valued activities.

Tax rebellions do not break out most often or most ferociously where hardship is most acute. Really miserable people devote so much of their energy to survival that they have none left for revolt. In order to understand why the North American colonists mobilized massively to resist unjust taxes in the decade before the American Revolution, we have no need to invoke material hardship, clever manipulation, or short-sighted greed. We can even take the colonists' own word for it: they believed the new taxes imposed by the British violated American rights and principles of good government. So believing, they resisted the British assault on American rights.

The same general observation applies to other characteristic forms of rural rebellion: the food riot, the land occupation, anti-conscription movements. Their common denominator is the redress of specific violations of rural rights. In these cases the prior rights of the village to food produced or stored locally, to local land, to the labor power of its young men are at issue. When those rights are well established, when merchants or landlords or officials violate those rights, and when the village has enough organization and resources to resist, some form of rebellion occurs. The grievances are concrete, specific, well defined. Yet they vary from rebellion to rebellion just as the patterns of local rights and of exploitation vary from place to place.

I have written as though rural rebellions were always defensive, always reacting to someone else's disruption of the established order. "Always" overstates the case. For rural Europe over the last few centuries, defensive rebellions are the general rule, but not the iron law. Two crucial qualifications apply.

First, some rural rebellions which begin defensively change direction or become tied to a major movement of social or political transformation by allying with other groups of rebels, with different grievances, outside the rural area. In his *Peasant Wars of the Twentieth Century*, Eric Wolf has shown how a number of our era's greatest rural movements—including those of Russia, China, Mexico, and Viet Nam—began with a strong orientation to the redressing of local grievances, yet developed through the play of coalition and opposition into powerful forces for revolution. Wolf's analysis holds for rural participation in major European revolutions.

The second qualification is that genuine offensive, forward-looking move-ments asserting new rights rather than simply defending old ones *have* arisen in some rural areas, and have sometimes provided the bases of important rural rebellions. Spanish rural anarchism and Italian rural socialism are examples. In these cases and others like them the movements themselves began defensively, but had acquired a new offensive orientation before the point of rebellion. Again coalitions with outsiders, especially organized craftsmen and radical intelligentsia, have played a crucial part in the swing from defensive to offensive.

An inverse process worked itself out in the Vendée. A series of local conflicts which had much in common with the standard local conflicts of the old regime evolved and coalesced into a rebellion which was emphatically counter-revolutionary. This book traces the development of the counter-revolutionary movement from 1789 to 1793, and relates its pattern to the social structure of local communities in western France. It shows grievances similar to those which had long activated tax rebellions, food riots and anti-conscription movements becoming the fuel of a mass movement against the Revolution. Indeed, it shows grievances and forms of action which worked for the Revolution in other parts of rural France working powerfully for the counter-revolution in the Vendée.

The book's resolution of that contradiction is not the obvious one: that grievances and forms of action are simply irrelevant to the revolutionary or counter-revolutionary character of a rural movement—either because rural people absorb whatever specific grievances they have into their estab-lished world view or because manipulative leaders direct the diffuse anger of the countrymen to their own ends. Instead, the book implicitly invokes an old political principle: the enemy of my enemy is my friend. It portrays a coalition of peasants, rural artisans, priests, and nobles lining up in dif-ferent ways, at different times, for different reasons, against a bourgeoisie which had been gaining economic strength during the eighteenth century, and which rapidly seized control of the local and regional political apparatus during the early years of the Revolution. As they did elsewhere in France, the bourgeois who came to power in the Vendée received strong support from their fellow bourgeois in the national government. Unlike their counter-parts in most other regions, they lacked the allies and power base in the countryside to crush their enemies, neutralize the disaffected, and generate active support among the rest of the population. Why and how that happened are the book's central problems.

On its own ground, *The Vendée* has stood up well to the dozen years of scholarship and criticism which have passed since its publication. Subsequent scholarship has generally confirmed the conclusions of the book concerning its main area of concentration, southern Anjou. For example, C. Petitfrère's new analysis of the participants in the counter-revolution of 1793 adds evidence from post-revolutionary pension applications to the documents

from 1793 I had studied and examines both bodies of evidence closely;
Petitfrère comes to essentially the same conclusions concerning participation
as you will find in the book.

Scholarship concerning other counter-revolutionary sections of western
France has been less kind to any hopes for a simple extension of *The Vendée*'s
findings elsewhere; other students of the subject have confirmed the importance of local anti-bourgeois coalitions, but they have shown that those
who lined up against the rural bourgeoisie varied greatly depending on the
character of the region. In Brittany, for example, T. J. A. LeGoff and D. N. G.
Sutherland find that the entire rural community tended to oppose the "petty
notables" who opted for the Revolution.

The Vendée's critics have complained mainly about the book's analytic
framework and about its incompleteness. I deliberately cast the book as an
analysis of community structure, of urbanization, and of related political
processes. Some historians found that the definitions, analogies, models, and
reiterated arguments cluttered an otherwise intelligible analysis of the
counter-revolution. Many social scientists claimed that the emphasis on
urbanization distorted an otherwise interesting account of the political
impact of modernization, or centralization, or some other major social
process.

After years of reflection, I find myself unshaken on the first charge, but a
bit rueful on the second. Were I to rewrite the book today, I would be at
least as careful as before about definitions, analogies, models, and explicit
statement of arguments. An author aids his readers, including other students
of the same subject, by stating the nature of the problem, identifying the
connections he wants to make with existing work on that problem, and
laying out the criteria of proof and disproof he regards as appropriate.
The book's concern with concepts is correct.

I have, on the other hand, lost some of my confidence that urbanization
was the best possible analytical focus. The growing and changing influence
of cities unquestionably played an important part in shaping western France's
response to the Revolution. As I see it now, however, the emphasis on
urbanization obscures the influence in the Vendée of two other processes
which have strongly influenced the development of rural rebellions in the
western world: the expansion of capitalism and the concentration of power
in national states. Cities and urbanization have fundamental roles in both
processes. Too great a focus on urbanization (or too broad a definition of
urbanization) nevertheless draws attention away from the independent
effects of capitalism and statemaking. In the Vendée itself, it is valuable to
learn the place of cities and city-based merchants in the growth of the
cottage textile industry. It is also important to realize that the property
relations which developed were not those of "city" or "country" but of
classic mercantile capitalism.

As for the incompleteness of this book, I was the first to lament it. Scattered through the chapters you will find apologies that I was unable to carry out a more detailed analysis of changing property relations in eighteenth-century Anjou, of the revolutionary sale of church properties, of a number of other crucial topics. I regret now that the book says so little about the implications of what happened in the Vendée for our understanding of the course of the French Revolution as a whole. I would be happier if it contained a more sustained treatment of counter-revolutionary movements elsewhere in France during the same period. Any one of these improvements, however, would have added months or even years to the eight years it took me to prepare the book that actually appeared. It is not certain that the improvement would have justified the additional investment of time.

In the light of the excellent studies of rural history and rebellion which have been published since the appearance of *The Vendée*, some other problems which the book neglects now deserve attention. Let me mention only two examples.

First, where did the rural proletariat come from, and what was happening to it in the years before the rebellion? The book devotes quite a bit of space to documenting the importance of rural textile artisans in the Vendée's population and in the counter-revolution. It also shows in passing that something like a tenth of the adult male population consisted of essentially landless agricultural laborers. As studies of the proletarianization of the rural population in other parts of Europe begin to come in, it becomes clearer, however, that my treatment neglects a significant problem and a fine opportunity. Where did those landless workers come from? Was rapid population growth or the consolidation of land in the hands of noble and bourgeois propertyholders forcing the children of peasants to choose among emigrating, remaining single on their family farms, or taking up work as weavers or day-laborers? If so, we might better understand the pressures on the rural population at the start of the Revolution, and the cooperation of peasants and artisans in the counter-revolutionary movement.

Again, the book neglects the daring expansion of the central government the French revolutionaries sought to accomplish from 1791 to 1793. Not only did they integrate the structure of the Catholic Church into that of the French government (a stormy process which the book does discuss in detail), but also they made the unprecedented step of extending the purview of the national government to everyday life at the local scale. Although Louis XIV had gained a great reputation as a state-builder and his successors continued the work of centralization, their efforts to penetrate local communities had been partial, tentative, and often unsuccessful. They had succeeded mainly in the realm of taxation — and even there the method of collecting the major taxes was to assign a quota to the whole community and let the local council do the assessing and collecting. For the rest, a kind of indirect rule via local landlords, priests, and professionals subordinated the rural community to the sovereign.

The substitution of direct for indirect local rule has happened many times and in many places since 1789. It is a process which has repeatedly produced conflict in European colonies both before and after independence. Revolutionary France was the first large western country to try it on a national scale. This book describes the impact of that effort on local elections, religious practice, routine record-keeping, and a number of other activities. But it does not seriously analyze the technical and political conditions under which the effort could succeed. Studies of the Terror in other parts of France, for example, bring out the widespread use (whether intentional or unintentional) of two interim solutions: first, mobilizing the local population against a small number of presumed enemies of the Revolution; second, substituting indirect rule via local networks of trusted bourgeois for indirect rule via priests and nobles.

Proletarianization and state centralization are important problems on which *The Vendée* touches, but only touches. There are others: the nature of revolutionary leadership, the roots of violence, the effects of repression, the rise and fall of political rights. Yes, *The Vendée* leaves a large agenda unfulfilled. Let me take refuge in a self-serving homily: a good book opens doors, and makes people want to enter them. If *The Vendée* opens the way to places other people want to explore, that will be reason enough for its writing.

C. T.

October, 1975

Selected References Since 1964

Accati, L. "Vive le roi sans taille et sans gabelle: una discussione sulle rivolte contadine," *Quaderni Storici*, 7 (September–December, 1972), 1071–1104.

Ardant, Gabriel. *Théorie sociologique de l'impôt*. Paris: SEVPEN, 1965. 2 vols.

Bercé, Yves-Marie. *Histoire des Croquants*. Paris: Droz, 1974. 2 vols.

—— Croquants et Nu-Pieds. Paris: Gallimard/Julliard, 1974. Collection "Archives."

Blok, Anton. *The Mafia of a Sicilian Village*. New York: Harper & Row, 1974.

Calvert, Peter. *A Study of Revolution*. Oxford: Clarendon Press, 1970.

Davis, Natalie Zemon. *Society and Culture in Early Modern France*. Stanford: Stanford University Press, 1975.

Dunn, John. *Modern Revolutions*. Cambridge: Cambridge University Press, 1972.

Fletcher, Anthony. *Tudor Rebellions*. London: Longmans, 1968.

Gratton, Philippe. *Les luttes de classes dans les campagnes*. Paris: Anthropos, 1971.

Hilton, Rodney. *Bond Men Made Free. Medieval Peasant Movements and the English Rising of 1381*. London: Temple Smith, 1973.

Hobsbawm, E. J., and George Rudé. *Captain Swing: A Social History of the Great Agrarian Uprising of 1830*. New York: Pantheon, 1968.

Hoerder, Dirk. *People and Mobs: Crowd Action in Massachusetts during the American Revolution, 1765–1780*. Berlin: privately printed, 1971.

Huizer, Gerrit. *Peasant Rebellion in Latin America*. Harmondsworth: Penguin, 1973.

Landsberger, Henry A., ed. *Rural Protest: Peasant Movements and Social Change*. London: Macmillan, 1974.

LeGoff, T. J. A., and D. M. G. Sutherland. "The Revolution and the Rural Community in Eighteenth-Century Brittany," *Past and Present*, 62 (1974), 916–119.

Lewis, John Wilson, ed. *Peasant Rebellion and Communist Revolution in Asia*. Stanford: Stanford University Press, 1974.

Lida, Clara E. *Anarquismo y revolución en la España del XIX*. Madrid: Siglo, 1972.

Lucas, Colin. *The Structure of the Terror. The Example of Javogues and the Loire*. London: Oxford University Press, 1973.

Mazauric, Claude. *Sur la Révolution française*. Paris: Editions Sociales, 1970.

Mitchell, Harvey. "The Vendée and Counterrevolution: A Review Essay," *French Historical Studies*, 5 (autumn, 1968), 405–429.

Mollat, Michel and Philippe Wolff. *Ongles bleus, Jacques et Ciompi. Les Révolutions populaires en Europe aux XIVe et XVe siècles*. Paris: Calmann-Levy, 1970.

Moore, Barrington, Jr. *Social Origins of Dictatorship and Democracy. Lord and Peasant in the Making of the Modern World*. Boston: Beacon, 1966.

Mousnier, Roland. *Fureurs paysannes: Les paysans dans les révoltes du XVIIe siècle (France, Russie, Chine)*. Paris: Calmann-Levy, 1967.

Peacock, A. J. *Bread or Blood: The Agrarian Riots in East Anglia, 1816*, London: Gollancz, 1965.

Petitfrère, C. "Les grandes composantes sociales des armées vendéennes d'Anjou," *Annales historiques de la Révolution française*, January–March 1973: 1–20.

Scheiner, Irwin. "The Mindful Peasant: Sketches for a Study of Rebellion," *Journal of Asian Studies*, 32 (August 1973), 579–591.

Shelton, Walter James. *English Hunger and Industrial Disorders*. London: Macmillan, 1973.

Soldani, S. "Contadini, operai e 'popolo' nella rivoluzione del 1848–49 in Italia," *Studi Storici*, no. 3, 1973: 557–613.

Stevenson, J. "Food Riots in England, 1792–1818." In R. Quinault and J. Stevenson, eds., *Popular Protest and Public Order*. London: George Allen & Unwin, 1974.

Thompson, E. P. "The Moral Economy of the English Crowd in the Eighteenth Century," *Past and Present*, 50 (1971), 76–136.

———— " 'Rough Music': Le Charivari anglais," *Annales; Economies, Sociétés, Civilisations*, 27 (1972), 285–312.

Tilly, Charles. "Food Supply and Public Order in Modern Europe." In Charles Tilly, ed., *The Formation of National States in Western Europe*. Princeton: Princeton University Press, 1975.

———— "Revolutions and Collective Violence." In Fred I. Greenstein and Nelson Polsby, eds., *Handbook of Political Science*. Reading, Mass.: Addison-Wesley, 1975. Vol. III.

———— Louise Tilly, and Richard Tilly. *The Rebellious Century, 1830–1930*. Cambridge: Harvard University Press, 1975.

Tilly, Louise A. "The Food Riot as a Form of Political Conflict in France," *Journal of Interdisciplinary History*, 2 (1971), 23–57.

Wallerstein, Immanuel. *The Modern World-System. Capitalist Agriculture and the Origins of the European World-Economy in the Sixteenth Century*. New York: Academic, 1974.

Wolf, Eric. *Peasant Wars of the Twentieth Century*. New York: Harper & Row, 1969.

Acknowledgments

Many people and many organizations helped me make this book. The Social Science Research Council, the American Council of Learned Societies, the Faculty Research Committee of the University of Delaware, and the University of Delaware Library Associates all helped finance the necessary research, and Princeton's Center of International Studies gave me the leisure to complete the manuscript. Maître Guy Fleury of Chemillé, MM. Gilles de Maupéou and André Barré of Nantes, Professor Joseph Sonnenfeld of the University of Delaware, M. d'Herbécourt, Chief Archivist of Maine-et-Loire, M. Bernier and Mlle. Héno, his two associates, the abbé Tricoire, archivist of the bishopric of Angers, and a number of my students at the University of Delaware — notably Nancy Lambert, Roger Kelsey, and Patricia Mackey — contributed in various indispensable ways to the gathering and analysis of data. The staffs of the Archives Nationales (Paris), of the departmental archives of Indre-et-Loire (Tours), Vendée (la Roche-sur-Yon), and Loire-Atlantique (Nantes) also lent kind assistance.

I am grateful to the Librairie Armand Colin for permission to quote from *Le Bas-Maine*, by René Musset (1917), and *Tableau politique de la France de l'Ouest sous la troisième république*, by André Siegfried (1913), to Professor Paul Bois for permission to quote from his *Paysans de l'Ouest* (1960), and to the editors of *French Historical Studies* for permission to draw on material from two of my articles published in that journal: "Civil Constitution and Counter-Revolution in Southern Anjou" (1959) and "Local Conflicts in the Vendée before the Rebellion of 1793" (1961).

When it comes to advice, criticism, and encouragement, the list of bene-factors is even longer. George C. Homans and Barrington Moore, Jr., shared the burden of directing my dissertation, and kept on helping after it was finished. Laurence Wylie and a whole host of his students, by their informed responses to my work and by their own exciting research on western France, have offered an unending stimulation to my investigations of the Vendée.

The members of a delightful special seminar held at Harvard during the summer of 1961 — Samuel Beer, Norman Birnbaum, William Chambers, Harry Eckstein, Klaus Epstein, George Nadel, Melvin Richter, and Michael Walzer — successfully challenged many an ambiguity in the formulations and findings. At the University of Delaware, my colleagues R. K. Burns, Jr., Roger Hahn, Walther Kirchner, Arnold Feldman, F. B. Parker, and Irwin Goffman devoted their considerable talents to the criticism of many drafts and fragments of this study. At Princeton, Robert Palmer, Gil Alroy, Karl Von Vorys, and Klaus Knorr helped me through the last stages of the book. Among the many French scholars who have generously aided this study, Marcel Faucheux, François Lebrun, Paul Bois, and Louis Merle deserve special mention.

My wife, Louise, not only bore with me through the seemingly interminable preparation of this study, not only surveyed its progress with her exceptional combination of perseverance, deftness, and high intelligence, but also did a very important part of the verifying, counting, tallying, and editing. To her and to all, my deepest thanks.

Contents

Chapter 1 · Introduction   1

The Counterrevolution in Capsule   2
The Traditional History of the Vendée   6
A Sociological View   9
Prospectus   14

Chapter 2 · Urbanization in Western France   16

The Idea of Urbanization   16
The Idea Applied to France   20
The West   26

Chapter 3 · Cities and Subregions of Southern Anjou   38

Southern Anjou   38
Cities   42
City Life   48
Town and Country   53

Chapter 4 · Rural Communities and Classes   58

Variation and Differentiation in Communities   59
Subdivisions of Southern Anjou's Communities   65
Land   73
Poverty   77
A Review of Class Structure   79

Chapter 5 · The Rural Neighborhood   82

Layout   83
Marriage   88
General Patterns of Affiliation   98

Chapter 6 · Curés and Clericalism   100

Parish Organization   100
The Curé   103
Religious Relations   110

Contents

Chapter 7 · Rustic Economics   113

The Agricultural Complex   114
The Control of Land   119
The Industrial Complex   132
Consequences   140

Chapter 8 · Power   146

Political Modernization in Southern Anjou   147
Change and Conflict   156

Chapter 9 · Revolution   159

The Revolution of 1789   159
The West's Experience   162
Response to the Revolution   167
Local Attitudes toward the Revolution   175
Statements of Grievances   177
Military Service   186
Emigration   192
The First Year of Revolution   195

Chapter 10 · Revolutionary Economics   199

Changes in Economic Policy   200
Sales of Church Property   203
Effects in the Two Complexes   212
Textile Troubles   215
Political Consequences   223

Chapter 11 · Religion in Revolution   227

Ecclesiastical Politics and Political Ecclesiastics   228
The Clergy's Choice   231
The Civil Constitution   233
The New Clergies   242
Refractory Religion   252
Control of the Refractories   257
Subregional Contrasts   260

Chapter 12 · The Political Crisis   263

The Revolution's New Politics   263
In the Commune   273
Divisions by Class   279
Modes of Party Conflict   282
Some Local Cases   290

Chapter 13 · Counterrevolution   305

Anticipations 306
Conscription and its Aftermath 308
The Coalescence of Local Rebellions 316
Who Were the Antagonists? 320
The Warriors and their Warfare 331
Putting Down the Rebellion 336
Final Thoughts 339

Appendix A · Procedure for Estimating Occupational
    Distribution   345

Appendix B · Occupational Classification Scheme   348

Appendix C · Textile Production in the Mauges   350

List of Writings Cited   353

Index   365

Tables

1. *Urban population, by district* — 45
2. *Ecclesiastical population and revenue, by district* — 47
3. *Occupations of adult males in three communities of southern Anjou* — 66
4. *Class distribution in three communities* — 67
5. *Estimated occupational distribution for rural communes of southern Anjou, by district* — 69
6. *Estimates of land ownership for sections of southern Anjou* — 74
7. *Estimated proportion of nobles, by district* — 76
8. *Local endogamy, by district* — 89
9. *Local distribution of marriages, by occupational class* — 90
10. *Intermarriage index for communities of southern Anjou* — 95
11. *Gross income of curé of St. Macaire, 1790* — 106
12. *Percentages of total land, according to use* — 114
13. *General position of Grievances, by district* — 178
14. *Taxes: percent of statements mentioning the Grievance, by district* — 179
15. *Government: percent of statements mentioning the Grievance, by district* — 180
16. *Lords: percent of statements mentioning the Grievance, by district* — 182
17. *Clergy: percent of statements mentioning the Grievance, by district* — 184
18. *Enlistments, by district, 1791–1793* — 189
19. *Occupational distribution of recruits, 1792* — 190
20. *Emigrants, by district* — 194
21. *Value of textile production, in livres, 1786–1790* — 216
22. *Number of curés affected by income changes under the Civil Constitution* — 234
23. *Percent of clergy taking the oath* — 241
24. *Occupational distribution of cantonal representatives, 1789–1792* — 271
25. *Occupational distribution of active citizens in the canton of Chemillé* — 291
26. *Executions in the Vendée, during the Terror* — 322
27. *Comparisons of rebel rosters with estimates of occupational distribution* — 326
28. *Occupational distribution of men named as bearing arms, by type of source* — 326
29. *Occupational distribution of men named as bearing arms, by district* — 327
30. *Occupational distributions of different types of participants in the counterrevolution* — 328
31. *Cloth marked at bureaux de marque of southern Anjou, 1752–1790* — 351

Figures

1. *Western France in 1790*   3
2. *Southern Anjou*   43
3. *Le Petit Foüy*   82
4. *Patterns of Occupational Intermarriage in Southern Anjou*   97
5. *Mean Income of Curés of Southern Anjou in 1790, by Canton*   107
6. *Cantonal Distribution of Winegrowing in Southern Anjou, 1880*   117
7. *Value of Textile Production, 1753–1790*   134
8. *Estimated Proportion of Textile Artisans in Cantons of Southern Anjou,*
   1780–1790   138
9. *The 1791 Ecclesiastical Oath in Southern Anjou*   238
10. *The 1791 Oath in the Area of the Rebellion*   240

CHAPTER 1

Introduction

In 1793 a great uprising in the West of France threatened the very life of the Revolution. Country people in adjacent sections of Poitou, Anjou, and Brittany seized staves, scythes, pitchforks, and muskets, then joined to attack the forces of the Republic. They remained masters of their territory for more than six months, and a threat to the authority of successive political regimes in the West for more than six years. We call the uprising of 1793 and its aftermath the War of the Vendée, the Vendée counterrevolution, or more simply, the Vendée.

The memory of the Vendée has never stopped inspiring histories in great volume and variety. In the minds of its many devotees it looms as large as the Civil War does in the United States. No doubt there is room in their enthusiasm, as well as in the technical literature of the Revolution as a whole, for new and more accurate general accounts of the Vendée. But this book says very little about what happened once the counterrevolution began. Instead, it fixes on the nature of eighteenth-century society in the West and on local developments between the coming of the Revolution in 1789 and the outbreak of the counterrevolution in 1793.

I have reversed the usual recipe, one part background to ten parts military history, out of a triple interest: in the effects of modernization on rural areas, in the sources of resistance to the Revolution, and in the origins of the Vendée. These interests have much more to do with each other than is apparent at first glance. They keep overlapping, intertwining, melting into each other; when we come to that trenchant question, "Why the Vendée, and not somewhere else?" we shall find that they are indistinguishable. Because these concerns have brought the book into being, most of its pages deal with events and social arrangements before the great rebellion. Even here, however, it may be useful to begin with a review of the events that made the Vendée memorable.

The Counterrevolution in Capsule

The counterrevolution known as the Vendée began in mid-March, 1793, breaking out almost simultaneously in several parts of the area between Nantes, La Rochelle, Poitiers, and Angers. Although observers were astonished at the rapidity, force, and apparent spontaneity of the uprising, it was the climax of four years of growing tension. As elsewhere, in the West the convocation of the Estates General, proclaimed late in 1788, caused great commotion. The establishment of Provincial Assemblies in 1787 had already helped form the nuclei of revolutionary parties; the local and regional meetings of 1789 crystallized the "bourgeois" and "noble" factions. Although the people of some of the West — especially the cities — received the Revolution quite eagerly, resistance to political change soon developed in the rural areas south of the Loire. The sale of church property caught the enthusiasm of only a few, and the Revolutionary reorganization of the church aroused widespread opposition. The parish clergy were soon uniformly opposed to the Revolution, and the great majority of their parishioners stood with them.

In 1791 and 1792, numerous local incidents — meetings, processions, even armed attacks — showed the growing restiveness of local feeling. Most of these fracases involved the priests named to replace those who had not accepted the church reforms, and almost all of them showed that the officials charged with local administration lacked the confidence and support of the rural population.

For many of their troubles, the administrators blamed the rebellious clergy. As a result, law was piled upon law to control the clergy, until the climax of August, 1792: the decree of immediate deportation of all priests who had refused the oath of submission. But with the deportation of a large portion of the nonconformist clergy and the disappearance of the rest into hiding, agitation only grew. The Revolutionary chiefs in the Vendée were talking fearfully of counterrevolution long before March, 1793. In fact, six months before then their fears were justified by a full-scale attack on Bressuire and Châtillon (in the department of Deux-Sèvres), an attack foreshadowing the counterrevolution in both motives and personnel.

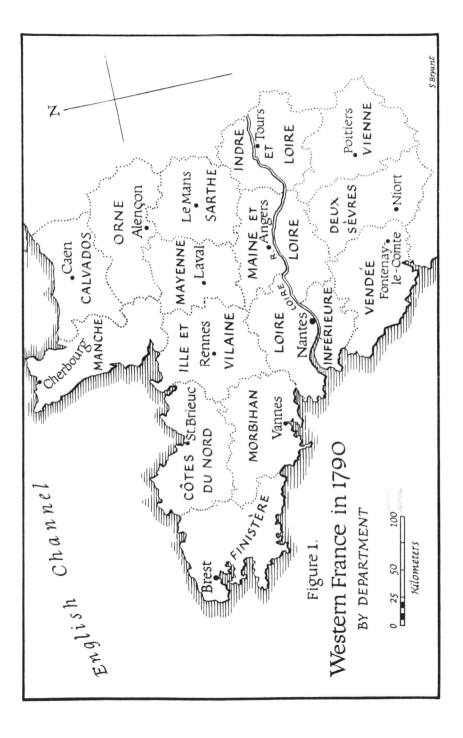

English Channel

N

Cherbourg

MANCHE

Caen
CALVADOS

Brest

FINISTÈRE

CÔTES
DU NORD

St.Brieuc

MORBIHAN

Vannes

ORNE
Alençon

MAYENNE
Laval

ILLE ET
Rennes
VILAINE

LOIRE
Nantes
INFÉRIEURE

LE Mans
SARTHE

MAINE ET
Angers
R. LOIRE

LOIRE

INDRE
ET
Tours
LOIRE

DEUX
SÈVRES
Niort

POITIERS
VIENNE

VENDÉE
Fontenay-
le-Comte

Figure 1.

Western France in 1790

BY DEPARTMENT

0   25   50   100

Kilometers

S.Bryant

The great rebellion came in short order. The government's call for 300,000 men to meet the menace on France's frontiers caused bitter agitation in the Vendée. The publication of the call to arms in the first days of March, 1793, was the signal for armed demonstrations, rioting, disarmament of patriots, and the flight into the country of the young men eligible for service.

For the first few days of March, everything rumbled, but nothing exploded. Riots at Cholet on the 4th cost a few lives, without becoming open warfare. On the 11th, 12th, and 13th everything seemed to blow up at once. At St. Florent, Chanzeaux, Machecoul, and Challans, armed troops appeared to the ringing of the tocsin, shouting of war and vengeance. The rebellion soon found leaders, and rapidly swept the region.

It would be an exaggeration to say the rebels stormed and took towns in the first days of the rebellion: they swarmed over them unresisted. By the fifth day, they had moved into St. Florent, Tiffauges, Beaupréau, Montaigu, Mortagne, Chemillé, Cholet, Challans, La Roche-sur-Yon, Clisson, La Roche-Bernard, Vihiers — almost every important town in the whole region. By that time the rebel mass had not only a name (the Catholic, or Catholic and Royal, Army) but also a body of recognized leaders (Bonchamp, d'Elbée, Stofflet, many others).

There were three stages in the great war of 1793: 1) rebel expansion (until the end of June), 2) check and attrition (until mid-October), 3) flight (until year's end). The dividing points are the defeats of the Vendeans at Nantes (29 June) and at Cholet (17 October).

Rebel expansion was in fact fairly well contained after the first few weeks of the revolt. After that, it was basically a tale of capture, relinquishment, and recapture of cities along the borders of the Vendée, culminating in the taking of Saumur (9 June) and of Angers (12 June). The Vendeans did not occupy these cities; they took them, sacked them, organized shadowy provisional governments, then decamped. During all this period the Republican government was changing plans, placing and replacing generals, shouting treason, sending investigatory missions, generally failing to meet the rebellion firmly and directly.

During the period of check and attrition, after the failure of the Vendean attempt to take Nantes, the Republicans became more decisive and more successful. Never again did the rebels carry an important victory outside their own territory. The high command of the Catholic and Royal Army increased in organization and decreased in daring. The gradual encirclement and exhaustion of the Vendeans ended in their defeat at Cholet, which drove the despairing rebels into exile north of the Loire.

Then came flight: the hopes of the counterrevolution were broken, the armies shattered. In a blind drive up to Granville, "to meet the English," the rebels — now an inchoate mass of men, women, children, carts, animals, household goods — entered and then left Laval, Mayenne, and Avranches. Turned away at Granville, the remaining fragments moved back toward the Loire. They were repulsed at Angers, but still were able to take La Flèche and then Le Mans. After trying to recross the Loire into their homeland, the remaining Vendeans were smashed at Savenay just before Christmas. That was the end of the great war.

It was not, however, the end of the Vendée. The remaining leaders patched together an army that troubled the Republicans for another year. This "second war" ended with an amnesty and the treaty of La Jaunais (February, 1795), but soon after, the leaders — spurred by promises of aid from *émigrés* and English — began again. Moving only from disaster to disaster, they were quieted definitively by March, 1796. Neither of these insurrections, nor any of those to follow, approached the first war in magnitude.

North of the Loire, the Vendée left more than a memory. About the time the rebel remnants were wandering in that neighborhood, late in 1793, *Chouannerie* began. The Chouans were guerrilla bands, aiming to harass the Republicans whenever and however possible. In its mood and its personnel, Chouannerie had a great deal in common with the more general warfare south of the Loire. But it was more varied in form, on a smaller scale; it flourished (unlike the great counterrevolution) in Brittany, Maine, Normandy, and northern Anjou.

Militarily, Chouannerie has almost no history. Its heyday was the period 1794–1796, but it might be said to begin with incidents in 1791 and to end with the collapse of the Republic. The height of its menace, as well as the point of its disintegration, was the disastrous landing of the émigrés at Quiberon (Brittany) in July, 1795. Even before then, these right-bank rebels were not one group but two: a body of high-ranking leaders busy with plots, missions, organization plans, and messages to Britain, and the mass of independently active local partisans. As the organizations disintegrated (particularly after 1796), sheer banditry loomed larger and larger in the motives of the Chouans.

Even south of the Loire, rebellion was not stilled forever in 1796. France heard of the Vendée again in 1799, 1815, and 1832. In 1799, it was a weakened imitation of the earlier revolts; in 1815, a confused protest during the Hundred Days; in 1832, an ill-conceived Legitimist uprising. Each of these later rebellions was a small-scale affair, agitated by a single small group with specific political aims. It is the great explosion of 1793 that interests us; the later troubles were consequences, reflections, imitations of '93, but not its equals.

The Traditional History of the Vendée

With such a splendid series of adventures, it is not surprising that there is a rich folklore and an abundant literature concerning the Vendée; Balzac, Hugo, Dumas, Scott, Trollope, Michelet, Carlyle, and Taine all devoted melodramatic pages to its pageantry. It is not even surprising that scholars and laymen alike continue to argue their favorite heroes, battles, and causes. Yet the importance of the counterrevolution is not simply that it was colorful. It is an essential part of the history of the Revolution itself. In 1793, Bertrand Barère called it "the political fire consuming the heart of the nation" (Walter 1953: 225).[1] In the opinion of Albert Mathiez (1954: II, 201), the counterrevolution had the "gravest consequences for the further development of the Revolution." Charles Seignobos (1934: 359) saw in the counterrevolution and the events that led to it the origin of one of the fundamental divisions in subsequent French politics, the division between the "Patriot" East and the "counterrevolutionary" West. And Alphonse Aulard (1910: II, 306) declared, "It is a classic saying, but a true one, that the Republic was stabbed in the back by La Vendée while the foreign armies and the émigrés attacked her in front." For these reasons alone the systematic study of the counterrevolution promises real rewards.

On first inspection, the Vendée does not seem very difficult to

[1] Citations in this form refer to the List of Writings Cited at the end of the book.

explain. Peasants opposed the Revolution. Why? The easiest answer is to stuff a standard mentality and a standard set of motives into the skulls of all the peasants of the region, preparing the mentality and motives mainly from general ideas of peasant character and the motives that could have opposed people to the Revolution (see Tilly 1963). The analyst's attitude toward the Revolution as a whole is likely to govern his choice of appropriate motives.

The assumption of this procedure is that the counterrevolution was the result of the mental state of the peasantry at the point of rebellion, and that the causes one must look for are those influences or events which brought about that mental state. As evidence of the mental state, the historian may take the observations of witnesses and the statements of the rebels themselves. Tradition has called for the recognition of only a few possible "motives" for the counterrevolution: 1) royalism, 2) resistance to conscription, 3) support of religion (variously called "fidelity," "fanaticism," and "subservience"), 4) self-interest among the leaders, plus uncritical loyalty among the bulk of the rebels (see Bois 1960b: 579–594). Each writer has made his choice among these "motives," or offered some combination of them.

There was no great delay in assigning causes to the counterrevolution. By the year III, Lequinio, a member of the Convention, was declaring:

The first causes of that disastrous war are known; 1. the ignorance, fanaticism and subservience of the country people; 2. the pride, wealth and perfidy of the former nobles; 3. the criminality and hypocrisy of the priests; 4. the weakness of the government administration, the special interests of the administrators and their illegal favors to their relatives, farmers and friends (Year III: 10–11).

The assertion that the causes of the counterrevolution are well known is among the most common introductions to its histories. Nevertheless, it is precisely on this question of motivation that the great debates on the Vendée have arisen.

The thesis of *royalism* has taken this form: the peasants were oppressed by the new regime and shocked by the abolition of the monarchy and the death of the king, so they revolted. As can well be imagined, only writers strongly identified with both the nobility and the counterrevolution have presented this theory in pure form (e.g., de Beauchamp, 1820; Lucas de la Championnière, 1904; Poirier de Beauvais, 1893).

Conscription, on the other hand, is a relatively nonpartisan cause. It has occasionally been used to suggest that the motives of the peasants were not so lofty as lyricists of the counterrevolution have claimed. Said Édouard Lockroy (1893: vi) "At first, the Vendeans fought neither for God nor for the King. They simply revolted against the fatherland; they did not want conscription." On the other hand, their distaste for military service has also been taken as a sign of the peasants' unwillingness to serve the evil Republic, or as evidence of their homely attachment to their native soil (e.g., Baguénier-Desormeaux, 1916; de Romain n.d.).

The various forms of the *religion* thesis have been the most popular, but with a different significance for clerical and anticlerical writers. The diligent abbé Uzureau published two journals (*Anjou historique* and *Andegaviana*) almost singlehandedly for over forty years, and the most persistent theme in those journals remained the spontaneous defense of wronged religion by the peasants of Anjou in 1793. The anticlerical approach has likewise attributed the peasant's position to his attachment to religion, but has emphasized the blindness and folly of that attachment (e.g., Bonnemère, 1866; Dubreuil, 1929–1930; Savary, 1824). A special version of the religion thesis is the argument that the peasants were attached less to religion in general than to their own parish priests. This, too, is an argument which can be turned for or against the Revolution, since such attachment can be called either "loyalty" or "servility."

This last version of the argument for religion as a motive is only one step from the more complex analysis which separates the mentalities of leaders and followers. It generally assigns self-interest to the leaders (priests and nobles, in varying combinations), but accounts for the participation of the great mass of the rebels on the grounds of their uncritical loyalty, or gullibility. There are several variations possible in this thesis, depending on how much concerted preparation for counterrevolution one discerns among the priests and nobles. In this respect, one may speak of 1) their general influence, 2) their agitation, or 3) a plot. Sound and sensible Léon Dubreuil (1929–1930: I, 20) decided that ultimately the clergy, "hungry for theocracy," was to blame for the counterrevolution. Eugène Bonnemère, not noted for his soundness or sensibility, averred that: "the nobles and the clergy pushed the peasant into the excesses and unheard-of hardships of a total war so that he would continue to pay the one the tithe and the other the corvée, and, thanks to his ignorance, the peasant went along, thinking he fought for religion and a threatened social order" (1866: 19). And a traditional formula has been the far-flung noble plot originating in Brittany: "At the beginning of the Revolution a vast and formidable royalist conspiracy developed in Brittany . . . composed of the nobility of that country and of the neighboring provinces. Its branches spread through all the West of France" (Jeanvrot 1894: 2). This theory, I need hardly add, has been the exclusive property of writers favoring the Revolution.

What unites these various explanations of the Vendée is that they all claim to identify the motives, by and large, the conscious motives at that, of the participants in the rebellion of March, 1793. No doubt every reconstruction of historical events implies some propositions about human motives; no doubt part of the historian's burden is to describe the motives of participants in crucial actions of the past. Yet it is possible to shift the emphasis. One may begin with questions about the organization and composition of the groups that supported the Revolution and the counterrevolution, about the relations among the principal segments of the population before and during the Revolution, about the connection between the rapid, drastic changes of Revolution and counterrevolution and the more general, more gradual social changes going on in eighteenth-century France. These questions occur naturally to a sociologist faced with an ebullient social movement. These questions have guided my inquiry into the origins of the Vendée.

A Sociological View

A concern with social organization calls for a comparative approach. We need a systematic comparison of the counterrevolutionary West with those sections of France that supported the Revolution. Such a comparison ought to include at least three elements: 1) most generally, the ways in which those major social changes which prepared France for revolution had affected the Vendée and the revolutionary segments of the country; 2) the major divisions of the population and the relations among them; 3) the organization, composition, and relations of the parts of the population that supported the Revolution, and those that resisted it. There is one more essential part of the analysis of the Vendée which does not require so direct a comparison: 4) the relationship between events before 1793 and the counterrevolutionary outbreak itself. These are the four problems one ought to solve in dealing with the Vendée.

This way of posing the problem of revolution and counterrevolution has a special virtue. It makes it easier to see the relevance for the Vendée of a great deal of sociological thinking on the nature of rural society and of social change. Applying the findings and formulations of contemporary studies to the society of eighteenth-century France clarifies some features of its revolutionary history. And contemporary studies suggest some useful comparisons with societies far removed from France. The reciprocal process is also rewarding. If we bring together the conclusions of modern observers and the facts of the French Revolution, we have a chance to judge the generality of those conclusions, and perhaps to modify them as well. At the very least, this procedure offers the adventure of posing outlandish questions about familiar matters. Outlandish questions often expose unsuspected ignorance, as well as inspiring sudden understanding.

Two lines of thinking about modern society form the frame of this analysis of the Vendée. The first concerns the set of broad social changes which has commonly accompanied the growth in size and influence of cities — the process of urbanization. The second deals with the organization of rural communities. Since I shall have to present detailed discussions of these matters in later chapters, there is no need here to do more than state the themes.

The growth of the size, number, and influence of cities is only one cluster in a set of changes that have occurred together in the growth of modern societies. I shall call the whole set of the changes "urbanization," but not out of any conviction that the growth of cities *causes* all the rest. There are three strong reasons for choosing this term for use in the present study over its chief competitor, "industrialization." First, despite the close correlation between industrial expansion and urban growth in recent years, in the past

there have been other important centralizing activities than industrialization, which have stimulated city growth together with a
number of the other social changes we shall discuss. Second, the
term "industrialization" casts a queer, anachronistic light on the
economic changes going on in most of France during the eighteenth
century. Finally, the emphasis on "urbanization" will draw our
attention to changes whose earliest and strongest effects appeared in
the cities of the West, and to the special importance of activities
based in the cities of that region. Nevertheless, the reader will undoubtedly recognize in the discussion of urbanization a reformula-
tion of many themes — the growth of large-scale, centralized activities, increasing differentiation, the development of rationalized,
impersonal rules of conduct, and so on — that he has noticed elsewhere under the headings of "industrialization," "modernization,"
"centralization," "rationalization," or "the growth of the nation-
state."

The first big task of this study is to show how the set of changes
called urbanization affected the social organization of western France.
The crucial questions will concern the differences in the ways urbanization affected various regions and segments of the population of
the West.

A general view of urbanization serves very well in the analysis of
the relationship between general features of the social organization
of western France and the nature of its response to the Revolution.
But it leaves out the means by which general social changes touch
the individual. It is convenient to deal with this part of the analysis
through a conception of community organization. The immense
majority of the citizens of the West lived in rural, predominantly
peasant, communities. I shall stress the divisions and relationships
within the rural community, and the ways they varied from one
type of community to another, from region to region, in western
France.

This is precisely the point at which the two lines of analysis come
together. Urbanization implies changes in community organization.
The changes that will command our attention are ones that follow
from the increased involvement of the members of rural communities
in sets of activities, norms, and social relationships that reach be-

yond the limits of their own localities. For example, production for a national market, participation in politics, and exposure to mass communication seem to have crudely regular effects on the organization of rural communities.

In order to determine the generality of these effects, and their relevance for the political orientations of rural areas, it would be best to study changes in rural communities within urbanizing societies over long periods of time. Out of necessity, this study will follow the more static, and more common, procedure of comparing communities at roughly the same point in time *as if* they were at different stages in a progression from a common origin.

Now we are in a position to review what there is to explain, and how to explain it. The essential problem is to identify the elements that set off the segments of the society of western France which opposed the Revolution from those which supported it. These "segments" we may view geographically, as the regions in which most of the population took part in counterrevolution, and those in which most people cooperated with the Revolution. How did they differ? We may also look at the "segments" socially, in terms of the responses of various important categories of the population to the Revolution. How did *they* differ? We may also take a more political view and ask what differentiated the groups of genuine activists — the Revolutionary and counterrevolutionary parties — from each other. Finally, we may push these static comparisons into motion, and try to learn how these segments of western France's society acted, interacted, and changed during the early Revolution.

The general idea of urbanization helps bring order into this analysis. The segments of western France's society which supported the Revolution were those which urbanization had enveloped; the segments in which opposition appeared were those which urbanization had touched but little. This is, of course, no more than an approximation. I shall have a number of occasions to qualify it. Furthermore, it depends on a peculiar and multifarious definition of urbanization. It will be convenient at times to shift the emphasis in that definition from one element to another. Despite these signs of inexactitude, the basic thesis seems to be valid, and to be a helpful guide to further questions about the Vendée.

One further question to which this path leads us is the nature of the changes in western France during the Revolution itself. Some of the most important changes — the centralization of governmental power, the increase in importance of the bourgeoisie, the redistribution of property, and so on — were in many respects accelerated continuations of the general process of urbanization. But they were in large measure introduced or imposed from outside the West, and the groups which brought them in tried to make them operate more or less uniformly throughout the region. Where the prerequisites for such a further, rapid transformation already existed — that is, where urbanization had gone furthest — the process went relatively smoothly, but where the prerequisites were missing, it produced ardent conflict. Now, this statement is also no more than an approximation, and one with an air of circularity to it. Yet it, too, helps bring some order into the study of the Vendée and social change in the West.

This sort of analysis provides some interesting by-products. Several of the by-products are corrections of serious inadequacies in the traditional accounts of the Vendée. First, the skepticism this approach raises about the view of the counterrevolution as the unanimous action of a monolithic Vendée brings us to examine local affairs more closely, and eventually to understand that the division of allegiance reached to the heart of the countryside, and that the adherence of localities, groups and individuals to one party or the other followed some fairly regular principles. Past historians have not appreciated the great importance of local party conflicts in the development of the counterrevolution. Second, an interest in the systematic study of social organization itself eventually forces us to recognize the emptiness of many of the debates over the spontaneity of the Vendée, or its dependence on a plot, or the assignment of praise or blame for its occurrence. Finally, a conscious concern with social change alerts us to how early in the Revolution open conflict between the parties that were at war in 1793 began, and how much continuity there was between the events of the great counterrevolution and those that preceded it, both immediately and at a distance.

Prospectus

In trying to answer the kinds of questions I have posed here, one might seek to assemble detailed information on all sections of the West from published sources, and thus learn the answers for all the region at once. I found the published sources too unreliable and too incomplete to make this course feasible. One might also try to glean an essential minimum of information about each section from both archival and published sources. But that procedure assumes that the investigator begins with a detailed master plan, knows in advance what information will be both crucial and available, and can easily reach a wide range of sources. The present study met none of these conditions. I chose a third course: to go far into the records available for one small, but important part of the West, and even farther into the records of a few communities there, and then to determine how well the most significant conclusions reached this way applied to other sections of the West. This study is based largely on the analysis of documents, and the documents deal mainly with the part of Anjou south of the Loire river. Southern Anjou offers the advantage of including one section whose inhabitants generally cooperated with the Revolution and avoided the counterrevolution, and another which was the very homeland of the rebellion. In addition to studying this one area intensively, I have devoted a good deal of effort to ascertain whether the conditions which appeared in southern Anjou also appeared elsewhere in the West. This effort, however, relied more heavily on published sources than did the rest of the study, and bore especially on the area in which large-scale counterrevolution appeared. For these reasons, at their best the conclusions of this study are firm for southern Anjou, tentative for the rest of the area below the Loire, and no more than hypothetical for Brittany, Maine, Normandy, and northern Anjou.

The chapters to follow will proceed from a general discussion of social organization to a specific discussion of the rebellion. First will come a fairly broad view of urbanization in the West (Chapter 2). Next will come a discussion of the role of cities, and of variations from one region to another (Chapter 3). After that, a closer look at the rural communities of southern Anjou (Chapters 4–8). The following chapters will deal with the first years of the Revolution from a regional point of view (Chapter 9) and in terms of the lives of rural communities (Chapters 10–12). Finally, we shall reach an analysis of the rebellion of 1793 itself (Chapter 13). If I have done my task properly, by the time we reach that point together, the reader will know something more about why a great armed rebellion burst out in western France in 1793, what it had to do with social organization and social change in that region, and how a sociological perspective helps in understanding the turbulent events of history.

CHAPTER 2

Urbanization in
Western France

It is all too easy to stumble into the assumption that the Vendée counterrevolution was simply the natural response to the Revolution of a backward region. This convenient formula explains nothing. It fails because it begs three crucial questions: What do we mean by "backward"? What is the "natural" political behavior of backward regions? Was the Vendée significantly more backward than sections of France which did not rebel? An examination of urbanization in western France provides some of the elements of answers to these questions.

The Idea of Urbanization

"Urbanization" is a collective term for a set of changes which generally occur with the appearance and expansion of large-scale coordinated activities in a society. These activities may consist of the operation of a centralized state, or the conduct of a religion with a professional priesthood, or the control of water for irrigation and flood prevention, or the production of goods in a factory system, or the channeling of exchange through a pervasive market. Too often recent students of urbanization have taken a narrowly economic view of the process, compounding the fault by assuming a monumental disjunction between "industrial" and "preindustrial" urbanization. There are differences, to be sure. But the changes based on the appearance of these various large-scale activities have a good deal in common. The development of any one of them implies the appearance of social positions (such as official, priest or merchant) devoted to their coordination, the establishment of extensive lines of communication, and the proliferation of social relationships which cross the boundaries of kinship, locality, and traditional alliance.

Coordinators, communication lines, and crosscutting relationships are parts of the definition of large-scale activity. From them, we may distinguish a series of common effects of their appearance. The first is *differentiation* — the formation of social positions specialized in different segments of the activity, and the subdivision of existing social positions into more specialized ones. (Adam Smith's famous example is the evolution of pinmaking from one-man craft to mass production.) The second effect is *standardization* — the development of uniform procedures, vocabularies, norms, and forms of organization throughout the range of impact of the large-scale activity. (The multiplication of stereotyped staffs of civil servants throughout the expanding provinces of the Roman Empire is a pleasantly apt illustration.) Third is the *change in quality of social relationships* so much discussed by sociologists, the shift toward impersonal, instrumental relations among men involved in carrying on the large-scale activity in question. (Lewis Mumford reserves some of his most acrid phrases for the transformation of the many local, personal, medieval markets into the abstract, rational, inhumane Market of merchant capitalism.) Finally, there is the *concentration of population* at the points of coordination and control of the large-scale activity, by which I mean mainly the growth of cities. (A case in point is the effect of the flourishing of international religious orders in the eleventh century on the vitality of such cities as Rouen, Caen, Dijon, and Tours.)

In a study of eighteenth-century France, the urbanizing activities which command our attention are market expansion and state centralization. The growth of a market is an increase in the volume, range, and proportion of goods and services exchanged by means of a generalized medium (money). By its very nature, it is a process which requires communication, specialists in coordination, and penetration of existing, traditional forms of social organization. Adam Smith, observing the very period which concerns us, went so far as to consider market expansion the fundamental cause of increasing complexity in the division of labor. State centralization — which in eighteenth-century France means mainly the extension of royal fiscal, judicial, and military control — has similar qualities. It encourages the rise of specialists in political coordination and manipulation, calls for more frequent exchanges of orders and information, draws formerly isolated regions and communities into greater contact with decision-making centers, and into greater dependence upon them.

State centralization and market expansion are city-building processes which leave their marks not only on the size, but also on the character, of a society's urban centers. Paris is the very model of Mumford's Baroque City, with its offices, showplaces, traffic, and means for display of military might. And the market creates the market place, the merchant quarter, the Bourse, the port.

Even more important than these features of the urban landscape are the rise to prominence of the administrators and the merchants, the division of the population into specialists in diverse phases of administrative and mercantile activity, and the development of the new forms of cleavage and solidarity that these changes entail. Furthermore, by their very specialization in communication, in response to far-off events, in the use of standardized and transferable techniques, and by the fact of their frequent recruitment from diverse and distant localities, a significant number of the inhabitants of mercantile and administrative cities are likely to be cosmopolitan in outlook, mobile, and sensitive to currents of thought and opinion. In short, even cities become more "urban" in urbanization.

Urbanization may also transform rural areas, without eradicating agriculture (cf. Gerth and Mills 1946: 363–385). The most usual form this process has taken recently in peasant societies is a shift from subsistence polyculture to mechanized one-crop production for the market. In this shift is a world of social change. The producer binds himself to distant and nameless consumers, adopts new standards for evaluating his work, requires for his yearly operation information from a much wider range of sources than before, and depends on market specialists both as sources of commodities he now needs and as means for the sale of the cash crops he now produces. Even in the absence of growing cities among the farms, we may properly say that an agricultural region in which these changes are occurring is "urbanizing."

One assumption about urbanization which is no doubt often convenient, but is invariably wrong, is that it permeates all segments of a society evenly. For the moment, it is not the important distinction between societies in which cities have a preservative influence and those in which they disseminate drastic social change that concerns us (cf. Hoselitz 1960; Murphey 1954; Redfield and Singer 1954; Sjoberg 1952; 1955). Rather, it is the fact that urbanization is necessarily selective, regardless of the society in which it occurs. This is because it is based on a limited range of human activities and because it touches the lives and positions of those involved in coordinating the activities more directly than it touches the rest of the population. Urbanization may utterly transform the situation of one class, or region, or community, while leaving others little affected. It is a truism, but a truism too often overlooked, that the expansion of trade in manufactured goods affects the situations of merchants and artisans more seriously and directly than it does those of peasants and landed gentry.

An important qualification is necessary. In the long run, urbanization in any sector of a society will affect all other sectors. The existence of cities — whether military, commercial, religious, or manufacturing centers — requires the presence of an agricultural surplus, and ordinarily presupposes a certain number of agricultural workers producing for the urban market. In fact, the usual conception of peasant society includes the presence of some cities, and at least a modicum of urban influence on the life of the peasant. That is precisely the point of Alfred Kroeber's calling the peasantry a "part-society" (1948: 284). Even in a society composed overwhelmingly of peasants, any kind of urbanization will eventually reshape all of the peasantry, by reshaping their relations with the other parts of the society. An example which is quite relevant to France under the old regime is the effect of the growing demands of an expanding state for taxes to finance its burgeoning military and bureaucratic apparatus: particularly where the tax bears mainly on land, these demands ineluctably persuade even the most self-sufficient peasant community to convert some of its products into the cash that alone will satisfy the tax collector (see Wolf 1955: 458). In this way, state centralization can draw peasant communities into the market.

Urbanization, then, is selective. Although its vigorous action in any segment of a society is likely eventually to change all other segments, at any particular time, some segments — regions, classes, communities, rural areas — will be more urbanized than others, and some will be urbanizing more rapidly than others. It is not enough to think of urbanization as a uniform change of a whole society.

I intend to show that this conception of urbanization is useful for understanding both political affiliation and political conflict. That it should be useful is not surprising, since it emphasizes changes in lines of cleavage and solidarity in a society, in the bases and distribution of power, in the forms of organization available for mobilizing many men simultaneously, and in the extent of communication and mutual awareness among the various segments of society. Equally important, it draws attention to differences among social segments in each of these respects.

The Idea Applied to France

The emphasis on uneven change is particularly interesting because the predominant view of the French Revolution today contains an implicit idea of "political lag." In this view, the Revolution was the violent adjustment of French political structure to changes which had already occurred in other elements of the society. That is the true meaning of Mathiez' declaration that the Revolution ". . . developed from the divorce, more definite each day, between realities and laws, between institutions and ways of life, between the letter and the spirit" (Mathiez 1951–1954: 1, 1). This formulation of political lag, as imprecise (and implicit) as it usually is, remains not only the dominant view, but also the one that promises the fullest understanding of the Revolution.

This book is not an analysis of the French Revolution as a whole. That does not mean it escapes making some assertions and assumptions about the nature of the Revolution. The study of the Vendée has led me to modify the formula of political lag in two ways: 1) by expecting to find tension and conflict wherever two segments of French society in contact with each other were changing at significantly different rates, 2) by substituting urbanization for economic development in the proposition: political institutions were lagging behind X. And the two urbanizing activities to which I have given the greatest attention are trade and state centralization.

The impulses of trade and state centralization were working in

France throughout the century before 1789. Even Ernest Labrousse, to whom the idea of a crisis in the French economy at the end of the old regime is so important, concedes that the crisis occurred in an expanding economy. Too often, other historians have mistaken one question about the eighteenth century ("Were the masses miserable?") for a quite different one ("Was the economy growing?") with an ease that Marx's and Engels' observations about the state of the English working class in the heyday of industrial growth should have made impossible.

Not that we should call the French eighteenth century a period of "industrial" growth, if we mean by that the arrival of a factory system. The market expansion of that time consisted very largely in the increased sale and wider circulation of agricultural products such as wine, grain, or hides, and of the portable products of domestic handicrafts — notably textiles. The most remarkable increase was in international trade via the Atlantic and channel ports, a fact which meant that participation in this expansion was uneven, concentrated in the ports and the areas which supplied them. In money value, French international trade increased by 900 percent in the century before the Revolution (Reinhard 1949: 93–94; cf. Marczewski 1961). But internal trade grew as well. As Henri Sée (1948–1951: I, 316) pointed out, the decline of the great fairs during the eighteenth century was a sign of the substitution of frequent, continuous, permanent commercial intercourse for the episodic meetings of buyers and sellers which had predominated earlier. Despite the many hindrances, physical and fiscal, to trade, despite the immense numerical preponderance of peasants in the nation, despite the later sluggishness of French industry, France before the Revolution was second only to England as a commercial and industrial power.

If Frenchmen were being drawn incessantly into market production and consumption, they were also coming into greater and greater contact with the central government and its proliferating agencies. I do not mean to say that royal absolutism increased after the reign of Louis XIV. Nor do I mean to deny the importance of the eighteenth-century "feudal reaction" of an important section of the nobility against royal claims. The important thing is that the government bureaucracy was growing, was extending its local influence and its sphere of jurisdiction, was making increasing demands on French citizens for funds, for information, for attention, for cooperation. Central government expenditure sextupled in the century after 1685 (Marczewski 1961). "The central power," said Alexis de Tocqueville (Tocqueville 1955: 41) "had taken to playing the part of an indefatigable mentor and keeping the nation in quasi-paternal tutelage." The founding of royal agricultural societies, the state-regulated division of common lands, the increasing assignment of secondary officials (*subdélégués*) to localities within the Généralités, the imposition (just before the Revolution) of a common organization on every commune in France, are so many examples of the penetration of the state into the lives of its citizens.

It may seem strange to claim, on the one hand, that state centralization was part of the process of urbanization and, on the other, that a major element of the Revolution was the obliteration of the lag between urbanization and political arrangements. It sounds as though the political structure were lagging behind — the political structure. There are two justifications for this apparently ridiculous assertion. The first is that leads, lags, and inconsistencies often appear within the political structure itself: the Court of 1787 was entirely out of step with the provincial assemblies created in that year. The second is that vigorous state action transforms far more than the internal, formal structure of government, and at times undermines its own bases of power: Colbert's determined encouragement of manufacturing probably hastened the day when the bourgeois beneficiaries of industrial expansion shook down the state Colbert sought to strengthen. Political systems sometimes nurture the seeds of their own destruction.

Of the two major eighteenth-century urbanizing processes — state centralization and market expansion — one would have to say that, in the long run, market expansion was the more influential in the transformation of French society. Fortunately, there is no need to undertake the weighing of one against the other, for it is their combined effects that matter. There were some unmistakable symptoms of these effects. One is the energetic growth of French cities during the eighteenth century. Although even at the end of the century the population in cities of any size at all was no more than 15 percent of the French total, it was in growing metropolises like Lyon,

Marseille, Bordeaux, Nantes and, of course, Paris, that one could see a new society being shaped.[1]

If we agree not to take the figures too seriously, it is possible to work out some estimates of urban growth during the eighteenth century. From the enumeration in Saugrain's dictionary of 1726 to the national survey of 1789, the population in cities of 50,000 or more rose about 30 percent, and that in cities of 20,000 or more, almost 60 percent (Mols 1955: 514–515). If correct, these figures would mean that about 4 percent of the French population at the time of the Revolution was in cities of 50,000 or more, and about 7.5 percent in cities of 20,000 or more.

The interest of these calculations lies not in their specious precision, but in the fact that they suggest with what modern countries we ought to compare eighteenth-century France. They are the poorest, most agricultural nations of the West, and the great awakening "undeveloped" nations of the East. India, Ceylon, Haiti, and the Dominican Republic are nations which now have approximately the proportion of urban population that existed in Revolutionary France (United Nations 1952: Table 7). They are nations in the early and most turbulent stages of urbanization.

This comparison suggests a further one. A large share of France's urban population was concentrated in one great metropolis, Paris. This is a condition — very common in Latin America, for example — which in the twentieth century is often associated with instability. If we calculate the proportion of the total urban population (i.e., in cities of 20,000 or more) living in the largest city, we find eighteenth-century France, with about 30 percent in Paris and Versailles, below the very high proportions of such volatile contemporary nations as Haiti (85 percent), Egypt (58 percent), or Cuba (48 percent),

[1] Marcel Reinhard (1949: 95–96) estimates the number in settlements of 2,000 or more at the end of the old regime as 4 million of the 26 million total population. The categorical disagreement between two recent and expert statements on the eighteenth-century growth of Paris is a fair warning that the statistical base of generalizations about population change before the Revolution is still quite flimsy. Roger Mols (1955: II, 513) argues that "the topographic expansion of the city, as well as all its history, show that the seventeenth and eighteenth centuries were periods of great growth. The contrary would be astonishing for the capital of Europe's most powerful state, for the City of Light of western culture." But Louis Chevalier (1958: 205) asserts that "whatever method of evaluation or coefficient is used, the growth of Paris' population during the seventeenth and eighteenth centuries appears slow and weak." The national role of Paris, the considerable growth of France's subordinate cities, and the many contemporary observations of Paris' vigor combine to make the hypothesis of substantial growth more convincing.

far above stable western democracies of the type of England (11 percent) or the United States (13 percent), and coupled with fairly turbulent countries like Hungary (30 percent) or Greece (about 30 percent).[2]

The numbers in themselves mean very little. But a high ratio is a rough indicator of the presence of a preeminent, politically active center containing the nation's principal organs of control, differing widely from the rest of the country in interests, organization, and awareness. De Tocqueville (1955: 76) identified France's administrative centralization and the resulting predominance of Paris as major causes of the Revolution. "Thus Paris had mastered France," he declared, "and the army that was soon to master Paris was mustering its forces."

Such a concentration of control no doubt encourages struggles for power within the capital. The existence of a dominant metropolis is also often associated with another set of politically significant circumstances. In labeling "over-urbanized" those countries (for instance, Egypt, Greece, Korea) in which the urban population is far greater than the degree of industrialization would lead one to expect, Kingsley Davis (1954; cf. Hoselitz 1960: 228–229) has described a number of special features of overurbanized societies. Overurbanization commonly implies not only the presence of an unusually dominant city, but also: forced migration off the land, "idle, impoverished and rootless masses" in the cities, and acute discontent. These conditions favor political instability.

The remarkable thing about this contemporary syndrome, as described by Davis, is that it corresponds so closely to the situation of France on the eve of Revolution, as described by Marcel Reinhard (1949: 98–99). Here are the elements: the appearance in the countryside of unattached, drifting, marginal "wanderers," the movement of surplus rural population toward the cities, the growing power of the metropolis, and the intensification of both conflict and mutual awareness between rural and urban. These are circumstances that many modern commentators have called revolutionary, circumstances which surely increased the revolutionary propensities of France to-

[2] United Nations 1952: Tables 7 and 8. Assuming that Mols (1955: II, 514–515) has given a complete enumeration of cities of 20,000 or more, the various statistics from 1787 to 1801 yield figures for France of 30, 29, 29, and 33 percent, the last (1801) percentage being very likely the most accurate.

ward 1789. These circumstances help explain the contribution of the indigent, the unattached, and the recent arrivals from the country to the Parisian malaise of the early Revolution. They constitute the most powerful evidence of the influence of rapid urbanization on the political temper of the French people.

Another, less dramatic, sign of urbanization was the proliferation of internal communications. From the time of Colbert on, France never ceased its construction of the finest network of roads in Europe. As Henri Cavaillès puts it, the road system became

. . . the expression both of a political situation and of a civilization. With every one [of the roads] leaving from Paris, running to the frontiers and to the seaports, linking the old provincial capitals directly to the Court, to the government, to the ministries, their starlike web stated with perfect clarity the territorial and political unity of the kingdom, at the same time as it made possible the insistent and continuous action of the [central] power (1946: 164).

Cavaillès (p. 166) adds that the new roads serve to circulate far more than government orders: "Via the same routes were distributed the gazettes, memoirs, philosophical novels, volumes of the Encyclopedia." They disseminated new ideas as easily as administrative instructions. The same may be said of the rapid expansion of the postal service, for which the value of the monopoly rose from 1.2 million livres in 1673, to 3.1 million in 1713, to 8.8 million in 1777[3] (Sée 1948–1951: 223, 299).

No doubt the most important sign — and far more than just a sign — of the urbanization of France was the rise of the bourgeoisie, that group of specialists in administration, coordination, and communication. For a small-town notary like Jean-Charles Prévost of Chemillé in Anjou, as well as for a great banker like Jacques Necker of Geneva and Paris, the eighteenth century was a time of both influence and affluence. Despite the gradual closing of their access to many of the most honorific positions in French society, the bourgeois were rising irresistibly to preeminence. The substance of these observations is that France was urbanizing rapidly during the later

[3] Some indications of the value of the livre in Anjou: Toward 1789 an ordinary farm hand could earn a livre in a day and a half or two; with it he could perhaps buy 3 pounds of butter, or two capons, or two geese, or a pound of wax, or close to a bushel of rye. A farm of average size was likely to rent for 500 livres per year, and all the household goods of the farmer were likely to be worth 200 livres.

eighteenth century, and that urbanization contributed immensely to its revolutionary potential. But there is one crucial qualification to keep in mind. Although the elixir of urbanization transformed whatever and whomever it touched, it did not touch all at the same time or with equal force. Just as it was the national capital and the trading cities of frontier and seacoast (rather than the venerable provincial capitals of the interior) that grew during the eighteenth century, it was the regions most firmly tied to those cities that were most thoroughly changed. Industries sprang to life in some provinces, but slept on in others. Social classes, occupations, various types of agriculture, diverse branches of industry, regions, even individual cities, differed emphatically in the extent to which they participated in the great transformation. The result was not to homogenize the nation, but to accentuate its internal contrasts. These contrasts are at the heart of the problem of the Revolution. Reinhard (1949: 99) speaks of the "opposition between citydwellers and countrymen," and Paul Bois (1960b: 623) of the "penetration of the revolutionary spirit, imported by the cities." Themes that will echo through the rest of this analysis. Indeed, they are conclusions that the two authors reached after long, shrewd, and expert appraisals of the situation of the West itself.

The West

The West, that is, the sixth of France west of Tours and north of Saintes, has often been treated by writers on the Revolution as a backward, isolated, and impoverished region. This is at most a half truth. To be sure, by any standard, the region taken as a whole was much less urbanized than the East or the Parisian hinterland. But the West of the eighteenth century exhibited contrasts in urbanization quite as sharp as those in France as a whole. After all, the region claimed a good share of the nation's flourishing cities: Nantes, La Rochelle, Angers, St. Malo, Brest, Le Mans, Rennes are on the roster. The vigor of these cities led to a certain invigoration of the territories surrounding them.

On the other hand, it is correct to recognize that much of Brittany and some other rural sections of the West were both administratively neglected and socially isolated. One of the special traits of the West's physiognomy was the juxtaposition of profoundly rural territories with prosperous cities. However, this statement does not do justice to the subtlety of the situation. It was actually a kind of coexistence — without coalescence — of rural and urban. One might picture the West as a patchwork of blatantly contrasting rural areas, overlaid with an irregular grille of linked cities, separate from the patchwork but touching it at many points. Even that discordant model would not indicate the uneven effect of urbanization on diverse institutions and elements of the population. The important thing to see is the constant confrontation of urban and rural, and the possibility of violent conflict between them.

Considering the common prejudice that the Vendée rebellion was the product of pure backwardness, it is probably more important to establish the presence of urbanity, than of rurality, in the West. There are a number of indications of its presence; a brief enumeration of them will also give a preliminary idea of the principal variations from place to place within the region.

The West juts into the sea, divided by the Loire. Along the shores of ocean and river, in the eighteenth century, stood a few great, growing cities, and many more which were less significant but equally filled with life. Nantes took first place, and even today her architectural core reveals that the eighteenth century was the city's moment of supremacy. But Sables d'Olonne, La Rochelle, Lorient, Brest, St. Malo were among the other western cities that shared the same spirit and activity.

For the study of the Revolution, the distinction between the sections north and south of the Loire is important. The counter-revolutionary movement of 1793 stirred all the principal provinces of the northwest: Normandy, Maine, Brittany, Poitou, and Anjou. However, the rebellion known as the Vendée itself only mastered part of that territory. It originated in western Poitou and in the parts of Brittany and Anjou south of the Loire. In modern terms, its theater was made up of fragments of the departments of Maine-et-Loire, Loire-Inférieure, Deux-Sèvres, and Vendée.

The sporadic warfare called Chouannerie prevailed north of the Loire, in parts of Maine, Brittany, Normandy, and northern Anjou (in the modern departments of Maine-et-Loire, Sarthe, Mayenne, Ille-et-Vilaine, and Côtes-du-Nord). By more than coincidence, the strong points of Chouannerie were those at which vigorously independent peasants came in contact with the inhabitants of such trading cities as St. Malo, St. Brieuc, and Le Mans.

From another angle, the counterrevolutionary theater may be divided roughly into sections of bocage, coastal marsh, and river valley, flanked to the south and east by broad plains. The bocage — of which there will be much more to say later — occupies almost all the area between the Loire and Luçon, Parthenay and Thouars, to the south, and west of Le Mans and Alençon, to the north. Travelers in the bocage are struck by the impression that there are trees everywhere, that houses, farms, and villages are lost in one great forest. In fact, forests are insignificant in the bocage. The most obvious difference from the rural plains of the East is that here cultivated fields are usually surrounded by tall hedges of bushes and trees. The bocage is a landscape formed by hedge-enclosed fields, narrow, sunken roads, and dispersed villages, hamlets, and single farmsteads.

The marshes are no more than small indentations along the maritime edges of the bocage. Most of them are the scenes of intensive and specialized agriculture — truck gardening and cattle — plus fishing or salt production. Despite the fascination of the coastal marshes, riddled with canals, varying widely in their dealings with cities and the sea, famed for their independence, they will occupy very little of the analysis to follow, since their place in the origins of the counterrevolution was secondary, and their inclusion would require an elaborate separate study.

The valleys of the Loire (by far the most important), of the Sèvre Niortaise, and of the Loir were already intensively cultivated in the eighteenth century: wine grapes, wheat, flax, hemp, hay, and garden crops predominated. The land was rich, and the contact with the cities of the interior and with the sea of long standing. The powerful cities of the region that were not on the Atlantic coast were almost entirely clustered in the river valleys.

Plains, named not so much for their topography as for their unenclosed fields and concentrated rural villages, stretched out from the sides of the bocage that did not meet the Loire or the ocean. The plains of southern and eastern Poitou, Touraine, Beauce, and eastern Normandy bound the bocage in its corner of France. Their peasant landowners raised wheat or livestock in abundance, for sale in the nearby market town.

As a first approximation, one may say that after 1790 the valleys and plains were favorable to the Revolution, the coastal marshes variable but energetic in their political affiliations, and most of the bocage counterrevolutionary. Much of what follows will consist of an examination of the contrast between rebel bocage and Republican plain and valley.

This description gives the stuff of the rural patchwork, but it does not sufficiently specify the form of the network of cities superimposed upon it. Albert Demangeon (1946: I, 231–232) remarked that many of the influential medium-sized cities of the West marked the frontier between plain and bocage; below the Loire, Sables d'Olonne, Fontenay-le-Comte, Niort, Parthenay, Thouars, Montreuil-Bellay guard the bocage's borders. Demangeon also noticed the proliferation of small cities, combinations of local markets and secondary centers of manufacturing, throughout the bocage. This is a fact whose importance has been neglected, for it belies the assumption that the bocage was purely rural. How can we write the history of the bocage without mentioning cities like Mayenne, Le Mans, Cholet, Bressuire, or Montaigu, all points of light within its shadow? The shading of the sections of the bocage that most concern this analysis of the counterrevolution was not a monotone of rusticity, but a complex and irregular pattern of rural and urban. Once again, the "average" is deceptive. On the average, or on the whole, the bocage was less urbanized than the surrounding plains and valleys, just as the West as a whole lagged behind the East. Yet in the bocage the contrast between rural and urban and the tension between them was of enormous significance.

There are, of course, many other signs of urbanization than the sheer location of cities. Administrative activities, governmental and ecclesiastical, were unevenly distributed in the West. Below the Loire, all the regional capitals (Poitiers, Tours, Angers before the Revolution, Fontenay, Niort, Angers, Nantes during the Revolution) were outside the bocage. The cities of the interior were at most secondary administrative centers. Therefore, the centralization of the French state during the century affected the interior less directly than it did the already favored sections. Likewise, the seats of power within the church were Poitiers, Angers, La Rochelle, Luçon, Nantes. Furthermore, although the West as a whole was well provided with monks, the bocage was not. Monastic wealth and activity were heavily concentrated in the river valleys, along the principal trade routes, and in the largest cities. It was more than coincidence. Roger Dion (1959: esp. 26–61, 181–187) has well noted the interdependence in France of trade, cities, commercial winegrowing, and monasticism. All of these were part of the way of life of valley and plain, while their appearance in the bocage was much more selective and irregular.

The major lines of transportation made up a similar picture. "Qui aime la ville," says Jean Brunhes, "construit la route" (Brunhes and Deffontaines 1926: 143). His observation is well substantiated by the pattern of eighteenth-century roads, radiating from Paris, sparser in the West than in the East of France, and, within the West, linking the major cities via paths lying mainly in plain and valley rather than bocage. The prefect of Deux-Sèvres observed that "the plain is crossed by a number of major highways, and its inhabitants are more civilized" (Dupin 1801–1802: 59). Only one of the roads in the quadrangle formed by Tours, Nantes, La Rochelle, and Poitiers actually ran through the bocage, and that was the last to come into heavy use. As before, this general contrast between the bocage and its surroundings was significant, but not absolute. The secondary roads that did pass through the bocage gave a special importance to such trading centers as Montaigu, Cholet, and Bressuire, as well as to those placed at the junction of bocage and plain, such as Thouars, Chantonnay, Parthenay, and Montreuil-Bellay.

While these observations on the locations of cities and roads are very useful as indications of the state of the West before the Revolution, they do not provide much information on changes in urbanization during the eighteenth century. Unfortunately, we have no sound information on changes in traffic and urban population. We may, however, draw some conclusions from the fact that the commerce of the West expanded immensely in the century before the Revolution. The prosperity of the Atlantic ports is the clearest sign. Nantes was at the peak of its participation in the slave trade when the Revolution began, as Jean Meyer (1960) has shown. The success of the coastal cities encouraged greater commercial activity in the towns that linked them with the interior (as Fontenay, Niort, and Luçon served La Rochelle), as well as in the country areas that produced their seagoing merchandise (as the textiles of Bas-Maine went to St. Malo). In general, even if internal trade was rising simultaneously, it was the towns and rural regions most closely associated with the great ports that were most strongly influenced by the eighteenth-century surge of urbanization in the West.

There are some important distinctions to make among the products that entered this expanding commerce. Trade in agricultural products does not call forth the same social arrangements as trade in manufactured goods, even if they are produced in the country. The arrival of cash-crop agriculture is certain to transform a peasantry, as well as to assure the livelihood of a variety of merchants, but, so long as it is based on the work of a distinctive group of craftsmen, rather than on the part-time labor of the farmers, the growth of small-scale manufacturing need not seriously affect the traditional organization of agriculture. On the other hand, the rise of manufacturing will necessarily affect the power and numerical weight of the peasants as opposed to other occupational groups, even if the peasants remain uninvolved in the new crafts. In the West (to speak very generally), specialized, commercial agriculture was of long standing in the valleys and plains but rare in the bocage. By contrast, if manufacturing outside the bocage was concentrated in the cities and relatively uncommon in the countryside, inside the bocage it was rapidly spreading out into the rural areas from its bases in the small cities.

The principal products of commercial agriculture in the West were wine, grain, cattle, and raw materials for the textile industry. Commercial winegrowing was unknown in the bocage. Along the Loire and its tributaries, on the other hand, wine reigned supreme. The wine of Anjou has an ancient renown. In addition to the great vineyards of the Loire, there were lesser winegrowing areas near La Flèche, to the north, and below Niort, to the south. This is important not only because winegrowing fosters a distinctive type of peasant character — alert, calculating, supple, egalitarian — but also because it calls forth a distinctive form of rural social structure, with fractionation of the land, peasant proprietorship, specialization, agglomerated settlement, constant mercantile activity. The character and the social structure are, of course, related by more than coincidence. Perhaps the most significant feature of the wine-grower's situation, for the present discussion, is his powerful interest in the business of his region's largest cities, as well as in trade, both national and international. The port of La Rochelle first grew up as the point of departure for the wines of its hinterland, and that of Nantes was a favorite stopping place for the wine merchants of Holland, eager to buy the esteemed products of Anjou and Touraine. The state of agriculture in the Loire valley was practically inseparable from the state of the market in general, so much so that "the winegrowers of Saumur, in 1687, claimed that they were ruined, or almost so, when the war hindered their commerce with Holland" (Dion 1959: 453).

Wine is the market product par excellence, but the production of grain can share some of the same characteristics. The great bulk of the cultivated land of the West was in grain: rye, wheat, barley, buckwheat, oats, in something like that order. There was, however, a great difference between the areas in which the "rich" crop, wheat, dominated, and those where "poor" grains like rye and buckwheat ruled. As in so many other cases, the eighteenth-century distinction between "rich" and "poor" in this case actually refers mainly to the fact that wheat was the only grain which instead of being consumed locally was widely shipped, traded, and sold for cash. Wheat was suitable for the bread of nobles, monks, bourgeois, and city-dwellers. Now, it was only the most economically advanced sections of the bocage (for example, the Sarthe, so well described by Bois 1960b) which devoted themselves to wheat; rye and buckwheat were the bocage's typical grains. Yet throughout the plains, wheat was the favorite crop. It was the peasants of the plain who specialized in producing the grain that traveled to the market and beyond, and who therefore shared many of the concerns of those other peasants who grew grapes for profit.

So far, the situation has seemed fairly simple: commercial, specialized agriculture outside the bocage, noncommercial polyculture within. The third case, cattle, disturbs the symmetry of this distinction. The bocage has often been advertised as a cattle-raising country. It is true that every farm of any size had some oxen and some cows. But the farmers were neither dairy farmers nor specialists in beef cattle. The oxen were essentially for the work of the farm. A well-informed official of the Vendée described the usual arrangement as follows:

Grain-raising is the principal asset of the bocage; however, it has another abundant source of revenue in raising and fattening cattle. Each middle-sized farm has six, eight or ten oxen. There are ordinarily half as many cows as oxen. Each year the peasant raises as many calves as he has cows. Each year he sells two oxen, which he replaces with others he has raised, and sometimes he also sells a pair of yearlings. Sometimes, besides, he very profitably sells two other oxen he has bought for fattening, when fodder is plentiful. From time to time, he sells a cow which he replaces with a calf he has raised (Cavoleau 1844: 521–522).

The common misconception that the bocage was covered with herds of cattle was due to the fact that the few steers the average peasant did sell were his principal source of *cash* income. Even if livestock sales were a minor part of the total farm operation, he paid taxes and money rents with the proceeds. He pastured his oxen on the portion of his land that was currently idle; he used the manure on the land that was in cultivation; he yoked the oxen (and sometimes a cow) to the plow or the cart; as they aged, he eventually fattened up a few for the market. The net result of the pursuit of this routine on thousands of farms throughout the bocage was the movement of a great many cattle, via the markets of such cities as Parthenay and Cholet, to Normandy for further fattening and to Paris for slaughtering. Yet we could hardly call the process specialized cattle raising. Still less could we think of the widespread practice of raising a few hogs, sheep, or chickens along with the oxen as a form of commercial agriculture.

In these respects, the contrasts between plain and bocage were not so great as in the case of wheat. In the valleys, it is true, cattle raising was almost unknown. And in some parts of the plain (Normandy for beef cattle, sections of southern Poitou for mules and, to some extent, sheep), livestock production was already a major agricultural activity. But elsewhere there was the same subordination of cattle to grain, and the same periodic sale of surplus draft animals, as in the bocage.

The textile crops, flax and hemp, present a rather different picture. In many parts of the bocage, the peasants planted small plots of flax or hemp to meet their own needs for cloth, and, at times, to supply the local weavers. This habit seems to have been more common north of the Loire than to the south. In any case, we ought to distinguish sharply between occasional production of this sort and the specialized raising of textile crops which was the preoccupation of only a few sections of the West. A 1781 report on the Generality of Tours (A.D. Indre-et-Loire C 82)[4] showed that the only elections producing substantial amounts of hemp were those of Angers and Le Mans, with the elections of Château-du-Loir, La Flèche, and Saumur running far behind. The distribution of flax was similar: true commercial production of flax was the business of part of the Loire valley (near Angers) and of the vicinity of Laval. In the area below the Loire, the remarkable fact about the textile crops is that they were not grown intensively in the same areas where cloth production was most active, but were imported from the fertile river valley.

This short list — wine, grains, cattle, and textile fibers — covers the major agricultural products produced for the market in the West. What we have seen is that their production was far from evenly distributed in the region. The great contrasts were among the plains, with commercial graingrowing and a certain amount of livestock production, the valleys, with wine and textile fibers, and the bocages, with grain grown mainly for local consumption complemented by livestock used both as draft animals and as occasional sources of cash income. The really important difference was between the subsistence agriculture of most of the bocage and the commercial agriculture of both valleys and plains. Eighteenth-century observers were so well aware of the effects of this distinction that they separated the two sections of the West into "rich" and "poor," "fertile" and "infertile," "advanced" and "backward." And, indeed, they could see very well that in the areas where commercial agriculture predominated, the land was already moving into the hands of peasants and merchants in the form of small parcels, the farmers were more willing to innovate and to adopt productive methods, the peasants were more alert, more rational, more citified.

[4] Citations in this form refer to dossiers of French departmental archives (Archives Départementales). "A.N.," when it appears, stands for Archives Nationales. The largest single group of documents analyzed came from the departmental archives of Maine-et-Loire in Angers, which are abbreviated "A.D. M-et-L."

Despite all this, it is not enough to tag the greater part of the bocage as an underdeveloped area. Rural industry brings in more complications. Nowhere in the West was there more than a foretaste of modern big industry, and only in the largest cities were there a few establishments that deserved the name of factory. Nevertheless, a complex of workshops, traders, local markets, and individual craftsmen reached far into the countryside of the whole region, and drew out load after load of finished goods for the merchants of the nation and the world. There is no need to tarry over Angers' slate industry, or Niort's production of gloves, or the tanning that flourished near the principal cattle markets, for it was textiles that were the fundamental rural industry. The decline of this industry after the Revolution, the concentration of what remained of it in the cities, and the consequent shriveling of the small towns it had activated have tricked many later commentators into exaggerating the homogeneous rurality of the region. Yet, as René Musset described the situation in one section of the West:

Bas-Maine, during the seventeenth and eighteenth centuries, had become an industrial region. It was a rural industry . . . but one which held an exceptional place in the life of the area: it produced not only for local needs, or even for those of the nation, but also supplied a great export trade; Bas-Maine was one of the most important *manufactures* of France. Moreover, the industry was not, as elsewhere, simply an adjunct to agriculture, but took precedence over agriculture, to the point of impeding its progress (1917: 250).

Similar statements, if not quite so hyperbolic, could be made for substantial parts of Brittany, Maine, Anjou, and even some of Poitou.

The rise of this rural industry was part and parcel of the commercial expansion that enriched the West's Atlantic ports and multiplied their contacts with Africa, the Americas, and the rest of Europe. The middlemen of the industry maintained relations with the shippers of Nantes, La Rochelle, or St. Malo, and some had agents as far off as the West Indies (Furet 1950: 94; Sée 1926).

Within the region, the best term for the industry is not actually rural, but semiurban. The most important merchants, as well as the fairs and markets through which the raw materials and finished goods were exchanged, were located in the cities and the larger towns. The workers who turned out the goods were to be found, along with the lesser merchants, not only in the cities and larger towns, but also in the villages and hamlets sprinkled all over the map. They were rare in the open country, and increased in frequency with the urbanity of the settlement, but compared with modern workers they were widely dispersed.

I shall have a great deal more to say about the textile industry. There are two points I must emphasize now. The first is that this form of rural manufacturing was absent from plain and valley, was almost entirely concentrated in the bocage. The plains and valleys were more single-mindedly devoted to agriculture than was the bocage. The second point is that within the bocage the cohabitation of traditional subsistence agriculture and a lively, growing industry produced some remarkable contrasts, inconsistencies, and opportunities for conflict. The difference between the "demanding, mutinous, improvident and intemperate" industrial workers and the phlegmatic inhabitants of the farms (Baudrillart 1888: II, 6) proved quite important in the Revolution.

This contrast between subsistence agriculture and growing industry, which epitomizes the distinction between urbanized and unurbanized sectors of a society, forecasts the general conclusions I have to offer about urbanization in the West. The plains and valleys of the region, permeated with commercial agriculture and enclosing almost all the seats of royal administration, had long been exposed to the great urbanizing influences at work in France. Angers, Tours, and Poitiers were ancient capitals; as early as the sixteenth century the fairs of Niort and Fontenay were attracting products from throughout the plain and merchants from throughout the country, while Nantes continued its long-standing trade with the Loire valley's winegrowers (Trocmé and Delafosse 1952; Raveau 1931: 34, 35; Tanguy 1956). On the other hand, by far the greatest part of the bocage kept on in unspecialized, noncommercial agriculture, while in the last century or so before the Revolution an industry full of vitality grew in its midst. The West was a territory of striking variations, of highly uneven urbanization, and the bocage — the chosen land of counterrevolution — displayed the greatest inconsistencies of all.

If I belabor the fact of inconsistency, it is because the apologists of the Vendée's counterrevolution have so often presented the whole region as a virtuous relic of dulcet, bucolic old France. Taken as a whole, the West was far from the most "backward" section of France (the term could have fit the South much more snugly), and even the sections of the West which favored the counterrevolution had been affected by urbanization. Throughout the nation, in fact, outright resistance to the Revolution or to the currently dominant faction within it was less the tendency of the most "backward" sections than of those in which recent social change had been both turbulent and uneven. The Atlantic coast and the valleys of Rhone and Garonne are the outstanding examples (Greer 1935: ch. III). It may not be irrelevant to point out that the main bases of Girondin strength in 1793 were cities, in the midst of agricultural regions, whose commerce and population had been growing apace during the previous century: Bordeaux, Lyon, Marseille, Toulon, Nîmes, with Caen a more doubtful case. Furthermore, many of the same cities — rather than the staid inland capitals — were the scenes of the White Terror of 1795. Finally, Paris itself produced more violent opposition and conflict than did any retarded province in France. For these reasons, it would not be preposterous to hold that violent resistance to the party in power was most likely to occur where interests were most deeply divided, factions most sharply defined, change most recent, drastic, and disproportionate. In short, to return to the viewpoint of this study: where urbanization had been both vigorous and uneven. The chapters that follow will contain no attempt to test this hypothesis on the whole of France, but they will suggest that it is a useful approximation for events in the West.

CHAPTER 3

Cities and Subregions
of Southern Anjou

So far, the object of our attention has been the entire West, or even all of France. It is time to narrow the focus and step up the magnification. Let us put southern Anjou under the lens. Southern Anjou, because it is small enough to examine closely, because it encloses sufficient contrasts to make internal comparisons possible, because it was the home of the rebellion of 1793. This undertaking will require the extensive analysis of archival documents, as opposed to the use of published sources which has guided the discussion up to this point. Amid the thousands of writings which treat the military history of the Vendée, only a paltry few offer any solid information on the social organization of southern Anjou. The investigator must go to the archives, and even there he is often disappointed.

Southern Anjou

Southern Anjou is the part of Anjou south of the Loire. Its traditional subdivisions are the Mauges, to the southeast of the river Layon, and the Saumurois (after the city, Saumur), to the northeast. Although the label does not have the wide recognition of the other two, geographers and local folk alike are inclined to identify a third subdivision, the Val (i.e., Anjou's segment of the Loire valley), along the south bank of the Loire. Southern Anjou, then — Val, Mauges, and Saumurois together — will monopolize our attention. Furthermore, it is with the Mauges that we are most concerned, since that area rebelled in '93, while in general Val and Saumurois were faithful to the Republic.

No observer of southern Anjou ever escapes the necessity of

speaking of Val, Mauges, and Saumurois as separate entities. I shall call each a *subregion*, on the grounds that each is part of a larger homogeneous area, or region, and that the three larger regions — plain, valley, and bocage — meet in southern Anjou. The Mauges (the term is plural, the area singular) are part of the bocage, the area of fields enclosed with hedges, of subsistence agriculture, of the blossoming textile industry. The Val is the area along the Loire, composed of relatively compact villages of peasant proprietors engaged in intensive cultivation of the flood plains' rich soil. Away from the river, the Saumurois belongs to the plain. It is an area of open fields with somewhat larger-scale farming centering on wine and wheat. Despite changes in agricultural methods, these subregions have remained fairly constant for centuries.

The division between Val and Saumurois is somewhat more difficult to delineate than that between the Mauges and their neighbors, and is indeed irrelevant to the purposes of this study. Where eighteenth-century political action is concerned, the important difference is between the Mauges on one side, and Val-Saumurois on the other.

In dealing with matters of social organization, it is no doubt more than fastidious to demand sharply surveyed borders; it is nevertheless useful to develop a working definition of the line between Val-Saumurois and Mauges. Fortunately, the testimony of a great many observers, from many points of view, is available and in great agreement. The river Layon, from Cléré to its mouth at Chalonnes, is the main dividing line between the two subregions. From the area of the Mauges, which fades indefinitely into similar areas of Brittany and Poitou on the west and south, one must also subtract that bit of river plain which includes Montjean, intersects St. Florent and Champtoceaux, and forms a thin line between Mauges and Loire.

The distinction between Val-Saumurois and Mauges is more than just a convenient fiction. The boundaries have been in place for centuries. Without being able to state with any precision, or even any agreement, of what the difference consists, generations of observers have noticed that life in the one section differs greatly from life in the other. Most commonly, they have put it in terms of "character" or "mentality." A nineteenth-century prefect of Maine-et-Loire, after giving a lugubrious sketch of the oppressed, ignorant inhabitant of the Mauges, observed, "Character changes as one comes to the communes on the Loire. The population, more concentrated and closer to cities, is lively, bright, Gallic, less ignorant and freer from prejudice. Independence accompanies the division of properties there" (Uzureau 1919: 89). Much of André Siegfried's description of southern Anjou is in the same style:

The Vendean insurrection never went, in any stable fashion, beyond the valley of the Layon. That little river is certainly a frontier. We know already the areas to the south: Bressuire, Cholet and the royalist Vendée. What a contrast with these small proprietors of the Saumurois, closely attached to the soil they own, independent of any lord! These are real revolutionaries, in the limited but solid sense in which the new regime guarantees their property (1913: 40).

As in so much that Siegfried wrote, the intuition is unerring, even when the facts remain vague. The Layon is a frontier between two different kinds of rural society. We shall see that the territories it separates differ in such various and critical respects as the distribution of property, the type of agriculture, the intensity of religious practice, the nature of nineteenth-century political preferences, and even the character of family life. We shall see, in fact, the fundamental opposition between the deeply urbanized social order of Val-Saumurois and the shallow, recent, uneven urbanization of the Mauges.

The bridge between these diverse social orders is the area of the Layon. It is an intensive winegrowing area, and was so in the eighteenth century. But it is a winegrowing area with a difference. Generally, the vine means small property, concentrated settlement, and political independence. In these regards, as in geographic position, the Layon stands between the Mauges and the Saumurois. Property is large for a vineyard area, the population relatively dispersed, and the political temper reactionary. While the winegrower of the Layon is quite independent, according to Le Theule (1950: 208; cf. Wagret and Le Theule 1954), he differs from other vintners in being more religious and distinctly farther to the right. Even within the small area of the Layon, however, there is variation from great similarity to the Mauges to close attachment to the Saumurois. Churchgoing is one index that follows this pattern, and parochial school attendance is likewise highest in the communes to the west, on the side of the Mauges. In short, on most of the important lines of difference between Mauges and Val-Saumurois, the area of the Layon stands between the two; it is the buffer, the zone of transition.

Today, when natives cross the Layon from Saumurois to Mauges, they often say, "I'm going over into Vendée." They mean that they are moving into a different landscape, a different atmosphere, a different social order. Perhaps the most remarkable fact is that there are similar areas of swift transition around most of the bocage's rim. Everywhere bocage and plain meet without mixing. Everywhere there is the same sharp contrast in the quality of life as there was in response to the Revolution. Because of this we have some right to apply conclusions drawn from a study of variations within southern Anjou to the whole of the West below the Loire.

In many of the subregional comparisons to follow, it will be helpful to redefine the divisions of southern Anjou in terms of the administrative units that existed during the Revolution. As part of the revolutionary transformation of France's territorial organization, the department of Maine-et-Loire (a shrunken successor of the old province of Anjou) was divided into eight districts averaging about 60,000 in population. Below the Loire were the districts of St. Florent, Cholet, and Vihiers, plus a small part of the district of Angers, and almost all of the district of Saumur. Each of these districts was subdivided into about ten cantons, ordinarily consisting of three communes or more, for a total of roughly 3,000 to 6,000 people per canton.

Much of the information available on the Revolution in southern Anjou falls neatly into these divisions by district and canton. Wherever possible, I have regrouped other data according to the 1790 arrangement of districts and cantons. This provides a standard set of units for a wide variety of comparisons. When convenient, the data appear for individual cantons. In those cases, it is possible to reconstruct with fair precision the boundaries of Mauges, Val, and Saumurois. In other analyses, it is only feasible to present summary information for whole districts (for the districts of Saumur and Angers, this means the segments south of the Loire). Then the social boundaries do not appear as neatly. The following summary may be helpful:

The district of Cholet was entirely in the Mauges.

The district of St. Florent was almost all in the Mauges, with the exception of the strip along the river, which was in the Val.

The district of Vihiers was divided fairly evenly among Mauges, Layon and Saumurois.

The district of Angers was essentially Val, with fragments that could be assigned to Mauges and Saumurois.

The district of Saumur was, as its name indicates, mainly Saumurois, but included a strip of Val to the north.

For most purposes, this list comprises a kind of scale, with the district of Cholet, the pure example of bocage, at one end, and the district of Saumur, a combination of valley and plain, at the other. Comparison of the districts along this scale will provide many of the most important conclusions about the subregions of southern Anjou to be offered in the pages to come.

Cities

So far I have followed the traditional distinction of regions in terms of agriculture and rural landscape. But we cannot forget the cities. In the eighteenth century, there were a number of settlements in southern Anjou it is correct to call cities, both because they had the legal right to the title and because their inhabitants specialized in other pursuits than farming. The cities of the Mauges in 1789 were Cholet (population 6,000), Beaupréau (600), Chemillé (1,100), Maulèvrier (475), Montfaucon (550), Montrevault (675), Vihiers (1,100), St. Florent (1,100). In Val and Saumurois were Saumur (10,900), Ponts-de-Cé (1,650), Doué (2,000), Brissac (875), Chalonnes (2,500), Montreuil-Bellay (1,800), Montjean (1,000). Just across the Loire to the north of Val-Saumurois, of course, lay Angers (31,500). Most of these figures will lead modern cosmopolites to sniff, "Small-town stuff!" Yet these places were cities in character, in tempo, in the nature of their relations with life outside their boundaries.

For administrative and methodological convenience, sociologists have commonly identified all settlements with more than a certain number of inhabitants as cities, just as they have defined urbanization as an increase in the proportion of a population in settlements

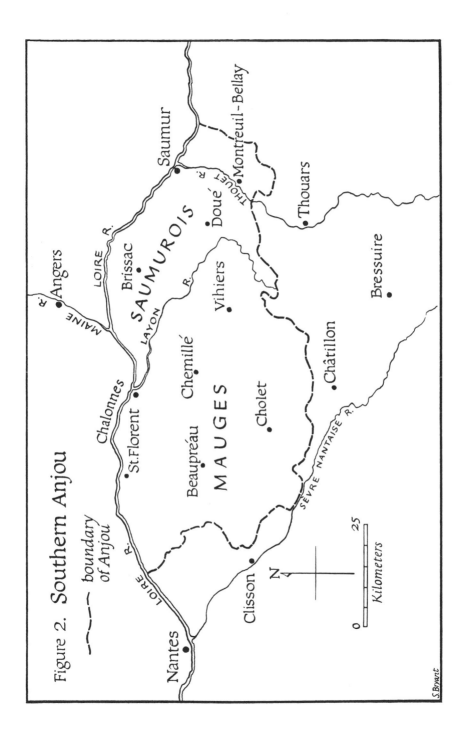

Figure 2. Southern Anjou

— — — boundary
of Anjou

of the minimum size or larger. The fact that the United States Census (with, it is true, an increasing number of exceptions) draws the line between rural and urban at agglomerations of 2,500 people has shaped a great deal of American research on the nature of the city. Of course, there are other justifications than sheer simplicity for the use of such a criterion. The larger a settlement grows, the smaller the proportion of his fellow residents a given individual can know intimately or, eventually, can know at all. The larger the scale of an enterprise, the more elaborate its administration is likely to be. These observations in themselves explain some of the differences between small-town and big-city life. But our sharpest methodological analyses and our most sophisticated approaches to a theory of urbanism (e.g., Duncan 1957; Mumford 1961; Weber 1958; Wirth 1938) agree in assigning a secondary rank to sheer size in the explanation of the special properties of cities. Furthermore, they tend to agree in identifying as cities those communities that combine a differentiated population with a coordinating role in activities that transcend the community itself. This touchstone serves very well in the present study, where a good deal of information about the population and activities of the settlements is at hand; it is less workable for the more usual research situation in which the investigator has scanty statistical data about a large number of communities.

In the present case, it is almost a joke to apply the statistical criterion of urbanization. The areas are very small, and the patterns of settlement vary (as we shall see) from concentration of all inhabitants within a single village in the Saumurois to a combination of central village, hamlets, and scattered peasant farms in the Mauges. Yet it is interesting to consider the implications of calculating "percent urban" by district, using two different criteria: 1) the proportion of the population in the settlements actually known as cities; 2) the proportion of the population in communes of 2500 or more people. A small table, using 1790 population figures, shows this distribution of population (A.D. M-et-L 1 L 402). There are more discrepancies between the two sets of figures than are apparent, since a number of the cities had less than 2500 people, and a number of the settlements of 2500 or more were not cities. The two sets agree in suggesting that St. Florent and Vihiers had the smallest share of urban residents, and the two extremes, Cholet and Saumur, the largest share. What the statistics cannot show is the great difference in both the form and the recency of urbanization in the two polar districts.

If the civilizing presence of cities over a long course of time is the important thing, Val and Saumurois were clearly more urban than the Mauges. The avenue of the Loire was already an old and favored thoroughfare in the twelfth and thirteenth centuries, those times of Angevin splendor. The tombs of Henry II, Richard the Lion-hearted, Isabelle of Angoulême and Eleanor of Aquitaine, at

Table 1. Urban population, by district.

District	Total population	Percent in cities	Percent in communes of 2,500 or more
Cholet	55674	14.6	26.0
St. Florent	45650	7.4	6.3
Vihiers	41271	4.8	6.1
Angers (south of the Loire)	24532	16.9	23.7
Saumur (south of the Loire)	48473	30.3	24.4

Fontevrault, attest the Saumurois' venerable pedigree. Saumur, Ponts-de-Cé, Chalonnes, Doué, Brissac, Montreuil-Bellay, and Montjean had ancient titles to distinction, while the cities of the Mauges were generally parvenus. The cities of Val-Saumurois had lived in intricate interdependence with the surrounding countryside for centuries, while those of the Mauges only began making their most strident claims for preeminence in the dozen decades before the Revolution. This is another way of saying that during those decades Val and Saumurois were already more thoroughly urbanized, even if the Mauges were urbanizing faster.

The cities of Val and Saumurois were at once more settled, more urbane, and more firmly integrated with the surrounding countryside. Industry played a relatively small part in their lives, and was not growing notably. There was, it is true, some woolen manufacturing at Doué, but Doué is said to have been a declining town in the years before the Revolution. Chalonnes was also involved in the textile industry, but not as a center of manufacturing. It was via Chalonnes that the flax of the Val reached the merchants and master weavers of the Mauges. Chalonnes was the most purely commercial city of Val and Saumurois: ". . . it conducted a very active commerce with Nantes, and even further, and therefore had some notable merchants" (Chollet 1952: 46). The city's greatest commercial advantage was its position at the mouth of the Layon, and its consequent role in the export of wine. In fact, as early as the eleventh century Chalonnes was known as a source of fine white wine: *peroptimam*, says Dion (1959: 279).

The trading activities of Chalonnes represented those of all the cities of Val-Saumurois in being devoted to agricultural products. These cities were exceptional in increasing rapidly in the later eighteenth century, with the dredging of the Layon and the continuing rise in Dutch demand for that little river's wines. Earlier, Ponts-de-Cé had been the principal entrepôt in the commerce with Holland.

Except for Saumur, the other cities of the subregion played a lesser part in the wine trade, but they busied themselves with diverse cash crops. It was reported of Brissac that ". . . it only subsists by its Friday markets, where all sorts of grain, a good deal of hemp and some flax are sold" (A.D. M-et-L C 211). Similar reports came from the other cities. There are two significant traits that set off this trade of Val-Saumurois from that of the Mauges: it was a long-established interchange between city and country which did not change drastically during the eighteenth century; and it took in the products of agriculture, not industry.

Trade was by no means all the life of these cities. As one might expect, there was a much greater load of royal and religious administrative activity in Val-Saumurois than in the Mauges. Saumur and Montreuil-Bellay alike were seats of Elections, with all their apparatus of courts and officials. Saumur was the headquarters of a *sénéchaussée*, a *prévôté*, and of numerous other units of the royal bureaucracy. Furthermore, Saumur, Montreuil-Bellay, Ponts-de-Cé, and Doué were thick with ecclesiastical establishments.

One very crude indication of the state of affairs is given in Table 2 by calculating the number of monks, nuns, and canons, and the livres of annual income of their establishments per 1,000 population for the districts of southern Anjou toward 1770 (computed from Uzureau 1901 and 1903). St. Florent's peculiar combination of few monks and much income was due to the one wealthy abbey in St. Florent-le-Vieil. The great contrast was between the District of Saumur, heavy with monasteries, convents, and chapters, and the rest of the area. It is true that the abbey of Fontevrault, which was not actually in a city, dominated the district with some 175 monks and nuns, receiving reported revenues of 250,000 livres per year. Still, Saumur was well supplied, with 140 people in major ecclesiastical centers living on revenues of at least 70,000 livres. These figures inevitably underestimate the extent of religious bureaucracy, since they omit not only priories, schools, and the parish priesthood, but also the army of civilian officials and workers the Church formed around itself.

Table 2. Ecclesiastical population and revenue, by district.

District	Ecclesiastics per 1000 population	Livres of ecclesiastical revenue per 1000 population
Cholet	2.0	559
St. Florent	1.7	1371
Vihiers	0.3	61
Angers	1.1	306
Saumur	7.9	7392

The difference between the subregions was far from absolute, however: almost every city had some clergy besides its parish priests. At the edge of the Mauges, St. Florent, with its Benedictines, had shared in the affluent monasticism of the Loire valley. Farther into the Mauges, Cholet, Chemillé, and Montrevault all had small religious establishments. Nevertheless, it was mainly the areas washed by the Loire that had flowered with wealthy centers of the Church.

Added together, these various observations amount to saying that in the Val and Saumurois the cities were examples of a species quite common in France: the old, established combination of administrative center and market for the crops of the hinterland. Their influence in that hinterland was of long standing. Indeed, one of the features that set them off from the towns of the Mauges was the antiquity of their existence as cities. Saumur was already a place of maturity and distinction when Saint Louis sojourned there. The handsome châteaux of Brissac and Saumur dated from the fourteenth century. Every one of the cities of Val and Saumurois was already notable in the Middle Ages, and some, like Montjean, lived their most brilliant moments then. With the possible exception of Beaupréau, none of the cities of the Mauges could present such claims of ancient urbanity. Their urban life was largely a creation of the seventeenth and eighteenth centuries. This is another element of the basic contrast: the old, fairly settled urbanization of Val-Saumurois versus the new, turbulent urbanization of the Mauges.

City Life

The cities of the Mauges were not primarily centers of administration. Yet it is true that the cities and the largest towns were hosts to the lowest echelons of the royal government. Courts, fiscal offices, police headquarters, and salt stores were in the cities, and many of their officials prominent members of the local bourgeoisie. The same was true of the administrations of the largest fiefs, such as Maulèvrier, Beaupréau, Cholet, and St. Florent. Their top positions attracted lawyers, notaries, and administrators of all kinds; they, too, were city-dwellers. The internal political structure of the cities was a complex of municipal offices, agencies of the central government, and seigniorial bureaucracies, with the order of importance varying from place to place. Many individuals occupied positions in more than one of these types of organization, but all of them were essentially bourgeois in composition.

Economic life was also dominated by the bourgeoisie. The major economic activities of the cities of the Mauges fall under the headings of local marketing, trade, and manufacturing. Each city had weekly markets and periodic fairs, the markets serving mainly to supply the townsmen, but the fairs attracting buyers from miles around. Chemillé had a weekly market, as it does today, but it also had the traditional right to hold fairs on the days of St. Eutrope (30 April), St. Madeline (22 July), St. Radegonde (13 August), St. Giles (1 September), St. Léonard (5 November), and St. Clement (23 November). The number of fairs depended on history, population, and royal favor, but the same kind of schedule existed in each of the cities, and each had its own specialities and its own regular concessionaires.

Most of the fairs and markets not only met the needs for local exchange, but acted as junctions in commercial channels that went far beyond the immediate vicinity of the city. As one might expect, the important items exchanged in the Mauges were cattle and textile products. Thus it was that the merchants of Beaupréau, Cholet, and several other towns between them appealed in 1786 for better hours for Beaupréau's market, on the grounds that ". . . for a number of years the thread market which takes place at Beaupréau every Monday has been growing in respect both to the volume of thread and to the number of clothiers an interest in trade attracts here . . ." (A.D. Indre-et-Loire C 129). And not long afterward, Montrevault was urging its prior claim to the establishment of a tribunal there rather than elsewhere: the great importance of its cattle market (Uzureau 1940). Cholet, Chemillé, and Beaupréau also dealt actively in cattle as well as in textiles. In fact, except for a small amount of trading in grain and wine at Montfaucon, the markets of the Mauges were essentially specialized in two commodities: cattle and cloth.

This trade was inextricably related to manufacturing activity. While textile manufacturing was scattered widely through the Mauges, its control was concentrated in a few cities and large towns. This fact takes on great importance when coupled with another: that the cloth production of the Mauges grew unceasingly during the eighteenth century. It came close to doubling between 1755 and 1785 (see Chapter 7). The result was that the few centers of the textile trade were bursting with energy and their influence extending swiftly, incessantly, but unevenly, into the surrounding countryside.

Of course, there was some variation in the relative weights of industry and administration in the cities of the Mauges. St. Florent, for example, was primarily an administrative center, with its life centered around a convent and a monastery. As the city fathers of St. Florent themselves avowed in 1790, up to the Revolution St. Florent had ". . . neither trade, nor manufacturing, nor fairs [and] only lived on its consumers. . . ." (A.N. D IV bis 26). Beaupréau and Maulèvrier were somewhat more specialized in seigneurial administration than Montrevault, Chemillé, Vihiers, or Cholet. The important point, however, is that where urban expansion *was* occurring in the Mauges during the eighteenth century, it was tied to the expansion of the textile industry. This means that, although the bourgeois dominated all the cities, the merchants, rather than the lawyers and administrators, gave the movement direction in the cities which were reaching out most actively. These circumstances brought increasing influence to men whose activities minimized their concern with agriculture and the peasantry and drew their attention outward, toward great cities and national affairs. In many ways, the ebullient textile centers were in, but not of, the country. This combination of expansion and partial detachment from the hinterland became critically important during the Revolution.

The center of the vortex in the Mauges was the city of Cholet. The second largest city of southern Anjou in 1789, it had been insignificant, "governed like a simple town," a century before. The story of its growth is a combination of noble initiative, general economic changes, and bourgeois enterprise. René Barjot, Marquis of Cholet, began the promotion of the city in mid-sixteenth century. Despite the common theory that it was a less well known brother of the great Colbert, briefly holder of the fief, who established the weaving industry and brought in the necessary equipment and artisans, most of the credit is due to the Marquis de Broon and the Comte de Rougé, later seigneurs whose conscious policy was to build up the commercial activity of Cholet.

This activity centered about the textile industry. There are records of weaving in Cholet well back into the Middle Ages, but its importance for commerce developed with expansion of France's colonial trade in the seventeenth century. The cloth made around Cholet left via Bordeaux and Nantes for the Americas and the slave trade. As Dion remarks, "At Cholet, there was only a commercial concentration," based entirely on the domestic system, and drawing finished work from weavers stationed in dozens of nearby communes (1934: 598). The city was the headquarters of the cloth merchants and clothiers, whose goods came from miles around, from the perhaps 40,000 workers involved in the industry.

At the same time, Cholet was a regional market and a major meeting place in the cattle trade. Altogether, according to one of its chief officials, the city was ". . . the metropolis of a famous commerce spread through the world; capital of an industry that occupies parts of three departments; the rendezvous of 100 parishes; celebrated for its cattle fairs" (A.N. D IV bis 26).

Changes since the Revolution have erased some of the traces of the position Cholet occupied during the eighteenth century. Then the city was essentially the chief of a number of linked commercial and industrial centers spread through the country. The merchants of Cholet had close associates in many of the surrounding towns. After the Revolution, the industry of the Mauges began to concentrate first in the larger settlements, then in Cholet alone. The result was that Cholet grew at the expense of the surrounding settlements (its population going from 5,000 to 22,000 between 1820 and 1920, while that of surrounding communes was declining: Furet 1950: ch. IV). More important, Cholet was absorbing what industrial activity there was, while its hinterland was returning to a more purely agricultural state than it had been in at the time of the Revolution. The later deindustrialization of the countryside should not blind us to the growing influence of Cholet in the territories around it during the eighteenth century.

At that time the clothiers of Cholet and environs depended heavily on the superior raw materials raised in the Val, so much so that the mayor of Chalonnes was moved to declare, "The industries of Cholet and Chemillé owe us their existence" (Dion 1934: 61). The contact of the merchants of Cholet with the river towns, the ocean ports, and even with their overseas' outlets was constant and voluminous. Their goods went off to Africa and America ". . . sent all these places by the shippers of Bordeaux, Nantes, La Rochelle and other cities in maritime commerce" (A.D. Indre-et-Loire C 135). It was in the fortunes of Nantes that the fortunes of Cholet were particularly involved; the merchants of Cholet dealt especially with the merchants of the great shipping center.

As a result of all this activity the population of Cholet quintupled during the eighteenth century. With its commercial development, Cholet became a center for government, eventually undermining the positions of Beaupréau and Montreuil-Bellay. The salt office established there provided official titles and revenues which were eagerly sought by the local merchants, and a number of other agencies added to both the income and the luster of the city. The agency that affected the merchants most directly was probably the *bureau de marque*, established by the *Intendant* (roughly speaking, the provincial governor) to grade and mark the cloth produced locally, in order to insure quality to the consumer. But the most important office, and one of the best indications of the growing importance of Cholet, was that of the subdelegate, the direct representative of the Intendant, established there in mid-eighteenth century.

The commercial development of Cholet meant perforce the growth of a substantial bourgeoisie. Toward 1760 they were wealthy enough for the innkeepers to claim, speaking of the wealthier bourgeois, "The greater part of Cholet and of the properties around the approaches to Cholet belongs to them" (A.D. M-et-L C 55). It was naturally the cloth merchants and the clothiers who profited most from the expansion of the textile trade, the merchants particularly. Trade prospered enough that by the late eighteenth century Cholet was the base of a well-established and well-heeled bourgeoisie of which a number of members had attached the high-sounding prefix "de" to their names, built country homes, and bought offices bringing them into the nobility. The prominent Béritault family, for example, was just making the transition in the 1720's. While René, the father, had been Béritault de la Chesnaye, merchant of Cholet, Alexandre, his son, was ". . . Esquire, lord of Le Coudray, Counselor Secretary of the King . . ." (A.D. M-et-L E 1651). Some of the later members of this family were almost indistinguishable from the older landed nobility. The majority of the bourgeoisie, however, remained essentially bourgeois even as they accumulated titles and wealth.

As the bourgeois became prominent, the nobles, even the lords of the city, faded from the scene. The lords were absentees, while the bourgeois ran the city. It was a bourgeoisie vigorous, enterprising, and wealthy, with a constant eye to the improvement of commerce. It was the bourgeois of Cholet who made one of the primary requests of the city in 1787 more and better roads (A.D. M-et-L C 192). It was the same bourgeois who were able to report a few years later: "Public spirit has undeniably made more progress here than in any of the surrounding parishes and cities" (Uzureau 1934: 94). By that time, public spirit, zeal for the Revolution, and urbanity were close to synonymous in the Mauges, and Cholet was the epitome of all three.

No other city in the Mauges was the equal of Cholet, but there were several cities and towns whose development was similar. Chemillé, for example. Chemillé was not only attached to Cholet by many bonds of business and communication but was its miniature in many respects. It was likewise a cattle market, a minor administrative center and, most of all, a focus of the textile industry. The population of the city proper had probably doubled during the eighteenth century, bringing the bourgeoisie to greater power and prominence. And the city's demands for consideration in the parceling out of Revolutionary offices sound like echoes of Cholet's: ". . . considering that a great deal of trading of all sorts of cattle, merchandise of Cholet [i.e., fabrics], thread and other things takes place here each year; and that Chemillé has always been very famous . . ." (A.N. D IV bis 26). Again, as we shall see in some detail, the patriotic sounds that emanated from the larger cities of the West reverberated at once in the little city of Chemillé.

Town and Country

Cities the size of Chemillé (little over a thousand in the main settlement) were by no means the last step in the path of urban influence in the Mauges. It is important to understand that throughout the bocage the ground plan of the rural community consisted of several different units: the *bourg*, generally the largest agglomeration, containing the church, the inn, the shops, the homes of the merchants, and most of the industry; *villages*, smaller clusters including some nonagricultural population; *hamlets*, composed of two or three adjacent farms; and *isolated farms*. It was uncommon for half the population to live in the bourg. But the bourg was the outpost of the city.

The merchants of Cholet, Beaupréau, or Chemillé had allies in the bourgs of each of the surrounding communities — other merchants, master weavers, and occasional professionals or officials. Through them the country felt the power of the city. Here, in the relations of the small cities of the Mauges with the surrounding rural territories, the condition of uneven urbanization begins to show its significance. It will be the business of later chapters to analyze the divisions and conflicts within the peasant community. No one could understand them without first considering the community's relation to the city.

The essential point is this: in most respects, the life of the countryside was quite insulated from that of the cities, but the commercial expansion of the eighteenth century dramatically heightened the impact of the cities on part of the rural population and some of its activities. Subsistence agriculture continued to dominate the country, hardly affected by the change in the cities. But weaving was prospering, attracting more of the rural population, and extending the influence of the urban markets in the countryside. At the same time, the bourgeois scattered through the country increased in importance and sought to secure for themselves a larger political role, as well as landed property. They were the nuclei of urban influence in communities still populated mainly with peasants. As never before, the forces of rural and urban life met within the bocage.

They did not meet as equals, however, so long as agriculture and the people involved in it remained untouched by city and industry. In many respects the peasant communities remained independent. In religious matters, for example, there was almost no liaison between city and country. Some urban abbeys, like that of Saint-Florent, were lords spiritual and temporal of country parishes, but their direct participation in local affairs was sporadic and capricious. There was a nominal secular hierarchy, with rural deans holding cures at such places as Chemillé, but there is no sign of any administrative connection whatsoever between these officials and the country curés. The curé made the religious contacts outside the community, and they were more likely to be with the bishop in Angers or La Rochelle than with the monks, canons, or curés of the cities.

Politically, there may have been a little more interdependence of city and country, but not much. The cities were the seats of the agencies of government, but country communes had very little contact with those agencies. Most of those contacts, moreover, were by means of a limited number of intermediaries. The economic problem is more complex, since the degree of contact depends on the people and activities discussed. To begin with, we might expect urban influence on agriculture and bourgeois ownership of land to go together. The available knowledge on land ownership in southern Anjou is far from firm. However, the information at hand indicates that the bourgeois had only a small share of the land: R. H. Andrews (1935: 12) gives a summary figure of 16.5 percent by area for his quite irregular sample of manors in the Mauges. This proportion, if correct, is insignificant compared with the more than 50 percent that Bois (1960b: 47) found in bourgeois hands in the Sarthe. Furthermore, the bourgeois holdings Andrews identifies were greatest in the immediate vicinities of the cities: near 30 percent around Cholet, 25 percent at Chemillé, and 20 percent at St. Florent. One may draw from these figures both a negative and a positive hypothesis about bourgeois property in the Mauges. Negatively, it seems that bourgeois landlords were virtually absent in the open country; positively, that they were probably acquiring land around their bases of operation as the cities grew during the eighteenth century. This would be in accordance with a time-honored pattern, well described by Gaston Roupnel (1955: 199–249) for the vicinity of Dijon. It would also be consistent with their eager acquisition of confiscated Church and noble lands during the Revolution.

It appears that the influence of urban landlords on the countryside was not very great. About the same may be said of the urban market for agricultural products. The cities drew their subsistence from the country, but of the major farm products, cattle alone were of more than local commercial significance. Most farmers drove oxen to the city for sale at one time or another, but few sold more than one or two a year. In general, peasant contact with city-dwellers via the market was at a minimum.

We have seen enough of the textile industry to realize that it established many more contacts between city and country, but that these contacts were selective. Geographically, it promoted relations between the cities and the bourgs of the rural communities, while neglecting the outlying areas. Socially, it set up connections with the merchants, clothiers, and — to a limited extent — the weavers of the countryside. Furthermore, if we take the major centers as the points of origin, weaving had spread quite unevenly in the Mauges. Villedieu-la Blouère, for instance, had essentially two bourgs, the "old" economy of subsistence agriculture centered around one, and the "new" of textiles and trade around the other, the curé dominating one, and the bourgeois the other. The same was true of St. Georges-du-Puy-de-la-Garde, with its twin centers of St. Georges and Les Gardes. There is no doubt, then, that many country bourgs carried on a steady interchange of industrial products with the nearby cities, but other bourgs were hardly affected, and the influence of this commerce rarely went far beyond the bourg.

The role of the bourg was very important. It was in two ways the transition between city and country. First, it was a physical compromise between the two, with its complement of shops, services, and administrative centers. In size, the bourgs of the Mauges ranged from 50 to 2,000 people. Second, the bourg was the actual social link between city and country. It was the home of those who had the most contact with the city: the priests, the artisans, and the bourgeois. It was the point of intersection of the two types of social organization, roughly "urban" and "rural," which are represented by the money-market-manufacturing and land-agriculture complexes within the rural community.

Le May is a case in point. It is a community not far from Cholet, well known for its commercial activity. Although Cholet's development was favored over Le May's, apparently as a matter of policy, the bourg still became a center of manufacturing. The eighteenth-century situation was this: "The bourg . . . formed the center of a concentration of merchants, clothiers, wool-spinners, tanners and smiths, having a sort of monopoly on the special, and then quite important, manufacture of spindle-liners . . ." (Port 1878: II, 360). The population of the commune grew enough that two of its subsidiary villages (Bégrolles and St. Léger) became seats of new communes after 1789. Roughly three fifths of the estimated 3,500 population of the commune lived in the bourg and these two principal villages; this was an exceptionally high concentration for the Mauges. The people of the bourg demonstrated an outlook akin to that of the leaders of Chemillé and Cholet, interested in anything that would favor trade, and demanding roads (A.D. M-et-L C 192). However, the prosperity of the bourg only served to heighten the contrast with the rest of the community. The two parties — "rural" and "urban" — were in militant conflict during the Revolution.

All this goes to show that the traditional cultural separation of city and country in peasant societies was in full force in the Mauges. At Beaupréau, the division was symbolized by the two parishes, Notre Dame (city) and St. Martin (country). Early in the Revolution the latter pleaded not to be incorporated into the city, on the ground that it was "distinct in character and geography" from Notre Dame, a claim corroborated by the fact that its municipality of 1787 was all peasants, while that of the city was predominantly bourgeois (Uzureau 1931: 22–29). The divergence is underlined even more definitely in a letter written by the notables of Cholet in 1789, commenting on the protest of a "faction" [i.e., the countrymen] that they had been prevented from taking part in the recent election:

> Since the parish is composed of inhabitants who differ a great deal among themselves in customs and interests, a sort of jealousy, which one might even call hostility, has developed. The people of the town, all bourgeois, merchants, clothiers, ordinarily more intelligent, richer, and therefore more suited to business than the country people, are smaller in numbers than the latter. It is possible that these good farmers, perhaps irritated by the small attention given them during the first election, might take advantage of their majority to choose representatives solely from people of their own cloth. The fact that they pay the greater part of the taxes could also enter into their reasoning, and justify these politics in their eyes (A.D. M-et-L C 187).

At this point, the distinguished citizens proposed a statutory limitation on the number of rustics who could be elected.

Rural and urban were in tension in the Mauges. On the one hand, the ties binding most of the country to the cities were both tenuous and of recent origin. On the other hand, the small cities were growing, full of *élan*, reaching out through the commercial bourgs, claiming more influence and recognition. The cities and their bourgeois were ready to assert their leadership, but their relations with the rural communities were not extensive or durable enough to make that leadership prevail against opposition.

Across the Layon, the tension of rural and urban was much less evident, the role of the cities basically different. In Val and Saumurois, the cities were the markets through which the produce of the region passed, the targets of peasant production, the centers of local influence through long centuries. They were the seats of the monasteries that had been such a force in local history. They were more readily accessible by superior roads. Saumur was in the midst of the region, and the great city of Angers lay only four miles beyond the river. Val and Saumurois, to return once again to the refrain, were more thoroughly and evenly urbanized than the Mauges. They were to that extent more susceptible to bourgeois leadership, less liable to the ancient agon of rural against urban.

CHAPTER 4

Rural Communities and Classes

A community is a group whose use of a particular territory is a major element in the social relations of its members.[1] Except in the (perhaps imaginary) extreme case, a community is always a segment of a larger society. The community's political, religious, or economic norms and relationships are essentially localized versions of those of the society as a whole, and there is ordinarily a great deal more communication across any community's boundaries in these respects than the customary, hermetically sealed model of the rural community would lead us to expect.[2]

In this regard, analysts of community organization have been surprisingly willing to draw tough, stanch boundaries around their objects of study, and to argue as if they were self-contained systems. They have shared the inclination of those students of industrial organization, the "plant sociologists," who have so often depicted the factory in the image of an isolated aboriginal village. Curiously, even theorists of urban structure, aware as they are of the constant flow of migrants, messages, and goods across urban boundaries, have customarily conceptualized the communities they have investigated as tightly bounded systems: The justly renowned essay of Louis Wirth (1938) on the essential character of cities pays almost no attention to the implication of cities in regional, national, and international networks of norms and social relations. Likewise, the assumption that each community has its own autonomous class order, based on

[1] This apparent truism (which finds its inspiration in Hiller 1941 and Reiss 1959) leaves conveniently open two elements which are often taken to define a community: the existence of a solidary feeling, or the presence of a formal political structure in control of the territory in question. For discussions of definitions and concepts of community organization, see Hawley 1950; Sanders 1958; Chiva 1959; Blackwell 1954; Heberle 1941; Hill and Whiting 1950; Hillery 1955; Lefebvre 1949; Loomis and Beegle 1950; Soboul 1957; Sutton and Kolaja 1960.

[2] See the valuable discussions of the interpenetration of community and society in Wolf 1956; Vidich and Bensman 1958: ch. 4.

mutual acquaintance, continually tempts analysts of social stratifi-
cation, and their critics just as continually condemn them for neglecting the national ramifications of the rank system that appears in
any particular community. They, too, need a conception of the interpenetration of the national and the local. Except perhaps at the
aboriginal extreme, a major élement in the structure of any community, and a major determinant of its characteristics, is the set of
social relationships that cuts across it and extends into the society
beyond its boundaries.

Variation and Differentiation in Communities

This does not mean that all communities, or even all peasant
communities, are equally involved in the world outside them. One
of the major respects in which communities vary is in the extent and
type of their external involvements. Cities grasp the outside world
hungrily, while villages timidly extend their antennae. The whole
swarm of ideas connoted by the phrase, "folk-urban continuum,"
clusters around the proposition that variation in such characteristics
of communities as their homogeneity, integration, or religiosity is
closely related to variation in the volume of their external contacts
(Redfield 1941 and 1947; Gross 1948; Miner 1952; Duncan 1957).
The untenably global scope of this assertion (and the sentimental
view of rustic virtues it may conceal) should not divert us from the
insight it conveys. Communities which differ in extent of outside
involvements also tend to differ in degree and form of internal differentiation, as well as in the quality of personal relationships. Much
of the discussion that follows will be an elaboration of this observation.

The fact of outside involvement makes it sensible to distinguish
between "internally" and "externally" oriented activities and individuals, a distinction which is gaining currency in a surprising variety
of studies (see Merton 1957: 387–420; Sykes 1951; Gouldner 1957 and
1958; Redfield 1956: esp. II; Wolf 1956; Hughes 1955). For example,
Julian Pitt-Rivers (1960) has portrayed the segregation of two worlds
of activity in a French village from one another: the one, the world
in which *patois* is spoken, embracing farming, animals, weather,
proverbs, family matters; the other, the world in which French is
spoken, embracing politics, fashion, learning, commerce, national

affairs. The world of French absorbs the citizens of the central village, but the peasants are profoundly bilingual. They live in both worlds. Now, the fact is that all peasants are to some extent bilingual — or, better, bicultural. All peasant communities participate simultaneously in activities and norms which pervade the entire society, and other activities and norms which are quite localized. The roles within them (merchant, day laborer, squatter, priest) vary in their involvement in the two kinds of activities. There are therefore some roles and some activities in every peasant community which are incomprehensible without some attention to the world outside.

The roles in a community which are most fully ambivalent we may call *elite* roles. Such individuals as the merchant, the curé, the political official gain much of their significance from the fact that they are mediators, actively and simultaneously participating in both the national and the local structures (Redfield 1956; Wolf 1956; Geertz 1960; Eisenstadt 1951; Sanders 1949; Sutton 1959). When the peasants or rural artisans do participate in such national structures as the market or the church, they generally do so under the control of the local elite, maintaining little contact with the outside agents of these structures. The elite themselves have much more extensive and lasting relationships with the outside agents. Their positions, furthermore, are much more transferable — have meaning in many more social contexts, depend less on particular memberships or traditional attachments, permit their occupants to move more freely among comparable positions in different communities. Relatively mobile, urbane, flexible, knowledgeable, the elite stand out from the rest of the peasant community.

One must not infer from the similarities in their social positions that the members of the elite are necessarily solidary. In so far as the elite positions in different systems — religion, government, and so on — are differentiated from each other, their occupants may be in heated conflict. Long before the time of Don Camillo, many a village had witnessed the spectacle of open rivalry between the local churchman and the "progressive" politician. Sociologists have developed a penchant to presume collaboration, if not collusion, on the part of the elite (e.g., Hunter 1953; cf. Greer 1962: 152–163). Instead of assuming the existence of solidarity, they would do well to investigate the conditions under which the elite of a community *is* able to act as a bloc.

The nature of its involvement in the society around it, then, profoundly influences the internal structure of a community. The contacts of a rural community with the cities of its nation are of peculiar importance. Cities are the control centers of the pervasive systems which crosscut the rural community and form its elite. Bureaucracy, market, church, and national language — as much as they may grow into the lives of rural communities — all are co-ordinated and stimulated by the city. The city is also, of course, the countryman's favorite illustration of original sin. Why?

On the surface, it seems natural to attribute the frequent eruption of rural-urban hostility to mutual ignorance or to utter incompatibility of outlook. Furthermore, there appears to be something to the idea that groups which are isolated from the rest of society and homogeneous, and whose members bear suffering in common are more likely to act collectively against a common enemy (Marx and Engels 1947: 43–69; Kerr and Siegel 1954; Kornhauser 1961). One might therefore assume that rural opposition to the ways and works of the city would be greatest where the insulation between country and city was toughest. Working from the notion that two groups which never meet cannot fight, nevertheless, it is possible to proceed to a contrary conclusion: genuine hostility awaits the establishment of a substantial amount of contact between the city and the peasant community, is reinforced by the presence in the country of insistent representatives of the urban viewpoint, and intensifies precisely when the intercourse between city and country is rapidly increasing. In these circumstances, urban-based norms and sets of social relationships lay increasing claims to control the actions of community members, a shift in the positions of the elites occurs, and the standard mechanisms for conflict resolution are likely to be inadequate. The struggle, it follows, is likely to center on the areas of behavior and the elites which the incursions of "urban" norms have affected most seriously. Certainly we commonly observe the resistance of rural populations, not so much to those urban institutions which are entirely alien to them as to those which are all too familiar. (Witness the curses American agrarian radicals used to hurl at banks, railroads, or bureaucrats.) Perhaps this formulation summarizes the matter adequately: Given substantial separation of rural and urban, outright warfare between them is most likely to break out when and where contact between them is most rapidly increasing.

This discussion leaves an interesting residue: the realization that even in a predominantly peasant society the conditions of city and country depend intensely on each other. If peasants are by definition aware of cities and influenced by them, however, they are by no means equally aware or influenced. When Max Weber (Gerth and Mills 1946: 378) remarks that ". . . nothing can be substituted for that educating influence which is exerted upon the peasant by an intensive formation of urban communities . . . ," he is underscoring the differences between rural communities that are much involved, and those that are little involved, in urban life. By a similar token, the growth of cities within a region or a society inevitably reforms its peasant communities. It is this fact which makes it reasonable to speak of the "urbanization" of peasant communities.

At its least complicated level, the urbanization of peasant communities consists of some fairly direct consequences and prerequisites of the growth of cities. First, urbanites must eat. Urban growth generally means the production of an agricultural surplus through increased efficiency, the expansion of the market for farm products, and a corresponding increase in the share of rural production destined for the market. Increased production for the market generally implies increased use of money and increased purchase of goods and services in the market, on the part of the producers themselves. Urban growth is also likely to lead to increasing imposition of taxes (which may be in the form of tribute, feudal payments, religious dues, tolls, or direct governmental taxation). And the imposition of taxes, as Eric Wolf (1957) has pointed out, frequently forces a compensatory reorganization of the peasant community and draws it farther into the market. Urban growth generally calls forth some improvement in the efficiency of communication and transportation; to some extent it therefore facilitates the traffic of ideas and men between the rural community and other points in its society. Finally, the growth of cities is so closely joined to the development of large-scale, coordinated activities that we may regard the increasing influence within rural areas of officeholders operating according to relatively impersonal standards on behalf of complex organizations as a nearly inevitable feature of urbanization. Increased involvement in markets, more taxes, enhanced communication and mobility, greater intervention by bureaucrats — urban increase in its society is likely to mean all these changes to the average peasant community.

Markets, taxes, communications and bureaucrats are, however, forces working on the community more or less from the outside. We ought to pay some attention to the internal changes of the peasant community that deserve to be grouped with these other elements of urbanization. All too often critics of mass society, with much wringing of hands, have announced this process as the "breakdown of community." It is much more than that. Under the denomination of "fragmentation-pervasion," Arnold Feldman (1962) has analyzed the standard process in which technological change in a society leads to 1) the increasing differentiation of sets of work-related norms and social relationships from each other (so that the standards and the principal agents of the labor market, for example, become quite distinct from those of line production); 2) the penetration of these standardized and specialized sets of norms and relationships into the multitudinous firms involved in industrial production (so that the criteria and procedures for hiring and firing, for example, become increasingly uniform, wherever a particular kind of worker is concerned); and 3) the subdivision of roles within the firm itself, each role being increasingly identified with one or another of the systems intersecting the firm (so that the factions of production bosses, product engineers and personnel specialists, for example, come to apply decisively different standards to their own and each other's work, and to compete for the firm's resources). An exactly parallel process appears in the urbanization of the peasant community.

The parallel changes are, of course, the local corollaries of the changes I have already identified as constituting the urbanization of a region or a society. With the pervasion of standardized, specialized norms throughout a society, localism necessarily declines. On the one hand, this means that more people and more behavior are involved in "national" norms; on the other, since pervasion necessarily advances unevenly, it means that in the short run the division between the "local" and "national" aspects of the community is actually sharpened. But even more important than this division between internal and external orientations is the fragmentation of roles within the community through the differentiation of the normative systems which intersect them. Religious behavior becomes separate from political behavior, political from market behavior, specialists explicitly devoted to the coordination of one or the other of them appear. And the differentia that prevail in the society as a whole — occupation, education, and so forth — supplant those that are peculiar to the individual community.

At the same time, the quality of the norms of the peasant community changes. To the extent that large-scale, coordinated activities generate impersonal, rationalized norms (and the extent seems to be great), urbanization means that an increasing share of social relations within the community will be governed by such standards. The range of behavior controlled by the diffuse obligations of kinship and neighborliness will shrink, while the range subject to the narrower definitions of commodity market or bureaucracy will swell. One apparent further consequence of this process is the segmentation of the behavior of each member of the community into the multiple roles he occupies.

If all this is so, we must conclude that the nature and the position of the elite also changes in urbanization. Elite roles fractionate and multiply. Seen from the present perspective, what Julian Steward and associates (1956) call the decline in the mediating activities of a community's "local hierarchy of power" is the *specialization* of mediating activity; whereas the large landowner in a backward Puerto Rican village is the intermediary between community and society for a wide range of problems, as the community becomes more absorbed in the cash-crop market the merchant, the politician, and the union leader each become prominent as middlemen with distinctive tasks. Who is the middleman depends on the task.

The fragmentation of the elite raises the possibility of new kinds of conflict within the peasant community, reinforced by the divisions within the whole society. Indeed, the process of urbanization facilitates the reforming of persistent local rivalries along lines that have some significance throughout the society (just as the divisions between Guelphs and Ghibellines absorbed a host of entirely local factional rivalries in Italy). It also probably increases the likelihood that new fissures that form in the community will separate groups whose major activities are in different crosscutting systems, and will thus extend to fissures within the elite. I would hazard the hypothesis that the likelihood of such a situation is further reinforced when the division in question also separates the most strongly externally-oriented segments of the community from the rest — an interesting parallel to the frequent disputes within colleges which polarize two parties around, say, the departments of English and Engineering.

Certainly it remains open to question and investigation whether the whole set of changes touched on during this discussion of the urbanization of peasant communities actually all belong together and invariably appear in each other's company. It is enough for the purposes of the present analysis that they often do so, and that their concomitant variation provides the basis for the classification of communities as 1) more or less urbanized, and 2) more or less rapidly urbanizing. If there is some validity to the previous discussion, ar-raying communities in terms of the extent of their involvement in pervasive, large-scale systems ought to permit an investigator to make some correct inferences about variations in their internal struc-ture. Furthermore, such an analysis ought to make some sense of the conflicts, internal and external, in which a given kind of com-munity is involved. That is, of course, the purpose immediately at hand.

Subdivisions of Southern Anjou's Communities

We may begin the application of these general ideas to the case of southern Anjou with a recapitulation: The rural communities of the Val-Saumurois (which were generally responsive to the Rev-olution) were much more urbanized, but the rural communities of the Mauges (which generally took part in the counterrevolution) were urbanizing more rapidly during the eighteenth century. The Val-Saumurois was an area of cash-crop farming, extensive and frac-tionated peasant property, large numbers of agricultural day laborers, long exposure to the influence of markets, monasteries, royal admin-istration, and cities. The Mauges' peasants, who gained most of their cash income from the occasional sale of cattle, were largely engaged in subsistence farming on land rented from nobles. In the same subregion, however, especially in the vicinity of Cholet, a textile industry incorporating a separate class of artisans and a prosperous group of merchants was growing up rapidly.

Throughout southern Anjou, even if their proportions and their relations varied, there were five distinguishable classes into which the members of rural communities fell: nobles, priests, artisans, bourgeois, and peasants. There are a few social positions, such as miller and carter, which are hard to place in such a scheme, but the immense majority of adult males, and their households, were well identified with one or another of these classes. Each of the five labels represents, as we shall see, a distinctive cluster of power, productive role, market position, prestige, property, and social relations. As a preliminary sample of the variation in the composition of the rural communities of southern Anjou, comparison of some fairly detailed data for three different localities is illuminating. The estimates are based on an enumeration of the entire population of one commune early in the Revolution, and on the frequency of appearance of various occupational groups among the fathers of newborn children in the parish registers of two other communities for 1780–1784, supplemented with information from other sources on nobles, priests, and total population (see Appendix A).

The first community (Grézillé) is a winegrowing village not too far from Saumur and the Loire. The second (La Pommeraye), in the section of the Mauges near the Loire, is largely in traditional subsistence grains. The third (St. Pierre-de-Cholet) is an important rural textile center adjacent to Cholet. The adult males in these three communities were employed approximately as shown in Table 3 at the time of the Revolution.

Table 3. Occupations of adult males in three communities of southern Anjou.

Category	Grézillé	La Pommeraye	St. Pierre-de-Cholet
Nobles	2	1	0
Parish clergy	2	3	5
Peasants renting large farms (*métayers, laboureurs*)	11	231	184
Peasants renting small farms (*bordiers, closiers*)	18	77	30
Winegrowers	46	0	0
Hired hands	41	38	102
Officials	0	0	12
Doctors, lawyers, and other professionals	0	4	7
Merchants, manufacturers, and innkeepers	3	14	86
Weavers and other industrial artisans	13	45	390
Smiths, bakers, millers, and other nonindustrial artisans	19	95	133
Total	155	508	949

Some important facts emerge when the numbers in Table 3 are translated into percentages and broad classes, as they are in Table 4. In the rural Saumurois, peasants were a resounding majority, whereas they were actually a smaller part of the rural population in the Mauges. However, most of the peasants of the Mauges were placed on good-sized family farms, while many more in the Saumurois were either working small plots, hiring out their labor, or both. There were fewer nobles residing in the Mauges (even if the nobles did own a great deal of land). Finally, rural industry, with its attendant artisans, merchants, and manufacturers, absorbed much more of the population of the Mauges, particularly in the vicinity of Cholet. On the one hand, differentiated and market-oriented agriculture; on the other, polarization between family farms and small industry.

Table 4. Class distribution in three communities.

Class	Grézillé	La Pommeraye	St. Pierre-de-Cholet
Nobles	1.3%	0.2%	0.0%
Clergy	1.3	0.6	0.5
Peasants	74.8	68.1	33.3
Bourgeois	1.9	3.5	11.1
Artisans	20.6	27.6	55.1
Total	99.9	100.0	100.0

Estimates for the entire area may inspire more confidence than three isolated examples. The analysis of parish registers and full population enumerations from 41 rural communities distributed throughout southern Anjou yields the results shown in Table 5. (See Appendix A for the basis of these figures.) There is every reason to suppose that the table records the variations from one section to the next faithfully, even if it may systematically inflate one category or deflate another.[3] *Caveat:* the estimates intentionally exclude the

[3] Where there is a reasonable basis for comparison, the analysis of the occupations of Active Citizens of the fourteen communities for which there is adequate occupational information (A.D. M-et-L 1 L 444) corroborates the conclusions to follow concerning differences within southern Anjou, except that it does not show the variation in the numbers of textile artisans. Since there are no such lists for the District of Saumur, and only one for the District of Angers, and since there is room for grave doubt as to the representativeness of the Active Citizens, the results of this analysis do not appear in the present tabulations. For a more confident use of such lists for the analysis of occupational distribution, see Bois 1960b: 224–237, 444–447.

cities, whose inclusion in the District of Saumur would, for example, immensely swell the proportion of bourgeois.

The districts of Cholet and St. Florent, the reader will recall, comprise the Mauges, while the district of Angers encloses some of the Val and a bit of the Mauges, Saumur is entirely Val-Saumurois, and Vihiers is split between Mauges and Val-Saumurois. Table 5 and the data on which it is based convey some additional conclusions: 1) Family subsistence farming (as indicated by small numbers of hired hands, and large numbers of leaseholders) was common throughout the Mauges, especially in the area of St. Florent, and much less frequent in the rest of southern Anjou. 2) Although they were numerous enough everywhere in the Mauges, the textile artisans (mainly weavers) were a particularly impressive part of the rural population in the district of Cholet; their presence, furthermore, was a reliable sign of a proliferation of rural manufacturers and merchants. In their absence, the local bourgeois were more likely to be officials or professionals. On the whole, the great contrast was between Mauges and Val-Saumurois, but within the Mauges the district of St. Florent (except the strip along the Loire) put more of its total energy into traditional farming, and less into industry, than did the district of Cholet.

Because of this significant variation among the subregions of southern Anjou, any general characterization of the classes for the entire area is bound to be misleading. The major classes I have distinguished, nevertheless, were present, distinct and, to some extent, aware of their identities throughout the area. The distribution of property is a good place to begin.

Although sheer monetary net worth does not distinguish the five classes, since it simply divides them into the two groups noble-bourgeois-clergy and peasant-artisan, a study of inventories taken by notaries at the deaths of their clients is illuminating.[4] They list the possessions of the household and give an idea of their arrangement and value.

Noble inventories reflect a comfortable life: hunting, gaming,

[4] The summary presented here, which ought to be verified systematically by someone with a great deal of time, patience, and access to notarial records, is based mainly on the study of the private archives of Maître Fleury (Chemillé, Maine-et-Loire) and the fairly slim notarial holdings from south of the Loire in the departmental archives of Maine-et-Loire (esp. E 4189–4192, E 4218–4219, E 4249, 5 E³ 58–59, 5 E³ 70–71).

Table 5. Estimated occupational distribution for rural communes of southern Anjou, by district.

District	Number of households	Estimated percentage of adult males								
		Noble	Priest	Bourgeois	Hired hands	Other peasant	Total peasant	Textile artisan	Other artisan	Total artisan
Cholet	10755	0.16	1.10	8.43	11.26	41.13	52.39	21.27	16.64	37.91
St. Florent	8686	0.28	1.50	11.07	7.88	43.82	51.70	7.93	27.52	35.45
Vihiers	9291	0.30	1.04	8.73	15.26	47.39	62.65	9.76	17.35	27.29
Angers	5784	0.36	1.22	9.90	11.12	43.34	54.46	2.44	31.62	34.06
Saumur	11923	0.47	1.42	1.69	29.19	51.11	80.30	2.35	13.77	16.12
Total, southern Anjou	46439	0.29	1.28	8.03	14.28	44.77	59.05	10.62	20.73	31.35

and drinking amid furnishings and fine table service. At the château of the future Vendean hero, Bonchamp, a listing of the property included rugs, tapestries, gaming tables, books, fine and plentiful dishes, horses, guns, and, in the cellar, the unbelievable total of 12,000 liters of wine (A.D. M-et-L VIII B 445).

At first glance, the possessions of the richest bourgeois were not much different. They had many of the accouterments of good living, including wine and fine furnishings. In fact, the similarity of the inventories of the great bourgeois to those of the nobles of the region is a sign of their tendency to join the nobility. In the case of the deminoble Béritault family, of the vicinity of Cholet, the possessions' inventories were about the same as those in the households of long-established nobles. Perhaps one sign of their assimilation is the fact that at their château of la Jumellière, a full quarter of the total worth of 15,000 livres was in wine (A.D. M-et-L E 1650). However, almost none of the bourgeois had hunting equipment, and their best furnishings were usually concentrated in their town houses. In any case, the great bourgeois families are less important to us, because they lived mainly in Angers and dealt with another world than southern Anjou. The "village bourgeoisie" lived in good houses in the bourgs, more comfortably than anyone else except perhaps lord or curé. The great difference between them and the rest of the population was that they usually had a good part of their total wealth in business credits. In 1764, the inventory of a merchant at Chemillé came to a total of 17,543 livres, but of that only 3,091 livres and 5 sous was household goods. The rest was the balance between his debts and credits (Étude Fleury). Frequently, depending on his line of business, the bourgeois had a good deal of money in goods for the market. Even the professional and administrative bourgeois (doctors, lawyers, officials, and so on) ordinarily had a much greater proportion of their wealth in liquid assets than did members of other classes. The bourgeoisie, judged by the composition of its wealth, was the moneyed class, the one tied up most in the cash nexus.

Inventories of the parish clergy prove them comfortably outfitted, in houses much like those of the professional men of their communities. They had more books than other people and often had good clothes and fine tableware. Frequently much of their total worth was in small rents and tithes (both money and kind) due them: The curé of Montilliers was worth 3,343 livres 7 sous in 1716, but only 1,725 livres was in household goods and cattle (A.D. M-et-L E 4219). More often than the bourgeoisie, the clergy had grain for the market on hand and owned farm equipment and animals. More often than the peasants, they had horses, books, and wine.

Artisans were, of course, poorer than the three classes already discussed. At Chemillé (Étude Fleury), their total worth rarely went beyond a few hundred livres, and that was largely the equipment of their trade. Their inventories give an impression of meager living — a few pots and pans, a few chests, an old table. But they also show that there were differences among the trades. A smith generally had a great deal more invested in his shop than a weaver, and millers were usually so substantial that they seem more like bourgeois than artisans. The artisans often owed money, but rarely had much due them. Witness the not unusual case of the poor mason of Chalonnes who in 1776 died with possessions valued at 113 livres and debts at 450 (A.D. M-et-L 5 E³ 58).

Even if many writers have jumbled them together, the artisans were quite distinct in character and situation from the peasants. To be sure, almost all the artisans, or their ancestors, had been recruited from the peasantry. But even though many artisans were worse off in every respect than the bulk of the peasants, the transfer from one group to the other operated in one direction only; in poring over the faded scrawls of the parish registers (to offer one small but diagnostic sign), one often encounters weavers named the equivalent of Farmer, but never a peasant named Weaver. Furthermore, the doubling of small farmers in money-making crafts, so common elsewhere in France, was relatively rare in southern Anjou. It is true that many artisans supplemented their basic incomes with the products of small plots of ground near their homes. That did not make them peasants.

The peasants were the largest group in the population, and the most information is available about them. In their case, one must be more than ordinarily alert to variations in wealth within the class. In examining the class distribution of the population, we have already seen that there were rather different *kinds* of peasants in Val-Saumurois and Mauges. In Val-Saumurois, there were few of those leaseholders of farms 20 to 40 hectares (45 to 90 acres) in size who were prevalent in the Mauges. There were, however, important distinctions among the winegrowers, the smallholders (*bécheurs* and *laboureurs à bras*), the day laborers and hired hands (*journaliers* and *domestiques*), the larger farmers (*cultivateurs* and *laboureurs*) — and the middlemen, *fermiers* and *marchands fermiers*, whose involvement in management and commerce has led me, not without misgivings, to classify them as bourgeois. In the Mauges, the labels corresponded rather more closely than in Val-Saumurois to the amounts of land controlled. Ordinarily that meant the amount of land leased. The *laboureur* (*labour*, I should remind the reader, refers to plowing, and not just to any toil) had so much land that he was obliged to have a number of oxen on hand for plowing. The middling farmer, the *métayer*, ran a *métairie* of some 20 to 30 hectares, a farm whose name, left over from another epoch, has misled many people into thinking of the eighteenth-century Vendée as a region of universal *métayage* — sharecropping. The *bordiers* and *closiers*, consistently enough, worked *bordages* and *closeries*, smaller farms which rarely maintained their own plowing cattle, and which were often fractured into several scattered pieces of land.[5] Finally, there were day laborers and hired hands in the Mauges as well as in Val-Saumurois, although in smaller number.

The differences in wealth among day laborers, bordiers, métayers, and laboureurs were reflected in farm equipment and livestock more than in home furnishings. The biggest difference was between farmers who owned oxen and those who did not. A métayer, for instance, usually had six or eight oxen and some other cattle; his farm animals alone amounted to at least 200 livres, and generally accounted for

[5] Contrary to the situation that Merle (1958: 194–196) discovered in the nearby Gâtine, the bordiers of the Mauges were distinctly poorer than the métayers. A postrevolutionary inquiry into farming in the Mauges (A.D. M-et-L 59 M 28) gives a view of the situation: "Small farming is done by hand; we call the farmers *bordiers* and their farm a *bordage*. The size of the bordages varies from a half hectare to five or six hectares of arable land plus one or two hectares of meadow. The quality of the fields and meadows determines the number of cattle fed, ranging from one cow to three cows and as many calves. It takes one man to run a small bordage and two for a large one. In the bordages the land is under cultivation; but since it is badly fertilized, the yield is small and the cost much greater than where the plow is used. This kind of farm requires proportionately more buildings and, generally, in every respect wealth is rarer and the abundance of children brings misery until they reach working age. . . . The farms known as métairies are run by three or four men per plow. . . . The best size is thirty hectares of arable land, and four of meadow, per plow. A properly situated métairie is ordinarily run by two family heads in collaboration; each one has either a son or a hired hand fourteen or fifteen years old, and they need four women to help them out and take care of the cows and calves."

from two fifths to one half of his total worth. A day laborer might have no more than a single cow. Like the artisans, the peasants had one or two rooms of old furniture, the bed by far the most valuable piece. But unlike them, they often had some grain stored away, and their debts were for arrears in rents and money due to the proprietor on their cattle.

Land

Dry, routine inventories of personal property, then, have a great deal to say about the lives of the various classes in southern Anjou. They do not, however, have anything to say about land ownership. They therefore obscure the fact that the wealth of the nobles was basically land, while that of the bourgeois was largely money, credits, and goods.

In studying southern Anjou and the surrounding territory, Siegfried was deeply impressed with the correlation between the control of land and political orientations in the regions of the West. He showed that toward 1880, the only cantons of southern Maine-et-Loire in which there were more than 25 landowners per 100 inhabitants were in Val and Saumurois.[6] That is, there were many landowners in Val-Saumurois, few in the Mauges. The division between small and large property in southern Anjou, according to Siegfried's observations, followed the border between Mauges and Saumurois faithfully, with a ribbon of small property all along the Loire. The small property was largely in peasant hands and worked by its owners. The large property was largely in noble hands, but still worked by peasants.

The same impression is unmistakable in comparing the transactions of notaries of the Saumurois (e.g., at Thouarcé, A.D. M-et-L E 4189 ff.) with those of the Mauges (e.g., Étude Fleury, Chemillé): the former are always dealing in halves of strips and fractions of small fields, while in the Mauges one rarely sees anything involving less than a whole field. The same records show frequent exchanges

---

[6] Siegfried 1911; see also Siegfried 1913. Considering the way Paul Bois (1960b) has laid waste Siegfried's assertions about landholding in the Sarthe, it is high time to test Siegfried's conclusions about Maine-et-Loire more rigorously. I have been unable to undertake that task. However, Siegfried's general conclusions about variation in the fractionation and control of property are borne out by Leclerc-Thouin 1843: 70–72; Sée 1927; Dion 1934. Similar descriptions of adjacent areas appear in Garaud 1954; Merle 1958; Baudrillart 1888, vol. II.

of property among peasants, artisans, and bourgeois outside the Mauges, but only rare sales within, and those largely small purchases by bourgeois.

Andrews' (1935) analysis of fifteen terriers — compendia concerning the lands controlled by different manors — opens another avenue. It is an avenue one must tread warily, because the terriers are very unevenly distributed over the territory, because there are no ecclesiastical fiefs in the group, because the use of terriers inevitably emphasizes the kinds of property controlled by large landlords, and because the analysis itself shows signs of haste.[7] Nevertheless, the uneven distribution can be turned into something of an advantage, since it makes it possible to divide the manors easily between those on the Loire or Layon, and those in the interior of the Mauges.

One can form a small but illuminating table by regrouping Andrews' findings in terms of the section of the Mauges involved and the percentage of the total land owned by each of the major classes.[8]

Table 6. Estimates of land ownership for sections of southern Anjou.

Area	Peasants	Artisans	Bourgeois	Clergy	Nobles	Total hectares in fiefs analyzed
Loire Valley, near Chalonnes	41.8	7.4	11.9	3.5	35.5	453
Layon area	79.3	0.0	8.7	6.6	5.4	26
Northern Mauges, near St. Florent	14.4	0.0	21.0	7.4	57.2	1628
Southern Mauges	14.1	0.6	14.3	4.1	67.0	2326
All areas combined	17.2	1.1	16.5	5.1	59.8	4433

The over-all figures are vulnerable to a variety of doubts, but some general conclusions and some observations on variations within the area surveyed merit attention. First of all, the figures for the Layon, even if based on a ridiculously small amount of land, do not fit badly with Joseph Denecheau's estimates for the section of the Dis-

[7] E.g., Andrews' analysis of the terrier prepared for the fief of La Houdrière around 1780 (A.D. M-et-L E 666), in which he almost certainly classified all the owners whose statuses were unspecified (including eleven entitled "Sieur," an appellation ordinarily reserved for bourgeois) as peasants.

[8] The regrouping: 1) Loire Valley: fiefs of Basse-Guerche, Turpinière, La Grand-Pé, La Houdrière, Long-homme; 2) Layon: La Hinière; 3) northern Mauges: Montmoutier, Gué-de-Vallée-et-du-Port; 4) southern Mauges: Barboire, Parigné, Montbault-Papin, Petit-Riou, Les Granges, Bouzillé-Melay. I ought to add that it did not fall within Andrews' intention to analyze terriers from the Saumurois.

trict of Vihiers across the Layon river from the Mauges: 6.3 percent for the clergy and 9.8 percent for the nobility (1955: 9). The nobles held an immense share of the land at the interior of the Mauges, but were less important landlords on its rim. In the Val, there were many more proprietors among the peasants and the artisans. The nature of the sources (as Andrews points out) forbids any conclusions concerning variations in ecclesiastical property. All the other evidence, including the sales of church properties during the Revolution, suggests that various units of the church owned much more of the land along the Loire than in the Mauges.

On the whole, these scattered sources agree on the control of land in southern Anjou. In the Val-Saumurois, especially near the Loire, property ownership was spread wide through the population, even if major religious establishments were extremely influential landlords. In the Mauges, the nobles owned a huge proportion of the land, the artisans were virtually landless, the bourgeois were landlords mainly in the vicinities of the cities, and the peasants relied mainly on rental, rather than ownership, for the use of the land.

There is a bit of a paradox in these observations: if the nobles owned so much land in the Mauges, why were there so few of them? The evidence assembled earlier shows that nobles were more common in Val-Saumurois. A troubling finding, since many historians have attributed great importance to that solidarity between peasants and nobles in the bocage that presumably developed from their everyday association in the use of the land. Because estimates of class distribution prepared by the methods employed in this study may not warrant perfect confidence, I have checked the conclusions by compiling a list, theoretically encompassing all nobles actually residing in southern Anjou, from the rolls of the *capitation nobiliaire* (literally, and fairly accurately, the noble head tax) up to 1789 and the responses of communities to a questionnaire asking, among other things, the identities of their "privileged" residents in the years just before the Revolution.[9] Unfortunately, there are no returns for about half the communities of the District of Cholet, including the city of Cholet itself, or for the canton of Saumur. The communities covered en-

---

[9] A.D. M-et-L C 192 and IV C 3, with identities of nobles verified in A.D. M-et-L II B (procès-verbal de la sénéchaussée de Saumur), Carré de Busserolle 1890; de la Roque and Barthélemy 1864; cf. Bois 1960b: 409–422.

closed only about 31,000 of the 46,000 households of southern Anjou, and the rates are corrected for that fact. The compilation is therefore indubitably incomplete, but there is no obvious reason for it to exaggerate the proportion of nobles in one section at the expense of another.

The results of this investigation are set parallel to the findings from the already reported study of class distribution in Table 7.

Table 7. Estimated proportion of nobles, by district.

Measure	Saumur	Angers	Vihiers	St. Florent	Cholet	Total
Nobles as percentage of adult males (from Table 1)	0.47	0.36	0.30	0.28	0.16	0.29
Noble households per 100 households	0.67	0.36	0.49	0.28	0.39	0.42

The basic data for the two statistics come from the same sources. The differences lie in the bases used for their computation. The first refers only to cantons for which detailed occupational distributions could be calculated, while the second includes all communities for which information on the presence or absence of nobles was available. The second statistic therefore probably represents the district-to-district variation more accurately. Altogether, it seems fair to conclude that there were many more nobles actually living in Val-Saumurois than in the Mauges, and that many more of the gentleman landowners were absentees than tradition has said.

True, there is an immense difference between the influence of a numerous but impoverished nobility and the influence of a rarer but wealthy nobility. Nevertheless, the relations between very powerful landlords and their tenants are rarely intimate, particularly if the landlords spend much of their time elsewhere. Images of the period after the Revolution, when many of the nobles of the West had returned to lead the lives of country squires on their estates and to dabble in local politics, have probably confused our vision of the eighteenth century, when many more nobles were at Court, serving in the army, or at least residing in their town houses. We even find the Gibot family — presented by its chronicler (Duhamonay 1942: 15–16) as part of the "old, landed and sedentary nobility, profoundly rooted in the soil" — at last "giving in to the movement

that was tearing the majority of gentlemen from their estates''
around the middle of the century. A casual muster of landlords
of the Mauges, furthermore, identifies as absentees the masters of
such diverse manors as La Boullay (in Trémentines); La Giraudière
and La Haute-Sauvagère (in La Tourlandry); Maulèvrier; Montbault-
Papin (in Mazières); Cholet; Le Coudray Montbault, and La Séverie
(near Maulèvrier); Parigny (in Montilliers); La Rocheferrière (around
Montrevault); and Le Sap (in St. Crespin and vicinity) (A.D.
M-et-L E 192, 604–610, 782–783, 800–806, 1200–1208, 1284–1286,
1302–1308, 1 E 234–242, 996–998).

In point of fact, it appears that a very large share of the agricultural land owned by the nobles was in the careful hands of bourgeois
overseers, managers, and middlemen, while the nobles spent most of
their time elsewhere (cf. Merle 1958: ch. VIII; Forster 1963). It is
certainly chiefly in the rural communities of the Mauges that the
analysis of occupational distribution shows up traces of the swarm
of officials needed to keep large estates going.

Is this so new? More people should have listened when Célestin
Port (1888: I, 21–23), who knew the Mauges well, denounced the
doctrine of noble omnipresence in that region which joined the
counterrevolution. The gentlemen dominated the land, to be sure,
but they dominated it through their hirelings, and not through
persistent and loving intervention in the everyday work of the fields.

Poverty

There was another problem in which Port came close to some
very important observations, even if *parti pris* seems to have kept him
from resolving it. That is the extent of poverty in southern Anjou.
In his great desire to show that the ''peasants'' of the Mauges had
many reasons to welcome the Revolution — and therefore, despite
their later being duped and agitated into a counterrevolution, could
not have been fundamentally hostile to it — he claimed that ''hardship was universal and hopeless, even the rich having barely enough
to live on'' (1888: I, 28) and peppered his account with citations
from the declarations of woe that so many communities registered
around the beginning of the Revolution. Furthermore, he detected
traces of ''invasions of nomads, wandering tribes, true Bohemians''
(1888: I, 28). What he did not do is test the claims against other

evidence, separate signs of misery among the peasants from signs of misery elsewhere in the population, or show the variation from one section to another. If he had done so, he would have seen many of the facts (and fraudulent claims) he presented so well fit together somewhat differently.

What about the presence of homeless, drifting, squatting, desperately marginal families in the countryside? It is true that reliable historians have shown the existence of such unfortunates elsewhere in the bocage (e.g., Merle 1958: 94–95; Bois 1960b: 233–235). It is also true that they are precisely the people whose identities are likely to disappear, like salt through a sieve, in the gaps of the surviving documents. Nevertheless, it is interesting to examine what the local officials of southern Anjou replied when asked explicitly to report the number of beggars and vagabonds in their localities. This they had to do in response to the inquiries of the National Assembly's Committee on Mendicity in 1790 (A.D. M-et-L 1 L 402; cf. Bloch and Tuetey 1911). Of about 160 communities reporting — excluding the District of Vihiers, whose detailed *statistiques* I have been unable to turn up — only 14 enumerated any beggars or vagabonds at all. Two or three figures (Montfaucon's 312, Montrevault's 276, and possibly Mozé's 55) stand out as likely frauds; aside from them, there were less than 100 drifters reported in all of southern Anjou. Although eighteenth-century village elders may have had motives for concealment of the existence of beggars and vagabonds which are no longer apparent to a twentieth-century reader of the documents, these figures hardly support a conclusion of general misery and rootlessness.

We should attend even more seriously to the sections of the same reports that deal with the number of "needy" and, better yet, the number listed as too poor to vote under the Revolutionary constitution by virtue of paying too little in taxes. In all of France, this latter group comprised just over 10 percent of the entire population (and consequently a much larger proportion of the males of voting age). In southern Anjou, the proportions in percentages by district were: Cholet, 9.1; St. Florent, 5.4; Angers, 6.0; Saumur, 5.4. The reports of the needy form a similar pattern. At first glance, these percentages seem to belie some earlier statements. Although they are all below the national average, they seem to indicate a genuine problem of peasant poverty in the District of Cholet, the southern part of the Mauges. Closer inspection of the reports by canton shows the situation more accurately and suggests what is involved. Except for the irritating absence of information on the District of Vihiers and the considerable number of disfranchised citizens in the vicinity of the declining city of Montreuil-Bellay (near Saumur), the map of poverty effectively outlines the principal precincts of the textile industry. The highest rates of all, 14 percent and 17 percent, are at the textile centers of Cholet and Chemillé. To anticipate a conclusion I shall fortify in the following chapters: in the Mauges, the very poor were often weavers and they were commonly plentiful, despite other signs of local prosperity, where weaving flourished. In Val-Saumurois, the very poor were found among the nearly land-less agricultural laborers. But almost nowhere in southern Anjou were the very poor a predominant part of the population.

A Review of Class Structure

The distance from the abstract discussion of community organization and change at the beginning of this chapter to these minute observations on poverty may seem very great; that is only because we have traveled a devious path from one to the other, in order to get the lay of the nearby land. For now we can see more distinctly that the class composition of a rural community of the Mauges was quite different from the composition of a community of Val-Saumurois and can sense that the contrast was related to the differences in their involvement in French society as a whole. For one thing, the great subdivision of the peasantry of Val-Saumurois by agricultural specialty, income, and property corresponds to the subregion's greater participation in the market; money and market position were the common denominators there. For another, the very incompleteness and partiality of the urbanization of the communities of the Mauges led to a deep dualism in their class structure. There were two complexes of class positions: those based on land and agriculture on one side, those based on commerce, manufacturing, and administration on the other. Nobles and peasants were in the first complex; bourgeois and artisans, for the most part, in the second; while priests (and a certain part of the bourgeoisie) occupied positions in both complexes. No doubt this way of putting the situation jibes badly with the common assumption that any class system must be built around a unitary rank order. It is not, however, incompatible with Karl Marx's distinction of classes on the basis of relationship to a means of production or with Weber's criterion of decisive differences in life chances for control of goods, services, and living conditions. Each of these leaves open the possibility of a set of classes which do not form a single scale.

The class situation, like the other features of social organization surveyed so far, forbids the easy splitting of southern Anjou into "traditional" and "modern" communities and the facile explanation of their political differences via the convenient dichotomy. Moreover, it posts an unmistakable warning against the treatment of the communities of the Mauges as homogeneous, simple, isolated, folkish. What we know about the elites of southern Anjou redoubles the warning.

The elite of a peasant community, it may be well to recall, consist of those who simultaneously carry on active roles in the community and in the national structures that intersect it. The elite are the mediators, the brokers, between those national structures and the relevant activities within the community. They gain power through their extraordinary access to information and to powerful individuals on the outside, and frequently have a good deal of influence over the contacts of other community members with "outsiders." As a rule, the fewer the elite roles and the less the specialization of those roles in one form of mediation or another, the greater the local power of the elite.

The national structures that call for attention in the analysis of southern Anjou's rural life are the market, the state, and the church — each much more manifold than the deceptively unitary term suggests. Throughout the area, the principal mediators between market and community were the bourgeois, the principal mediators between church and community, the parish clergy. Even in these respects, however, there were differences. The great extent of cash-crop production among the peasants of Val-Saumurois, as opposed to subsistence farming in the Mauges, enhanced the significance of the merchants in peasant life, and likewise elevated the number of peasants who were at least part-time merchants and thereby marginal members of the elite. In the Mauges, on the other hand, the bourgeois were all-important as mediators between the international market and the local textile artisans, and controlled as well what efflux of agricultural products there was. Their position gave them relatively little direct influence over the peasantry.

So much for the market. On the side of the church, the higher clergy (monks and canons especially) were much more influential in the rural communities of Val-Saumurois than in the Mauges, where the curé usually was the sole religious authority. As with commerce, there seems to have been more frequent contact between community members and outside authorities in connection with ecclesiastical administration in Val-Saumurois than in the Mauges.

That leaves the state. The curé of the Mauges, as we shall see, dominated the dealings of his community with the government before the Revolution; the local noble landholder, however, was often the spokesman when the community had to address very high levels of the government. The bourgeois played a part, but a subordinate one. In Val-Saumurois, the bourgeois, despite their smaller numbers, were more prominent as political intermediaries, while the positions of curé and noble shrank accordingly.

The following chapters will elaborate on this spare summary. For the moment, it is enough to recognize the complexity of the "simple" peasant villages of southern Anjou; to observe the general relationship between the degree of urbanization of the rural community and both its internal structure and its class composition; to notice the difference between the relatively large and differentiated elites of Val-Saumurois, and the more compact and monopolistic elites of the Mauges. Each of these elements will take on fuller meaning as we study in detail the operation of the rural community.

CHAPTER **5**

The Rural Neighborhood

Even though the reader who is accustomed to a glorious sweep of global ideas in his discussions of revolution may find it an intolerable descent to detail, the chapter now beginning will have to deal even more closely than the last with particular elements of the rural community. Only with this examination over can we proceed with any confidence to the analysis of the Vendée's counterrevolution. Like a fine firearm, a community can be better understood in its moments of explosive energy if one has already broken it down and then reassembled it into a working whole.

For the purposes of analysis, we may distinguish four systems of social relationships within the community, essentially political, economic, religious, and affiliational. When analyzing political relationships, those that pertain to the distribution of power, I shall speak of the *commune*. Relationships built around the production and distribution of goods take place in the *economy*. Relationships that have to do mainly with the control of belief form the *parish*, the religious aspect of the community. And those that center on personal access and intimacy belong to the *neighborhood*.[1] Each of these is the basis of division, solidarity, ranking, and influence within the community. Each of these constantly interacts with the others. These systems together constitute the complex structure we call the community.

This chapter and the following three will treat the neighborhood, the parish, the economy, and the commune, at first separately and then together. The neighborhood first, but by no means in the fullest

---

[1] These categories, of course, have a good deal in common with the traditional rubrics in descriptive community studies, as well as with the "subsystems" Talcott Parsons (1952, esp. ch. III) sees as inherent in the structure of any social system. However, in treating community structure, Parsons himself has preferred to conceive of it as the spatial aspect of all social systems (1960, ch. 8).

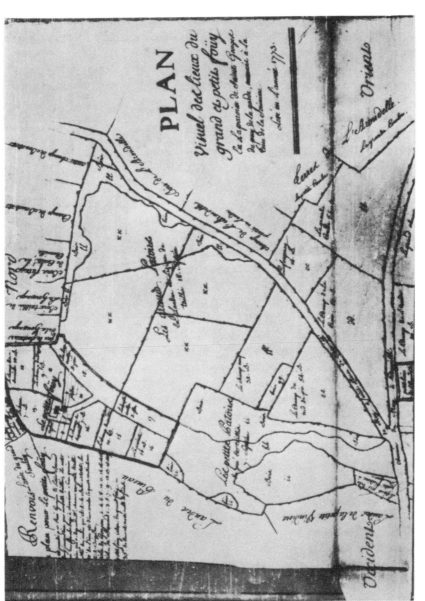

Figure 5. Le Petit Foüy

detail. Except perhaps for the private lives of the powerful, historical records generally contain fainter traces of affiliation, of personal access and intimacy, than they do of the other aspects of community organization. Sad, but true: In the world of history, true love leaves fewer memorials than the sale of a sow. Even so, love is sometimes formalized by marriage, enmity sometimes leads to recorded crime, personal alliance sometimes crystallizes into duly registered residential proximity, and each then joins the data of history. Documentary evidence of these kinds is more abundant than most analyses of the state of eighteenth-century France suggest.

Layout

Certainly the physical layout of a community in itself reveals something of its social organization. Just as the band of sociologists inspired by Robert Ezra Park have sought to discern the shadow cast by a city's social structure on its ground plan, students of rural communities still have much to learn from agricultural settlement patterns. Paul Vidal de la Blache (1926: 301) went so far as to say that the landscape formed around scattered hamlets "is characteristic of an entirely different type of agriculture, of another mode of life, and of a totally different arrangement from that of clustered villages." We have to look no farther than southern Anjou to find the contrast exemplified. For on the whole the people of the Mauges were in dispersed settlements, while the inhabitants of Val and Saumurois huddled in villages surrounded by unpopulated fields. This is the very core of the ancient contrast of bocage and plain, of woodland and champion. Toward Cholet, bocage. Toward Saumur, plain.

The face of the bocage is unmistakable. An experienced traveler of the last century spoke of the "few villages, but an infinite number of farms lost beneath the trees, linked by narrow roads bordered by hedges, often arched over by them" (Ardouin-Dumazet 1898: 74). The essential feature of the bocage is the farm whose small fields are surrounded by tall hedges.

The map of the farm called Le Petit Foüy, in the community of Saint-Georges-du-Puy-de-la-Garde, illustrates some of the features of bocage properties (A.D. Maine-et-Loire E 460). This métairie was not "typical," since it had just been formed a few years before the map was drawn in 1773. But it had all the usual characteristics. The land was assembled from the uncultivated portions of a larger métairie, Le Foüy, on condition that the tenants build a house on the new property. In 1773, two day laborers, René Goujon and Louis Besnard, farmed the métairie in common. They had about forty hectares, the greater part of it almost equally divided into pasture and cultivated fields. The map shows two small houses, each described as having one room with attached stable. Near the houses are the garden, the orchard, and the smallest, most intensively cultivated, fields. Each field that takes the plow has a name: Magpie's Nest, Newfield, The Point, and so forth. There are rather more small clumps of trees than on the average farm. The map carefully traces the courses of the narrow, gullied, hedge-bordered roads, and even follows the tall hedges around the irregular fields in painstaking detail. The hedges are important. They announce the private property of planted fields, forbidding access at any season to gleaning women or foraging cattle. They keep the farmer's own cattle in place. Furthermore, they supply him with firewood, lumber, and litter for the stable (see Poirier 1934: 22–31).

The necessity of hedgerows was so ingrained in custom and law that in 1769, on hearing a complaint that cattle were getting into the nearby vineyards, the senechal of St. Florent ordered that:

landowners, leaseholders, and tenants of vines throughout this jurisdiction shall enclose them the day after the publication of these presents in such a way that cattle will be unable to enter; we also forbid all persons to let their cattle wander or pasture in such places, or even to cut or pull out grass there to feed the aforesaid cattle, all this on pain of three livres fine levied against each lawbreaker, plus seizure and confiscation of the cattle and damages, interest, and costs (A.D. M-et-L VIII B 440).

Such an order would have been utterly antithetical to the open-field customs of England's champion country or France's East. A number of other characteristics go along with the essential hedge-bounded type of farm: little forest area, numerous brooks and rivulets, winding and constricted roads, and expanses of land temporarily or permanently out of cultivation.[2]

[2] Merle's erudite researches (1958, cf. Bloch 1952: 57–63 and 1956: 64–68; Dion 1934a and 1934b; Le Lannou 1950) indicate that many of the apparently ageless elements of the bocage landscape are actually post-Medieval creations of consolidating landlords. Earlier, the countryside of the West was probably even more like the hamlet-studded surface of Britain's woodlands (see Mogey 1947: 15; Homans 1941: 26–27; Rees 1950: 100 ff.; Seebohm 1896: 187; Meynier 1958: 22–31) than

More to the point is the division of the dwellings within each bocage community among the bourg (the central agglomeration, the emplacement of church, inn, shops, and, in an agreeable etymological coincidence, the homes of the rural bourgeoisie), an occasional secondary village or two, the spread-out hamlets, and the isolated farms. A useful case is the small community of St. Quentin-en-Mauges (at the northern edge of the Mauges, toward St. Florent: the tag "en-" followed by a place name usually indicates a location on the periphery of a named region). Good fortune has put into the archives a complete list of St. Quentin's inhabitants at the time of the Revolution, presenting age, sex, and precise residence within the community (A.D. M-et-L 6 L 19). The document shows that 375 of the 1090 men, women and children lived in the bourg, 90 in one village, 41 in another, and the other 584 people were scattered among 52 named hamlets or individual farms. Outside of the three largest settlements, the average cluster of houses therefore contained about 11 people. Not concentration, but dispersion.

The denizens of Val-Saumurois, on the other hand, were villagers. The average rural community actually had a smaller territory and fewer citizens than a community of the Mauges, but the residents were much more often grouped in a single solid settlement. Paul Wagret (1951: 32–33) says of the winegrower of the Val-Saumurois that "he is sociable and he likes to live with his neighbors in the big bourgs that follow one another along the foot or the side of the slope: Montsoreau, Turquant, Parnay, Dampierre along the Loire; Varrains, Chacé, Saint-Cyr, Brézé above the Thouet." One concomitant of the settlement pattern was somewhat higher population

---

it is today. Indeed, there seems to have been a standard evolution which occurred at varying times and rhythms throughout the West, in which substantial landlords assembled odd lots of land into the characteristic métairies, sometimes breaking up existing villages and hamlets in the process. At first they let these medium-sized farms on shares to responsible peasants, but eventually the direct intervention and interest of the master in the individual farm declined, the overseer or agent became more important, and the conversion of share tenantry into leaseholding for fixed payments (in kind and in cash) spread relentlessly. There may be one more phase: the gradual breaking up of old estates, and their piece-by-piece purchase by newcomers, including peasants. By the eighteenth century, the process was already far advanced in much of Anjou and Maine, yet still quite close to the original stage in the remoter sections of Poitou and Brittany. There may well be a direct connection between the extent to which the nobility of an area had left the land for the cities and the stage this process had reached. According to this hypothesis, first stage created the landscape, but the later stages modified it as they transformed the social relations originally associated with it. Today, in consonance with further social evolution, the bocage is thinning and even disappearing in much of the West.

densities toward Saumur (and particularly in the vineyard areas) than by Cholet or St. Florent. Some crude estimates of density measured in persons per square kilometer, in 1792, are:[3] in the Districts of Cholet and St. Florent together, 63; Vihiers, 55; Saumur, 100; and all four Districts combined, 69. Although high densities may be important in themselves because they generate more intense communication, it is the fact that the population congregated in compact villages that matters most. Of the social significance of such an arrangement, Vidal de la Blache wrote: "As narrow as the horizon may be, as muffled as the outside sounds which arrive there may be, the village forms a little society accessible to general influences. Instead of being dispersed in molecules, the population there is a nucleus; and that rudiment is enough to make it amenable to influence" (1903: 311). Siegfried (1913: 385 ff.) took up the same theme, under the inspiration of this very passage from Vidal, maintaining that collective movements more easily find followers in villages.

No doubt the truth is less simple: the strongest farmers' movements in nineteenth-century America took place amid the most dispersed habitat imaginable, that of the Wheat Belt; the Vendée's counterrevolution, which ought to qualify as a collective movement, bypassed the villages and found its home among the hamlets and isolated farms. Still, it does seem that ideas, programs, and movements from outside reach all inhabitants of agglomerated villages more rapidly and uniformly, and in that way are more likely to incite a collective response — not necessarily a favorable one — in such communities. In the same way that participation in nonpolitical associations draws people into political opinionating and action (as latter-day interpreters of de Tocqueville, e.g., Lipset, Trow and Coleman 1956; Kornhauser 1959; Greer 1962, have shown), membership in a concentrated rural village probably reduces one's chances for political apathy. Recent analyses of French political geography, for example (e.g., Dupeux 1952; Dogan and Narbonne 1954), have uniformly shown the tendency for "agglomerated" communities to have higher proportions voting in national elections than "dispersed" communities do.

In the absence of well-defined factions, membership in a concen-

[3] Based mainly on A.N. D IV bis 51, with no correction for the greater number of city-dwellers in the districts of Saumur and Cholet; cf. Châtelain 1956.

trated rural village probably also reduces the possibility of public and individual dissidence. Where there is a controlling clique, the villager finds it harder to escape the clique's surveillance or its retaliation than the inhabitant of a distant hamlet does. That does not mean at all that there will be no opposition in a concentrated village, but it does mean that political opposition and personal alignments with a minority will be closely associated, and that the voice of opposition will probably speak more loudly in the privacy of the polling booth than in the publicity of the town meeting. Conclusion: Vidal was right. Village living enhances responsiveness, political awareness, collective action, and [forced] unanimity. The effectiveness with which the villages of Val-Saumurois formed patriotic clubs and National Guard units during the Revolution is an excellent illustration.

Now it is time to recall that the dispersion of the population in the Mauges did not amount to simple scattering, but consisted of partition of each community to several types of settlement. Most important, the principal agglomerations differed in character from the rest of the community. Bourgeois, artisans, and clergy almost invariably lived in the bourg or a subsidiary village. Nobles never did, while among peasants only day laborers were likely to have houses in the population centers. How much of a community's people lived in the bourg was, consistently enough, a function of the vigor of its commercial and industrial activity. The extremes in the rural Mauges were cases like 1) sleepy St. Laurent-des-Autels, with only 23 percent of its thousand inhabitants in the bourg, and less than 4 percent of its men in bourgeois occupations or 2) lively La Tessoualle, where more than 900 of the community's 1500 inhabitants lived in the bourg, and 26 percent of the men were bourgeois. The commerce, administration, and manufacturing of each community were the business of the central settlements, so that within each one appeared a miniature division into "rural" and "urban." To this extent, the geographical divisions within the community were also class divisions. We shall see later how trenchant the distinction between bourg and countryside became during the Revolution.

All this said, let us not inflate the importance of the settlement pattern. There was in western France, it is true, a rough correlation between bocage settlement and 1) inefficient subsistence agriculture,

2) noble landholding, 3) counterrevolutionary activity from 1791 to 1800, 4) political conservatism in the nineteenth century. The bocage landscape is related to a particular way of using land, a particular brand of agriculture, and that kind of agriculture is related to a certain set of social conditions. Hence a correlation. Yet Bois (1960b) has demonstrated that the correlation was far from a perfect correspondence: both the revolutionary and the counterrevolutionary sections of the Sarthe were predominantly bocage, and important sections of Brittany and Normandy refuse to fit the formula. In southern Anjou, the contrast between dispersed and concentrated habitats did reinforce the deep differences in social experience between Mauges and Val-Saumurois, but it did not account for them.

Marriage

In any case, the evidence on solidarity and informal relations that the pattern of settlement provides is rather indirect. The pattern of marriage, on the other hand, offers precious direct evidence 1) because marriage itself is ordinarily a powerful sort of alliance between families as well as individuals, 2) because the frequency of marriage suggests which groups were able to treat each other as approximate equals, 3) because even where rank is not involved, the frequency of marriage between two groups generally corresponds to the warmth and frequency of other, less binding, social relations.

The parish registers already used for the estimates of occupational distribution include records of all marriages which took place in eighteen communities during the years 1780–1784. About half the time, the curé or vicar who performed the marriage registered not only the names and residences of the newlyweds, but also their ages and occupations, and enumerated as well the parents and the witnesses by residence and occupation. As a result, the records contain an immense range of information on both kinship and friendship. The only unfortunate fact in the present case is that the parish registers analyzed include, by the most liberal definition, only four or five small communities (yielding no more than a hundred marriages) from areas well within the Val-Saumurois.[4] On the other hand, they

[4] A.D. M-et-L B, parish registers for 1) *District of Cholet:* Chanteloup, Gesté, Vezins, La Tessoualle, La Romagne, St. Pierre-de-Cholet; 2) *District of St. Florent:* La Poitevinière, La Pommeraye, La Chapelle-du-Genêt, La Chapelle-St. Florent; 3) *District of Vihiers:* Chanzeaux, St. Lambert-du-Lattay, Beaulieu, Vauchrétien, Trémont; 4) *District of Angers:* Soulaine, Chalonnes; *District of Saumur:* La Chapelle-sous-Doué.

do include a fairly wide range of communities from the rest of southern Anjou. Conclusions concerning subregional differences will have to come from comparisons of the districts of Cholet and St. Florent with the combined results from the districts of Saumur, Angers, and Vihiers. They are, consequently, tentative.

I have drawn information concerning four problems from the parish registers at hand. The problems are: 1) the extent of marriage outside the local community, 2) occupational differences in tendency to marry outside the community, 3) the extent of marriage across occupational boundaries, 4) patterns of preference in those marriages that do cross occupational boundaries. Residence refers to the homes of the bride and groom just before marriage. When it comes to occupation, it is the habitual employments of the groom (or of his father, when his own is not specified) and of the bride's father that count. Altogether, there are 961 marriages to analyze. Of the 1922 individuals marrying there is residential information for almost everyone (including 941 couples), but occupational information for only 1079.

The first question is the extent of local endogamy, that is, the frequency with which individuals marry others from their own community. The greater the tendency to local endogamy, the more likely it is that other social relations are highly localized. The results are no more than suggestive. They are summarized in a small table:

Table 8. Local endogamy, by district.

Districts	Percent of marriages			Number of marriages analyzed
	Bride and groom were both from the community	One was from elsewhere in the same canton	One was from outside the canton	
St. Florent	64.6	7.9	27.4	277
Cholet	60.5	5.8	33.7	481
Vihiers, Angers, and Saumur	57.4	11.5	31.1	183
Total	61.1	7.6	31.3	941

The fact that two fifths of all the marriages crossed community boundaries is a strong counter to any notion that the communities were tightly sealed off from one another. The proportion marrying out of the canton may seem incredibly high, in fact, until one realizes that many adjacent communities were not in the same canton, especially in the districts of St. Florent and Cholet, where there were fewer communities per canton.

The table hints that local endogamy was greater in the Mauges than in Val-Saumurois. The rate of marriage within the community was highest for the District of St. Florent, and lowest for Vihiers, Angers, and Saumur put together. However, the summaries camouflage great variability from place to place within each district, as well as some very high proportions in Angers and Saumur. And the over-all differences are not very great. This part of the analysis, then, produces no more than an interesting hypothesis for further verification.

The analysis of local endogamy by occupational class produces more definite results,[5] and is given in Table 9. On the whole, the

Table 9. Local distribution of marriages, by occupational class.

| | Percent of marriages in which: | | | |
Occupational class	Bride and groom were both from the community	One was from elsewhere in the same canton	One was from outside the canton	Number of marriages analyzed
Large farmers	53.3	8.5	38.2	199
Small farmers	55.1	18.4	26.5	49
Hired hands	66.2	9.9	23.9	71
Total peasant	56.4	10.3	33.2	319
Total bourgeois	52.8	1.9	45.3	53
Industrial artisan	76.0	5.4	18.6	129
Other artisans and millers	62.4	11.2	26.4	125
Total artisans	69.3	8.3	22.4	254
Unidentified	59.5	9.0	31.5	333
Entire sample	60.7	8.9	30.4	959

Note: There were two marriages of nobles, in both of which one of the newlyweds was from outside the canton.

proportion marrying out — and presumably the extent of social relations outside the immediate locality — rises with rank. Among the peasants, for example, the rate of marriage outside the canton goes from under a quarter among the low-ranking hired hands to

[5] The comparisons derived from rural parish registers alone are weakened by the virtual certainty that the nobles and the highest-ranking bourgeois (both of which categories are greatly underrepresented in these rural marriages) often both staged their marriages in the city and married far outside the locality.

almost two fifths among the large farmers. By far the most localized group, by this measure, were the industrial artisans. Not only were they, economically, the most precarious element of the population, but they were also the element whose social relations had the narrowest scope. Their masters, the bourgeois, were far different. Bourgeois social relations, interests, and aspirations were much broader than the boundaries of a single rural village. In this sense, the bourgeois were well qualified to serve in the local elite.

An interesting amplification of these findings comes from the analysis of the lists of Active Citizens (that is, registered voters meeting the property qualifications) from 13 communities of southern Anjou in 1790 and 1791.[6] Among other things the lists ordinarily indicate how long the individual had lived in the community, and thus lend themselves to a comparison of occupational groups in terms of their mobility.

Because of the greater numbers involved, it is possible to use somewhat finer distinctions than in the analysis of marriage records. The proportion of each category who had lived in their communities all their lives (with the number of cases analyzed in parenthesis) is shown in a small table.

Priest	6.7%	(15)	Industrial artisan	68.8%	(218)
Large farmer	59.8	(748)	Other artisans	49.5	(305)
Small farmer	45.6	(318)	Millers	41.4	(58)
Hired hand	50.0	(168)	Other skilled and		
Total peasant	54.8	(1234)	service occupations	48.6	(74)
Administrative and			Total artisans,		
professional			millers, and		
bourgeois	31.7	(60)	others	55.1	(655)
Commercial bourgeois	54.3	(254)			
Total bourgeois	50.0	(314)	All occupations	53.9	(2220)

If we think of the measure of exogamy as dividing the population into "wide-range" and "narrow-range" groups, and this measure of

[6] A.D. Maine-et-Loire 1 L 444: Chaudefonds, Beaulieu, Neuil, Coron, Somloire, St. Hilaire-du-Bois, Beaupréau, Chemillé, Tourlandry, St. Georges, La Tessoualle, Chanteloup, Montfaucon. I have excluded a list from Chavagnes because it appears to indicate how long the individuals had been heads of their own households, rather than how long they had been in Chavagnes. As usual, there are some important qualifications to attach to the findings. The list systematically excluded the poor, the dependent, and those who had already declared their opposition to the Revolution. This set of 13, although well enough scattered through the other districts, does not include any communities from the District of Saumur.

origin as dividing it into "insiders" and "outsiders," we can set up four types: wide-range insiders, narrow-range insiders, wide-range outsiders, and narrow-range outsiders. In these terms, the contrast between the industrial artisans and the bourgeois for whom they worked reappears as a contrast between wide-range outsiders (the bourgeois) and narrow-range insiders (the industrial artisans). Not only by their skills and local economic power, but also by their origins and continuing social relations, the bourgeois were in a position to act as intermediaries between the industrial artisans and the outside world. Even if the local origins of the weavers and their confreres may have enhanced their sense of membership and even given them a measure of parochial power, their narrow social range made them more amenable to control by the wide-ranging bourgeois.

The other artisans were in a somewhat different position. They married out more often (even if they, too, did so less than the community average) and were much more likely to have come from elsewhere. Most likely these characteristics are closely related to the greater wealth and power of such artisans as smiths, carpenters, or coopers, and their more direct involvement in the market through the sale of their own goods and services.

The hired hands shared a number of traits with the nonindustrial artisans, but, more constricted in scope, were closer to the pure type of narrow-range outsiders. This suggests that they had less attachment to the local community than other groups and little power to influence it. Their situation was in some ways like that of recently arrived ethnic minorities in large cities.

The most interesting comparison is between the large farmers and the bourgeois. The bourgeois, especially the ranking members of the rural bourgeoisie, frequently married outside, and were often themselves from elsewhere; they were wide-range outsiders. The large farmers, on the other hand, were natives often enough, and married out often enough, to be called wide-range insiders. One can see the possibility of a struggle between "insiders" and "outsiders," with bourgeois and large farmers in the front lines of opposing teams. Formations of this type were common during the Revolution.

Let us reassemble the findings of this phase of the analysis slightly differently. On the whole, 1) the higher the rank, the greater the range of social relations, 2) the greater the involvement in market activity, the greater the likelihood of being an outsider. Market involvement facilitates mobility, but it is high rank that is the basis of continuing participation in activities and relationships that surpass the limits of locality. Not only are these conclusions plausible on general grounds, but they recall strikingly the earlier discussion of urbanization and community structure. Once again it appears that the extent of market involvement is a powerful denominator within the peasant community as well as among communities. Once again it seems essential to distinguish the outward looking elite from the rest of the community. And in this context it is clearer than before that elite position, in the sense of simultaneous engagement in national and local roles, and high rank go together, even if they are not the same thing.

There are some obvious companion questions to these inquiries about local endogamy. What about class endogamy? What forms of preference show up in marriages among different occupational groups? The extent of class endogamy should indicate the degree to which the class distinctions used in this analysis separate groups which were truly distinct in status. The forms of marital preference should give some idea of the main lines of solidarity within the community and should help identify those groups which were able to treat each other as approximate equals. When it comes to honor and social access, rather than power or wealth, there are few sources more precious for understanding the class structure of villages distant in time or space than well-kept marriage records.

Class endogamy is the first question. The simplest answer is the proportion of each category marrying within the same category. Weakness: with such a statistic, the finer the distinctions one uses, the lower the rates of endogamy he arrives at (the limit being the situation in which every person is in a separate category, and every marriage thereby exogamous). The proportions of individuals within each category marrying within the same category were, in percentage: large farmers, 77; small farmers, 24.6; hired hands, 48; total peasant, 84.3; total bourgeois, 58.3; industrial artisan, 58.1; other artisans and millers, 30.1; artisans and millers combined, 63.2. The low percentages among the small farmers (unexpected, but largely due to their propensity to marry into the families of hired hands and of "other artisans") and among the other artisans and millers (expected, because here they actually serve as the "miscellaneous" category) raise some doubt as to our right to think of them as separate and solidary subdivisions. The other categories stand up fairly well. Even this simple statistic shows the relative insulation of the peasants from the rest of the community. If we add the unsurprising observation that nobles almost always married nobles, then the figures suggest that the major classes — nobles, priests, bourgeois, artisans, peasants — were distinct in solidarity as well as in wealth and power.

Such simple percentages, however, are affected by the size of the group in question, and do not reveal the choices that individuals make when they do venture outside their own group. For this, something subtler is called for. One way to handle the problem is to use an index which compares the actual number of pairings of a given type with the "expected" number — the "expectation" being that choice will be independent of occupational class, and therefore that the chances of an individual X's marrying a Y are exactly proportional to the fraction of the total population who are Ys, just as the chances of an X's marrying another X are proportional to the fraction of the total population who are Xs. We may call it the Intermarriage Index. Its formula is:

$$100 \times \frac{\text{Number of marriages between groups X and Y} \times \text{Total number of marriages in the sample}}{\text{Number of persons in group X} \times \text{Number of persons in group Y}}$$

An index of 50 means that there were exactly the expected number of marriages of the given type; the higher the index, the greater the surplus over the expected number.[7]

Table 10 arrays the results for the entire sample, using the finest occupational distinctions possible with the data at hand. The top diagonal line shows the index for marriage within each category, and the rest of the table presents scores for pairs of categories. The top diagonal figures indicate that the young men of every occupational category, with only one small exception, strongly prefer the

[7] One evident drawback of this index is the ease with which it becomes astronomical where the total number of persons in one of the groups is very small. For that reason I have not reported results for categories with 10 persons or less. Marriages involving such groups (consisting of 2 "other peasants," 4 professional bourgeois, and 5 innkeepers in the computations for the entire sample) are, however, included in the class totals.

Table 10. Intermarriage index for communities of southern Anjou.

Occupational category	Not given	Large farmer	Small farmer	Wine-grower	Hired hand	Total peas.	Admin. bourg.	Comm. bourg.	Total bourg.	Ind. artis.	Agric. serv. artis.	Gen. serv. artis.	Total artis.	Miller	Other
Not given	80														
Large farmer	18	157													
Small farmer	41	59	114												
Winegrower	19	20	97	2656											
Hired hand	35	27	108	148	295										
Total peasant	24	117	78	107	89	106									
Admin. bourgeois	48	20	0	0	0	13	0								
Commercial bourg.	13	15	15	101	22	20	101	643							
Total bourgeois	17	15	12	84	19	19	168	560	508						
Indust. artisan	29	12	35	0	45	21	40	43	41	210					
Agricultural service	31	65	78	0	0	53	0	161	134	32	850				
General service	40	26	23	0	9	22	232	70	107	84	0	180			
Total artisan	33	19	33	0	31	23	101	57	67	160	61	112	140		
Miller	41	78	0	0	0	51	0	48	40	0	0	37	12	918	
Other	28	24	85	194	43	39	0	0	0	106	155	45	89	0	455
Number of persons	833	393	82	12	108	597	12	79	95	198	15	103	315	25	41

daughters of men in the same occupational category (or perhaps it is the daughters who prefer the young men). Of the major classes, the bourgeois exhibit the strongest tendency to marry within their own group.[8]

The table also shows well defined preferences among those members of each category who marry outside their group. Only a glance, for instance, will reveal that the large farmers favored millers, agricultural service artisans, and small farmers, and shunned the rest. The small farmers lavished most of their attention on other peasants, but they also married the daughters of agricultural artisans and of "others" (i.e., such miscellaneous types as gendarmes, messengers, boatmen) fairly often. The hired hands rarely married outside the less substantial peasantry. And so on through the table. A review of every pair is informative and diverting, but it is unnecessary here. The significant contents of the table may be summarized in a few remarks: 1) Generally speaking, the strongest attachments between groups are within the same broad class, a fact which, once again, confirms the presence of a measure of class cohesion in southern Anjou. 2) There is a tendency for marriages which do cross class boundaries to unite groups which are similar in power and wealth: industrial artisans seek "others," large farmers seek millers. 3) There is also a tendency for groups which the demands of economic life throw together as approximate equals (even when they are unequal in other respects) to intermarry: the marriages of commercial bourgeois and agricultural service artisans (i.e., blacksmiths, coopers, and the like) illustrate this tendency. 4) This last point can be generalized to say that there are actually two clusters of marriages, one based on the agricultural complex and the other based on the commercial complex; even in affairs of the heart, the division cut the community in two.

A complicated table is a maze in which one can easily lose his way. For that reason, I have prepared Figure 4, which is no more than a graphic translation of the stronger relationships in the table of intermarriage indexes. The diagram illustrates all the points already

[8] The apparent discrepancy between this statement and the results of the inquiry into the percentage of each group marrying out is due to the fact that the present index corrects for the sizes of the groups involved — saying, in effect, that it is less remarkable that 50% of group X, which constitutes half the entire population, marries within its bounds, than it is that 50% of group Y, which has only a tenth of the population, does so.

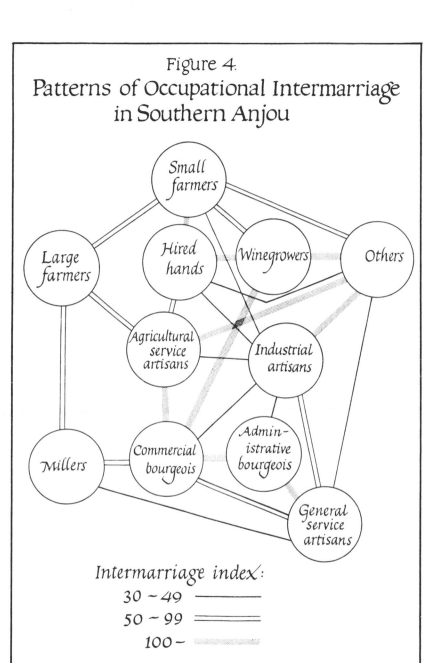

Figure 4.

Patterns of Occupational Intermarriage in Southern Anjou

Small farmers

Large farmers

Hired hands

Winegrowers

Others

Agricultural service artisans

Industrial artisans

Admin- istrative bourgeois

Millers

Commercial bourgeois

General service artisans

Intermarriage index:

30 – 49 ————

50 – 99 ========

100 –

S Bryant

made concerning the general table and suggests some new ones. It confirms the partial separation of the agricultural and commercial complexes, but suggests some useful qualifications and elaborations: 1) The winegrowers and, to a lesser extent, the hired hands were closer to the nonpeasants than were the large or small farmers; these were, in fact, the peasant categories most regularly involved in buying and selling. 2) Millers and agricultural service artisans (and perhaps the "others") held positions intermediate between the peasants and the rest of the classes, a fact which likewise corresponds to the social relations their occupations demanded.

The diagram has some other rewards to offer. First, it has sometimes been asserted that the small farmers and industrial artisans (largely weavers) of southern Anjou were essentially the same people, shifting from one activity to the other as season and demand dictated. If this were the case, we might expect the marriage records to reflect an exceptional number of alliances between the two groups, and to give them very similar relations to the rest of the community. Not at all. Although they apparently maintained some cordial contact, the two groups were quite distinct. The observation is a good reminder of the importance of maintaining the distinction between peasants and artisans.

A second observation — and one which could probably be better substantiated if we had adequate data for each subregion — is that marriage seems to follow the residential pattern of the community. For example, the three most typical categories of bourg-dwellers — the commercial bourgeois, administrative bourgeois, and general service artisans — frequently intermarry. The relations of the other artisans, the hired hands, and the small farmers seem to bring together the categories that were most likely (in the Mauges) to live in the villages and hamlets. These apparent effects of proximity do not override those of class or of relations generated by work. Instead, their importance lies in their support of a point already presented: that in the Mauges the geographic divisions of the community actually reinforced the class divisions.

General Patterns of Affiliation

There is one more interesting implication of the patterns of marital preference. If there were a single, well-defined, rank order of classes of the type that Lloyd Warner's careful dissections of American communities inspire other investigators to seek elsewhere, it would surely show up in the marriages. For precisely such questions of social access and acceptability weigh most heavily in the Warner analysis. But the reality registered in the thousand marriages considered here is a hard one for the enticing vocabulary of Upper, Middle, and Lower. Although there are clearly rank differences within each complex, they cannot be squeezed into a scale. The reality returns us to the conclusion that genuine classes can exist which do not form a unitary rank order.

Considered as a whole, the findings of this analysis nicely amplify some of the vaguer assertions about class structure and solidarity made earlier. The pattern of marriages confirms the division of the rural community of southern Anjou into major classes, corroborates its broader division into agricultural and commercial complexes, and urges the conclusion that these divisions extended to personal friendship, access, and alliance. Indeed, the findings are sufficiently definite and provocative to leave one longing for an adequate number and distribution of cases to make an adequate comparison of the subregions of southern Anjou. The limits of the present sample, however, leave that admirable objective unattainable.

Despite their inescapable weaknesses when it comes to matters of personal affiliation, the records have told us some important things about the structure of the rural neighborhood. We can see the simultaneous significance of class and geographic location for informal social relations. We can see how the absorption of parts of the communities of the Mauges by the market accentuated the division of the agricultural and commercial complexes, and how participation in the commercial complex fostered mobility and wider experience outside the community. We can see the presence of a genuine set of elite positions, combining higher rank with wide social relations, within each of the complexes. And, finally, we come away with a stronger presumption that the agglomerated settlement pattern of Val-Saumurois fortified the responsiveness of its citizens to ideas and political movements from abroad. It will be interesting to see how many of these conclusions find their counterparts in parish, economy, and commune, the other three systems of social relations in the rural community.

CHAPTER **6**

Curés and Clericalism

The *parish* is the portion of a community's social organization built around beliefs and their control. As it happens, an eighteenth-century Angevin was likely to refer to a rural community as "the parish" whether he was considering it from a religious angle or not. The parish church was the community's identifying monument, as the prevalence of such community names as St. Christophe-de-la-Couperie, St. Macaire-en-Mauges, St. Georges-du-Puy-de-la-Garde, Notre-Dame-de-Chemillé, or St. Florent-le-Vieil testifies. The feeling that the church supplied an identity for the community was so strong that bewildered protest arose from every part of southern Anjou when Revolutionary officials sought to close down and consolidate redundant parishes in the interests of economy and efficient administration. This is the chauvinistic side of local loyalty or, as the apt French phrase has it, of *esprit de clocher*.

Parish Organization

More than diffuse sentiments attached the Angevin to his parish. Almost every formal organization that a countryman could participate in — school, brotherhood, vestry, charity, and, of course, church — was manifestly religious. The parish assembly, charged with such worldly concerns of the local church as rental of pews or repair of the steeple, was virtually indistinguishable from the secular council of the community. The parish was the largest grouping in which the countryman was likely to be strongly conscious of membership.

The parish was also the basic local unit for religious administration. The curé, its head, was often practically independent of the rest of the hierarchy; he was responsible not only for the oversight of the parish church and its lands, but also for charities, midwives, schools, and what we might call the keeping of vital statistics. The vicar was the curé's appointed assistant. (Pity the poor translator: *curé* and *vicaire* reverse the meanings of curate and vicar, their English cognates.) Chaplains, priors, and regular clergy (that is, monks) did not occupy places in the formal parish organization. However, local chaplains were usually subordinate to the curé, and the others were relatively rare in the countryside.

In the sense of occupying dual roles within the community and in the international structure of the Church, all the clergy qualified as members of the local elite. Yet monks, canons, and even priors were often no more than peripherally (and parasitically) involved in the local affairs of the rural community, while the chaplain was likely to be wholly absorbed in them. It was the vicar and — especially — the curé who were fully and simultaneously involved both in the life of the parish and the goings on of the outside world. The position of the curé as intermediary is apparent in even the briefest enumeration of his varied activities: as a prime witness for wills and marriage contracts; as a writer of recommendations for peasants seeking to lease farms outside the community; as the man who announced upcoming auctions of land and private property; as the recorder of all births, deaths, and marriages; as the local scribe; as the writer of appeals to the royal functionaries of Angers, Tours, or Paris.

This much was true of the whole of southern Anjou. Within these limits, there was considerable room for variation in religious practice and clerical influence. Religiosity and clericalism are not the same thing. Clericalism, as Siegfried (1913: 363) declared, is the decisive condition for the political influence of the church in France. Strong clericalism and intensive religious practice, nevertheless, tend to occur together, just as anticlericalism, religious indifference, and radical politics tend to coincide. Bois (1961 and 1960b: 99–116 and 589–594; cf. Faucheux 1960) has confirmed Siegfried's observation of a general correspondence in the West among the territories of 1) strong religious practice, 2) conservative voting in nineteenth-century elections, 3) counterrevolution in the period 1791–1799. Likewise, the diligent researches of Gabriel Le Bras (1955–1956: I, esp. 120–194, 302–310; II, esp. 526–545) have produced evidence of the same correspondence, of a remarkable similarity between the

boundaries of the West's "practicing regions" today and the outlines of the insurrections against the Revolution. This is true not
only in gross, but also with the small compass of southern Anjou.
Le Bras gives the following summary: "The region of the diocese
of Angers which touches Touraine is completely indifferent. Suddenly one crosses, after Saumur, a Eucharistic frontier, and one
enters into hallowed ground" (1955–1956: I, 122; cf. Châtelain
1956; Denecheau 1955; Lancelot and Ranger 1961, p. 142). The line
Le Bras draws splits the District of Vihiers, as it was in 1790, and
is a satisfactory approximation of the division between Val-Saumurois
and Mauges, between revolutionary and counterrevolutionary, and
(as we shall see) between the territories whose priests generally accepted the Revolution's religious reforms and those whose priests
generally rejected them. To corroborate this, the zone of transition
between Mauges and Val-Saumurois, the vicinity of the Layon, is
reported to lie between them in terms of religious practice and
political opinion as well (Le Theule 1950).

Other facts about the Mauges of this century testify to the vigor
of the heritage. Outside the cities, state schools are almost unattended in the Mauges. Sunday church attendance is near 100 percent.
The birth rate is high and large families are common. Even in the
process of demonstrating that the religious life of a community at
the edge of the Mauges has been transformed since the old regime,
Laurence Wylie (1959: 544) demonstrates its continued, or renewed,
vitality. He reports a conversation with ". . . the head of the tiny
Communist cell in Chanzeaux. 'The Communist Party is dying out
here,' he said. 'Only a few of us older people really understand the
class struggle. The priests keep the young people so busy that they
don't even have time to realize what is wrong with society.' "

The evidence from the period of the Revolution is not so solid,
but it leans in the same direction. Early chroniclers of the Vendée
rebellion, including those who knew the region before 1789, agreed
in depicting the bocage as a region of exceptional religious fidelity
(or fanaticism); when they thought to mention it, they usually
described the plain as a region of religious indifference (or enlightenment). J.-J.-M. Savary (1824: 31–32), for example, claimed that "the
people of the Vendée are perhaps those of the whole of France who
. . . have lost the least of their former habits and primitive lib-

erty. . . . The priests had at their disposition the keys to Heaven and Hell . . . [They] could do what they wanted with the spirit of the countryside." Many writers have attributed the pace of religious activity — pilgrimages, sodalities, special devotions, the erection of wayside crosses — to the influence of an extraordinary eighteenth-century missionary, Grignion de Montfort, and his followers at St. Laurent-sur-Sèvre; Ch.-L. Chassin (1892: I, 43) grumbled that Grignion had "fanaticized" the whole region. And when a post-Revolutionary prefect, in a report already cited (Uzureau 1919: 88–89) contrasted the peasant of the Mauges ("The ignorance he wallows in and his hereditary prejudices throw him at the mercy of his curé, who has always held a despotic influence over him.") with the peasant of Val-Saumurois ("The population, more concentrated and closer to the cities, is lively, bright, Gallic, less ignorant and freer from prejudice.") he was making exactly the same point.

By linking the concentration of the Val-Saumurois population and its "freedom from prejudice," the prefect may have been recording a more telling observation than he realized. I have already mentioned some reasons for thinking that the clustered conformation of the Val-Saumurois communities enhanced their sensitivity to exotic ideas. In a slightly different way, dispersion may have reinforced religion in the bocage. With fewer everyday, secular occasions for meetings among the community's scattered citizens, the religious affairs, which drew together people from all the hamlets and farms, were probably magnified. There were an enormous number of local *frairies*, religious brotherhoods, in the Mauges, but no other detectable clubs or associations. Religious activities provided the only settings in which men could express their gregarious impulses. If there is something to this explanation, it is undoubtedly fortified by the frequent observation that the inhabitants of bourgs are less attentive to religion than are those of the hinterland.

The Curé

The community's collective business was transacted in assembly after Sunday's Mass, "before the portal of our Holy Mother Church," as the timeless formula ran. The curé was almost always there, and the minutes show he was never silent. The custom of the Sunday meeting was commanding enough that the great majority of the communal assemblies convened in the Mauges to prepare for the Estates General of 1789 formed as the parishioners filed out of church on Sunday, 1 March or Sunday, 8 March. And the habit of the curé's chairmanship was so strong that the next year, when it came time to elect local officials to carry forth the work of the Revolution, the curé was generally named president of the electoral assembly.

Bois has summarized the position of the parish priest as follows:

The role of the curé in the bocage was, without any doubt, immense, and it would be difficult to overestimate it. One can hardly see how any conflicts, rivalries, or mistrust could arise between him and the peasants. While [the peasant's] relations with artisans or the bourg's merchants were often in terms of material interests . . . his relations with the curé were in spiritual terms. The tithe, to be sure, was irritating, and the parish *cahiers* are almost unanimous on this point. But it was rarely a matter of the curé's tithe; it was the upper clergy, the chapters and monastic orders, that drew the complaints. . . . Nor was there any intellectual rivalry. . . . Only the petty bourgeois of the village, lawyer or merchant, could take umbrage at the curé's claim to intellectual superiority. . . . Finally, the moral surveillance of the curé was not overly inhibiting. He could not maintain close control over what happened on the farms or in the distant hamlets, whereas in the bourg, or, elsewhere in France, in concentrated villages, his surveillance . . . has sometimes seemed tyrannical and has encouraged distrust and the beginnings of an anticlericalism which had no *raison d'être* in the bocage . . . [The curé] was for peasants confined in their scattered groups . . . the only center, the only means of spiritual life (1960b: 614).

In the small parish of the Mauges, the curé was unquestionably the moral, charitable, and intellectual chief. Even if the seigneur gave money for good works, he let the priest administer them. The curé was scholar and scribe. The "late Master Jacques Pigeol, in his lifetime curé of the parish of les Cerqueux-de-Maulèvrier," as a 1727 inventory reads (A.D. M-et-L E 1303), had owned the grand total of 104 books, about evenly divided between theology and pastoral practice, plus one solitary volume of the *nouveau theastre du monde*. Like Master Pigeol, other curés generally had the largest, if not the only, libraries in their bourgs. In addition, they controlled the schools, the almshouses, and often a great deal more.

One easy hunch which has sometimes been taken for an established verity is that the curés of the Mauges were generally local boys who had made good. If "local" means anything narrower than birth in the same diocese, not so. Of the 110 curés (a little over half of the total) serving in southern Anjou in 1790 whose birthplaces I have been able to trace, only 23 percent had grown up in the same canton as their present parish, or in an adjacent one.[1] And only 31 percent were even from the same district. Furthermore, the proportion of home-grown curés was, if anything, higher in Val-Saumurois than in the Mauges, the percentages born in the same district being: Cholet 18, St. Florent 40, Vihiers 19, Angers 36, Saumur 54. In trying to explain the greater authority of the parish clergy in the Mauges, the argument that it was based on the solidarity of insiders does us little good. I suppose we may discount the opposite explanation: that a prophet is without honor in his own country. That leaves us with a clearer realization that the prestige of the curé depended not on the accident of his origins but on his position in the structure of the community.

It is important to realize that in material terms the curés of the Mauges were men of substance indeed. Their net incomes were in the same range as those of the country bourgeoisie. Old Father Jacques Galpin of Melay netted 2520 livres 17 sous 2 deniers in 1790. His nearby colleague, Retailleau of Cossé, was receiving 2244 livres, Delacroix of St. Macaire 3288 livres, Coulonnier of Le May 3444 livres, Fontenau of Tilliers as much as 4073 livres, at a time when a good-sized farm rented for 350 livres, a chicken sold for 6 sous, a bushel of rye for a livre, and the net worth of the average farmer was under 500 livres (A.D. M-et-L 1 E 1371, 16 Q 82–86).

These substantial incomes were not from direct control of the land. If the sale of church properties during the Revolution is a good indication, the glebe of Melay included only about 8 hectares formed into a single bordage, and the glebe of St. Macaire about 10 hectares (A.D. M-et-L 6 Q 1, 12 Q 53, 12 Q 281). Rather than coming from land owned outright, the greater part of the curé's income was likely to be in the form of incidental rents of tithes in kind, collected on scores of properties scattered throughout his parish and even beyond. The tithe, despite its name, varied between 5 and 10 percent of the harvest of certain traditional crops in each community. At St. Lambert, a winegrowing community on the Layon, the curé collected

---

[1] Based mainly on information in Queruau-Lamerie 1899, augmented with notes on individual curés compiled from a wide variety of other sources. Gallard (1960: 16–17) estimates that 60% of all the clergy of the Saumurois in 1789 — curés, vicars, monks, and all the rest — were natives of the area.

14 *busses* of wine which he sold for 1,130 livres, 60 percent of his income (A.D. M-et-L 16 Q 148). In mid-Mauges, the main crop and the most important tithe was rye.

An analysis of the curé's income in St. Macaire, presented in Table 11, will show how these various sources fit together. By far

Table 11. Gross income of curé of St. Macaire, 1790.*

	Value
A. Tithes	
114 septiers rye	3596 livres
10 septiers wheat	417 livres 6 sous 10 deniers
6 septiers bran	129 livres 12 sous
43 bushels oats	35 livres 9 sous 6 deniers
Other minor tithes	400 livres
Straw from tithed grains	400 livres
B. Rents	
4 septiers rye	110 livres
C. Total return from lands of the glebe	150 livres
Gross revenues	5238 livres

* (A.D. M-et-L 16 Q 86).

the largest part of this curé's income was in the form of tithes. The curé of St. Macaire had to pay certain fixed charges which included, in livres 1) harvesting costs (for tithes and rents), 400; 2) pension for his retired predecessor, 1,200; 3) vicar's salary, 350. These were his legally deductible expenses, according to the 1790 law. The curé had claimed 700 livres for his vicar's salary and about 500 livres for alms and the wages of his hired hands, but these claims were disallowed. His legal net income was, accordingly, 3,288 livres. According to the curé's own computation, it was about 2,400 livres. Even at the lower figure, his income was ample.

There are two striking facts about this income. First, the preponderant element by far was the tithe of the principal local crop, rye; this portion of the curé's income varied with the abundance of the harvest. Second, almost all the curé's revenues were in kind. For both these reasons, he was at once concerned with the condition of local agriculture, and alert to the state of the market. The welfare of practically every farm in the parish affected his welfare. Whether the curé farmed out the tithe to a local entrepreneur or his own men handled the collection and resale of the farm products, his welfare also depended on agricultural prices.

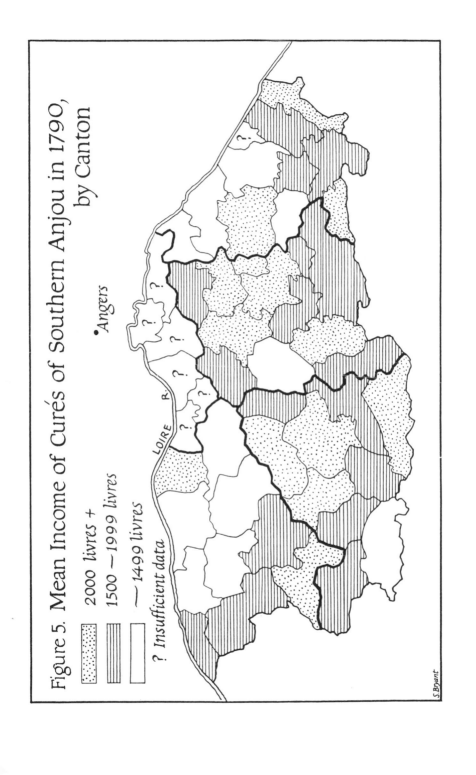

Figure 5. Mean Income of Curés of Southern Anjou in 1790, by Canton

• Angers

LOIRE R.

2000 livres +
1500 — 1999 livres
— 1499 livres
? Insufficient data

S. Bryant

Exactly what income the curé received from the various possible sources depended on a multitude of historical accidents. The greatest variable was the presence or absence of a *gros décimateur* — literally, a Big Tither, but actually an outside agency which took the bulk of the local tithe. The abbey of St. Florent-le-Vieil, for example, laid claim to tithes all through its vicinity, and the nearby parishes were correspondingly less opulent. Several of the curés under its influence were on *portion congrue*, which means they got meager salaries in lieu of the tithe which the abbey carted out of the parish. In fact, the number of curés on portion congrue is not a bad index of the strength of abbeys and chapters in southern Anjou: in the Districts of Vihiers and Cholet there were none among the curés who reported their 1790 incomes, while in St. Florent there were 4 out of 37, and in the thoroughly monasticized District of Saumur 11 out of 49 (A.D. M-et-L 16 Q 80–156).

Beyond this, however, there was no clear correlation between the social characteristics of the subdivisions of southern Anjou and the incomes of their curés. The District means for 1790, in livres, were for Saumur, 1735 livres; Vihiers, 2130 livres; St. Florent, 1525 livres; Cholet, 2254 livres. The map of mean 1790 income by canton (which unfortunately lacks information for the District of Angers) does indicate the greater average wealth of the priests around Cholet and Vihiers, but it also outlines patches of both high and low income in each district. So far as the parish clergy were concerned, the line between Val-Saumurois and Mauges was not a division into rich and poor.

The division was more trenchant when it came to the higher clergy. I have already shown that establishments of monks, nuns, and canons — and their properties — were much more common in the District of Saumur than in the rest of southern Anjou. They, and not the parish clergy, were the great landowners. Their property, more than the property of the curés, was coveted by the bourgeois and finally bought by them during the Revolution. By the eighteenth century, the religious energy which centuries before had made of the Loire Valley a garden of monasticism had faded. If anything, monasteries, priories, and chapters turned people away from religion. It is surely more than coincidence that the few places in the Mauges

where they were found — Cholet, Chemillé, Les Gardes, Le May —
were Patriot centers after 1789. Says Émile Gabory:

> The forebears founded abbeys for pious purposes; the descendants looked for
> profits. Where the secular priest had influence, he upheld Catholicism by his
> example; there, the peasants took part in the uprising. Where the monk was
> master, the people became skeptics; they supported the Revolution. The rich
> abbeys of the Vendean plain succeeded only in creating a spirit hostile to
> religion (1925: I, 12–13).

He does not explain how this happened, but any bad name their
private lives gave organized religion was compounded by envy of
their properties, irritation with their wealth and their intervention
in local affairs, as well as geographic coexistence with areas of vine,
commerce, and peasant property, in themselves breeders of independence.

A lawsuit originating not long before the Revolution in Le Puy-
Notre-Dame, south of Saumur, illustrates the point (A.D. M-et-L
C 35). There, the titulary prior was the Dom de Cressac, of whom
it was said that "he lives at the abbey of Montiersneuf in Poitiers,
rather as a pensioner than as a monk. The revenues of the benefice
he has at Le Puy-Notre-Dame as well as of several other big benefices
he has are all to his profit." The parishioners argued that they ought
to be able to tax this rich absentee, because he was actually farming
his land and using a house to store the grains of the priory. The
technicalities are less interesting than the whole implication of
resentment and resistance.

Take the community of St. Lambert-du-Lattay, astride the Layon,
for another example (de Menil 1962). The temporal seigneur was
the abbess of the convent of Le Ronceray, in Angers, who had some
200 tenants in the area. She made many claims for jurisdiction over
local affairs, and her agents were ever present in the community.
The abbess and the curé were in continual contention over the rights
to the local tithe, and, according to the communal cahier of 1789,
the abbess was maneuvering to grab the nearby common fields (Raimbault n.d.; Andrews 1935: 93). Is it a great surprise to learn that the
same cahier asked for the expropriation of the monasteries?

The case of St. Lambert is not quite ordinary, but it is diagnostic.
On the one hand, the abbess was rich enough, influential enough,

and attentive enough to local affairs to excite genuine irritation and envy. On the other, her presence in person or proxy weakened any of the curé's claims to hegemony in religious affairs. These were fairly general effects of monastic influence: resentment, covetousness, a weakened parish clergy, the ingredients of anticlericalism.

In the absence of such active competition, the curé was in a stronger position to dominate local affairs. Indeed, the curé of the Mauges was often said to "govern" his community. By custom and by law he was a leader in all parish affairs, the old regime's closest approximation of a mayor, the usual spokesman in contacts with the outside. The discussion of economic and political organization will identify some other supports to his power. But the curé's domination is impossible to explain on the basis of his administrative position alone. It has lasted long after the institution of modern government, after the loss of many of his civil powers. It rested and rests as well on his intellectual monopoly and on the tremendous importance of religion to his parishioners.

Siegfried, speaking of the twentieth century, declared:

. . . in the Vendée, it is the priest who remains as in other days the peasant's real chief. [The peasant] is not only religious; he also feels a kind of sacred superstition regarding that priest toward whom ancestral habit prescribes passive obedience. Behold then the real leader of the Vendean region! It is for him, and not for the noble or for the king, that [the peasant] revolted in 1793. It is for him that today even the humblest go so far as to deprive themselves of necessities. Furthermore, he knows his prestige, knows that instead of asking he need simply say, "It must be done!" and be obeyed, without discussion or resistance. Fear, respectful affection, habit and devotion blend strangely to put that people at once passive and passionate, under the discretionary authority of the Church's representative (1913: 26).

What is hard to believe is that when Siegfried wrote, that authority had already been through the challenge of over a century's commercial growth and political turmoil.

Religious Relations

Not that the curé was never challenged. The lords caused many an imbroglio, and the bourgeois of many parishes carried on a constant, if covert, campaign to undermine the priest's power. The difficulties with the nobles were generally over the honors the Church should accord them, apparently a trivial matter, but just the sort of thing to touch the nerves of a rustic eighteenth-century noble. Occasionally the rights of the lords which affected the parish church had a faintly economic tinge, like the lord of Le Planty's ringing the bells of St. Quentin to signal the haymaking at his farm of Cul de Loire (A.D. M-et-L E 1057). But more often the rights that aroused arguments were the right to be called founder of the parish, the right to put the church into full mourning at the death of a local lord, the right to a distinctive type of aspersion with holy water, the right to put one's coat of arms on the wall of the church, and other "useless" prerogatives (e.g., the argument between the lords of La Séverie and Maulèvrier, A.D. M-et-L E 1303; cf. Arnault 1945: 7). The significance of these quibbles is this: the man in the château rarely meddled in local affairs, but when he did, he demanded deference. Perhaps he sensed and resented the independent power of the priest. In any case, there was a subtle balance between the economic dominance and honorific priority of the lord and the practical leadership of the curé.

There was no such balance between clergy and bourgeoisie. In the countryside, the manufacturing and commercial bourgeoisie had only come into existence late in the seventeenth century; it was still struggling for a stronger position in the communities of the Mauges late in the eighteenth. Too few and too weak (until the Revolution) to compete with the lord for control of the land, the bourgeois competed with the curé for control of the people. Generally, they led any resistance to payment of the tithe.

The bourgeois, with his relative wealth, his cosmopolitan experience, his daily dealing with affairs of concern to the entire community, and his influence over a substantial part of the population, was a growing threat to the curé's local hegemony. By the same token, the curé blocked the bourgeois' path to the power and prestige his skills and sensibilities might otherwise have brought him. "He's run this parish long enough!" shouted the bourgeois of Vauchrétien in 1790 (A.D. M-et-L 1 L 349). That motto was broadcast throughout the Mauges, and tells a good part of the history of the Revolution and of the counterrevolution.

This analysis of religious affairs is like a reupholstered chair: it may look new, but underneath stands the old, familiar frame. Once again, the conception of differential urbanization is the frame. The long, slow, thorough urbanization of the Val-Saumurois — of which the growth and decadence of monasticism was an essential part — reduced the independence and power of the parish priest by drawing his parishioners away from clerical religiosity, by decreasing their dependence on his mediation, by setting up rivals for his position, both as chief and as intermediary, both in religious affairs and in secular affairs. In short, urbanization sapped the priest's elite position.

The process had not gone so far, nor so evenly, in the Mauges. The population had not been so long, or so fully, exposed to the secular forces which seem to be the constant corollaries of participation in France's national society. Yet the rapid rise of a new elite, based on commerce and manufacturing, offered an eager alternative to priestly leadership, without seriously threatening the bases of that traditional leadership. There was the making of conflict, but not of successful revolution.

Unquestionably, "The church belongs to the conservative forces in European countries . . . ," as Weber said. He continued:

[Both the Roman Catholic and Lutheran churches] support the peasant, with his conservative way of life, against the domination of urban rationalist culture. . . . Likewise, a landed aristocracy finds strong backing in the church. . . . The church is pleased with patriarchal labor relations because contrary to the purely commercial relations which capitalism creates, they are of a personal human character (Gerth and Mills 1946: 370–71).

According to this formula, there is no question which of the two, Mauges or Saumurois, the Church would prefer. There is no question, in fact, where its influence — or rather, the influence of its parish priests — was stronger in 1789. On one side of the Layon was the Saumurois, "Catholic enough in its habits, but not clerical." On the other side were the Mauges, part of "the most Catholic provinces of France" (Siegfried 1913: 40, 55).

CHAPTER 7

Rustic Economics

The *economy*, the reader hardly needs reminding, is the set of social relations in the community built around the production and distribution of goods. More evidently than the neighborhood and, perhaps, than the parish, the economy is at once an essential element of the community's structure and a subdivision of a complex of social relationships spreading far beyond any individual community. The theoretical, self-contained village economy holds little interest for students of peasant societies, except as a pure, abstract standard for the appraisal of the impure reality.

The same is true of the imaginary homogeneous peasant community. Certainly the idea of such a community hangs awkwardly on the framework of even the most uncomplicated, or the most rural, community of southern Anjou. Behind a multitude of variations in specialty, wealth, and economic power lay a division between two economic complexes — *agricultural* and *industrial*. They could be called, in Marxian terms, modes of production. One set of social relations was built about tilling the soil; the other was built about manufacturing.

The somewhat separate development of these two complexes has been a nearly universal feature of the economic histories of modern European nations. Often, however, local manufacturing has grown up from the crafts — weaving, woodworking, tanning — indigenous in most peasant communities. Peasants have used their spare time for manufacturing. In recent centuries, the desire for the products of industry has often drawn peasants into market production, and consequently into dependence on industry. In both cases there is a measure of integration between the agricultural and industrial complexes.

One fact that set southern Anjou apart was that the integration of the two complexes was greater in Val-Saumurois (where there was little industry, but plenty of commercialized agriculture) than in the Mauges (where there was vigorous industry cheek by jowl with subsistence farming). The separation of the agricultural and industrial complexes in the Mauges was great enough to require that we discuss each quite separately before attempting to put them together.

The Agricultural Complex

To begin with, some simple, eloquent figures from the cadastre of 1844 (A.D. M-et-L VI P[1] 102). A table presents percentages of the

Table 12. Percentages of total land, according to use.

Arrondissement	Plowland	Meadow	Vines	Woods	Other
Saumur	56.4	9.3	9.5	10.7	14.1
Angers	59.5	12.8	6.8	6.5	14.4
Beaupréau	69.0	13.1	1.7	5.3	10.9

total land devoted to various uses according to the *arrondissements* that existed then.

Clearly enough, the Mauges (represented here by the arrondissement of Beaupréau) had more land under the plow, and therefore in grain, than did the Val-Saumurois. To feed the cattle, the Mauges also had more meadows. The Val-Saumurois maintained vineyards and forests instead. The statistics belong to the nineteenth century, but the general contrast is that of the century before.

The peasants of the Mauges were subsistence farmers. They raised a good deal of grain for local consumption, and a few cattle for cash sale. Just because the cattle were a prime source of cash, and perhaps because the inhabitants of Val-Saumurois have the habit of calling the Mauges the *pays de bœufs*, the ox country, many commentators have been moved to describe the Mauges as mainly a stock-raising area. For example, Andrews wrote that "throughout the region the farmers concentrate their efforts on raising cattle rather than field crops . . . any growing of grains or vegetables is secondary to the principal industry, stock-raising" (1935: 108–109). But this is an illusion. On a farm of 20 to 30 hectares (50–75 acres), a peasant was likely to fatten up two or three steers for sale each year (see Uzureau 1941: 45–46). Some of them were superannuated draft animals. Some were bought in Poitou or Brittany, specifically for fattening. Some few were raised especially for the market. In any case, the peasant made about two hundred livres on his sale, and perhaps another two hundred from cows, sheep, and other products. At times, he fattened cattle on half shares with his landlord, the tenant supplying the labor. The tenant was likely to meet most of his needs for cash — including taxes and the rents that were not in kind — from the annual sale of a few animals, but his family actually lived on the other products of the farm.

These few cattle being readied for the butcher were by no means the only ones on the farm, and that fact probably explains some of the confusion about stock raising in the Mauges. Oxen were the draft animals, and they were needed in good number. A 25-hectare farm often had 10 oxen for plowing. But these oxen often belonged to the landlord, as did a good deal of the farm equipment. This is particularly true of the smaller farmers, the bordiers and closiers, who were working from 5 to 10 hectares of land. Near Chemillé, inventories of their possessions rarely included more than a few cows (notarial minutes, Étude Fleury, Chemillé). The métayers, the middling farmers, often had half their gross worth in cattle. However, even they frequently owed money to their landlords for oxen the landlords had bought them.

In short, it is true that cattle were essential, but what they were essential to was the raising of grain. The grain of the Mauges was rye. In Val-Saumurois, on the other hand, it was wheat. The difference matters. It matters because, as I have already mentioned, wheat was the commercial crop, the grain more suitable for the bread of manor, monastery, or *hôtel de ville*, while rye was the humble crop for local consumption. In the districts of St. Florent and Cholet, the only place where more than a third of the cultivated land was devoted to wheat was along the Loire, in the vicinity of St. Florent (see Andrews 1935: 110–111; Millet 1856). Wheat predominated in the grain-growing sections of Val and Saumurois. The difference in crops, then, is one significant element of the contrast between the commercial farming of Val-Saumurois and the subsistence agriculture of the Mauges.

A second, equally significant, element is the abundance of winegrowing in Val-Saumurois, and its virtual absence in the Mauges (see Dion 1934: esp. 621 ff.; Dion 1959: esp. 274 ff.; Le Theule 1950; Wagret and Le Theule 1954; Maisonneuve 1925). Figure 6 is a simplified version of a map of southern Anjou's winegrowing areas in 1880, a map which does not differ in essentials from the information available for 1789 (A.D. M-et-L 59 M 4; cf. 59 M 2; Andrews 1935: 115). Except for the minor string of vineyards along the western flank, near the Sèvre Nantaise, it could hardly outline the Mauges more clearly. It was in the winegrowing areas of Val and Saumurois that both peasant ownership and fractionation of the land were at their extreme. It was likewise in the winegrowing areas that the villages were most concentrated.

The difference between the work of the traditional cultivator and that of the winegrower is important in itself. As Labrousse (1944: 210) has put it, "The vineyard's labor force consists of what one might call the craftsmen of agriculture." The winegrower is a merchant by necessity and by inclination; he must calculate costs, prices, and the probable effects of distant decisions. He is inevitably sensitive to governmental policies affecting commerce (the vintners of the eighteenth-century Val and Saumurois could not fail to notice the effect of the major toll barrier between them and Nantes, on the Loire at Ingrandes). He keeps up communication with the cities that consume or ship his output. He is a specialist whose product is delicate and uncertain, whose welfare is determined by the gyrations of an international market. His occupation gives him a great deal of common ground with the petty bourgeoisie. It is not surprising that during the nineteenth century the rural sections of France that most consistently voted for traditional republicanism — the "radical" republicanism of small property, personal independence, political equality — were the winegrowing areas. It was true of the vineyard areas of Anjou as well as of the rest of France. And in the century before, the differences between the "ox country" and the "vine country" were fundamental.

One more significant set of agricultural products to consider is the pair that fed the textile industry of the Mauges: flax and hemp. According to Dion:

   . . . the principal function of the agriculture of the valleys, during all the eighteenth century and most of the nineteenth, was to supply raw materials

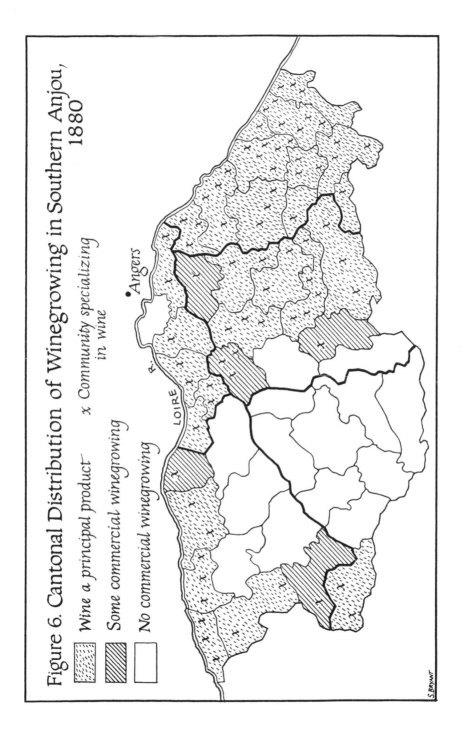

Figure 6. Cantonal Distribution of Winegrowing in Southern Anjou, 1880

x Community specializing in wine

Wine a principal product

Some commercial winegrowing

No commercial winegrowing

LOIRE R.

• Angers

S. BRYANT

to the industries created or regenerated by Colbert. In 1699, flax and hemp ranked, with wheat and beans, among the essential products of the Loire valley. The mildness of the climate, the depth, lightness and freshness of the arable land, the abundance of fodder, leading to the abundance of manure, allowed the cultivation of textile plants on a large scale and with rare success (1934: 600).

The burgeoning textile centers of the interior drew their raw materials not from the nearby farms of the bocage, but from the small, intensively cultivated plots crowded into the strip of river valley from Champtoceaux to Ponts-de-Cé (see A.D. M-et-L 59 M 33–34). The bustling city of Chalonnes, that focus of the wine trade, was also the geographical center and the principal entrepôt for these profitable and eminently commercial crops.

That leads to an observation worth reiterating: the cities of Val and Saumurois were not simply administrative or industrial centers, but agricultural markets. Consider the reasons that the chiefs of Vernoil and Vernantes, two communities north of the Loire, gave for wanting to be attached to the District of Saumur in 1790:

Since time immemorial the two parishes of Vernoil and Vernantes have formed bonds of commerce with the city of Saumur on the Loire, bonds which it would be damaging to destroy. They take wheat, oils, timber for ships, firewood and dried fruit there, and it is assuredly Saumur that is the main source of wealth and the principal market for these two parishes, which cannot belong to another district without ruin and detriment (A.N. D IV 40).

Although none could match Saumur, the other cities of Val-Saumurois maintained similar relations with their tributary areas.

The facts of agricultural production and trade, it is clear, pile up to confirm what we already knew in a general way about the differences among plain, valley, and bocage. The differences in crops have some potent concomitants: 1) in Val-Saumurois, more intensive use of the land, greater specialization, considerable fractionation of property, many peasant landowners, a peasantry involved as a matter of course in the world of business; 2) in the Mauges, inefficient land use, extensive idle land, polyculture, concentration of property in large (mainly noble) holdings parceled into medium-sized tenant farms, a peasantry with only a peripheral involvement in commerce. Their intensive, energetic, flourishing, commercial agriculture set

Val and Saumurois in sparkling contrast to the somber wastes of the bocage.

The Control of Land

The differences in agriculture were inseparable from the differences in property. The two together shaped many other features of social organization. Siegfried described Val and Saumurois as forming a society of small peasant proprietors, independent, egalitarian and democratic. But in the Mauges, he said, "That coexistence of large properties and small exploitations, which could deceive by a false appearance of fractionation, actually constitutes the most anti-democratic property regime; by exaggerating the importance of proprietors by comparison with the humbleness of their leaseholders, it contributes essentially to create that hierarchical and feudal atmosphere we have said to be that of the Vendée" (1913: 24). To Siegfried's way of thinking, the essential elements of the contrast between the republican Saumurois and the royalist Mauges of the Third Republic were 1) the immense respect of the peasants for their parish priests and 2) this difference in the control of the land.[1]

We should take care not to make the easy inference from Siegfried's analysis, or from the fact of noble land ownership itself, to a notion of "absolute" domination of local affairs by the eighteenth-century lord. A counterquotation gives a good reason for caution:

Many great landlords had hardly lived on their domains . . . before 1830; they were in Paris, at Court, busying themselves with politics, serving in the army; those who had remained in the country were not all interested in agriculture. In 1830 came the first return to the land: the Legitimist nobles of Bas-Maine and Anjou left the Court, abandoned politics and came back to their properties; with little to do, many nobles became interested in agronomy. In 1852, after the *coup d'état*, a second and more extensive [return to the land] occurred . . . (Musset 1917: 326).

There is every reason to think that this description fits the Mauges

[1] Of course, ownership is by no means the only aspect of control of the land that deserves attention. I must confess that, as a critic of a study such as this one, I would be quick to bemoan the neglect of the *transfers* of property going on during the eighteenth century, of changes in rent, and of variations in agricultural prices. The necessary materials are in the archives, notably in the *fonds d'enregistrement* (e.g., A.D. M-et-L 15 C). I can only plead the inconvenient fact of having to work mainly in the United States rather than in France, and cheer on other investigators who undertake to spend the several years in the archives that the proper analysis of these matters will require.

as well as the areas farther north, and that Siegfried was therefore observing, among other things, the effects of changes that occurred *after* the Revolution. At the end of the eighteenth century, the frequent absence of the landlord, combined with the notion that parish politics were degrading, hindered any desire he may have had to control everyday affairs; the voting that concerned Siegfried was, in the last analysis, external to the day-to-day life of the community.

Nevertheless, from the point of view of honor, his land and the privileges attached to it gave the noble of the Mauges a position he could not hope to attain in Val or Saumurois. The local lord retained at least vestiges of feudal justice. He had the honored seat in the parish church, and his coat of arms was displayed on the wall of the church. He often collected a share of the profits of the local market. He received the rough equivalent of sales and inheritance taxes on the properties held from his fief. If the possession of a given fief carried with it the title of lord of a given community, as it often did, the lord gained a seat on the communal council which was organized not long before the Revolution. Although his ancestors had generally relinquished the right to appoint the curé, the lord was often able to name the local chaplains. These varied privileges, however, were bagatelles compared with the prestige that accompanied the sheer fact of being a great landowner where land was all-important.

There were noble landowners in Val-Saumurois, too; in fact, in sheer number more of them than in the Mauges. But almost none of them had great, concentrated holdings in the area. (Indeed, at times it must have seemed rather crowded on the land to the six noble households in Le Puy-Notre-Dame or the six others in Nueil-sous-Passavant.) Even collectively the nobles were not unrivaled: they were squeezed between ecclesiastical magnates and the sizable number of peasants who owned enough land to assure their independence. The nobles of Val-Saumurois could well envy their brothers of the Mauges their unchallenged domination of the land.

It was more than a local contrast. In all of prerevolutionary France it was rare to find a section where the nobles owned more than 35 percent of the land (Lefebvre 1954: 201–222; Sée 1948: I, 173–177). In the Mauges, if Andrews (1935: 15) is correct, the proportion was

60 percent. France was already becoming a nation of smallholders, but the Vendée remained the citadel of great noble landlords.

Who owns the land, however, is not the only question: how it is parceled out also matters. The holdings of a noble family in a given section of the Mauges — which ordinarily had a collective name, and were still said to constitute a "fief" — were likely to be divided into a small "domain," containing château, park, gardens, and perhaps a little cultivated land, and a number of métairies. The métairies, the familiar farms of 20 to 40 hectares, were leased to peasants with sufficient capital, equipment, and experience to run them, for periods of 5, 7, or 9 years. There was a sharp difference between the rents on these properties, which generally ran into the hundreds of livres (or the equivalent in grains) and the nominal "feudal" dues of a few sous or deniers owed to the fief by the owners of various properties, small and large, in its vicinity.

To take an example: the male head of the family Maumusson de la Béraudière held the fief of Bouzillé-Melay from the Count of Chemillé, which means he owed the absentee Count a symbolic profession of loyalty and a few equally symbolic sous of annual dues. As holder of the fief he was lord of the community of Melay. The fief consisted of the 100-odd hectares surrounding the château, 300 hectares made up of 7 métairies, 4 smaller bordages, three mills, and a few other incidental pieces of land. There were a multitude of properties around Melay whose owners paid token rents to M. de la Béraudière. This lord also held the fiefs of Belligné and La Gruéchère, near the Layon, but he lived in the château of Bouzillé-Melay (A.D. M-et-L E 193).

Whether absentees or residents, few such noble landlords actually administered their properties themselves. A whole layer of officials stood between them and their tenants (see Andrews 1935: 44 ff.). Let us neglect the bailiffs, clerks, archivists, notaries, and other petty officials who jostled each other in the anterooms of the large estates. The ones that mattered most were those who ran the business of a whole manor. Some were hired, full-time managers (commonly called *régisseurs*) and some were farmers-general (who made their livings by subletting the properties composing the manors they rented *en bloc*), while most were local lawyers, notaries, or merchants who kept their own affairs going, perhaps better than those of the land-lords they served. Considering a section of the bocage not far from the Mauges, the astute Dr. Louis Merle (1958: 92) speaks of "those merchants and bourgeois, long experienced in handling landed property, who had enriched themselves at the expense both of the nobles whose properties they ran and of the métayers they rack-rented."

Marcel Garaud, discussing the same section of the bocage, offers an equally significant comment:

[The rural bourgeoisie] was ready to seize the greatest advantage from the Revolution, which accelerated its social rise by abolishing feudal privileges and by putting ecclesiastical and émigré properties on the market. Merchants, farmers-general or overseers, they rushed to put in their bids. Within the commune, the Revolution had no more active agents, nor any more un-compromising advocates of its reforms (1954: 659).

This does not mean that they were "revolutionaries" from the begin-ning. The greatest among these managers of property were strongly identified with the manorial regime that had treated them so well. They led the opposition to the bright lawyers and wealthy merchants of Angers during the provincial Estates of 1789. They were in a position of uneasy moderation during the later clash of revolution-aries and counterrevolutionaries (see Boutillier de Saint-André 1896: esp. xxiii). Still the group as a whole, in the company of the rural merchants and manufacturers, took great advantage of the changes of the early Revolution.

It does not take an undue amount of perspicacity to recognize that these circumstances might put peasants and bourgeois at odds with one another both before and during the Revolution. There are some impressive analogies between the situation in the Mauges of 1793 and the situation of the Calabria of 1799, whose violent counter-revolution Gaetano Cingari (1957) attributes in large part to the hostility of peasants to the bourgeois managers of the land they tilled. Reflection on these analogies brings a bonus: the realization that in both cases the arrangements for control of the land diverted the blame for iniquities in the system from the noble landlord to his bourgeois agent. The noble could continue to play his part as a dis-tant but beneficent patron, while his overseer or farmer-general exacted from the tenants the rents and farm products which allowed the noble to live nobly.

As I have already said, the misleading label métairie ("sharecrop-pery") disguises the fact that in the eighteenth-century Mauges the farm of this name was ordinarily rented for a fixed sum in money and/or farm products, even if it just as surely betrays the fact that in earlier centuries the same farm had been run on half shares (see Merle 1958). Elsewhere in the bocage, sharecropping was much more common than in the Mauges; it seems to have been most common where noble absenteeism was least common, and had very likely declined as the nobles moved away from the land.

Typically, the peasant who owned no more than a few small pieces of land rented a farm of 5 to 30 hectares from a local lord. His lease most likely ran for nine years, beginning either on St. George's Day (23 April) or All Saints' Day (1 November). The lease probably included the following conditions (see Leclerc-Thouin 1843: 55–57):

1. Pay specified rents in cash, kind, and labor.

2. Pay the taxes, tithes, and endowed rents due on the farm.

3. Run the farm "as a good father of a family should."

4. Plow, fertilize, and seed according to the proper (i.e., tradi-tional) procedures.

5. Use all the hay, straw, and dung on the farm and for the good of the land.

6. Make all necessary repairs, including transporting materials supplied by the landlord.

7. Keep up the hedges and replant them at specified intervals, commonly every five or seven years.

8. Trim only certain trees, and those only when they are old enough.

9. Keep up the ridges on which the hedges grow.

These were the general conditions for renting in the Mauges. Many leases, however, added other obligations. According to their 1776 lease, for example, the tenants of a métairie, La Grande Simonnière, in Cholet, had to plant four trees each year (A.D. M-et-L E 800). In 1773, André Deneschere and René Banchereau signed a nine-year renewal of their joint lease of the métairie of Parigny, owned by the lord of Parigny. In addition to paying the rent and hauling four loads at the pleasure of the lord each year, they were to "plow and enrich the soil of said métairie, sow it with the quantity of seed it customarily bears . . . mow and ted the hay in the accustomed manner, clear out the brambles that grow in the meadows, rebuild the hedgerow ridges, keep up the irrigation ditches and streams and make the meadows ready for mowing from hedge to hedge at the end of this lease" (A.D. M-et-L 1 E 996).

One thing is clear about the detailed conditions of these typical leases: they left the tenant little room for either innovation or maneuver. Even if, as Demangeon (1946: I, 147) declared, tenant farming was commonly an accompaniment of advanced forms of agriculture in other parts of France, in the Mauges it maintained the same unproductive traditionalism that prevailed in the rest of the bocage. The choices open to the tenant were further curtailed by another set of obligations, petty but binding. Because of the penchant of earlier generations for the endowment of individuals and institutions with small and various annuities, most tenants paid a miscellany of rents in kind to chapels, churches, priors, and individuals as well as the landlords. In 1764, René Bernier, tenant at La Crillière in Cholet, owed 40 bushels of rye, 8 of wheat, 24 of oats, one capon, two hens, and 20 livres 18 sous cash to a number of individuals, plus 215 livres cash, one lamb, two capons, four young chickens, and a pound of wool to the landlord (A.D. M-et-L E 800).

There were also services to be rendered that limited the autonomy of the tenant. The manorial *corvée* (forced labor) was dead, but peasants in the Mauges often held their farms on the condition that they also work the lord's fields periodically. At Coudray-Montbault the tenants of one small farm had to provide:

. . . thirteen sous, four capons at All Saints', a man with his pitchfork to help pitch hay in my meadow until all of it is in the barn at my château of Le Coudray, to which man I must give two deniers and must feed him, and they also owe a man's labor on the four Wednesdays of the month of January for the repair of the hedges at my property of Le Coudray (A.D. M-et-L 1 E 238).

Very often, a lease called for the labor of a man with oxen. At times, it even called for that labor at the pleasure of the landlord, rather than on specified dates for specified tasks. In short, calling this kind of tenure "rental" obscures the numerous obligations and restrictions in which it enclosed the tenant.[2]

---

[2] It is only fair to say that in an earlier analysis (Tilly 1958), from which these examples are taken directly, I pictured these many obligations as enhancing the solidarity of lord and tenant.

The amount of change in rents in the period before the Revolution is obviously an important question. Only a massive statistical study will resolve the question. My opinion is that they did not, on the average, rise very much. At manor after manor it is possible to find leases renewed regularly at the old price. Rents at the manor of Montbault-Papin, near Cholet, for example, appear to have risen an average of 20 percent during the eighteenth century (A.D. M-et-L E 800). Rents in kind hardly changed at all. The increases that did occur there came when the manor was changing hands through inheritance.

On the whole, despite the fact that they were renters, not owners, the larger farmers were also able to hold on to the land they worked for long periods, sometimes even for generations. The fact that the analysis of mobility already reported showed the large farmers to be natives of their community more frequently than almost any other group suggests as much. In lease after lease appears the phrase ". . . who say they know the land well because they have worked it for long years." Where continuous records of the tenants of a given farm are available, they generally show the regular renting and rerenting of the farm to the same family (e.g., at the manor of Le Planty, A.D. M-et-L E 1057 and at Montbault-Papin, A.D. M-et-L E 800 ff.).

The whole system conspired to keep agricultural technology at a primitive level (see Leclerc-Thouin 1843; Millet 1856; Sée 1927; Andrews 1935). Consider some of the elements: distant landlords treating their properties as sources of fixed income, middlemen with no particular incentives for increasing the productivity of the land, peasants who might well conclude that the most likely consequence of an increase in productivity would be a rise in rent, for whom, in the absence of an active market to stimulate and measure their efforts, the standard of success had to be: enough to eat, and enough to pay the year's debts.

The corollary of this devotion to traditional, subsistence farming was a degree of insulation from the effects of fluctuations in the agricultural market. From the point of view of cash, it is true, the

---

The extent of absenteeism and the importance of the bourgeois middleman, neither of which I recognized at that time, now make that conclusion seem more doubtful. Likewise, Merle's detailed researches on the nearby Gâtine (1958: esp. 91–92) have sapped some of my assurance about the stability of tenure in the Mauges.

situation looks bleak. Between the taxes and money rents, it was a rare peasant who had a cash surplus at the end of the year (see Uzureau 1941: 146; Andrews 1935: 227; Merle 1958: 92). The cattle he sold were his usual source of cash, which means his gross income was generally no more than a few hundred livres. Rent and taxes (in a ratio of roughly 2 to 1, rent to taxes) took most of that.

This sort of calculation, however, leaves out most of what matters to the well-being of subsistence farmers. The evidence that would permit a confident evaluation of the relative well-being of the peasants of Mauges and Val-Saumurois is elusive in principle and hardly available in practice. We do have some indirect evidence; the fact that the communities that issued the sharpest complaints about their poverty-stricken citizens just before the Revolution and during its first two years were either those which were most active in textile production or those which were engaged in the most intensive cash-crop farming, especially wine, flax, or hemp (A.D. M-et-L C 191–193, 1 L 402). That is, the communities with many weavers or many day laborers — in short, many wageworkers. These communities were more vulnerable to the vagaries of the market and more likely to have a wide range from rich to poor. But on the whole, the economic state of the peasantry seems to have been neither prosperous nor impoverished (see Le Moy 1915: I, xxviii).

That vague and tentative estimate, even if correct, leaves open the question of the rigor of the manorial regime. This has traditionally been the fundamental question to ask when trying to explain the response of a rural area to the Revolution. Undoubtedly its explanatory power (along with the importance of the *droit du seigneur*, the corvée, the hunt, and other "feudal" rights) has been greatly exaggerated. An "explanation" in terms of the beneficence or maleficence of the local nobles is persuasive because it is simple and dramatic, and because it conveys an implicit judgment about the value of the Revolution itself (see Tilly 1963). Writers favorable to the Vendean cause, and especially writers of a royalist tint, have had their reasons to point up the virtues of the old regime. The most famous passage of the most famous description of the old regime in the Vendée, attributed to Madame de la Rochejaquelein, but actually written for her by the Baron de Barante, runs as follows:

The mutual relations between the lords and their peasants did not resemble those one saw in the rest of France. There reigned between them a sort of union unknown elsewhere. . . . Since the domains are quite broken up, and a fair-sized property included twenty-five or thirty farms, the lord was in regular contact with the peasants who lived around his château; he treated them paternally, visited them often at their farms, talked with them about their affairs, about the care of their cattle, was interested in their accidents and misfortunes, which affected him seriously as well; he went to the weddings of their children, drank with the guests. Sundays, people danced in the court of the castle, and the ladies joined in. When they hunted the wolf, the boar or the deer, the curé told the peasants from the pulpit. Everyone took his gun, and went gladly to his post. The horsemen placed the marksmen, who followed the instructions they were given carefully. Later they were led to combat the same way, and with the same docility (1815: 41–42).

"What tales," snorted Port (no royalist), "people have told of celebrations at châteaux and of that noble life of the lords, who spent their efforts for the welfare of the countryside, in sweet familiarity with peasant households!" (188: I, 21) This time he had a right to snort. In addition to the simple fact of absenteeism — which the good marquise's own memoirs actually document — there is evidence that the "feudal reaction" that is supposed to have soured peasants on the old regime elsewhere in France did not spare the bocage. Marc Bloch (1937) detected a number of signs of that tightening up of the manorial regime in Andrews' description of the Mauges.

A case in point is the fief of La Séverie. Monsieur Chevreux, a "feudist" of Cerqueux-de-Maulèvrier, left an interesting note in the summary (*dépouillement*) of the fief he assembled around 1770:

The properties indicated in articles 1, 29, and 30 do not exist any more. As for L'Espère, the métayer, an old man, told me that he had heard that there used to be many houses composing the village of Les Granges, which the lords of Maulèvrier had expropriated and destroyed and had built a métairie, still called Les Granges today, on the spot. The properties in question were at the end of the courtyard of that métairie, on the road which leads to Maulèvrier (A.D. M-et-L E 1308).

The note simultaneously illustrates the facts 1) that there was enough business to keep men like M. Chevreux, specialists in the preparation of terriers and the analysis of titles, going, 2) that the process of formation of métairies that Merle has described for the Gâtine to the south was also occurring at the lower edge of the Mauges, and maybe elsewhere, as late as the eighteenth century, 3) most important, that the lords were employing specialists to search out the titles to feudal dues that had fallen into desuetude. For, despite the obstacles our "feudist" encountered at Les Granges, there were plenty of properties which *did* still exist, and on which he was able to re-establish a claim to long-lapsed dues. Elsewhere in the Mauges, the considerable number of well-kept terriers, rent books, and minutes of assizes dating from after 1750 which appear in the archives (A.D. M-et-L, series E and 1E) testifies to the reassertion of fiscal rights during that period.

Another case helps put this observation in perspective. Louis François, Comte d'Aubigné, Lieutenant General of the Army, Director General of Infantry for the Government of Saumur, living in Paris, held the fief of La Rocheferrière, in and around Montrevault (A.D. M-et-L E 1215). In 1741 he obtained a letter in council permitting him to have a terrier made. In the years to follow, his agents made up a series of well-organized rent books and terriers, after collating all the old papers in the files to establish the legal claim to each rent. Through most of the century, the fief was rented to a farmer-general (in 1738, "Gabriel Chevalier, merchant" and again, or still, in 1777, "le Sieur Chevalier") at a rate that increased from 2700 livres per year plus 300 livres earnest money (*pot de vin*) in 1722 to 3460 livres plus pot de vin in 1767. That represents an increase in the rental of just under 30 percent in 45 years, a rise which does not seem excessive. After 1767, as we shall see, the rise was much more rapid.

The fief consisted in 1775 of a "château in bad condition, partly destroyed and the rest valueless" plus some adjoining grounds and woods, 15 métairies, 1 borderie, some income from tolls the lord had the right to levy on goods passing through six nearby bourgs, and a variety of small rents and dues. At that time, the usual métairie was bringing the farmer-general between 200 and 400 livres in cash, and another 100 livres or so in farm products, mainly rye. And the rents on the métairies, which appear to have been set by the lord, rather than by the farmer-general, provided the bulk of his revenue.

A breakdown of the 11,320 livres in income of La Rocheferrière in 1784 states the matter clearly:

Money rents from farms........... 7,960
Rents from farms in rye........... 2,400
Rents from farms in oats.......... 105
Rents from farms in wool.......... 75
Rental of vineyard at Chalonnes.... 180
Sale of wood.................... 500
"Feudal" rents.................. 100

The dues on properties outside the domain of La Rocheferrière formed a trivial part of the fief's revenue. Even if the lord did reassert his right to dues on properties owned by others, that is, the returns were not nearly as important to his income as were the rents on the properties he owned himself. This was generally true in the Mauges; it would be interesting to know whether the situation was different in Val-Saumurois, where there were many more properties of bourgeois, artisans, and peasants on which the nobles could collect dues.

The other side of the coin is clear: Unless it entailed the systematic inflation of regular rents, the "feudal reaction" could only affect the local economy seriously where there were many commoners owning land (cf. Forster 1963). But what about the inflation of rents at La Rocheferrière? By 1775, the fief had passed into the hands of Louis Henri de la Forêt, Comte d'Armaillé. He, too, was an absentee, as testifies not only the dilapidation of his château and the obligation of the farmer-general to feed the horses "when Mr. d'Armaillé or someone representing him shall come to La Rocheferrière," but also a later note that "since his remoteness from the property did not permit him to use the 24 wagon trips the métayers had always had the custom of making [for the benefit of the lord], they agreed to pay him 150 livres in cash. . . ." But the Comte d'Armaillé, in 1786 — whether through choice or through inability to find a manager I cannot tell — rented the entire fief to a kind of syndicate of seven of his métayers for the grand total of 11,000 livres. The landlord's revenues from La Rocheferrière had risen handsomely over the previous twenty years.

The collection of leases in the well-kept files of the fief records that profitable period soberly but adequately. It shows rather little increase in rents from 1750 to 1767–1768. In the latter years the average tenant of a métairie paid about 250 livres, including roughly 90 livres worth of produce. In 1784, the average tenant on the same farm was paying 560 livres, including approximately 140 livres in kind. Rents more than doubled over the interval of sixteen years. At each new lease (which meant every seven years or so) the terms changed. A number of the minor obligations, like the "3 cartloads of 3 leagues, 2 days of woman's work, 5 days of man's work, 2 capons and the feeding of an ewe" due from the tenant of La Crocherye, disappeared from the contracts. Generally, the proportion paid in cash went up. The changes give the impression that someone was rationalizing the operation of the manor, turning it into a business.

If the case of La Rocheferrière turned out to be typical, historians would have to revise their accounts of eighteenth-century life in the bocage even more drastically than the rest of this chapter suggests they should. The wealth of the manor, the distinction of its owner, the very order and comprehensiveness of its records, compared with those of other manors, argue against its entire typicality. Nevertheless, the case has been well worth looking at, both for the questions it answers and for the questions it raises. La Rocheferrière's history contradicts the common conception of lords and tenants living together on the Vendean manor, working in close harmony, and reinforces the impression that absenteeism and the use of bourgeois managers were widespread. The evidence it gives on the importance of the "feudal reaction" is more ambiguous, but certainly far from negative. Finally, it provides some reasons for being tentative about the conclusion — which nevertheless remains the best summary of the other evidence now available — that rents rose only moderately during the eighteenth century in the Mauges as a whole.

All this said, we must still consider how the various exactions of the lord and his agents affected social relations in the rural community. First, we need to recall several things: 1) Peasant landowners were plentiful in Val-Saumurois, rare in the Mauges; 2) The manorial apparatus of overseers, farmers-general, and the like was generally more elaborate in the Mauges; 3) The "feudal" obligations we have been discussing affected mainly the owners, not the renters, of agricultural properties. The facts are strong enough to chase the cherished myth of idyllic solidarity from the history of the Mauges, but they cannot support an assumption of great hostility between lords and peasants.

Because of the coexistence of peasant proprietors and relatively weak but numerous nobles in Val-Saumurois, the "feudal reaction" and the petty privileges, fiscal and otherwise, of the local lords were more likely to put lords and peasants at odds there than in the Mauges. True, we might expect the few peasant landowners of the Mauges to rail against the nobles. But on the whole the system in that section of southern Anjou was destined to produce active resentment of the bourgeois intermediaries, and a kind of respectful fear of the distant landlord.

To sum up: There was an unquestionable difference between the varieties of agriculture practiced in the two halves of southern Anjou. On the whole, the Mauges was characterized by medium-sized farms, rented from a noble proprietor (often absent, and working through a bourgeois agent) and worked by one or two peasant families on nine-year leases, renewed from one time to the next with little change in conditions or total payment. Agricultural techniques were backward, and the system of tenure and control conspired to keep them that way. The great bulk of the grains grown went either into local consumption or rents, with hardly any surplus for sale; the annual sale of a few head of cattle from each farm met the needs for cash. As a consequence, the individuals most concerned with the state of the agricultural market were not the cultivators but those who received their rents — essentially the local merchants and managers of property.

The predominant situation was far different in Val-Saumurois, where agricultural production was much more specialized and much more uniformly intended for the market. Vineyards and the production of raw materials for the textile industry brought with them fractionation, intensive cultivation of the land, and widespread property ownership, while even grain production (with wheat, rather than the rye of the Mauges, the principal crop) was commercialized and associated with relatively small property holdings. The nobles of Val-Saumurois were far from that distant domination of the land which characterized their cousins in the Mauges and, indeed, sometimes acted as direct competitors of the peasants, farming their own land (as at Nueil-sous-Passavant, A.D. M-et-L C 193). On the other hand, ecclesiastical landlords were relatively powerful in Val-Saumurois. The widespread ownership of property and the permeation of the area's agriculture by the market economy were the bases of considerable differentiation within the peasantry; most notably, there were many more day laborers and individuals wresting their livings from very small plots (for example, the peasants called *bécheurs* — spaders) than in the Mauges, where three quarters or more of the peasants were operators of family farms (that is, laboureurs, métayers, bordiers, or closiers).

One more implication: only in Val-Saumurois, with the common denominator of the market, were peasants and bourgeois likely to develop similar perspectives and interests. The merchant was the cash-crop peasant's indispensable ally, although we need not elaborate that observation into a myth of untrammeled cordiality. The bourgeois, in fact, was essential to both the systems that met in southern Anjou, but in the Mauges he was almost inevitably cast as an exploiter.

To summarize even more compactly, the contrast was between commercial and subsistence agriculture, between efficient specialization and inefficient polyculture, between farming oriented to the needs of cities and national markets (and in that sense "urban") and farming no more than local in its scope (and in that sense "rural"). By now, these themes should echo familiarly.

The Industrial Complex

Agriculture dominated the economic life of southern Anjou. Nevertheless, the industrial complex meant a great deal to the cities, and to a substantial number of artisans and bourgeois. There was the usual complement of rural industries: coopers, smiths, potters, tilers, and other artisans plied their crafts, and tanning was quite active around cattle markets like Beaupréau, Montrevault, Chemillé, and Cholet. There were light industries in cities like Montreuil-Bellay, Saumur, and Vihiers. But the most significant industry by far was textiles — to be more exact, the manufacture of linen. Bustling Cholet was the center of a minor textile empire, with some 10,000 looms spread over a multitude of communities (Bonniveau 1923; Furet 1950: 96; Uzureau 1901: 92). In reality, Cholet's was not an industry of national importance, for it was not even in the first rank of the industries of the Generality of Tours (Bois 1960b: 497–502;

Dornic 1955: 158, 223; Dumas 1894: 161).[3] By contrast with its rural setting, however, it was impressive.

The *fabrique de Cholet* produced linen almost exclusively, most of it in the form of kerchiefs, some of it as colored cloth in twenty-yard lengths. The linen was an eminently commercial product. Let the chief of Cholet's textile inspection bureau describe it in his own words:

All the dress fabrics except for a small amount used in France are exported to the French and Spanish colonies and to New England by merchant shippers. The kerchiefs, especially the varicolored, the black and the gray ones, are sold in this kingdom [but] a large number of the cheapest ones go into the slave trade . . . [and] the red ones go to the French and Spanish colonies and to the United States. They are sent these various places by the merchant shippers of Bordeaux, Nantes, La Rochelle, and the other maritime cities, and sometimes our merchants ship them directly on their own account . . . (A.D. Indre-et-Loire C 134).

The industry's growth had been tied to that of Nantes as capital of colonial shipping and the slave trade.

Like the slave trade, Cholet's industry was growing substantially, if not regularly, during the decades before the Revolution. The reports of the local bureaux de marque (whose employees inspected goods brought to them and stamped them as suitable for commerce if they met the standards of size and quality) give evidence. Figure 7 puts together official production statistics for most of the years from 1750 to 1760 and 1770 to 1790, and connects them with conjectural lines which simply represent the directions of change during the gaps in the available information (A.D. M-et-L 1 L 546; A.D. Indre-et-Loire C 114, C 121, C 134, C 135, C 136; A.N. F[12] 564, F[12] 1427; see Appendix C and Dornic 1955: 223).

The graphs show, first of all, that production at Cholet ran about twenty times the volume of production at Vihiers. The area around

---

[3] Bois (1960b: 501–502), however, unduly minimizes Cholet's textile industry, perhaps not recognizing that in the average year only a quarter of the money value of the area's production was in yard goods, while three quarters were made up of kerchiefs. Considering that in the good years just before the Revolution the reported value of goods officially inspected at Cholet, Vihiers, and Maulèvrier ran well over 3,000,000 livres per year (A.D. M-et-L 1 L 546; A.D. Indre-et-Loire C 134, C 135, C 136) and that an unknown number of weavers and merchants took their goods to the office at La Tessoualle, in the Generality of Poitiers (A.D. Indre-et-Loire C 114), it seems quite possible that the industries of Cholet and of Haut-Maine were approximately equal in size.

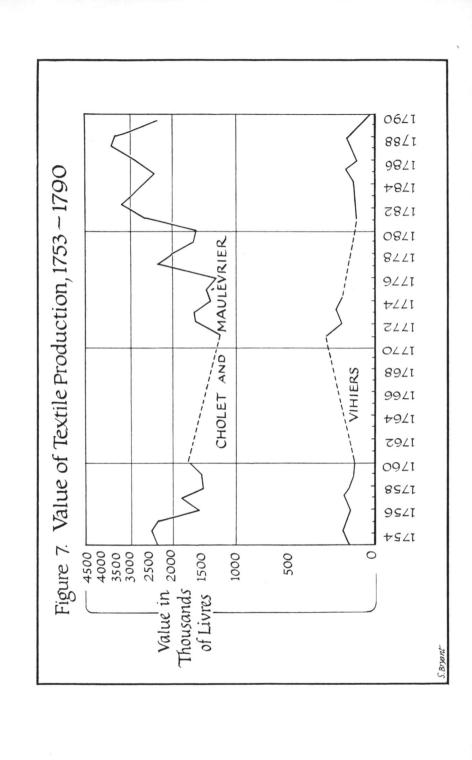

Figure 7. Value of Textile Production, 1753 – 1790

Value in Thousands of Livres

4500
4000
3500
3000
2500
2000
1500
1000
500
0

1754 1756 1758 1760 1762 1764 1766 1768 1770 1772 1774 1776 1778 1780 1782 1784 1786 1788 1790

CHOLET AND MAULÉVRIER

VIHIERS

S. Bryant

Cholet especially outweighed the territory of Vihiers when it came to the production of kerchiefs; even today the "handkerchiefs of Cholet" have a wide reputation. Furthermore, production around Vihiers changed rather little over the forty years under scrutiny, while the amount of cloth inspected at Cholet both fluctuated drastically and grew substantially during the same period. Cholet, that is, was the center of the industry's energetic advance.

Of course, these official production statistics show nothing like an even progression from year to year: wars, weather, and monetary fluctuations all made eighteenth-century international trade an uncertain adventure. Nevertheless, the average production of kerchiefs around Cholet in the 1780's was about double that in the 1750's, and the total value of cloth production was up some 75 percent (see Appendix C). While only as recently as 1719 a regional official had been able to call Cholet "a pretty center of manufacturing which is, so to speak, just beginning," by 1751 local output was over two million livres' worth, and by the time of the Revolution Cholet's boosters were ready to boast that it was "the metropolis of a famous commerce, spread through the world; capital of an industry which occupies parts of three departments; the rendezvous of 100 parishes" (A.N. F^{12} 553; F^{12} 564; D IV bis 26).

The shorter-range fluctuations in production include a drop for the Seven Years' War and some huge variations around the time of the American Revolution. They also indicate a drastic decline in production after 1788, a phenomenon which will attract our interest later on. The parts of the curves which are not based on simple interpolation correspond remarkably to the year-to-year fluctuations in the international shipping of Nantes (see Meyer 1960: 126). That correspondence underscores the fact that Cholet's industry was one with a vital concern for trade, and for trade on a global scale.

There had been weavers and spare-time peasant weaving long before the slave trade began. It took the commercial expansion of the later seventeenth century to organize the industry itself. Elsewhere in the West, weaving became the regular off-season peasant activity, just as wood carving and watchmaking did in the Alps. This was the case in part of Maine, where weaving replaced agriculture as the basic rural occupation (Musset 1917: 268). It was also the case in the sections of the bocage beyond the direct influence of Cholet's industry; in 1787, a report on La Mothe-Saint-Heraye (Vendée) declared: "It is a big town; they make very good cloth there; its territory is quite large; the industry occupies at least five hundred workers, who only want to spend their time on cloth manufacturing in the winter, which hinders the commerce of that community, since the merchants cannot fill the orders they get" (A.N. F¹² 564). But in the Mauges, weaving grew up somewhat independently of agriculture. Perhaps because of their greater satisfaction with farming, perhaps because of the resistance of their landlords or perhaps because the industry was introduced "from outside" by a few great lords, the peasants of the Mauges did not become part-time weavers. Yet many men of peasant stock became full-time weavers, leaving behind their agricultural preoccupations as they did so.

Eighteenth-century weaving was not the mass-production industry we know today. This was especially true in western France:

In rural industry as in agriculture, the West gives the impression of a backward country, evolving little and slowly. We have already given the reasons: it is an isolated region, sheltered by that fact from the influences which could have changed it, a region of difficult communications, hardly able to undertake other important industries than textile manufacturing, the products of which are light and not too bulky, and can be easily transported (Musset 1917: 262).

The essential production unit in agriculture was the family farm, a unit which operated with little reference to any other organization besides the manor. But even the poorly developed industry of the eighteenth-century Mauges involved a complex much broader than any local economy, related directly to a world market.

Within this complex, the domestic system made the local economy an essential operating unit. It was a system decentralized from the viewpoint of its distribution centers, but centralized from the viewpoint of any particular community. Individual weavers working in their damp, low shops in the bourgs and villages were linked together by the merchants who gave them their orders and took their products. That is, it was a *commercial*, not an *industrial*, organization:

At Cholet, there was only a commercial concentration. What people called *la manufacture de Cholet* during the eighteenth century was composed of a multitude of looms in private homes, scattered through about thirty rural parishes in which there had already been a number of weavers in the Middle

Ages. The new fact by which that industry, beginning with the last years of the seventeenth century, distinguished itself from the old domestic manufacture, was the preponderance of a group of rich traders who gathered the goods to organize their sale in far-off regions, and who oriented the work of the looms in the direction they judged best to assure the success of that exportation (Dion 1934: 597).

Cholet's industry, then, was not a set of large factories with a great, standardized labor force, but a network of artisans working individually or in small groups.

Where were these groups of artisans? The question matters because it is so easy to slip into thinking of the counterrevolution of 1793 as a purely peasant affair, when in fact it reached its greatest intensity where weaving was most important. We already know from the analysis of occupational distribution that textile artisans were much more common in the District of Cholet than in the rest of southern Anjou. The cantonal versions of those estimates agree almost perfectly with the other available sources in locating the industry.

Figure 8 presents the essential information.[4] It states unmistakably that the textile industry permeated the District of Cholet, and spilled over into the adjoining sections of the Mauges, but left Val and Saumurois untouched. Beaupréau, Chemillé, Cholet, Le May . . . most of the first foci of the 1793 rebellion were also foci of the eighteenth-century linen industry. Of course, the map, being restricted to Anjou, does not show the full extent of the industry. In 1810, 1200 spinners of linen were reported in the canton of Châtillon alone (A.N. F^{12} 631). In 1787, "two thirds" of Bressuire's population was said to work for the linen industry in the wintertime (A.N. F^{12} 564). Linen manufacturing à la Cholet was important in a substantial section of northern Poitou: the vicinities of Les Échaubrognes, Châtillon, Bressuire, Mortagne, Saint-Laurent-sur-Sèvre

[4] See Appendix C for sources and method. In the case of 17 scattered cantons, the estimate is calculated from the number of textile workers given in the enumerations contained in A.D. Indre-et-Loire C 114, by means of the regression of 1) the proportion of textile workers as given by the occupational distribution analysis on 2) the numbers given in those enumerations, over the cantons of the districts of Cholet and St. Florent for which both items are available. The relationship between the two is very close (Pearsonian r = .778). "Textile artisans" in this case are overwhelmingly weavers, but they include spinners, dyers, bleachers, and the like. The district totals, already given in Chapter 4, were: Saumur 2.4%, Angers 2.4%, St. Florent 7.9%, Vihiers 9.8%, Cholet 21.3%. If permitted to second-guess these computations on the basis of other evidence, I would say that they underestimate the amount of textile activity in the northeast corner of the Mauges, in the cantons of Chemillé and Jallais (see Bonniveau 1923).

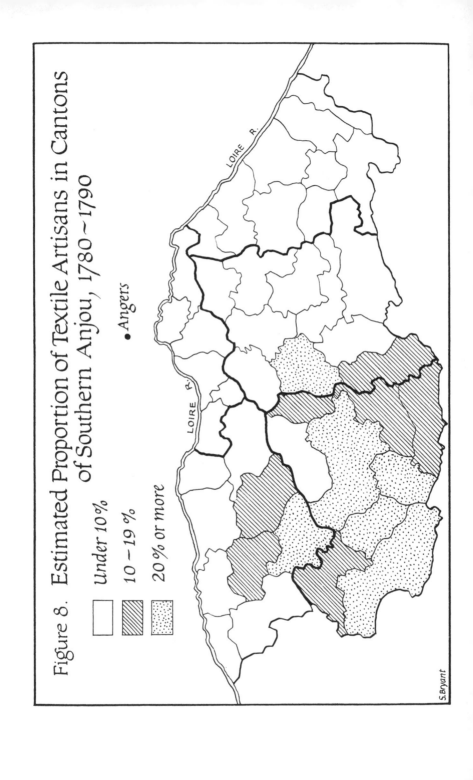

Figure 8. Estimated Proportion of Textile Artisans in Cantons
of Southern Anjou, 1780~1790

Under 10%

10 – 19 %

20% or more

●Angers

LOIRE R.

LOIRE R.

S.Bryant

(Dupin 1801–1802: 326; Cavoleau 1844: 661–662; Garaud 1954: 646). These, too, were names to reckon with during the counterrevolution. Nevertheless, southern Anjou was the industry's home, and Cholet its capital.

Although the kerchiefs and cloth were produced in the bocage, the raw materials came mostly from the Val. This meant that the farmers of the Mauges themselves did not produce crops for the industry and were not affected directly by its welfare. The farmers of the Val who produced the flax supplied fiber to spinners, who were often farm women. The spinners either had working arrangements with merchants in the Mauges or sold their products at local markets and fairs, the most notable of which were those of Chalonnes (see A.D. M-et-L 59 M 33–34; A.D. Indre-et-Loire C 82).

Some of the weavers worked independently and marketed their own products, but most depended on a master weaver or a merchant to commit work to them. Clothiers (*fabricants*) bought the thread and farmed out the work to weavers, bleachers, and dyers in turn. The weavers, bleachers, and dyers spread throughout the region. The amount and kinds of work the clothiers farmed out depended on the orders placed by the merchants (*négociants*), who actually sent or took the cloth to the great fairs and markets of the West. The merchants, not the clothiers, were the rich and powerful members of the industry. The merchants were often accused of combining to fix prices, manipulate standards of quality, and keep the clothiers under their control, just as the clothiers were often accused of producing such substandard goods as to degrade the international reputation of the fabrique de Cholet (A.D. Indre-et-Loire C 121, 128, 129, 134). Still, most of the clothiers were titans compared to the individual weavers, living only from their work and their occasional garden plots, spread through the region in bourgs and villages full of their humid, lightless hovels, completely unorganized, working or workless according to the state of the market. Towns with many weavers were most concerned about "mendicants." The 1788 report on local conditions at Saint-Laurent-de-la-Plaine (A.D. M-et-L C 192) declared that "the greater part of the inhabitants are employed by the industry of Cholet, whence comes a crowd of poor who beg in the winter."

Where textile activity was greatest, there were a few merchants accompanied by a number of clothiers, who farmed out work to a large number of weavers and other artisans. Where production was small, there was still a small concentration of clothiers in the bourg. They dealt with the merchants of the larger bourgs or of Cholet, on one side, and with textile workers living in their communities, on the other. Spatially, the few key figures in local industrial activity were settled in the bourg, while the workers stayed in the bourg or in the largest villages.

The relationship between the bourgeois and the artisan was fraught with potential conflict. It was in the interest of the clothier to keep the return of the weavers low and their production high. He had the power to give work to some and withhold it from others. The workers were isolated from each other and in a poor position to organize against the bourgeois. They were engaged in work that was seasonal to begin with, because of the growing season for flax and hemp. The orders that gave them work depended on the state of the international market as well. All in all, it was a marginal and uncertain existence for most weavers. Their uncertainty was likely to focus on the bourgeois who gave them, or failed to give them, work. These considerations may have been less important while the market was good, and even expanding. They became central during the industrial crisis of the early Revolution.

Consequences

Paradox, conflict, antithesis, antinomy: the two complexes of the local economies of the communities of the Mauges ran in two different directions: the one fleeing the market, the other pursuing it eagerly. Any declaration about the total involvement of these rural communities in the market calls for an immediate "but on the other hand . . ." The state of the roads illustrates the point. It is part of the ritual description of the Mauges to speak of

. . . the old roads of yesterday, here and there invaded by the people who live beside them, everywhere caved in, deeply rutted, buried in gorges fifteen to twenty feet deep, between thick earthworks, below dismal hedges, and occasionally even sowed with rockpiles which give way under one's feet as he tries to balance on them, or with great boulders on which every team breaks down (Port 1888: I, 14).

The Mauges, it is said, were held incommunicado by roadlessness,

". . . foreign to both the ideas and the ways of the rest of the department . . ." (Bouchard 1884: 14).

It is unquestionably true that Val and Saumurois were better provided with lines of communication: There were no navigable rivers in the Mauges, no postal routes went through it, and, up to 1786, the stagecoach had been unable to deliver any Parisian papers to Cholet and its hinterland (Marboeuf 1954: 38; Carte des postes 1791). Val and Saumurois had the Loire, a constant flow of movement between inland France and the sea. The Loire had brought the monks, and thus the vine (Dion 1934: 621 ff.). It was the Loire that carried away the wines of Anjou to Holland or Spain. It was the Loire that gave Saumur more contact with Tours than with Cholet. And to add to their advantages, Val and Saumurois had more roads than the Mauges, and better ones.

Yet in the Mauges there is the fact of the trading, thriving textile industry. Yet in the Mauges there is the very fact of widespread complaints about the insufficiency of the roads. The complaints were like those of a Gulliver, awakening, who finds himself fettered. Significantly enough, it was mainly the commercial bourgs and the cities which agitated for the building of new roads (A.D. M-et-L C 192, e.g., Le May). The merchants and manufacturers were acutely conscious of their fetters, as well as of their growing strength. They had to push aside the residues of centuries of commercial inactivity, based on an agriculture that — literally — was going nowhere. But they were beginning to push. Their push helped form the contrast of Mauges and Val-Saumurois: recent, shallow, uneven urbanization versus long, deep immersion in the urban currents of French society.

In terms of purely economic relationships, the contrast entailed bisection of the communities of the Mauges into nearly independent industrial and agricultural complexes, unification of the communities of Val-Saumurois by means of common participation in the market. Let us consider the implications of this situation for the local elite. To the extent that a society's economy is based on control of the land, the elite position of predominant landlords (or of those who control decisions affecting the disposition of land) in the community will be accentuated; to the extent that a market economy predominates, the merchant will move into the elite. Indeed, these statements are nearly tautologies. Nevertheless they make it easier to recognize that while the bourgeois dominated the external economic relations of the communities of Val-Saumurois, there was a dual economic elite in the Mauges, consisting of nobles and bourgeois, each with somewhat different bases of control.

It is true that the bourgeois of the Mauges were significant not only as the activators of industry but also as managers of property, and that the control the nobles exerted was largely negative and distant. But it is also true that each made — or at least transmitted — the decisions that most profoundly affected the relations of the one complex of the local economy and the other to the world outside, and thus deeply affected the state of the local economy. This bifurcation of the economic elite should not be confused with the increasing differentiation of function that accompanies urbanization. The criterion for differentiation of function ought to be the existence of several subsystems in which all members of the group in question participate more or less simultaneously, with specialized roles growing up for the mediation of each subsystem's relations with the "outside." (A concrete illustration of this rather abstract statement is the American rural community, with its grain elevator operator, feed merchant, tractor salesman, tax collector, county agent, banker, general store manager all specializing in somewhat different aspects of the community's external economic relations, while almost all the farmers, at one time or another, sell grain, buy feed, use tractors, pay taxes, seek technical advice, borrow or bank money, purchase goods made elsewhere.) If this is the criterion, we must say that differentiation of the elite had gone farther in Val-Saumurois.

There is another question about economic relations that comes naturally to mind: the probable loci of conflict. In Val-Saumurois, where property ownership was widespread, if uneven, and cash-crop production general, there was a real possibility of competition for land or market position and a genuine possibility of conflict between the many agricultural laborers and their employers. There were many parallels with the structure of the peasantry, eventually riven with internal hostilities after beginning the Revolution in solidarity, that Georges Lefebvre described in his justly famous study of the department of Nord:

It develops from all our study that the population of the village, solidary in the face of the king, of the privileged, and of the city-dweller, by no means formed a homogeneous class, but constituted a small society which had its proletariat, divided into day laborers and householders, its middle class formed by the farmers whose farms were able to support them, and finally its dominant class, the big farmers and the wealthy cultivators who made up, in very small numbers, the rural bourgeoisie (1924: 307).

The description is obviously much more applicable to Val-Saumurois than to the Mauges.

The response of the citizens of Distré, just outside of Saumur, to the complaint of the prosperous Sieur Alexandre Fournier that he was being charged 300 livres taxes whereas his father had only paid 150 livres, shows very well the kinds of conflicts that could develop in Val-Saumurois:

The inhabitants reply to the claims of the honorable merchant farmer that the parish of Distré is very poor and overburdened with taxes, that it is not in a position to pay all the taxes, being charged with a multitude of miserables who are not in a position to pay any taxes, and that furthermore, a large part of the properties of this parish being possessed by privileged parties [i.e., tax-exempt clergy and nobles], it is quite natural that the weight of the taxes should fall onto the persons in the easiest circumstances (A.D. M-et-L C 35).

Here are all the expected themes: the presence of the poor, the obstacles to justice set up by "privileged" property, the division according to wealth. In the Mauges, on the other hand, the preeminence of the métairie, the debility of the agricultural market, the relative equality of the farmers in the face of the great landholders set the conditions for what Bois (1960b: 442), in discussing the same problem, calls the "moral homogeneity" of the peasantry.

The "moral homogeneity" of the peasantry, however, is not identical with the solidarity of the so-called peasant community, of which the peasants are simply the largest part. Within the agricultural complex in the Mauges, the potential clash of interests was between the owners and the managers of the land and those who worked it — between the nobles or the bourgeois and the peasants. Given the frequent absence of the eighteenth-century landlords and their tendency to treat their manors as sources of fixed income to be governed according to traditional rules (even the "feudal reaction" was a reenforcement of traditional rights rather than a rational reorganization of the manor), the more immediate focus of conflict was the relationship between bourgeois and peasant.

There was also a silent struggle for control of the land, although not on the part of the land-hungry peasants who are commonly supposed to have made the rural Revolution in France. The leasehold system gave most peasant families in the Mauges as much land as they were capable of working with their limited technics and capital — the great extent of wasteland on each farm indicates as much — but, by the same token, kept them from accumulating the surplus necessary for the purchase of the fair-sized farms that were the principal form of rural property. The bourgeois, on the other hand, had money and could undoubtedly have bought more land when they wanted to — if there had been land available. The nobles, however, dominated the land. They were not selling. There was no way to make them sell. Here was an area of strong potential class conflict.

What of the peasants and the artisans? Surely the artisans moved into the agricultural complex more often than the peasants moved into the industrial complex. The "service artisans"— blacksmiths, toolmakers, bakers, and the like — occupied positions between the two complexes, a fact which the earlier analysis of marriage patterns reflects. Some of them were, in fact, part-time peasants. This was much less true of the industrial artisans, whose ventures in agriculture were limited to gardens, vines, and small plots for spare-time cultivation. None of these activities of the artisans of the Mauges put them into regular economic relations with the peasants, or into conflict with them. They were not competing for land or for market position. Neither controlled the other's economic activity in any way. In short, there was no significant economic basis for class conflict between peasants and artisans.

There was a chance of an economic clash between peasants and clergy, since the clergy's substantial incomes were drawn largely from the tithe on the major crops and from the innumerable petty rents with which the métairies were burdened, both of which directly and obviously reduced the resources available each year to the peasant family. There were, in fact, several disputes about (of all things) the turnip tithe in the Mauges just before the Revolution (A.D. M-et-L C 35). However, such contestations seem to have been much more common in Val-Saumurois, where ecclesiastical properties were more extensive, and small peasant proprietors, counting their sous and deniers, were likely to be highly aware of the effects of these payments on their own incomes (see A.D. M-et-L C 24, C 35).

When we move into the industrial complex of the Mauges, we find it easier to anticipate conflicts readily comprehensible to imaginations shaped by life in an industrial world. The Marxian conditions for a militant and class-conscious proletariat, it is true, had not developed in the rural industry of southern Anjou, but there was every possibility of a familiar, more primitive kind of protest on the part of the poor, vulnerable, boom-or-bust, industrial artisans. And the object of their protest was likely to be the figure who seemed to control their economic fate: the merchant.

The most likely loci of economic conflict in the rural communities of the Mauges were clustered, this summary indicates, around the position of the bourgeoisie. Of course, the analysis enjoys the incomparable advantage of hindsight. For it is perfectly clear that the most significant economic conflicts of the Revolution pitted segments of the local bourgeoisie against other classes of the rural community.

CHAPTER 8

Power

Inevitably and desirably, the discussions of neighborhood, parish, and local economy have touched on the distribution of power in the rural community. In eighteenth-century France, politics was not an enterprise separate from religion, economics, or personal affiliation. Perhaps I should say that they were even less differentiated than now, since a favorite sociological pastime in our own day is to point up the connections between politics and other elements of the social structure — interest groups, pressure groups, power elites. Although power and power struggles have been with mankind since Cain's *coup d'état*, the emergence of specialized political institutions distinctly separate from kinship or religious authority has been a rare event, confined mainly to recent centuries. One of the surest signs of the development of a modern nation-state is the formation and spread throughout the society of the role of "citizen": Consider, for example, the meaning of the frenetic attachment of the chiefs of the French Revolution to the word *citoyen* itself.

The conception of urbanization which has guided this study draws attention to the fact that the growth of political parties and associations, of standardized laws, taxes, administrative procedures, and civic obligations, as well as the rise of citizenship itself, inevitably occur in the company of changes in community organization. Changes, but not necessarily "breakdown," perversely satisfying as that word seems to be to those who find modern society out of joint. Within the community, participation in the growth of a modern state leads to the increasing differentiation of political activities and institutions from other activities and institutions. It increases the comparability of at least some of the means of wielding power from one community to another, not only by introducing uniform administrative arrangements, but also by fostering the growth of centralized political associations with members of several communities. It fosters the "politicizing" of behavior within the community, in the sense of making persons more aware (whether truly or falsely) of the relevance of local factions, problems, injustices, influences, not to mention their own desires, to national decisions and the national distribution of power. And vice versa. Finally, participation in the growth of a modern state also means change in the elite, ordinarily in the direction of greater differentiation and of specialization in political manipulation itself.

Political Modernization in Southern Anjou

By these criteria, the France we are concerned with here was just beginning its political modernization. Its Revolution — however little else scholars may finally decide it "accomplished" — immensely accelerated that modernization. Widespread suffrage, national legislation, universal conscription, national holidays, constitutions, nationwide societies of Jacobins or Girondins, standardized governmental organization, and the development of a political press did not all work as intended, nor did they all survive the Revolution, but they propelled France and Frenchmen toward modern politics. These revolutionary changes make it all the more interesting to look at the structures of control, those that make up what I have called the "commune," in the communities of southern Anjou *before* the Revolution.

In this chapter I shall argue that political modernization, as just described, had gone farther in Val-Saumurois than in the Mauges. The word "argue" is well chosen, since the evidence now available is less than adequate. Nevertheless, the information already presented on other aspects of community organization provides some basis for believing that political awareness was more widespread in Val-Saumurois than in the Mauges, and that the traditional elites met much more resistance and even competition there. Because the principal events of the Revolution, despite all their implications for belief, production, and personal relations, took place in the "house of power," this analysis of political organization will also be a summing up of the significance of differences in social organization for response to the Revolution.

These significant differences, in the nature of the case, could hardly appear in the formal organization of government. "Everyone knows well enough," says Andrews in his study of the peasants of the Mauges (1935: 1), "how France was governed during the eighteenth century. At first glance, there is nothing simpler. At the very top was the king with his advisers; then the intendants who represented the king in the 'generalities' and the subdelegates who represented the intendants in the 'elections.' But the governmental system of old France was far from being as homogeneous as one thinks at first glance." Not only were the broad administrative divisions of the nation confused, overlapping, and conditioned by local circumstances, but the legal position of each section was determined by the weight of centuries of its political history.

Endowed, like other parts of France, with its own Custom, Anjou was an "election country," which meant basically that it did not have provincial Estates to balance the control of the Intendant.

Before 1790, southern Anjou was divided among the Elections of Angers, Montreuil-Bellay, and Saumur, which were subdivisions of the Generality of Tours. This meant that the royal administrators who mattered most were the powerful Intendant, at Tours, and his representatives, the subdelegates, at Angers, Montreuil-Bellay, and Saumur, plus (after about 1760) two at Cholet and Maulèvrier. The ordinary citizen was undoubtedly much less conscious of these high-level officials than he was of the employees of courts, police units, salt administration, or tax bureaux. Outside the urban centers, the direct influence of the royal administration barely touched the individual communities; practical government was permeated by an extreme localism. The rural citizen — the word itself is a fascinating anachronism when applied to the period before the Revolution — was made aware of his attachment to a nation-state mainly by his tax obligation, his liability for military service and, to a lesser extent, his chances of recourse to the royal courts of law. Even these limited forms of political participation were commonly mediated by communal groups: village tax assessment and collection by appointees of the local elders, collective drawing of lots for military conscription by the community's young men, jurisdiction of manorial courts in legal disputes.

There are two sides to the problem of administrative localism: 1) the action of the royal officials, 2) the positions of the individual communities. Aside from tax receipts and occasional petitions, even the subdelegate rarely communicated directly with the chiefs of rural communities. There was no easy way for information about conditions in the countryside to get to the upper administrative levels. By the same token, high-level officials were not much concerned about the plaints or the needs of country towns. Their insouciance and the sheer crudeness of the administrative machinery put many a town in the position of Thouarcé, on the Layon, which waited until 1785 for the funds and the authorization to repair its bridge, already about to tumble when the townsmen began their pleas in 1778 — a full seven years before (A.D. M-et-L C 20). In general, the farther a place was from the seat of the Intendant, the less attention it received. Tours was beautified, pampered, favored, while cities in the Mauges rarely heard from the Intendant. And even those neglected cities received much more attention than did the country.

The other side of the problem of administrative localism is, of course, that local leaders learned to get along without the government; perhaps it would be better to say that local leaders never learned to depend on the government. Community political affairs were handled within the community, and almost all necessary contact with the "outside" handled through curé or lord. Indeed, it was a system that gave exceptional power to the individual who *did* have access to the higher reaches of the royal administration, a circumstance which often made the lord the crucial figure in the attempts of the community to get concessions, favors, or simple justice from the central authority (cf. Vidich and Bensman 1958: 100).

Much of this description would apply to rural France as a whole during the eighteenth century. The relevant question is therefore whether there were any significant variations in its applicability. What we know about the general nature of the external relations of rural communities in southern Anjou would make it plausible to believe that political localism was greater, and direct participation in national politics less, in the Mauges than in Val-Saumurois. In this case, however, the evidence is flimsy, and it is even hard to conceive of the kind of evidence that would settle the issue. It may be relevant to note, as a measure of their political ineffectiveness, that the communities of the Mauges bore an inequitable share of the Generality's taxes. Charles Colbert reported in 1664 that the Election of Montreuil-

Bellay, including most of the Mauges, had been "excessively over-charged" (Marchegay 1853: I, 157; cf. Andrews 1935: 208). In 1792, the District of Cholet's officers wrote that "the election of Montreuil-Bellay was more heavily taxed than any other of the Department; and the officers, careful to pay nothing, threw off the greater part of the taxes on the area formerly known as Lower Anjou, which now forms the District of Cholet. One could calculate the geographic distance from a parish to the seat of the election, simply by knowing the rate of *taille* that it paid" (District de Cholet 1792: 2). As evidence on political involvement, I must admit, these complaints are, at best, ambiguous.

Another possible indication is what happened during the Revolution itself. Then, political organizations, in the form of clubs, national guard units and, later, revolutionary committees, abounded in the communes of Val and Saumurois, while they were extremely rare in the Mauges (A.D. M-et-L 1 L 566–568, 1 L 745, 1 L 1152, 1 L 1169–1199, 1 L 1304–1318). The value of this observation as evidence is obviously weakened by the fact that it was precisely those communes of Val and Saumurois that were favorable to the Revolution. It may be strengthened again by the further observation that what there was of counterrevolutionary organization in the Mauges took the more archaic and sporadic forms of pilgrimages, religious ceremonies, and simple crowds, while the famous counterrevolutionary army consisted mainly of communal bands with only the most rudimentary of tables of organization. One may infer that there was less experience on which to base an effective political organization in the Mauges.

Seen as microcosms, however, the communities of southern Anjou did have significant political lives of their own. Let us begin with formal organization, and reserve the informal structure for later. In the Mauges, what we would normally call civil administration was largely in the hands of the curés up to the Revolution. But there were two other figures who had to be reckoned with officially: syndic and lord.

The syndic was the agent of the local assembly. The assembly itself was a centuries-old institution in Anjou, as elsewhere in France, an institution almost impossible to distinguish from its religious counterpart, the vestry (*fabrique*) (Spal 1886; Guinhut 1909: 79 ff.).

Legally, the separate post of syndic appeared shortly after 1700, but in fact the syndic and the churchwarden were usually the same person, and no distinction was made between the meetings of the two groups.

The assembly, until late in the eighteenth century, was simply the meeting of all the heads of households of the community after Sunday's last Mass. As a body, they had a number of legal powers:

They determined the sales, purchases, exchanges, and rentals of the commons; the repair of the church, the presbytery, the public buildings, the roads, the bridges; in addition to their syndics, they named their schoolmaster, their herdsman, their sergeant, their hayward, the tithe collectors, the assessors and collectors of the taille. Sometimes they fixed the conditions of the wine-harvest; in certain circumstances they even set the rate of pay for day laborers and the prices of certain products (Babeau 1878: 48).

With the subtraction of the herdsman, sergeant, and hayward (who did not exist) as well as the schoolmaster (who, if he did exist, was almost surely the curé's appointee), we may apply this enumeration, intended for France as a whole, to southern Anjou. In 1787, the assembly was replaced in Anjou and other provinces without Estates by a small assembly of notables, including the curé, the lord, and a small number of elected members. The same principle of local government by a small group of elected notables was continued through most of the Revolution.

Who actually took part in the assemblies may be more interesting than their formal organization and legal powers. In the vicinity of Chemillé, the average assembly seems to have been composed of about 19 persons, distributed as follows: 1 priest, 7 peasants, 4 bourgeois, 5 or 6 artisans, 1 or 2 others.[1] According to Jules Spal's report (1886) on a much wider range of assemblies, the curé or the vicar was almost always present, and the lord almost always absent. The substantial citizens, unsurprisingly, were in greater proportion here than in the general population. They often had a direct economic interest in the decisions of the assembly, they were by training and temperament more concerned with "civic affairs," and the assembly was in any case limited to established household heads. The bourgeois

[1] From the analysis of the minutes of 19 assemblies during the years 1749–1753 and 1769–1783 in the private archives of Étude Fleury, Chemillé. A comparative analysis of such minutes for the various subregions of southern Anjou would be an extremely valuable way of getting information on differences in the local arrangement of power.

do not seem either to have dominated the churchwarden's job, nor to have been kept from it.

There are some signs that the urban bourgeois felt that service as syndics or churchwardens was beneath their dignity. When the Provincial Assembly planned in 1788 to join the job of parish syndic with the higher-ranking job of municipal syndic in the city of Cholet, the correspondents of the District of Cholet wrote:

> You know that wellborn people will not wish to subject themselves to conducting the boys of their parishes to the drawing for conscription at the whim of a subdelegate, and to being at the service of an assembly, and that the greater part of them wish to decline the double office, which will not be any better filled in the future than it was in the past (A.D. M-et-L C 187).

They suggested giving the administrative details to the municipal clerk. To the "wellborn" urban bourgeois, public office was an honor, but the details of public administration an unwelcome burden.

Most of the meetings of local assemblies were for purely routine matters — appointment of tax collectors, renting of pews, apportionment of the corvée, election of a churchwarden. Occasionally there was a dispute with someone (generally rich) who did not think he should be taxed in the commune, or who felt he had been overcharged (e.g., the dispute of M. Reveillère, merchant farmer of the domain of La Treille, with the commune of La Séguinière, A.D. M-et-L C 35). Signs of open fights between members of the commune are very rare. One gets the impression from the rather laconic minutes that when the curé spoke, or on the rare occasions when the lord spoke, he was heard, and no further deliberation was necessary. The assembly was the only formal unit of local government, and even it was limited by the power of noble and priest.

Again we reach a weak, and sore, point in the information now available. There were no differences in the formal organization of the assemblies from one subregion of southern Anjou to another, but there is every reason to guess that participation and control in the assemblies differed significantly in Val-Saumurois and Mauges. It *ought* to be true that the curé's influence was lesser, the bourgeois' influence greater, and the general level of participation higher in Val-Saumurois than in the Mauges. If the reader will permit a little grasping at straws, there is one item of information that may indicate something of the sort: the fact that at the beginning of the

Revolution the curés were more often elected president of the local electoral assembly, or even mayor, in the Mauges than in Val-Saumurois (see A.N. D IV 9–13, D IV 40; A.D. M-et-L C 186–188). This was very likely a simple continuation of the habitudes of the old regime.

Informal local government was just as clearly the sphere of priest and noble. The priest was generally in control of local affairs, the noble likely to intervene in the political relations of the commune with the outside world. The lord acted as a symbol of the community and a bridge to the national government (cf. Sutton 1959). He mixed little in the details of communal administration, but it was often he who requested favors from the government, or influenced the government's plans to the advantage of the commune. Even if he was commonly absent, even if he had much less to do with the everyday affairs of the rural community than tradition has said, on those exceptional occasions when the community needed a symbolically appropriate and politically effective representative to the central government, the lord ordinarily played the part.

Karl Kautsky, surprisingly enough, gave a description of the bocage and other similar regions in France which exaggerated the point, but still had some substance to it:

We have already seen . . . that in France before the Revolution there were distant provinces where feudalism and those forms of Catholicism which accompany it still had their roots in the means of production, where that which had elsewhere become unbearable chains still served as a protective shield. In those provinces, each village still lived and produced for itself, in the old way. The peasant's allegiance went no further than the village bell-tower: what lay beyond the horizon was for him *l'étranger*, of which he had no need, with which he wanted no contact, expecting of it only disorder and pillage. Handling relations with that Outside and assuring the defense of the area against it were the affairs of the curé and the lord (1901: 99).

What we may now say, with the advantage of the half century of research that lies between us and this statement by Kautsky, is that it was not true, but was certainly truer of the bocage than of the areas outside it. Sixty years after Kautsky, F. X. Sutton (1959: 8) expanded a similar idea into a characterization of all preindustrial politics: "Most of the members of a local community have not been direct members of the political system in the sense that a modern citizen is.

They have entered into the political system through local representative figures who have normally held a diffuse high status" (cf.
Kornhauser 1959, 1961). The figures with this sort of "diffuse high
status" in the Mauges were the lord and, to a lesser extent, the curé.
The nobles of Val and Saumurois were more numerous, more often
on hand, and on the whole less wealthy, a set of circumstances which
probably bred both familiarity and contempt. The curés suffered the
frequent, and often overriding, competition of the higher clergy. And
long participation in a far-reaching market had both broken down
some of the local insensitivity to national affairs and built the class
of specialized intermediaries between local and national systems:
the bourgeois. In these respects, the communities of Val and Saumurois were already entering into modern political ways.

These differences in social arrangements may help explain the persistent strength of royalist candidates for representative office in the
bocage after the Revolution. We may put together a (hypothetical)
account of their implications for the years after the Revolution. The
nobles, still predominant landlords and now back on the land, could
build on their traditional roles as spokesmen for their communities
both in regional and national affairs. The title changed, the function
remained the same. In the republican plains adjoining the bocage,
goes the hypothesis, effective political participation was much more
widespread, representation more differentiated, the local relevance of
national political issues more apparent to voters, and the bourgeois —
qualified as representative, spokesman, communicator, and intermediary by the very essence of his social position — more capable of
claiming the right to elective office. If this speculation is correct, the
difference in apparent political affiliation was less a matter of sharp
disagreement in political philosophy than of differences 1) between
an essentially apolitical electorate and a politicized one, 2) between
two different kinds of linkage between communes and the national
political process. The hypothesis is piquant, since it suggests that the
fundamental beliefs of the two populations concerning the proper
government of France may not have differed nearly so much as the
public positions of their elected representatives. There is a significant
difference between this way of looking at the facts and that of
Siegfried (1950: 1) who argued that in the bocage "a social structure
of the old regime persists . . . on the whole, public opinion accepts

this type of social structure and prefers it to the one that France inherited from the French Revolution."

As for the priest, his activities in the administration of the commune were so varied and so closely mingled with his religious functions that the earlier discussion of religious organization necessarily dealt with them in some detail. The curé of the Mauges was essentially the master of his commune's internal affairs. Appointing the schoolmaster and reviewing the qualifications of the midwife, keeping the communal records and writing the reports, administering the charitable funds and running the multitude of religious organizations, the curé was more of a despot in his own community than any term like "mayor" can suggest.

The conditions for bourgeois power in eighteenth-century rural French communes were a market orientation, a certain level of economic independence among the peasants, the passing of land into other than noble hands. These conditions could be fostered by good communications, production of strictly industrial and commercial crops, the development of cities, the sheer numerical proliferation of the bourgeoisie, and common resentment against the exactions and pretensions of the privileged orders. In short, urbanization. Conditions were evidently more favorable to the bourgeois in Val-Saumurois than in the Mauges. In the Mauges, the bourgeois found it much more difficult to prevail against curé or lord.

André Siegfried saw the weakness of the bourgeoisie as one of the fundamentals of political life in western France:

The West is not a region of bourgeois strength. The rarity of cities and industrial centers, the scattered and particularly rural character of the population mean that the bourgeois find themselves squeezed between the nobles and the people. They are only on top in exceptional circumstances. This weakness of a class which is important almost everywhere else is a notable element in the political balance of the West (1913: 426).

We can use the exceptions to the rule of bourgeois weakness to put it to the proof. In the cities and in those bourgs where both bourgeois numbers and industrial activity were high, there was a greater tendency for the bourgeois to dominate the commune. This was true, for example, of Le May, Saint-Macaire, Chemillé, all active textile centers with a substantial number of clothiers and merchants. In these places, the curé was either the ally or the subordinate of the bourgeois in political affairs. The conditions that gave the bourgeois strength in these communities were unusual in the Mauges. Indeed, even in these places bourgeois strength was far from absolute: it was precisely such communities, as we shall soon see, that most often broke into angry political factions during the Revolution.

The political characteristics I have described were not things of the moment. They endured. Truly reactionary movements stirred the bocage until Napoleon clamped his iron hand on the region, and then, that grasp loosened, stirred again in 1815 and even, with a last ludicrous spasm, in 1832. Saumur, on the other hand, was a center of *republican* plots and rebellions in 1820–1822, in 1853, and probably in between. In the more peaceful ways of elections, parties, and plebiscites, too, the division between Mauges and Val-Saumurois persisted through the nineteenth century into the twentieth. Siegfried's celebrated work leaves little doubt of that. That division, a constant feature of the Third Republic, was still detectable under the Fifth: although there were signs of change in 1958, the Catholic MRP was still much stronger in the Mauges than in Val-Saumurois, and "the localization of the MRP still corresponds remarkably to the departmental map of religious practice" (Jeanneau 1960: 597–598; cf. Lancelot and Ranger 1961: 142).

The endurance of the political frontier that bisects southern Anjou is more than a local peculiarity. One of the principal points in Siegfried's argument was the constancy of the territorial correspondence among an "archaic" social structure, the presence of counter-revolutionary activity in the 1790's, and the electoral strength of the Right a century later. Paul Bois, in the very process of tearing a number of Siegfried's explanatory hypotheses to shreds, has confirmed the existence of such a durable frontier in the Sarthe (Bois 1954, 1960b: esp. ix, 35–59, 1961). For the department of the Vendée, a sophisticated study of the elections of 1869 by Marcel Faucheux (1960) testifies to the persistence of a division that had prevailed in the previous century.

Change and Conflict

Let us not be mesmerized by the vision of constancy. The fact that a boundary stays in place does not mean that nothing changes on either side of it. All the authors I have mentioned, and more (e.g., Goguel 1951: 281–282; Wylie 1958, 1959), have reported the political evolution of the bocage and the plain since the distant days of the Revolution. The assumption that the political situation of the West in the 1870's, or the 1950's, was nothing but the petrified remains of the situation of 1789 is not just foolish; it is pernicious. Pernicious, because it encourages retrospective inferences from 1870 — when the clergy had lost their lands, when the heirs of the purchasers of church property now had that property to defend, when the entire position of the nobility in French society had changed, when both the reality and the flourishing myth of the great counterrevolution had done their work — to the times of the old regime, to 1789. Pernicious, because it obscures a fundamental fact: the differences between areas in various stages of constant social evolution. If I insist on the obvious, it is because the temptations of the assumption of stasis are so great, because I have not been the least of the sinners in this respect (see esp. Tilly 1958).

There is another sort of static assumption it would be well to avoid: the assumption that each of the sets of political arrangements that appeared in the communities of southern Anjou was a harmonious whole which operated without conflict, real or potential. Far from it. Our examination of community organization has disclosed a number of likely sources of contention. Most important of all, there was the rise of a mercantile bourgeoisie in the Mauges, prosperous, competent, literate, aware of national affairs and responsive to them, aware of its own interests and responsive to them as well, but barred from the traditional path of landlordship and ennoblement (genuine or synthetic) by the lords' tenacious preservation of their extensive fiefs and barred from domination of communal decisions by the occasional intervention of the lord, by the unassailable prestige of the curé, and by the weakness of their means of influence over an uncommercial peasantry. A set of circumstances which significantly weakened one or the other of these competitors, or transformed the external situation of the community, could give the bourgeois an opportunity to increase greatly his local power and, in the long run, his prestige. I mean to imply, of course, that the Revolution brought such a set of circumstances.

Seen from an economic point of view, there were other latent conflicts around the position of the bourgeoisie. The industrial artisans of the Mauges were precariously dependent on the decisions of the merchants and manufacturers, as well as on the prosperity of the textile industry; economic crisis, increased exploitation, or an access of class consciousness among the artisans could mightily strain that relationship. And the relations of many of the peasants with a somewhat different group of bourgeois, the managers of property, were subject to stress and strain. No doubt all these latent conflicts were concrete manifestations of what E. J. Hobsbawm (1959: 67), in his fascinating essay on rural rebellions, speaks of more generally as the devastating effects of the "irruption of capitalism" into backward rural areas.

One more potential conflict, of a different order, ought to enter the inventory. That is the conflict of city-dwellers and countrymen. City and countryside were much more closely integrated in Val-Saumurois than they were in the Mauges. The chiefs of the Mauges' cities exercised very little influence, less than those of Val-Saumurois did, over the surrounding areas. Certainly they had precious little political control. It is not hard to see that an attempt to impose such control would present a serious threat to the whole organization of the rural community, and could rapidly activate a whole series of sources of rural-urban hostility.

These observations on potential conflict, made with all the benefits of hindsight, are as much anticipations of the analysis of the Revolution that is to follow as they are deductions from the analysis of community organization. The observations are important because they identify some of the most important links between the rural community organization of the Mauges and the largely antibourgeois, antiurban character of the counterrevolution of 1793.

CHAPTER 9

Revolution

So, at last, we arrive at the Revolution. In another sort of account, we would have been there from the very first page. But the object of this study is to place the events of the early Revolution in time and space, to fix their positions relative to the varieties of modern society and the predominant processes of social change. That is why the discussion of the Revolution — and, even more so, of the counterrevolution which is the special concern of this book — comes late. Even here, the account will contain very little chronicle, and a great deal of analysis.

A favorite tautology among students of political upheaval is that for a revolution to occur there must be a "revolutionary situation." Often this has been taken to mean that throughout the revolution-prone society (except, perhaps, in the incumbent elite) there are demands for radical change. However, a society is not like a cheese which, however thinly sliced, tastes like cheese throughout; a revolution is a state of a whole society, not of each segment of society. There is therefore no reason to expect the analysis of the performance of one class, one association, or one region to explain the outbreak of revolution.

The Revolution of 1789

Certainly it is hard to imagine that there would have been a great revolution in 1789 if France had consisted of the West, or of territories like the West, alone. It is hard, for that matter, to imagine a Revolution without Paris. De Tocqueville (1955: 76–77), fresh from the experience of Louis Napoleon's *coup d'état*, opined that "chief among the reasons for the collapse of all the various governments that have arisen in France during the past forty years are this administrative centralization and the absolute predominance of Paris. And

I shall have no difficulty in proving that the catastrophic downfall of the monarchy was largely due to the same causes." With the same intuition (if not the same set of explanations), subsequent historians of the Revolution have poured the overwhelming share of their energies into the study of events in the City of Light. Even Celestin Port (1888: I, 3) began his account of the Revolution in Anjou with a vignette of Angers' intelligentsia waiting for the news from Paris, and springing into action at its inspiration. The picture is true to the situation of most of provincial France through most of the early Revolution.

For these reasons, treatment of the Revolution as a series of "external" events to which southern Anjou had to respond is not only convenient, but accurate. That is how I shall treat them.

And what was the nature of the revolutionary changes that impinged on provincial France? Again Tocqueville is helpful. At least when discussing governmental institutions, he emphasized the continuity between the developments of the old regime and the changes of the Revolution. In a sense, the Revolution did not overturn, it accelerated. It accelerated the formation of a "modern" kind of property, free of multiple private rights and obligations, and speeded the transfer of property to the Third Estate. It fostered the preeminence of Paris. It hastened the construction of a centralized nation-state, uniform in its administration, demanding widespread participation. It added impetus to the growth of political associations, newspapers, means of communicating and opinionating. It extended a kind of economic rationalization and market expansion, combining the eradication of personal and local controls with the fortification of national controls. It intensified many of the general changes associated with urbanization. In these respects, the great French Revolution anticipated the powerful "modernizing" and "nationalizing" revolutions of such countries as Egypt, Japan, or Argentina.

Of course, the Revolution also *reversed* some trends in French society: the attempts of the high nobility to reaffirm its influence in French government and to shut off the access of new men to lofty positions of honor and power, the reassertion of fiscal rights by noble landlords, the decadence of monasticism. Still, on the whole, the Revolution continued the work of the old regime. It seems to be generally true that as a consequence the Revolution found its most willing reception in the most urban sectors of French society. Again, "urban" is an elastic term, for it applies to great cities more than small ones, city more than country, but also trading areas more than commercially stagnant ones, people involved in trade and industry more than those involved in the land, holders of "capitalistic" property more than holders of "feudal" property, communicators and coordinators more than those they served or controlled, the mobile more than the immobile.

No doubt the proper retort to such a sweeping summary is "Which Revolution do you mean?" After all, Georges Lefebvre (1947) distinguished four overlapping revolutions — aristocratic, bourgeois, popular, and peasant — without moving past 1789. Yet there is a rough kind of unity in the major changes of the early Revolution. That complex unity, in the last analysis, is probably best conveyed by the fabulous watchword: Liberté, Égalité, Fraternité.

One of the bases of this unity was surely the prominence of France's bourgeoisie in the events and reforms of the Revolution. There was continuity with the old regime in this respect as well. The bourgeoisie (the observation is at least as old as Guizot) was gaining strength and self-awareness throughout the eighteenth century; the Revolution swiftly augmented that class's political power. As Marx would have it, the "feudal" class system was crumbling, and the "capitalistic" class system arising from its dust. As Marx would also have it, the bourgeois were the principal agents and beneficiaries of the Revolution.

My reasons for stating these unsubtle and largely commonplace generalities are to put the experience of western France back into its historical setting, to characterize the external changes to which the West had to respond during the early Revolution, and to suggest that the Vendée was not the kind of region in which one could have expected to find enthusiastic support for the Revolution. One of the most self-consciously Marxist of recent historians (Guérin 1946: 10) summed up the distinction in this way: "The archaic conditions of land ownership and of agriculture in certain regions like the Vendée and Brittany had helped keep these provinces in the darkness of servitude." Hippolyte Taine (1876: 32), with an enormously different bias, spoke of the Vendée as one of the few "remnants of the good feudal spirit" left in the France of 1789.

Both statements are quite wrong in detail. Both statements are quite right in signaling the distinctiveness of the Vendée's social situation. Less urban as a whole than the rest of France yet supplied with newly growing cities, its bourgeoisie weaker than elsewhere yet aware of growing strength, the Vendée was not ready for revolution, but it was ripe for turmoil.

The West's Experience

We may begin the detailed discussion of the Revolution with the relatively unconventional date of 1787. In that year, Loménie de Brienne's reform established a series of assemblies, uniformly organized throughout France, at the level of the individual community, the election, the province, and the generality. In addition, there were "interim commissions," executive bodies designed to carry on the work of the provincial assemblies between their meetings. As precedent and as practical training, these new arrangements were exceedingly important. As precedent, because (even though the projected elections were never actually held) the reform established the principle of representative assemblies throughout the nation, as well as combined the double representation of the Third Estate with the vote by head instead of by estate. As practical training because (even though the assemblies generally accomplished very little, and were probably intended to do no more than ratify new taxes) the new arrangement gave a whole generation of the ambitious Third Estate its first taste of public office.

The functions of Anjou's Commission began modestly, but expanded significantly:

The task of the Interim Commission of Anjou was narrow at first. It tried to oversee the creation of municipal governments in the rural parishes, to multiply charitable efforts, to diminish beggary. It studied agricultural problems, asked for an increase in police protection, the abolition of the salt tax, and tried to supply the region with a new network of roads. But soon its mission became more complicated. It was given the responsibility for the assessment of various taxes: the tax substituting for the royal corvée, the supplementary tax rolls for the last half of 1789. Later it had to undertake the general assignment of taxes for 1790 (Réau de la Gaignonnière 1911: 44).

The Commission, furthermore, used a substantial questionnaire to collect a revealing mass of information on the administration, mate-

rial condition, and troubles of each community under its jurisdiction
(A.D. M-et-L C 190–193). In short, the Interim Commission was developing into a new and influential organ of regional government as
the Revolution began.

As for providing new men with political experience, the Commission was less important than the provincial and communal assemblies. I regard the communal assemblies as of particular importance,
for three reasons: 1) They established a formal organization for local
government, the municipal council, clearly distinct from other groups
in the community; the change almost inevitably challenged those
whose interests were vested in the old, relatively undifferentiated
mechanisms of local control. 2) They overturned the antique tradition of communal decision through the assembly of all heads of
households and concentrated the formal powers in the hands of a
relatively small number of *gros* —"big guys." To be sure, the curé
and the lord were still prominent ex officio members of the municipality. But the property requirements (10 livres in annual tax payments to vote, 30 livres to hold office — much more stringent than
the qualifications of the early Revolution) meant that such groups as
industrial artisans and day laborers were conspicuous by their virtual
absence from the voting lists. The lists for 40 communities of the
District of Montreuil-Bellay (A.D. Indre-et-Loire C 744) average just
over 50 names, while the same communities contained, on the average, over 200 households. And, of course, the municipal councils
themselves included only a half dozen of the most substantial of these
voters. 3) The selection of the municipal council gave the first formal
recognition to the small groups that were to govern the commune
during the Revolution. I suspect it also whetted the appetites of the
rural bourgeois for political power. It was not without self-satisfac-
tion that L. M. Larevellière-Lépeaux (1895: I, 60), an eminently
bourgeois revolutionary, reminisced that "they had just established
the provincial assemblies, and the former parish syndics, who were
generally simple peasants, were replaced by property owners who
mattered in terms of wealth or upbringing; they were called municipal syndics. In the commune of Faye, the choice of the provincial
administration fell on me; it was my first public office." As Port
pointed out, the reform greatly fortified both the power and the
prestige of the syndic:

Those agents, who up until then had been no more than the delegates of the residents, received only a mandate limited to keeping accounts, sending out notices for the corvée, taxes, conscription, under the authority of the royal officers, the subdelegate, even the lord, and at the risk of arbitrary fines. The new election made of them all at once true representatives of the community, intermediaries between it and the central power, endowed with their own authority, which left servile relationships to subordinates. Everywhere that it was possible, these modest functions, until then forced on simple peasants, were for the first time accepted proudly, even sought with eagerness by the small number of petty nobles, or officials, seneschals, rentiers, notaries, landowners "who mattered in terms of wealth or upbringing" in their parish 1888: I, 92–93).

The new-found eminence of "those who mattered" carried over into the first phase of the Revolution. The administrative reform of 1787 may have been much more important to the local history of the early Revolution — and not only in southern Anjou — than it has been customary to recognize.

No one, on the other hand, has missed the importance of the Estates General of May, 1789, the local and regional assemblies which preceded that national congress, or the drawing up of the *cahiers de doléances* — Statements of Grievances — that accompanied these meetings. In Anjou, the process brought to a head a dispute between a group of Anjou's most distinguished bourgeois (notably the famous Volney) and some of its wealthiest lords (notably the Count Walsh de Serrant). The specific issues, which began with opinions on the ownership of trees on the rights-of-way of public highways and then expanded to questions of provincial administration and the arrangements for the Estates General, are less important than the fact that their presence gave the preparation of the Estates in Anjou the atmosphere of a hard-fought electoral campaign. The fact that the issues had been widely debated in the province also gave the drafters of the local Grievances some points of reference in terms of which to define their own positions. Of the 89 Statements of Grievances from below the Loire which he analyzed, A. Le Moy (1915) was able to classify 34 as being strongly influenced by one of the two parties; a number of others show traces of the conflict.

At their meetings of early March, the communal assemblies of southern Anjou approved their Grievances and elected representatives to the Third Estate assemblies at Angers and Saumur. The local assemblies were usually conducted by the bourgeois of the vicinity, especially the notaries and bailiffs. The Grievances themselves were often prepared beforehand by a local leader and approved substantially as written, although there is no evidence of the wholesale preparation of the documents by the lords that Chassin (without convincing substantiation, 1892: I, 41) reported for the heart of lower Poitou. A number of the Grievances of the Mauges, for instance those of Le Pin-en-Mauges, Melay, and St. Macaire (A.D. M-et-L B) are in the hand of the curé or the vicar, which suggests that though officially absent the parish clergy played a part in the decisions made.

The bourgeois, and particularly the manorial officials, also played a substantial role. One indication is the frequency with which a whole series of communal assemblies presided over by the same official prepared similar Grievances. For example, the eminent notary from Chemillé, Thubert, soon to be a major figure among the revolutionary party of the Mauges, left his mark on the Grievances of Saint-Georges-du-Puy-de-la-Garde, La Salle-de-Vihiers, Vezins, Nuaillé, Saint-Lezin d'Aubance, and La Chapelle Rousselin. All of them, with similar turns of phrase, agreed on the suppression of the privileges of nobles and clergy, the abolition of the gabelle, the payment of the corvée in cash and not in labor, the ending of *franc-fief* (the tax paid by commoners who held noble fiefs), and a number of other matters (Le Moy 1915: II, 55–82). This sort of official influence went even further in the three assemblies presided over by the lawyer Pierre Baranger; Saint-Hilaire-du-Bois and Le Voide simply subscribed to the sentiments of the Grievances already prepared for Vihiers, without bothering to put their own together (Le Moy 1915. XI, 32–53).

On this point, too, the memoirs of Larevellière-Lépeaux provide an interesting elucidation:

I ran the assembly of my commune for the choice of electors; I was named first, and given the responsibility of drafting the communal Grievances. At first I had some trouble making my good villages understand that the Estates General could not concern themselves with matters peculiar to their commune; finally they understood that for the moment they had to deal with matters of universal interest and with general reforms like the abolition of every kind of privilege, of the tithe, feudal dues, benefices without parish duties, the religious orders, the gabelle, etc. They eagerly accepted the proposal I made that curés be chosen by their parishioners, that the celibacy of priests be abolished, that all religions have the same freedoms; and that, finally, to assure the success of these changes, forestall new abuses, and handle the nation's expenses, there be an annual representative assembly (1895: I, 60–61).

The proof of his success was the text of Grievances of his commune, Faye: like those of nearby Thouarcé and Rablay, it was taken almost word-for-word from a pamphlet that Larevellière-Lépeaux circulated in the heat of the preparations for the Estates General.

We shall return to the actual contents of the Grievances later, but there is one matter that deserves notice now, since it confirms the influence on the substantial bourgeois: the frequency of complaints about the franc-fief. The complaints were most common in the vicinity of Cholet, precisely where it was least likely that any peasant or artisan ever had to pay such a tax. I believe that they expressed the views of bourgeois who already owned some property, and wished that a good deal more were freely available. Savor the relevant article from the Grievances of Le Longeron (Le Moy 1915: II, 497): "The franc-fief is ruining most of the commoners who own noble properties, and individuals residing in areas where land is almost all noble stagnate in idleness and in the greatest poverty." The rich — and, apparently, the envious and impatient — were speaking.

The facts about their preparation raise some serious doubts whether the Grievances can be taken as ". . . the most authentic testament of the French society of yesteryear" (Sagnac 1906–1907: 341). Nor is it sure that every plaint recorded a heartfelt wrong, since the assemblies were specifically told to prepare proposals for reform. It is true that the assemblies of southern Anjou were almost unanimous in certain complaints, and those perhaps merit confidence. The cries against the salt tax were paramount and the pleas for tax reform widespread (see Le Moy 1915: I, xxvi; Bellugou 1953). Later I shall identify some interesting systematic differences between the Grievances of the Mauges and those of Val-Saumurois. So the contents of these documents are far from meaningless. The mistake would be to take them as direct expressions of "peasant opinion," without controlling for the influence of the local elite. Until the Revolution came along to stimulate one, I doubt that there *was* an articulated peasant opinion on most of the matters of national policy with which the Grievances dealt.[1]

That brings us to a major effect of the calling of the Estates General: that it helped "politicize" local issues and personal alignments, in the sense of making them appear relevant to national issues and alignments. It is a momentous day in the growth of a modern state when people in its rural villages begin to recognize the connection between what goes on at home and what goes on in the nation at large. A whole series of events of the early Revolution — the reorganization of local government, the Civil Constitution of the Clergy, the changes in taxes, universal military conscription, and frequent elections as well as the calling of the Estates General — made French villagers unavoidably aware of the fact of citizenship. In Anjou, as elsewhere, the sudden proliferation of pamphlets and newspapers reinforced the new awareness. During the first year of the Revolution, the *Affiches d'Angers*, the *Angevin patriote*, *L'observateur provincial*, and *Correspondance de MM. les députés des communes de la province d'Anjou* were all reporting the news of Paris. Most of the newspapers, and most of the early pamphlets as well, were of a patriotic persuasion. Together they made it likely that the great events in the nation's capital would not only be known, but also duly endorsed, in the cities of Anjou.

Response to the Revolution

When it comes to tracing the response of southern Anjou to such exciting events of the early Revolution as the storming of the Bastille or the "abolition of feudalism" on the Fourth of August, some problems appear at once. All the great days of Paris received their ritual recognition, and often more, in Angers, Saumur, and the other important cities. But no one has assembled whatever information may be available on who celebrated what, and how, outside the major cities. For that reason, the many claims that "the Revolution was greeted with joy" in Anjou leave tantalizingly unanswered the question "By whom?" It is clear that there was no substantial and vociferous opposition to the major reforms of the Revolution in southern Anjou before the end of 1790. It is not clear that this negative

---

[1] For another view, see Dorsey 1960.

fact tells us very much about the spiritual state of the countryside.

Another negative fact may be worth a trifle more: the absence of spontaneous rebellions against the privileged classes in a time when peasants elsewhere were vigorously overturning traditional obligations to the clergy and nobility, and violently attacking abbeys and castles. "While all around the tumults of sudden liberty had invaded city and country," wrote Port (1888: I, 85; cf. Chassin 1892: I, 42), "Anjou, thanks to the uprightness of public morality and especially to the leadership given the popular movement by resolute citizens, was free of any private violence or excess. Here there was no pillaging of castles, no burning of archives; neither insult, riot nor violence." Although the shiver of agitation that passed through the French countryside after the taking of the Bastille had no single "cause," the account that Lefebvre (1932: 118–144) gives leaves the impression that the areas most affected were particularly those of a sort of primitive Poujadism, where all kinds of public cash obligations — tithe, salt tax, manorial dues — were resented and those in which the lords had been encroaching on the traditional rights of the peasants in commons, forests, and the like. Although resistance to the tax collector was common enough (see A.D. M-et-L C 168, C 186), neither of these conditions was prevalent in southern Anjou.

The case of southern Anjou fits Lefebvre's observations in another interesting respect. Lefebvre (1932) established that most sections of the country not washed by the wave of agrarian uprisings after the fall of the Bastille were swept by the slightly later, but much different, Great Fear, that bizarre, hysterical reaction to reports that "they" (British, Poles, Bretons, Germans, or just plain "They") were coming. Southern Anjou was strongly affected by the Great Fear. More precisely, and more interestingly, the local version of the Fear began near Nantes and spread through the bocage, but hardly went beyond it:

. . . the area affected was limited by the Layon and the Thouet: the Poitevin plain was unaffected; likewise to the south: it would seem natural for the agitation of the bocage to have frightened the plain, but in fact everything happened as if the existing contrast between the two regions had forestalled the contamination of the "right-thinking" country (Lefebvre 1932: 202).

In fact, the Fear seems to have stopped exactly at the Layon, in

Saint-Lambert-du-Lattay, on 22 July. As a later parish priest of the town described it:

The day of the Feast of the Madeleine a stranger said as he went rapidly through the bourg that the Polish had landed at Sables d'Olonne, and were putting everything to the torch and the sword, and that he was on his way to Angers to announce the news. In an instant everyone came·to the square; many wanted to flee, but others proposed to send someone to Chemillé to find out what was up. MM. Dailleux and Gautier got on their horses and soon disappeared, leaving their compatriots in fear and hope. Every eye was on the road to Chemillé. After an hour two horsemen appeared in the distance, urging their horses to top speed . . . they were shouting "We're lost! Save yourself! There's an army at Chemillé, and Chemillé is in flames!" (Raimbault n.d.).

Need I say there were no army and no flames, that MM. Dailleux and Gautier had never gotten to Chemillé, just eleven kilometers away? That is how word spread through southern Anjou. But they did not pass on the word to the Saumurois, just to the east. Just as Saint-Lambert itself, stationed at the entrance to the Mauges, was first the stopping point of the Fear and then the very frontier post of the counterrevolutionary country, the panic as a whole fatefully traced the boundaries of the area that later joined the counter-revolution. The coincidence is informative because it suggests the presence of widespread uneasiness rather than stolid insensibility throughout the bocage at the beginning of the Revolution, and indicates the possibility of the rapid and spontaneous dissemination of a popular movement through the lines of communication already operating in the region. That possibility is interesting because of the common assertion that a rebellion could not have swept the whole bocage in a week in March, 1793, if there had not been a well-laid plan of insurrection in advance.

There was no concerted response in southern Anjou to other major events of the first half year of Revolution. I know of no particular reaction to the Night of August Fourth or the "anti-feudal" legislation that followed it. Nor does the nationalization of church properties seem to have incited a general hue and cry, despite the shouting that began a year later as the sales of those properties approached.

Taxes were another story. Many Angevins, like many other Frenchmen, felt that if there had been a revolution, then it followed obviously that taxes had been abolished. Especially the onerous salt tax.

At the end of August, 1789, the authorities at Beaupréau reported that "everyone is seeking to avoid any payment of taxes. There have been armed bands near the Loire which have engaged in every sort of violence toward the officers of the Gabelle, whom they have disarmed. People are going to Brittany to fetch salt, which they are selling publicly in a number of bourgs" (A.D. M-et-L C 186). When official word came that this extralegal abolition of the salt tax was not only premature but financially intolerable, communities throughout Anjou sent delegates to a meeting of protest on the 6th of October, and the protest was carried effectively to the top of the national government (Port 1888: I, 83–85). Likewise, the hopes for revolutionary revision or abolition of taxes incited not only increased resistance to tax collection but also numerous disputes over the proper distribution of the taxes. In the Saumurois, significantly, there were a number of demands that "former privileged persons," i.e., basically the nobles, should be taxed more heavily (e.g., Ambillou, Saint-Rémy-la-Varenne, A.D. M-et-L C 198).

Another set of revolutionary changes that received a decisive response in southern Anjou was the reorganization of the territorial arrangements of government. Like the changes in taxation, this reorganization provided a splendid opportunity for the "politicizing" of local affairs; local rivalries and ambitions took on national meanings (see Tilly 1961, 1962). During the year 1790, Anjou's Interim Commission followed the Constituent Assembly's directives, first, in revamping communal administration and, then, in replacing the incredible crisscross of provinces, bailiwicks, jurisdictions, and the like with the uniform system of departments, districts, and cantons.

Even though it was begun later, the reconstruction of provincial administration was completed before that of the communes, so I shall discuss it first. The ancient province of Anjou was transmogrified into the department of Maine-et-Loire by a bit of decapitation (to the advantage of what had been the provinces of Maine and Touraine on the north and east) and a bit of tacking on (to the detriment of what had been Poitou) on the south. After a good deal of tugging and hauling, southern Anjou was divided up among the districts of St. Florent, Cholet, Vihiers, Angers (most of which was north of the Loire) and Saumur (some of which was north of the Loire). And the districts were in turn subdivided into cantons, at first hardly mattering except for elections, whose boundaries, seats, and functions were all to change much more often than those of districts or departments as the Revolution moved on. This revolutionary redefinition of the territory has, of course, been the basis of a large number of comparisons already made in this study.

The redefinition either stimulated or uncovered a great number of local rivalries and a great deal of petty imperialism on the part of cities and bourgs. While farther south St. Maixent, Parthenay, Thouars, and Niort were all pressing their claims to be capital of the new department of Deux-Sèvres, Saumur fought a futile battle with Angers, first for its own department, and then for the alternation of Maine-et-Loire's capital between the two cities (see A.N. D IV 2, D IV bis 26). No city seriously challenged Saumur's claim to its own district, but many of them (like Montreuil-Bellay and Le Loroux-Bottereau, the latter proposing to group the vineyard communities on the border of Anjou and Brittany) sought to redraw the map to give themselves districts, or (like Beaupréau and Montrevault) insisted on their superior rights to be seats of districts, or (like Chalonnes and Montreuil-Bellay) argued that at the very least they deserved to have some of the district's administrative apparatus. Even the empty title of cantonal seat was enough of a prize that bourgs like Passavant and Nueil-sous-Passavant were willing to slander each other for it.

In a message to the National Assembly in September, 1790, Langlois, a lawyer of St. Florent, declared that "in the process of placing courts of justice in each district, you have robbed Saint-Florent-le-Vieil, capital of a district of 40 parishes, of that honor and advantage, and placed it in the mudhole which is the bourg of Beaupréau, where there is not a single house suitable for housing an honest man, and no public place for courtroom, office or prison" (Uzureau 1933: 201). So eager was Langlois, only one of the many from St. Florent who wrote to this effect, to deprecate Beaupréau that he was not even willing to call it a city. An earlier request of Clisson for a tribunal confided its hope that the city would take on "the size and area of cities of the third rank in the kingdom" (A.N. D IV bis 26). These two sample cases illustrate the facts that the territorial reorganization made available distinctions considered worth fighting for, and that the acquisition of these distinctions was felt to be essential to the size, power, prosperity, and glory of the city or bourg. There are more important implications. The very act of contending for the prizes committed the contestants to the revolutionary reorganization, gave them practice in a new variety of politics, and made them aware of the connection between the decisions of the national legislature and their own welfare.

The same was true, to some extent, of the remaking of the commune. There were two aspects: 1) changes in the formal organization, 2) changes in communal boundaries. The formal changes, which generally took effect in 1790, reduced the property requirements for voting and holding office from those of 1787 (but still did not broaden the potential electorate to what it had been before 1787), transformed the communal council into a group of elected "notables" and "municipal officers" with no members ex officio, and added the important office of mayor to that of communal procurator. The arrangements were a further break with the tradition of local government that had prevailed until 1787. Not only did they introduce more formal and elaborate mechanisms of government, not only did they turn away from the traditional authorities by excluding curé and lord from automatic membership, not only did they accentuate the difference between the new organization and any other (such as the vestry) that might exist locally, but they now installed an elected official, the mayor, as the designated spokesman of the community. The earlier syndic had been a dignified errand boy, but the mayor was truly a presiding officer. Even the formal change of name from "parish" to "commune" reflects the specialization of local government involved, and the undermining of the old, diffuse, undifferentiated structures of communal power.

The traditional arrangements did not give way easily. It is remarkable how many communities of the bocage bridged the chasm between the old system and the new by electing their curés mayor early in 1790 (see A.N. D IV 2, D IV 40; cf. Chassin 1892: I, 119–120). Although the point needs verifying, the curé seems to have been the people's choice much less frequently in Val-Saumurois. When he was chosen there, as at Le Puy-Notre-Dame (A.N. D IV 10), it was a hotly disputed event. Later on, the curé was to be legally barred from local elective office, a reform that would obviously have greater effects in the Mauges than in Val-Saumurois. But the short-range effect of the governmental changes was not to overturn the general distribution of power in the commune, even though they added an increment of strength to the new men, but to make it clear as never before that the national Revolution reached into local affairs, and made politics and political organization a distinct, dominant, and thoroughly renovated sphere of local life. Furthermore, the changes stimulated the formation of a new political elite, specialized both in local government and in linking the changing demands of a national Revolution with the exigencies of local life. That elite, as we shall see, was increasingly drawn from the bourgeoisie.

The other aspect of the reworking of the commune was the drawing of its territorial limits. Somehow under the old regime it had rarely seemed important to decide exactly where one community began and another ended. A modern Revolution, however, could not be so tolerant of imprecision — there are detailed piece-by-piece descriptions of the new communes in the archives to prove it (e.g., A.D. M-et-L 1 L 440; A.N. F 19 445). In addition to the specification of local boundaries, which was not overly controversial, there was the consolidation of previously independent communities into larger communes, which was absolutely explosive. At first, the objective was administrative convenience and efficiency. Later, in 1791, the dearth of priests loyal to the Revolution added a new reason for combining communes and shutting down redundant churches; the political reliability of the leaders of the communes in question was often taken into consideration in these later decisions (see A.D. M-et-L 1 L 970-976).

If the people of cities like St. Florent or Chalonnes were irritated when their rivals got the district or the tribunal, the chiefs of the rural bourgs were inconsolable when they were annexed to their neighbors. Hear the cry of Joué, threatened with absorption by nearby Gonnord: "What a triumph for some its neighbors and its inhuman, jealous, and ambitious enemies and what a shame for her, what confusion, what sadness, what pain! In short, the bourg will be no more than a hamlet, a desert without work, without money and without commerce, reduced to a piteous condition" (A.N. D IV bis 97). That local pride should be hurt by the prospect of civic extinction is not surprising; that the town fathers of Joué, and many other places, took the step of complaining to the National Assembly is evidence of growing political awareness. The annexation of a commune required, among other things, the closing of its church, the removal of the ornaments and, perhaps most inflammatory of all, the removal of the bells — those bells that had been solemnly named and baptized by the curé, and had tolled out the history of the parish, those bells which the sexton rang loudly and rapidly, to make the warning sound of the tocsin. By 1791, when the parties of revolutionaries and antirevolutionaries were digging into their positions, the closing of churches was not only a political issue but an occasion for violence on the one side, and the use of armed troops, on the other. Late that year, the prorevolutionary priest sent to assist in the removal of the ornaments from the supernumerary church at La Fosse-de-Tigné reported that the only thing that saved him from massacre at the hands of the crowd was the quick action of the National Guards who had come with him (A.D. M-et-L 1 L 360). By the time the Department of Maine-et-Loire sent out Larevellière-Lépeaux and Villiers to speed the "suppression of various parishes" and to reassure the patriots of the Mauges, at the end of January, 1792, the mission was a fairly dangerous one (A.D. M-et-L 1 L 976). The dangers were already accumulating imperceptibly two years before, with the first realignments of communal organization and boundaries.

The trivia of local history, it turns out, are not trivia. In the petty events of 1787–1791 we can see a new kind of political existence developing for the inhabitants of southern Anjou. A new group of connoisseurs of politics (whose identity we shall have occasion to discuss in detail) was forming. The course of the Revolution became widely known and of utmost interest, not so much through the Great Events that shook Paris, as through their consequences in local and regional administration. The apparent relevance of local affairs to national policies, organizations, and parties, and vice versa, rapidly and greatly increased. The men of southern Anjou were becoming citizens, political participants.

Of course, this was happening to some degree everywhere in France. The Revolution presented a relatively uniform set of external challenges to all kinds of provincial communities — which does not mean that it met uniform conditions or received uniform responses. Within southern Anjou, we have general reasons for thinking that the communities of Val-Saumurois were readier for the political changes of the Revolution than were those of the Mauges, and that those changes posed a greater threat to the existing structure of power in the Mauges. It would be well to look a little more closely at the evidence on the political orientations of the two sections.

Local Attitudes toward the Revolution

We are close to a question that has often, too often, been discussed, that of the "attitude" of the Mauges toward the early Revolution. Over the last century, historians of the Vendée have ordinarily argued that the region's population greeted the Revolution happily, but were later turned against it by something (e.g., Port 1888: I ch. 2; La Sicotière 1889: 7–16; Gabory 1925: I, 18; Dubreuil 1929–1930: I, ch. 2–5). In naming that *something* — the religious reforms, military conscription, a noble plot, agitation by the priests are the main choices — historians have neatly explained the counter-revolution, judged it, and taken a general position regarding the Revolution at the same time. There are three significant defects in such a procedure (see Tilly 1963). First, it smuggles in the risky assumption that one *can* identify a unitary "attitude" for the entire region and explain its history on the basis of fluctuations in that attitude. Second, it tempts the analyst to glance over the evidence on the response to the early Revolution, in order to get on to the real business: the state of mind of the rebels in the process of rebellion. Third, it draws attention away from the crucial problems in comparative social organization that have occupied so much of the present analysis.

One way to test the merits of these criticisms is to turn directly to the evidence most commonly given for the early enthusiasm of the people of the Mauges for the Revolution: 1) the purchases of church property, 2) the public ceremonies and declarations of 1789 and 1790, 3) the contents of the Statements of Grievances, 4) the formation of National Guard units and the frequency of enlistments in the army. The church property sales will be an important subject of the next chapter. For the moment, it is interesting simply to notice how often commentators favorable to the Revolution (and, it almost goes without saying, unfavorable to the nobility) have cited a few instances of church property sales in which future Vendean leaders like d'Elbée and Bonchamps were involved, and how often their opponents have worriedly minimized those sales (e.g., Port 1888: I, 109–111; Baguénier-Desormeaux 1916). It is also worth while to remark that some of the later historians of the Vendée (e.g., Gabory 1925: I, 47; Dubreuil 1929–1930: I, 61–62) have reported the nearly clean sweep the bourgeois of the bocage made of the purchases, although they have not attached any great significance to the occurrence. The *effects* of the sales remain elusive, but it is becoming clear that those sales went quite differently in the revolutionary and counterrevolutionary sections of the West. The importance of these differences and the estrangement of peasants and bourgeois over the sales have surely been underestimated.

Altogether, these observations — and the sheer fact that the sales did not begin until the end of 1790 — drain most of the value of the church property sales as evidence of the acceptability of the beginnings of the Revolution to the various sections of southern Anjou. The patriotic ceremonies and declarations of various communities in 1789 and 1790 are probably easier to interpret, but the testimony they give is not unequivocal either. The citizens of Beaupréau sent a stirringly patriotic message to the National Assembly as early as July, 1789. Likewise, Chalonnes had enthusiastic celebrations of all the great days of the early Revolution (Chollet 1952: 80). The external signs of allegiance to the Revolution were widely visible at Montreuil-Bellay (Charier 1913). Nor was Cholet left behind in declarations of loyalty (Port 1888: I, 80–81). These instances, and others like them, effectively contradict any notion that the people of the areas that later joined the counterrevolution never responded to the Revolution (for the department of Vendée, cf. Chassin 1892: I, 71 ff.). Unhappily for the value of the demonstration, no one has held such a naïve view for a long time. What the casual enumeration of such signs of support cannot show is the distribution of enthusiasm and antipathy for the Revolution among different segments of the population and among different sections of southern Anjou. That is precisely what we need to know before drawing firm conclusions about the "attitude" of the region in 1789.

Statements of Grievances

The Statements of Grievances carry with them the problem of deciding how they were written and whose viewpoints they represent. But they have the advantages of usually indicating who took part in the formal deliberations on their acceptance and of being sufficiently numerous and detailed to permit some interesting comparisons. For Anjou, the rich collection of Grievances published by Le Moy (1915) covers most of the territory; its only drawback for present purposes is that it practically excludes the Saumurois, whose Grievances have not yet been assembled, edited, or published.

I have already presented some reasons for hesitating to hear the Grievances as the Voice of the Peasantry. It would not be any better to assume without investigation that they were the Voice of the Elite. The assemblies that endorsed the Grievances were quite similar in size and composition to the better-attended parish assemblies of earlier years. The elite was overrepresented, while on the whole the poorer peasants and artisans were underrepresented. Nevertheless, 1) peasants and artisans generally formed the majority and 2) even where a ready-made document was brought to the assembly, changes or additions to the text were often made in the course of the deliberations. For example, at Saint-Lambert-du-Lattay the assembly, in which local merchants and officials were prominent but still outweighed in sheer number by peasants and artisans, adopted the Grievances of nearby Rochefort-sur-Loire, with six locally drafted articles added; the original set of Grievances was probably brought from Rochefort by an influential manorial official (De Menil 1962: ch. III). In short, the Grievances represent compromises among multiple points of view, like modern party platforms, or major bills as they finally leave the legislative machinery. As such, they are valuable evidence of the public political position to which the sum of all its internal forces brought the community, suggestive indications of the lines of influence within the community, but risky guides indeed to the thinking of any particular class, or to that of "the people" as a whole.

In Le Moy's appraisal (1915: I, xxviii), the Grievances of the Mauges showed more signs of the influence of manorial officials than those of any other section of Anjou. There were considerable concentrations of those Grievances which Le Moy classified as "favorable to the ideas of Walsh de Serrant"— that is, to the maintenance or extension of the power of manorial courts — in the vicinities of Cholet, Maulèvrier, and St. Florent.[2] Of course, some of these same statements, like those of Rochefort-sur-Loire and Saint-Lambert-du-Lattay, incorporated extensive demands for reform. Nevertheless, one can use a consolidated version of Le Moy's categories, augmented by an impressionistic classification of his "original" Grievances as reformist or not, to construct an interesting table. The table suffers

Table 13. General position of Grievances, by district.

| District | Number of communities in each category | | | | |
	Favorable to Walsh	Original, not reformist	Original, reformist	Influenced, and reformist	Total
St. Florent	7	4	12	7	30
Cholet	11	2	7	14	34
Vihiers	1	2	1	12	16
Angers	·1	0	4	7	12
Total	20	8	24	40	92

from the unavailability of information from the District of Saumur, but it still shows some significant variations from one section to another. The "influenced" Grievances are those which either 1) directly followed one of the models circulating in Anjou or 2) clearly endorsed the widely publicized "bourgeois," or antiseigneurial, position (cf. Dorsey 1960). Although there were a number of such Grievances in the District of Cholet, they were proportionally much more common in the Districts of Angers and Vihiers and relatively rare in that of St. Florent. By contrast, almost all the statements favorable to the "seigneurial" party came from the two districts of the Mauges. Finally the "original" Grievances, which may well reveal the lesser involvement of their authors in the political fights and factions of the province as a whole, were more numerous in the Mauges than outside.

[2] There is an interesting parallel here to the case of the Sarthe, where the communes in which Bois (1960b: 182) detected the influence of manorial officials were mainly in the western part of the department, the section that was to support the counterrevolution most vigorously.

The differences are impressive, the explanation elusive. Le Moy was probably right to claim that the presence of large manors in the Mauges gave their officials exceptional influence over the Grievances of that section. This reanalysis of his classifications also seems to confirm the greater involvement of the communities outside the Mauges in provincial politics, and the more frequent presence of an effective reform party in those communities.

The assignment of whole Statements of Grievances to major political tendencies in this way is useful, but it tells us little about the specific issues that mattered in 1789. For that reason, I have gone back to the Grievances to identify the most common complaints and proposals, and to see how *they* varied from one part of southern Anjou to another.

Let us take all the items mentioned by at least 10 percent of the Grievances, and add to them both the sale of church properties and the reform of "feudal" rights, which were not proposed very often, but are interesting anyway. That gives us a list of 24 items, which fall under four general headings: 1) taxes, 2) government, 3) lords, 4) clergy. A separate table for each heading will keep the number of items under discussion small enough to be manageable. (In evaluating the Grievances, I gave a full score on a given item to explicit proposals or complaints, and a half score to indirect ones; that is why some of the percentages in the tables to follow are based on 9.5 or 10.5 cases.)

The first, and most commonly discussed, category is taxes. Table 14 presents the distribution of complaints by district.

Table 14. Taxes: percent of statements mentioning the Grievance, by district.

Grievance	Angers	Vihiers	Cholet	St. Florent	Total
General reform of taxes is needed	67	94	76	47	57
All three Estates should pay the same taxes	88	62	85	67	75
The salt tax	100	94	92	93	94
Abolish duties on movement of goods within the country	83	59	89	88	83
Complaints against the tax on legal transactions	75	81	61	47	62
Complaints against franc-fief	67	53	88	70	73
Number of cases	12	16	33	30	91

The first message of the table is: everyone complained about taxes. There was far more agreement on these items than on any others that appeared in the Grievances. The salt tax, that infamous gabelle, was apparently the most unpopular of all. Complaints about duties on internal trade, the *Traites*, were also widespread, and three quarters of the communities inveighed against the inequitable distribution of taxes among the Estates. When it comes to the franc-fief, which burdened the commoner who held "noble" land, there is a plausible correlation between the intensity of the complaints and 1) the extent of noble property, 2) the presence of wealthy bourgeois managers of property. Almost 90 percent of the Grievances of the District of Cholet, where noble property was almost certainly the most extensive, protested against the franc-fief. Otherwise, aside from a slight tendency for the communities of St. Florent to complain less than the rest, there were no systematic differences among the four areas on the subject of taxation.

There were four common items among the Grievances that can be grouped under government: the objections to *jurés-priseurs*, military conscription, and the malfunctioning of the royal courts, as well as the need for general reform in government. The jurés-priseurs were the petty officials who seized property in cases of court judg-ments and indebtedness; they were the scourge of the poor. The question of military conscription deserves special mention because a number of authors (no doubt influenced by the knowledge that the first violence of the counterrevolution in March, 1793, was in the form of resistance to the draft) have postulated an extraordinary hatred of military service among the people of the Vendée. The other two items, the malfunctioning of the courts and the need for general reform, are perhaps self-explanatory. The distribution of grievances appears in Table 15.

Table 15. Government: percent of statements mentioning the Grievance, by district.

Grievance	Angers	Vihiers	Cholet	St. Florent	Total
Objections to jurés-priseurs	75	62	52	50	56
Military conscription	17	62	48	37	43
Malfunctioning of royal courts	67	69	39	65	57
The need for general reform in government	33	19	15	7	15
Number of cases	12	16	33	30	91

On the whole, the communities of the Mauges complained less about matters of government than did those outside. The courts and the jurés-priseurs came in for about the same amount of criticism, just under 60 percent of the statements commenting on their deficiencies. Less than half of them condemned military conscription, and the condemnations were no more common in the Mauges than outside. Port (1888: I, 74) was therefore wrong to say, in summarizing the same Grievances, that "almost as much as the salt tax, military conscription met general disapprobation." The complaints about conscription were numerous, but not nearly as numerous as those about taxes. Certainly they give no reason to suspect that the Mauges were peculiarly hostile to military service.

The "need for general reform" is a deceptive category, because a number of statements list a number of specific governmental reforms without making a general proposal for change. Nevertheless, there is a connection between readiness to speak of general reforms and willingness to see a change in the whole order of the old regime. By this principle, the spokesmen of the Val (District of Angers) were much readier for change than were those of the Mauges (District of Cholet and St. Florent).

The issues of taxes and government were mainly located outside the rural community. The questions concerning lords and priests brought the possibility of revolution closer to home. Many more of the questions that aroused bitter local controversy in the years following the Estates General were in these areas. So these complaints and proposals gauge especially well the desire of local leaders for changes in everyday life and local arrangements of power. The most common Grievances concerning the position of the noble landlords were: 1) explicit rejection of the claims of the great landlords (that is, those whose courts had jurisdiction extending to high justice) to trees in the rights-of-way of roads passing through their territories; these claims were associated with the party of Count Walsh de Serrant; 2) demands for reform or abolition of manorial courts; such demands could be, among other things, protests against the position of Walsh and his followers; 3) complaints about the hunting privileges of the lords including their dovecotes and game preserves; 4) proposals for reform of the monetary obligations to the lords with which commoners owning property were burdened; these were mainly proposals to let the landowners cancel the petty feudal dues they had to pay periodically by reimbursing the lord; 5) general demands for the reform or abolition of "feudal" rights, including banalities, hunting rights, ceremonial privileges, dues, and the like. In one way or another, the list covers the grudges rural people are usually supposed to have had against the nobles of the old regime. The distribution is shown in Table 16.

Table 16. Lords: percent of statements mentioning the Grievance, by district.

Grievance	Angers	Vihiers	Cholet	St. Florent	Total
Against claims of Walsh party that lords with high justice had right to trees in roadways	33	6	8	13	13
For reform or abolition of manorial courts	38	50	12	7	25
Against the hunting rights of the lords	83	50	9	22	30
Reform of monetary obligations of commoners to lords	58	56	12	17	27
General reform or abolition of "feudal" rights	33	18	0	8	9
Number of cases	12	16	33	30	91

Much more so than in the cases of taxes and governmental administration, there was a decided difference between the communities of the Mauges and those outside on the subject of the lords: distinctly fewer protests came from the Mauges. Generally speaking, the proportion of communities in the District of Angers calling for reform was at least three times the proportions in the districts of Cholet and St. Florent, while Vihiers was in between. While the proportions of the Grievances in the districts of Angers and Vihiers dealing with these matters were hardly lower than those discussing taxes or government, around St. Florent and Cholet there was a striking contrast between the wealth of comments on taxes or government and the dearth of proposals when it came to the nobles.

The "affair of the trees" was little noticed outside the District of Angers, where a third of the Grievances mentioned it. The related, and more general, problem of the manorial courts attracted more attention, but very little of it inside the Mauges. The hunting privileges of the nobles provided the most commonly discussed issue of this series. The Grievances of the Mauges, however, hardly mentioned them, while those from outside were vociferous about them. On the question of monetary obligations, there was a distinct split between the frequent complaints in the districts of Angers and Vihiers, and the fairly rare complaints in the districts of Cholet and St. Florent.

Plausible explanations are available for some of these differences. Lordly hunting parties may well have been more of a menace in Val and Saumurois, with their frequently resident nobles, their unfenced fields, and their intensively cultivated land. The wide distribution of property in those areas meant that many landowners were obliged to pay petty feudal rents, not to mention the payments, often substantial, when property changed hands. Yet there is no reason to believe that trees were more common in the roadways there, or that the manorial courts were more active or more faulty. How much did the influence of manorial officials on the drafting of the Grievances in the Mauges keep down criticism of the property system? How much were the assemblies of the Mauges intimidated by their great landlords? It is hard to say. What it seems safe to say is that in Val-Saumurois groups critical of noble power and privilege carried a good deal of weight in the local deliberations, while in the Mauges any parallel groups had much less influence. The summary of the whole set of comparisons is in the proposals for general reform or abolition of "feudal" rights — essentially the rights that were to be destroyed on the famous Night of August Fourth. A third of the Grievances of the District of Angers made such a proposal, while the proportion stepped down to zero around Cholet. There is no question that in this crucial respect, the public demands for reform were much greater in Val-Saumurois than in the Mauges.

The fourth, and final, phase of the Grievances consists of recommendations concerning the clergy. The range of such recommendations was wide, but there was less agreement on any particular proposal or plaint than there was in regard to taxes, government, or the nobility. Parish priests and higher clergy drew approximately equal attention, but some of the recommendations concerning the parish priests were meant to improve their position, while no such thought entered the comments on the higher clergy. For both the tithe and the sale of church properties, it is not hard to separate the Grievances directed at the parish priests from those intended for the higher clergy, so a rough comparison of attitudes toward the two groups is possible. Table 17 gives the relevant figures.

The division between the "reformism" of Val-Saumurois and the "conservatism" of the Mauges persists in these Grievances, but it is not nearly so marked as in the discussion of the noble landlords.

Table 17. Clergy: percent of statements mentioning the Grievance, by district.

Grievances	Angers	Vihiers	Cholet	St. Florent	Total
The revenues of religious communities should be reduced	21	50	39	20	32
Religious communities should be reformed or abolished	8	25	21	8	16
Against absentee holders of benefices	25	12	12	4	11
Against the tithe collected by curés	4	19	15	5	11
Against the tithe collected by outsiders	17	34	12	10	16
Properties of the higher clergy should be sold	12	12	2	7	7
Properties of the curés should be sold	0	0	0	0	0
Curés should have higher incomes	8	41	15	13	18
The lot of vicars should be improved	25	66	30	17	31
Number of cases	12	16	33	30	91

Here, it is the District of Vihiers that is most concerned about the clergy, and most hostile to the privileges of the higher clergy.[3] The communities of the District of Angers seem to have distinguished among the parish priests, whom they ignored, the religious establishments, which they treated gently, and the absentee clerics, whom they denounced. In the districts of Cholet and St. Florent, no religious issues attracted very much attention, except that the wealth of chapters, priories, and monasteries and the poverty of vicars drew the condemnation of a number of communities around Cholet.

In general, the statements were much more critical of the higher clergy than they were of the parish priests. Outside collectors of the tithe drew more fire than the curés who got their income from it, and there were at least a few plans to dispossess the landholding abbeys, but none to take land from the parish priests. There was more agreement that the impoverished vicars needed help than on any other point, except for the opinion that the religious communities were too rich. In this pair of propositions there might have been the beginnings of a program for religious reform. Otherwise, the communities of southern Anjou were not nearly so ready to discuss religious organization as a matter of public policy as they were to deal with taxes, government, or even the position of the nobles.

[3] Within the District of Vihiers, the criticisms of the higher clergy came almost exclusively from the Layon and the Saumurois, while the communities on the side of the Mauges were the main ones to express solicitude for the curés and vicars. So a rough formula — anticlerical in Val-Saumurois, pro-parish-priest in Mauges — applies a little better than the table indicates. Still, there were enough demands for religious reform in the District of Cholet (particularly in the communities which said least about the manorial regime) to upset any pat formulation.

The communities of the Mauges were even less ready to do so than those of Val-Saumurois.

What is the general significance of these cahiers de doléances? First, the comparison of Val-Saumurois and Mauges confirms the conclusions drawn from our earlier inspection of Le Moy's categories of Grievances. Opposition to the traditional privileges of the noble landlord was much more common in Val-Saumurois, as was outright support of the "bourgeois" party in the dispute between Walsh and his enemies. Furthermore, the Grievances of Val-Saumurois more commonly include comprehensive programs for reform. These programs probably reflect greater, politically focused, dissatisfaction with the old regime and greater participation in the political debates that preceded the Estates General, as well as the direct influences of the model Grievances that were circulating.

There are some important points that Le Moy's categories could not reveal. The issues closest to formal politics — taxes and governmental administration — attracted far more comment and far greater agreement than the problems of the nobility and the clergy. I think the explanation is that the authors of the Grievances were not so sure that the traditional positions of these classes were proper matters for legislation and public policy or safe matters on which to take a public stand. They were not, I suspect, simply less concerned about the priests and nobles. The place of these groups in French society was not yet clearly a political issue. Yet the spokesmen of Val-Saumurois were much more willing to treat it as such, and in that limited sense were much closer to making revolutionary demands.

That leads to the more general point: proposals for fundamental reforms were significantly more common in Val-Saumurois than in the Mauges. Judging from their Statements of Grievances, the Mauges were less ready for revolution.

All such statements are, of course, dogged by the two serious qualifications I have already presented: 1) Only a narrow slice of Val-Saumurois is actually represented in these Grievances; will those from closer to Saumur, when they are found and published, show the same tendencies toward reform? 2) We have no sure way of controlling for the variable influence of variable segments of the local elite; how much of the reticence of the District of Cholet on questions of noble property is the direct result of the influence of manorial officials? The first qualification does not bother me very much, since nothing about Saumurois in the first year of the Revolution detracts from the guess that its proposals had been widely reformist. The second qualification is grave, and ought to be kept in mind in all analyses of the Grievances of 1789. If we are willing to treat the Grievances as a *resultant* of local forces, and thus as a useful sign of the political position to which the local concatenation of power and opinion brought a community, then the conclusion stands: greater readiness in Val-Saumurois for the kinds of changes the Revolution was to bring. Certainly the findings give cold comfort to anyone who (like Gabory or Port) proposes the Grievances as evidence of the unanimous cry for comprehensive reform in 1789. Léon Dubreuil (1929–1930: I, 53) posed the question: "How is it that a good number of peasants, directly interested in the success of the Revolution, so rapidly turned against that constitutional regime which they had called for with all their might in their Grievances?" The problem deeply troubled Dubreuil. He finally sought to resolve it by arguing that the Revolution rapidly met all the needs and desires of the peasantry, and thus left them no stake in its continued success. A sophist's argument. Both its terms and its premises are mistaken. The Grievances were in no simple sense the voice of the peasantry. They did not unanimously propose fundamental reform. The peasants as a group never became strongly committed to the success of the Revolution, any more than they ever really became committed to its defeat as a political revolution. It is hard to see that the course of the Revolution up to 1791 satisfied many of the conscious needs of the peasants of the Mauges, as desirable as its reforms may have been. Finally, it obscures the entire problem to concentrate on a supposed rapid reversal of peasant sentiment.

Military Service

To return to the question of "attitude" toward the Revolution itself, we may investigate the willingness of citizens to enter the military service of the nation. Frenchmen had a whole series of opportunities to do so: in the militia units that formed in a number of cities as the first revolutionary news from Paris spread; in the various forms of the National Guard that were organized, more widely, later; then, in the enlistments for the revolutionary armies of 1791; still later, in the response to the draft of 1793 (which was the beginning of open civil warfare in the Vendée), and then to the *levées en masse*, the attempts at mass conscription for the prosecution of the European war. As an ensemble, the civilian response to these calls to service is still awaiting its historian, both for the French nation and for Anjou. When the accounts are written, they will surely be of interest to more than the military historian. The enthusiasm of enlistments must have something to do with the extent of working patriotism, and the response to conscription ought to be a gauge of the strength of the principle of citizenship.

The evidence I have been able to assemble for southern Anjou is distressingly weak for 1789 and 1790, the years before the struggle between prorevolutionary and antirevolutionary parties became so open and general as to transform the entire meaning of volunteering to serve the fatherland. It is much fuller for 1791 and later. As far as it goes, the evidence does not reveal unanimity or widespread enthusiasm. Instead, it anticipates the final chapters of this book in emphasizing the deep divisions of classes, subregions, and parties in southern Anjou before the counterrevolution broke into the open.

Before 1791, the organization of a Militia or National Guard was almost entirely the affair of the cities. Angers gave the cue, with its militia of 1789. By the next year, Brissac, Montreuil-Bellay, Beaupréau, Le Puy-Notre-Dame, Cholet, Chemillé, and most of the other cities of any size had their own National Guards. The higher ranks in these groups were prizes the citizens were willing to squabble over. And at times the squabbles had strong overtones of class, party, or factional conflict. For example, at Saumur in February, 1790, the citizens of the "districts des ponts et château" complained that the "aristocrats" had perverted the purposes of the Militia by forming a special, privileged group with distinctive uniforms, "looking on other citizens as scum" (A.N. D IV 10). About the same time, there were similarly angry reports from Montreuil-Bellay (A.N. D XXIX 58). There are signs that the substantial citizens of Cholet sought to exclude mere peasants from their Guard (A.N. D IV 40). Even if lamentable, these teapot tempests are not very surprising. Their only importance to us is that they tell us that in many of the cities of southern Anjou the distinctions the early Revolution had to offer were eagerly sought. There are some small indications that all cities did not participate equally in these patriotic displays, and that lasting gradations of "patriotism" among the urban centers appeared fairly soon. For example, toward the end of 1790, the National Guards of St. Florent and Beaupréau were reported (by, I admit, a biased source: their rival, Cholet) to be practically non-existent, while those of Cholet, Chemillé, and Vihiers were still going strong (A.N. D IV bis 67). In 1791 and 1792, it was Cholet, Chemillé, and Vihiers that were to have the reputation of being "patriotic" cities, while the positions of St. Florent and Beaupréau were much less definite.

These last observations do not permit any conclusions concerning subregional differences in response to the early Revolution. They do illustrate how much more actively the cities took part in the new, patriotic, organizational life than the countryside did. Even that point deserves further investigation, since the occasional traces of military units at such places as St.-Lambert-du-Lattay (Raimbault n.d.) or Bouzillé (A.D. M-et-L I C 4) in 1789 or 1790 makes one wonder whether such units, having little but ceremonial functions, simply slipped through the available records unmentioned. Yet even that circumstance would finally support the same conclusion: organized revolutionary activity was much greater in city than country.

The formation of National Guard units in 1791, in response to the directives of the National Assembly, was another matter. At least nominally, every commune had its Guard. Units were widely organized. Their longevity, however, depended on the number and determination of the local supporters of the Revolution. I cannot adequately describe the development of the National Guard from 1791 on until I have discussed the formation of local prorevolutionary and antirevolutionary parties, which I shall do in the following chapters. I can only summarize the most important facts. The National Guards of the cities remained especially vigorous and became the formidable enforcers of the laws of the Revolution. Lasting units of the Guard were much more common in Val-Saumurois than they were in the Mauges. In the rural sections of the Mauges, units lasted into 1792 only in the patriotic bourgs like Vezins, Les Gardes, St. Macaire, and La Tessoualle, which were mainly centers of mercantile activity and the textile industry. Furthermore, peasants were rarely active members of the Guard; it was mainly an organization of bourgeois and of some kinds of artisans. After 1790, the history of the National Guard in the Mauges was inseparable from that of the dwindling supporters of the Revolution.

The history of enlistments was not really very different. Enlistments tell us little about the response to the earliest phases of the Revolution, because they took place mainly in 1791 and 1792, when party lines were already sharply drawn in southern Anjou. For that period, they provide some rather interesting information. By the beginning of 1793, the Department of Maine-et-Loire had recruited about 2,700 men for three battalions of volunteers, from a population just under 500,000 (A.D. M-et-L 1 L 551). The area below the Loire, which had a little less than half the population, contributed about a third of the recruits. Table 18 gives the distribution by district

Table 18. Enlistments, by district, 1791–1793.

District	Number of volunteers	Enlistments per 1,000 population
Baugé	304	4.2
Segré	121	3.6
Châteauneuf	91	2.6
Angers	1,236	11.1
Saumur	581	7.0
Vihiers	183	4.2
Cholet	126	2.6
St. Florent	71	1.4
Total	2,713	5.6

both in raw figures and in enlistments per 1,000 population. There was a considerable correlation between the revolutionary fervor of a district and the frequency of its enlistments. In southern Anjou, with allowances made for the fact that the figure for the District of Angers includes the great city itself, the correlation was almost perfect. Similarly, the patriotic cities of Sables d'Olonne, Saint-Gilles-sur-Vie, and Fontenay supplied the bulk of the volunteers of the Department of the Vendée (Chassin 1892: II, 155–156).

It is rather interesting to look at the sources of the 126 volunteers from the District of Cholet. Sixty-seven came from the city of Cholet alone, and 32 from Chemillé. Once the 7 from Vezins, 4 from Les

Gardes, and 3 from Le May are accounted for, there are only 13 more enlistments to apportion among all the other communities of the district. That is, the cities and the principal bourgs of the textile industry, which were also the centers of revolutionary zeal, supplied almost all the recruits. The correlation between revolutionary fervor and enlistments holds up.

Outside the District of Cholet, the cities also predominated. The first battalion of volunteers (for which 28 of the 38 recruits in the District of Cholet came from the city of Cholet, 9 from Chemillé, and 1 from Les Gardes) drew 8 of its 14 members in the District of St. Florent from Montrevault and St. Florent, 16 of the 31 in the District of Angers from Chalonnes, and as many as 85 of the 94 men in the District of Saumur from the city of Saumur itself (compiled from Grille 1851–1852: I, 184–202). Only the District of Vihiers, where Joué, St. Lambert, Chavagnes, Luigné, Faye, Rablay, Brissac, and Vihiers all contributed to the 15 enlistees, escaped the pattern.

The next logical question is the identity of the recruits. It is possible to answer that question in great detail for the Second Battalion, which was recruiting from January to October, 1792 (A.D. M-et-L 1 L 598 bis). The well-kept registers described the recruits carefully, right down to the color of their eyebrows, sometimes even to the tint of their patriotism. The great majority were young men, and single ones. Of the 268 admitted to the battalion from southern Anjou, there is occupational information for 221.

Table 19 gives the occupational distribution of recruits by district.

Table 19. Occupational distribution of recruits, 1792.

District	Total number of enlistments	Percent of recruits*			
		Bourgeois	Artisan	Peasant	Other
St. Florent	30	5.9	94.1	0.0	0.0
Cholet	52	35.7	54.8	7.1	2.4
Vihiers	11	25.0	50.0	0.0	25.0
Angers	0	—	—	—	—
Saumur	175	29.9	55.8	4.6	9.7
Total, southern Anjou	268	29.0	58.4	4.5	8.1

* Calculated on the basis of the 221 recruits identified by occupation.

Considering the actual distribution of these occupational categories in the general population, it is obvious that the artisans and, especially, the bourgeois contributed much more than their share of recruits, while the peasants were greatly underrepresented. This is not a bad description of all kinds of support for the Revolution.

The data, and the conclusions they suggest, call for a pair of demurrers. First, there is no need to exaggerate the mechanical accuracy with which divisions of class or region separated the True Believers of the Revolution from the rest of the population. The tendencies revealed by the available information are impressive enough without being uncritically inflated. There were patriots on both sides of the Layon, in the open country as well as in the cities. Some bourgeois were avid counterrevolutionaries, and others were unable to make up their minds. There were peasants who supported the Revolution. Many features of the analysis of community organization in earlier chapters — for example, the investigation of marriage patterns — suggest other variables which unquestionably affected personal alliances and party alignments. The most microscopic information we have on communal politics in southern Anjou resists forcing into categories of class and locality alone, and calls for hunches about kinship, family friendships, the residues of old feuds, and the like. When Chemillé formed its tiny company of mounted guards in June, 1792 (A.D. M-et-L 1 L 567), it is true that all the volunteers were artisans and bourgeois, but it is equally true that four of them were members of the patriotic Briaudeau family, and most of the rest were from precisely those families which had been closest to the Briaudeaux in the local politics of the previous years. The lesson: categories of class, locality, and party explain a great deal, but they do not explain everything.

The second demurrer has to do with the character of the supporters of the Revolution. It is tempting to think of them as fiery-eyed, fearless "radicals." (After all, they were helping make a major revolution.) The fact is that, like all other political groupings, they displayed a tremendous range of zeal, conviction, and assurance. In regard to military service, one of the gripes of the first counterrevolutionaries of March, 1793, was that revolutionary public officials had neatly shielded themselves from genuine military service by assuming office. A diverting illustration of the cross-pressures in which many prudent patriots found themselves comes from the letter which Barbier, secretary of the District of Cholet, wrote in August, 1792, when he feared that he was to be called to the colors:

I am full of love for Liberty and the Constitution. I swear with all my heart to defend it to the death. But when I think that I have no fortune, and that if I leave for the front I will run the risk of returning stripped of all resources, I cannot keep from saying that the salvation of the country does not depend on my arm. If I do not combat foreign enemies I will combat the enemy within (A.D. M-et-L 1 L 567).

That the case of Barbier was not the rule is shown by the considerable number of young Patriots who *did* go to the front. All the more reason for hesitating to attribute a single type or intensity of motivation to a whole great segment of the population.

What do the various forms of military participation, then, tell us about the response of southern Anjou to the early Revolution? All they say with any clarity about the period before 1791 is that there was *some* enthusiasm in each major section, and that formal participation was much more extensive in the cities than outside. After 1790, military patriotism paralleled the other overt forms of allegiance to the new regime. It found greater favor in Val-Saumurois, in the cities, in the commercial and industrial bourgs, among the artisans and bourgeois, in the urban sectors of the society of southern Anjou.

Emigration

One other kind of evidence has a place in this discussion. Except for the deportation of many priests and the occasional return of the nobles of Anjou from the company of the émigrés, emigration has not been discussed in connection with the Vendée very often. It is hard to interpret crude rates of emigration. Do they measure antipathy to the Revolution? Or do they reflect the amount of internal conflict in the area?

I lean toward the second interpretation. Donald Greer (1951) has shown without question the general relationship in France between political turbulence during the Revolution and departmental rates of emigration. Revolutionary storm centers like Bordeaux, Lyon, and Toulon had many émigrés, just as counterrevolutionary departments like Mayenne did. The correlation deserves attention. People seem to have fled conflict as much as they fled the Revolution.

The departments of the West were a bloc with exceptionally high emigration; however their lists of emigrants were swollen both by the exceptional number of exiled priests and by the inclusion of many counterrevolutionaries who had not left the country but had fled their homes, gone into hiding, or died in combat. It is interesting to ask, therefore, whether it was the counterrevolutionary sections of these departments that supplied most of the names on their lists of emigrants. For southern Anjou, the answer is: No.

To find that answer, I have simply applied Greer's procedure in miniature to the cantons and districts of southern Anjou. That is, I have taken the general list of émigrés through October, 1793, for the Department of Maine-et-Loire (A.D. M-et-L 15 Q 271–280, 1 L 398 bis), and assigned the persons named to cantons and districts. I struck out the persons identified as being placed on the list for serving on counterrevolutionary committees in 1793. There may well have been more such nonemigrants left on the list; their inclusion would probably inflate the totals for the cantons of the Mauges, where the rebels were able to organize committees everywhere. But the great majority were surely genuine emigrants, for the great majority were priests and nobles. In this respect, southern Anjou seems to have followed the pattern of nearby Vendée and Deux-Sèvres (where about four fifths of the listed emigrants were priests or nobles) more closely than the pattern of Maine-et-Loire as a whole (where about two thirds were priests and nobles).

There were only 80 emigrants who could definitely be assigned to cantons of southern Anjou. Compared with an estimated population of 210,000, this number gives a rate of emigration of 3.8 per 10,000 people. The figure is lower than Greer's gross figures for Maine-et-Loire (4.4) and the departments of the West (e.g., Vendée 4.7, Deux-Sèvres 5.0, Loire-Inférieure 4.7). It is based on a paring down of the list (which includes not only members of counterrevolutionary committees, but also a good number of residents of Paris, Nantes, and the departments adjoining Anjou), and it includes no emigration after 1793. The conclusion that the rates were lower for southern Anjou than for the rest of Maine-et-Loire is therefore premature. Nevertheless, it is worth noting that a very large number of emigrants came, not from the counterrevolutionary sections of the department, but from the revolutionary center, Angers.

With the small number of cases involved (80 emigrants spread across 47 cantons), it would be foolish to analyze all the variations from canton to canton. The ten cantons with the highest rates of emigration per 10,000 population are given in order, with the district in parentheses: Montreuil-Bellay (Saumur), 18.8; Courchamps (Saumur), 14.8; Saumur (Saumur), 13.2; St. Georges-des-Sept-Voies (Saumur), 10.3; Le Puy-Notre-Dame (Saumur), 9.9; Cholet (Cholet), 9.5; Thouarcé (Vihiers), 8.7; St. Aubin-de-Luigné (Angers), 7.6; Vezins (Cholet), 7.3; Ponts-de-Cé (Angers), 6.8. The list is fascinating. Notice that the first five cantons are from the patriotic District of Saumur, and none from the counterrevolutionary District of St. Florent. All these cantons (with the possible exception of Courchamps) contained centers of exceptional revolutionary vigor. Almost all had more than their share of factional tussles during the period 1789–1793: Montreuil-Bellay, Saumur, Le Puy-Notre-Dame, Cholet, and Vezins are notable examples. In other words, the emigrants on the list came especially from sections of southern Anjou with 1) energetic groups of supporters of the Revolution, 2) unusual political agitation. Once stated, the proposition seems obvious. Yet it differs greatly from the equally plausible proposition that emigrants came from areas which as a whole were *hostile* to the Revolution. The district totals shown in Table 20 confirm this impression. Later on,

Table 20. Emigrants, by district.

District	Number of emigrants	Emigrants per 10,000 population
St. Florent	2	0.5
Cholet	23	4.1
Vihiers	13	3.2
Angers	8	3.3
Saumur	34	7.1
Total	80	3.8

we shall see that the emigration, or deportation, of priests was heavier from the Mauges than from the rest of southern Anjou. That makes the district totals all the more remarkable. Since they correspond, in a rough sort of way, to the proportions of resident nobles calculated for the districts earlier one might argue that these figures simply show that there were more of the kinds of people who ordinarily emigrated in the vicinity of Saumur than in the Mauges. The argument would not invalidate my main conclusion: the emigrants were especially likely to have left those areas where their view or social position put them at odds with a powerful group of local political officials. The numbers are small, the conclusion provisional. Provisionally, then, it confirms the differences in the response of the subregions of southern Anjou to the Revolution, long before the rebellion of 1793.

In summary, none of the conventional forms of proof — church property sales, public ceremonies, Statements of Grievances, enlistments, and National Guard memberships — really proves that southern Anjou thrilled unanimously to the first movements of the Revolution. On the contrary. They all come closer to showing that the principal differences in political position were there in embryo from the start. I do not mean there was no change from 1789 to 1793. At the beginning, groups like the peasants of the Mauges were not so much in opposition as unaware of politics altogether. Gradually, local life became more and more openly political. The pace quickened around the end of 1790, with the local application of major religious reforms. Opposition parties formed and filled out. Party positions hardened. The uncommitted found it impossible to remain uncommitted. Conflict between the supporters of the Revolution and their opponents became open and general. This is, in the last analysis, what it means to say that the "attitude of the people of southern Anjou toward the Revolution" changed deeply from the time of the Estates General to the time of the War of the Vendée.

The First Year of Revolution

While pursuing the problem of "attitude" I have had to wander beyond the bounds of the Revolution's first year. It may now be helpful to pause for a backward look. What was the state of Anjou a year or so after the Bastille fell? To commemorate the event, Federation Day of July, 1790, brought delegates from all over France to Paris for one of the first of the great modern political rallies. Southern Anjou's representatives were there — in what strength, it would be worth knowing. There were some things for Angevins to celebrate. The salt tax had disappeared. The tithe was gone (but the financial advantage of that change went mainly to the owners of property). The pettier vestiges of traditional noble privileges had been swept away. Some of the more irritating excise taxes were being abolished, even if the general tax load was far from being lightened.

There had been other changes that were less surely seen as unalloyed benefits, but even more surely made most people aware that they were living through a time of extraordinary political change. The 1787 reorganization of the municipalities, the Estates General, the revolutionary re-reorganization of the municipalities, the local elections of 1790, the formation of cantons, districts, and departments comprised the most drastic, thorough, and rapid administrative reformation Frenchmen had ever known. By the middle of 1790 the official correspondents of southern Anjou were already writing of The Revolution, although sometimes in the past tense. A new corps of public officials, from petty to great, was at work. Of course, the corps included many who had helped run the old regime, but it also included many whom the older traditions would never have called to public service. Villagers could now see their local notary, or the rich merchant of the bourg, serving as a member of the district's increasingly powerful administration. Lord and curé had been toppled from automatic eminence in the commune, and prosperous clothiers or wealthy farmers had often stepped into their places. Outsiders and newcomers were arriving in office. Furthermore, the administration with which the local political officials had to deal had been transformed, in personnel, outlook, and formal structure. It was an administration with which the traditional ways of mediation of lord and curé were decreasingly likely to be effective, with which the local bourgeoisie was well prepared, by taste, skill, and personal acquaintance, to deal. In other words, the commune — the political aspect of the community — was in the process of moving toward greater formal differentiation from other aspects of the community, greater specialization in its formal positions, greater involvement in political movements pervading all of French society, a new elite.

The events of the first year of Revolution probably disturbed the position of the lord more than that of any other figure in most communities of southern Anjou. They came close to destroying the social arrangements that gave him distinction and privilege outside the community. They also sapped his usefulness as liaison between community and outside, for influence with grandees, King and Court rapidly became insignificant in getting things done, and handsome traditional titles were fast becoming a liability. The response of most of the nobles was withdrawal. For a great many, it eventually became withdrawal to the place where the old social arrangements had been hastily, and somewhat shabbily, reassembled: the court of the expatriate princes, at Coblentz. Emigration had already gained plenty of momentum by mid-1790. For the rest, it was withdrawal to inconspicuous privacy in their town houses or manors. When they were once again able to function as leaders in activities that went beyond the mean and confining range of local politics, the nobles were ready to return. In the meantime, the political elite of the community was being transformed.

Both the national church and the individual parish were likewise being transformed. By the anniversary of the Bastille, the church properties were "at the disposition of the nation," already inventoried and under the surveillance of the local revolutionary administration. The preparations for their sale were underway. Monks, their vows dissolved by the National Assembly, were leaving their monasteries. Those who remained found local officials empowered to inquire with unheard-of freedom into the operation of the religious establishments. As far as the social position of the curé was concerned, the greatest changes were still in the future; I shall have my chance to analyze what Dubreuil called "the break of the lower clergy with the Revolution" in the next chapter. After a year of Revolution, the tithe had been abolished in principle, if not yet in fact, and the curé had an ill-defined promise of payment by the revolutionary authorities to replace it. He was now obliged to read governmental decrees at Sunday Mass (which was not really much of a change from his news-dispensing functions of before the Revolution, when he often announced auctions and decrees as well as blessed events). He no longer belonged to the communal council ex officio, but he still officiated in many communities as mayor or as president of the electoral assembly. His small properties had been enumerated and placed, at least technically, under the control of the government. And it was especially the local bourgeois, the ambitious ones, the upstarts, the outsiders, who were presuming to regulate the curé's actions. This was enough to make him abundantly aware of the scope of the nation's political changes. But the most serious attempts of the Revolution to intervene in the actual exercise of his functions, and the most serious threats to his position in the community, were not to begin until later in 1790.

If the direct effects of the early Revolution on the parish were less than those on the commune, the directly induced changes in the local economy were even less extensive. To be sure, the changes in taxes, the easing of internal trade, the seizure of church properties, and the disappearance of "feudal" obligations were all to transform the economic life of every community in France, in the long run. They had not had time to work by mid-1790. I do not mean to say that there were no economic circumstances worthy of attention. Célestin Port, that acute observer whose principles of interpretation so often counteracted his enormous grasp of the documentary evidence, long ago noticed the malaise, the dangerous unemployment, spreading through the Mauges in 1790 (e.g., 1888: I, 99–100). The matter is so important that I shall devote a major part of the next chapter to it. Suffice it to say now that textile production was in serious trouble, the workers restless, and the questions of bread, grain, prices, and work more ominous than ever. The situation was in no direct sense an effect of the Revolution. Yet it contributed a potent influence to the development of the Revolution, and the counterrevolution, in southern Anjou.

CHAPTER **10**

Revolutionary Economics

Alphonse Aulard was a member of the last generation of French historians who dared to write accounts of the Revolution without seriously considering the economic changes of the eighteenth century. By Aulard's time, Marx's use of the Revolution in his own historical scheme was already becoming an intellectual challenge to be answered, yea or nay. By now, even the least doctrinaire historians must somehow deal with the effects of economic growth in France before 1789, and be aware that events from that date on did not serve the interests of all French classes equally. A large component of what I have called the differential effects of urbanization in the West is essentially economic. In the long run, the economic differences between subregions and among classes in southern Anjou were of great importance in creating the alliances and the enmities that appeared during the Revolution. In Val and Saumurois, the widespread holding of fractionated land, the cash-crop farming, the "useless" wealth of the higher clergy, and the relative weakness of the nobility all helped form a situation in which bourgeois and peasant supporters of the new regime could act freely and vigorously. In the Mauges, the confrontation of subsistence farming (of land leased from eminent nobles and managed by bourgeois intermediaries) with a dynamic, erratic, textile industry, and the corresponding confrontation of intensely rustic territories with growing centers of commerce and industry, was unquestionably of the first importance. Faucheux has suggested that in the coastal sections of the Vendée the sections which stayed with the Revolution in 1793 were, in general, those in which the higher clergy had extensive economic interests, while the sections which joined the counterrevolution were those which owed little to any besides their parish priests. He concludes: ". . . facts of a material order, the question of ecclesiastical and civil taxes, the conflicts of interest [that question] aroused among the various classes of people . . . had a greater part in [the counterrevolution's] development than has been said until now" (1953: 85). In the long run, differences in the economic positions of the clergy from section to section were just as important in southern Anjou as in coastal Vendée. In the short run, we shall see that economic factors contributed both to the alignment of political forces in the West, and to the region's great unrest during the early Revolution.

This analysis of the impact of the Revolution on the local economy will cover the same time span as the later discussions of parish and commune. The order is not chronological, but analytical. I hope this necessary arrangement of the subject matter will not hide two essential points: 1) Events in each sector of the community constantly fed into the other sectors; the ways in which changes in economy, neighborhood, and parish impinged on the commune, became political problems and contributed to the struggle for power are of particular interest to this study. 2) The development of tension and conflict in the Mauges before the counterrevolution was long and continuous, if unsteady, and came to envelop all aspects of social relations. What we have to discuss here, then, is the contribution of economic division and stress to the political struggle in the Vendée.

Changes in Economic Policy

As a matter of course, every phase of France's economy was affected by the coming of the Revolution, just as every phase of the Revolution was affected by the state of France's economy (see esp. Garaud 1959; Godechot 1951; Lefebvre 1947, 1951 and 1952; Sagnac 1898; Sée 1951; Soboul 1962). But the major changes we may think of as following from Revolutionary *policy* fall under four headings: 1) the consolidation of "bourgeois" property, both by reducing the multiple rights of use and revenue which had commonly touched a single piece of property, and by fortifying the guarantees given to property; 2) the development of uniform taxation, regardless of traditional privilege; 3) the reduction of traditional controls and fiscal hindrances to commerce and industry; 4) the massive transfer of land expropriated from the Church and the emigrants, plus changes in the legal conditions for other transfers of land. Not all of these changes, however, affected the communities of southern Anjou strongly, immediately, or equally (cf. Sée 1927).

The abolition of the tithe, the eradication of lordly privileges like the monopoly of mill, oven, and winepress or the right to sell the manorial wine before any other went on the local market, and the authorization to amortize manorial ground rents worked mainly to the advantage of commoners owning land — which is to say that they were more important in Val-Saumurois than in the Mauges. In fact, the formal acts of amortization of ground rents and other manorial dues were much more common in the District of Saumur than in those of Cholet and St. Florent (A.D. M-et-L 1 Q 56–57). Furthermore, the landlords of the Mauges ordinarily upped their tenants' rents for 1791 by the amount of the abolished tithe, so the peasants made no saving.

So it seems that the reforms of property were mildly beneficial to the peasants of Val-Saumurois, and indifferent to those of the Mauges. It is almost certain that they meant greater actual changes to the landowners (whether peasant or not) of Val-Saumurois. The parish priests of all sections, on the other hand, were wrenched from their places by the new regime. On the whole, the sale of church property was less important to them than the abolition of ecclesiastical rents and the tithe, or the establishment of a salary. They went from rentiers to salaried officials in one jarring step. No other group's economic position (with the possible exception of those nobles who chose to emigrate, and were too imprudent to devise subterfuges for the retention of their land) was so profoundly affected by the economic reforms of the early Revolution.

The basic French taxes were not really overhauled until 1791. The salt tax, however, was defunct by the end of 1789, and a number of other incidental taxes perished with it. There was some reduction of exemptions and special allowances, which shifted some of the weight of taxation from the shoulders of the peasants, even if it did not lighten the total burden.

This redistribution of taxes within the community, combined with the increased accessibility of the outside officials making the crucial decisions, increased the salience of taxes as a political issue, but it does not seem to have affected deeply the conditions of the economies on either side of the Layon. In any case, the government canceled much of the benefit gained by the peasants, first by continuing to use the old regime's distorted regional apportionment of taxes in 1790, then by actually raising the rates in 1791 and 1792. Stinging letters from Cholet, Coron, and Chanteloup greeted the heavy tax burden for 1790 and the "coddling" of the taxpayers of Angers (A.D. M-et-L C 198). By 1792, the District of Cholet claimed it was being overcharged 210,000 livres in property tax alone (Port 1888: II, 44–45). But by 1792, it did not greatly matter how much the government demanded of the District, for the citizens were not paying. In November, 1791, the communal officers of St. Léger, Cerqueux-de-Maulèvrier, La Crilloire, and La Tessoualle had not yet prepared the supplementary tax rolls for the second half of 1789 (A.N.F^{1c} III Maine-et-Loire 5). A little earlier, the municipality of Chemillé had complained that "the métayers of our parish are unwilling to pay their taxes, on the pretext that there are no collectors in the countryside" (A.D. M-et-L 1 L 203). In the years to follow, refusal to pay taxes became quite general in the Mauges (see Port 1888: II, ch. 2). Nonpayment became another way of harassing the Revolutionary administrators, and a very comfortable way at that. To be sure, the officials of Maine-et-Loire had trouble collecting the taxes for 1791 everywhere in their territory. But in the Mauges, where resistance to the government in all regards was the strongest, the power of the administrators to force citizens to pay was the weakest. In short, the *political* effects of tax reform were probably much greater than its influence on production or consumption.

As for the dissolution of restrictions on production, consumption, and commerce, it is hard to detect any direct short-run effects on the economic life of southern Anjou. I suppose one might argue a priori that the removal of internal hindrances to trade (like the customs barrier at Ingrandes) and of controls over production (like the textile inspection stations of Cholet, Vihiers and Maulèvrier) should have most affected the sectors most involved in the market, but there is no solid evidence. Perhaps the lack of evidence in itself indicates that the immediate impact of these reforms was not very great.

Sales of Church Property

The immediate effects of the expropriation and sale of church properties were much greater. Most of the research that French historians have done on the sale of the national properties (as they were called) has been aimed at finding who got them: "Who, then, really profited from these sales?" (Lefebvre 1954: 224; see Marion 1908). The question is fundamental in the ever-lurking arguments about the ultimate work of the Revolution. Did the Assembly take the land from the wasteful hands of the nobles and ecclesiastics to put it in the industrious hands of the peasants and artisans? Did the Revolution establish small property, that foundation of democracy? Or did it take from the old rich to give to the new rich? These questions are important, surely. But there are other questions: How did the sales actually proceed? And what political significance did they have when they occurred?

These questions have taken on a new significance recently because of the stress that Bois (1960b) has given them in his analysis of politics in the Sarthe. In his view, the peasants of the western section of the Sarthe, prosperous and eager for land, already suspicious of the political ambitions of the urban bourgeoisie, deeply resented the domination of the local church property sales by the same bourgeoisie. At that point, according to Bois, the homogeneous peasant communities underwent a *prise de conscience* — the rapid awakening of a sense of unity, something like the transformation that Marx supposed would occur in an oppressed class suddenly becoming conscious of its inferior place in the mode of production, and of its separate identity. These communities turned against the urban agents of the Revolution, gave support to the counterrevolutionary Chouannerie, and stayed reactionary in politics throughout the nineteenth century. The hypothesis is inherently difficult to verify. When applied to southern Anjou, the model — homogeneous "peasant" communities responding to an external threat — hardly seems appropriate. The emphasis on the rural-urban conflict, however, is extremely important. And the thesis properly draws attention to the contribution of the church property sales to the partisan struggles of the region.

What *did* the sales mean to the communities of southern Anjou? There were few places where clerics held as much as a quarter of the land. There were therefore few places where the short-run economic effects could be revolutionary — the more so since the buyers of very large properties tended to maintain the same use of the land, the same system of tenure, and even the same tenants. The immediate effects were more likely to be ideological and political. An important part of the effect depended on whether the curé had pronounced against the seizure of the Church's lands, and when. Although the clergy of the Mauges seem to have been cool toward the operation from the beginning, the first solid evidence of anathemas against the purchasers of ecclesiastical properties comes from a time when the sales were already well begun. From that time on, and perhaps before, most countrymen of the Mauges who joined in the buying *ipso facto* separated themselves from their curés. In an increasingly bifurcated community, that meant that in effect they aligned themselves with the prorevolutionary opponents of the curé.

Why the curé might condemn the sales is another question. Not all did. In Val-Saumurois few did. One factor that could have figured in the subregional differences was the nature and extent of ecclesiastical property. The revenue declarations for 1790 (A.D. M-et-L 16 Q 80–125) indicate that the curés of the Mauges depended very heavily on the tithe for their income, while those of Val-Saumurois more frequently had their own lands to farm out. The same dossiers show that the higher clergy held more of the land in Val-Saumurois (cf. Denecheau 1958: 9). The sales were a more serious matter for the communities outside the Mauges, yet they were the ones whose priests more readily accepted them. Paradox? More likely a warning against using any simple interest theory as an explanation of these circumstances.

It makes greater sense to examine the symbolic challenge to the position of the curé posed by the sales of church property. For the first time, the National Assembly's abstract claims to regulate religious affairs concretely impinged on the parish. Moreover, the new revolutionary officials, precisely the persons who were contesting the preeminence of the curé, had to do the regulating. When it turned out that they were also the men who were to profit most by the sudden availability of all the property, the circle was complete. The sales sealed the arrival of the bourgeois-patriots in power. That was true both for the patriots of the rural community and for their allies in the cities and principal bourgs, who were generally the directors of the entire operation. The significance of these circumstances was not lost on those members of the community who were unable to acquire land, who were devoted to the curé, and who had their own reasons for unease at the commanding position of the local bourgeoisie. Their effects were greatest where the prestige of the curé was high, and where the local bourgeoisie came close to monopolizing the church properties. These conditions were met most often in the Mauges. In short, the transfer of the "national properties" did not in itself seriously affect the economic life of the community. The sales gained their significance from the context of political change and religious reform.

There are, however, two questions that this way of analyzing the situation may unduly minimize. The first is whether a large bloc of peasants and artisans interested in acquiring property (and to that extent, at least, cordial to the new regime) were turned away from their goal, either through the competition of wealthier bidders, or through the persuasion of counterrevolutionary propagandists (cf. Dubreuil 1912: 3). We shall see that there were, indeed, a number of ordinary people among the early competitors for the church lands, although they soon abandoned the field to the bourgeois. The second question is how often the change of landlords itself threatened the peasants with a much more enterprising supervision of their working of the land than before, or with a much more precarious tenure. The bourgeois had the reputation of being hard-driving landlords. Did that reputation frighten their prospective tenants?

Preparations for the sales in southern Anjou began in May or June of 1790. At that time, the districts began arranging expert evaluations of the properties to be sold, and began receiving preliminary bids (*soumissions*) from individuals and from municipalities. The preliminary bids probably give more information about the breadth of interest in the sales than the final purchases do. Sheer wealth, after all, often won out when the auctions began. The preliminary bids, unfortunately, have rarely been studied systematically. The range of persons making preliminary bids seems to have been much greater than the range of persons finally acquiring land (A.D.

M-et-L 12 Q 52–56). Although this was true throughout southern Anjou, preliminary bidding was, I believe, even more widespread in Val-Saumurois than in the Mauges. Among the bidders of Val-Saumurois, there were more artisans, more unskilled workers, more small peasants. In the Mauges, the priests were conspicuously absent, while in Val-Saumurois a number of them offered bids, mainly on properties they already controlled. So there are some signs of more general acceptance of the sales in the Val-Saumurois.[1] The larger peasants of all sections, on the other hand, put in bids. They were most often seeking to buy properties they were already leasing. Considering how rarely they succeeded in doing so once the sales began, this evidence of their aspirations is intriguing.

Despite the wide range of people who took part in the preliminary bidding, the merchants, notaries, lawyers, and other bourgeois were still most prominent among the bidders. They also helped persuade their municipalities to bid, in order to acquire properties for resale to individuals who might be squeamish about buying church properties directly. The letters of transmittal which accompanied the communal bids show what a public service and profession of patriotic faith the local leaders thought they were performing (see esp. A.D. M-et-L 12 Q 53). On the whole, communities with vigorously patriotic leaders (like Cholet, Montjean, Montreuil-Bellay, or Saumur) were much more likely than the rest to send in such blanket bids (A.N. Q 2 96). There were, in fact, many more communal bids from the District of Saumur than from the District of Cholet. It appears that in the differences in initial support for the church property sales there were some omens of the grave political divisions that were to appear in 1791.

By the end of April, 1791, the District of Vihiers had received almost a thousand bids on properties in its hands (Denecheau 1958: 25). The early sales had gone very well. Before April, the District had auctioned off 362 lots of property at an average of 65 percent above their estimated value; at Cholet, the mid-April score was somewhat lower, but still respectable: 116 lots at about 45 percent above posted value (Denecheau 1958: 29; A.D. M-et-L 12 Q 281). Around St.

---

[1] Qualifications: land was more fractionated in Val-Saumurois, more of it came from holdings of the higher clergy, cash was more readily available in its market-oriented communities, and there *were* more unskilled workers and small peasants in the subregion.

Florent, there were more sales of property recorded in 1791 than in the previous forty years put together (A.D. M-et-L XV C: Bureau de St. Florent). But the sales reached their peak early. By the middle of the year, they were fast diminishing. In the District of Cholet, where sales had averaged 386,000 livres per month from January to April and reached almost a million livres in May, they declined precipitously: June, 292,000 livres; July, 172,000 livres; August, 96,000 livres (A.D. M-et-L 12 Q 281). As the religious crisis rose, the purchases fell.

Some of the reasons for the apparent success of the sales of church properties come to light when we study the identities of the purchasers. At first, a number of peasants took part in the auctions, in the Mauges as well as in Val-Saumurois, and some succeeded in winning their prizes. In the District of Vihiers (and probably elsewhere) most of the farmers of large pieces of land who sought to buy the properties they were already leasing were outbid by others with more capital (Denecheau 1958: 42); surely this event soured many of them on the whole enterprise. A number of nobles (Colbert de Maulèvrier is a prominent example) took part in the purchases. But the increasingly dominant force in the sales of church property in southern Anjou was the bourgeoisie.

The only comprehensive study of the sales in Anjou available so far is Joseph Denecheau's analysis of developments in the District of Vihiers. His figures for all purchases up to the counterrevolution of 1793 include the following division of the total money value of properties auctioned, by percentages: nobles, 2.6; clergy, 4.3; professionals, 5.4; businessmen, 31.5; small merchants, 20; artisans, 11.4; cultivators, 18.6; winegrowers, 6.2. By this calculation, the bourgeois walked off with well over half the land. Of course, the District of Vihiers was about evenly divided between Mauges and Saumurois, so the percentages give no hint as to subregional differences. The rest of Denecheau's analysis does. In essence, he says that after the first burst of sales, and with the intensification of religious conflict, the representation of the Mauges at the auctions dwindled to a hardy remnant of Patriots. Almost all of them were bourgeois. On Saumur's side of the Layon, wider participation in the sales kept on. It seems reasonable to infer that in the Mauges the share of the bourgeois was substantially greater than the figures above show.

In the absence of systematic studies of the other districts, some brief glimpses of communities located in them may be helpful. In *Melay*, near Chemillé, there was not a great deal of property to sell; the monks and canons of Chemillé had a few farms and plots, and the curé of Melay a few more.[2] The appraisal of the properties dragged on late into 1790. There is no record of bids received until December, 1790. Soon after that, the sales began. The first purchaser was Tristan Briaudeau, a merchant of Chemillé, a prominent Patriot, and a diligent buyer of properties throughout the district. His first choice in Melay was one of the richest properties available, a farm renting from the church of Saint-Léonard-de-Chemillé for 400 livres, 8 capons, 186 bushels of rye, and threepence. Apparently no one was able to bid against M. Briaudeau, since the appraised value of the property was 16,100 livres, and that is the price he paid.

This first purchase marked the pattern of those that followed: important bourgeois from the manufacturing centers of the region bought with relatively little competition. No one from Melay bought any of the properties. Of the 9 lots sold in 1791, 4 went to residents of Chemillé, 2 to Vezins, 1 each to Cholet, Rochefort, and Paris. The first purchase is interesting in another respect. The buyer, M. Briaudeau, was one of the chief Patriots of the Mauges, a member of the departmental administration, as well as the principal figure in the textile industry of Saint-Pierre-de-Chemillé. The métayer who leased the farm which Briaudeau acquired, on the other hand, was Louis Clémot ("dit Jeremie"), who was to become one of the chief counterrevolutionary activists of the canton — and one of the tormentors of Melay's Constitutional curé. The curé was himself the son of the notary, Thubert, of Chemillé, a close ally of M. Briaudeau. To give one more twist to the kaleidoscope, it was Thubert and

---

[2] I have studied in detail the sales in seven communities of the District of Saumur (Ambillou, Antoigné, Courchamps, Distré, Grézillé, Vaudelenay, and Les Verchers) and eight in the districts of Cholet and St. Florent (Chemillé, Les Gardes, Le Marilais, Melay, Neuvy, Saint-Georges-du-Puy-de-la-Garde, Saint-Pierre-de-Chemillé, and Saint-Macaire-en-Mauges). The six cases discussed here illustrate the main characteristics of sales in those communities. I make no claim, however, that they amount to a representative sample. Sources for the descriptions: *Melay*, A.D. M-et-L 1 Q 47, 6 Q 1, 12 Q 14, 12 Q 54, 12 Q 281, 13 Q 114, 16 Q 86; *St. Macaire*, Déniau 1908; Spal 1887; A.D. M-et-L 1 Q 47, 6 Q 1, 12 Q 14, 12 Q 52, 12 Q 53, 12 Q 54, 12 Q 281, 16 Q 86; *Neuvy*, A.D. M-et-L 170 G 2, 9 Q 1, 12 Q 14, 12 Q 289, 16 Q 101; *Vaudelenay*, A.D. M-et-L 7 Q 5, 12 Q 55, 12 Q 56, 12 Q 282, 12 Q 283, 12 Q 284, 13 Q 148, 16 Q 125; *Distré*, A.D. M-et-L 12 Q 282, 12 Q 283, 12 Q 284; *Ambillou*, A.D. M-et-L 7 Q 1, 7 Q 6, 12 Q 55, 12 Q 56, 12 Q 282, 12 Q 283, 12 Q 284, 16 Q 107.

Briaudeau who kept sending copious reports concerning counterrevolutionary tendencies at Melay to the Department, and were instrumental in the investigation which sent Clémot to jail early in 1792. It is at least plausible that Clémot saw the change of landlords with no great pleasure, and let his displeasure reinforce whatever other reasons he may have had for opposing the agents of the Revolution. How many more cases were there of this kind?

St. Macaire, closer to Cholet, had more church property than Melay. The prior was the lord of the community, while the curé himself held two tiny "fiefs." Bellefontaine abbey and several other outside establishments owned farms and odd plots in St. Macaire. The total appraised value of church properties for sale was over twice that of Melay. St. Macaire was also a much more active manufacturing center than Melay, a fact reflected in the way the sales went there.

In St. Macaire not only was there apparently a good deal more local activity than in Melay, but also at least one peasant who bid for the property he was farming. Nevertheless, the bourgeois finally monopolized the land that was sold. The largest purchases were made by a merchant from Cholet, but those of St. Macaire did their share. In September, 1790, the bourgeois municipality had submitted a bid to buy most of the properties available as a block. When the sales began in March, 1791, a number of these municipal officers were among the buyers. In fact, the roster of local buyers of church properties in St. Macaire would serve as a list of its most important Patriots.

The experience of *Neuvy*, a peaceful town of fewer than a thousand souls in the District of St. Florent, was like that of Melay. The curé had only bits and pieces of land supplemented by a number of rents in kind ranging from rye to straw to faggots. A number of monasteries, priories, and chapters owned farms and smaller parcels; in fact, the eighteenth century saw many a squabble over various kinds of dues between Neuvy's curés and the representative of outside religious houses. These long contentions, however, do not seem to have left Neuvy's inhabitants eager to buy out the religious houses, for when these properties were put on the block, no one from the community bought. When the sales began in March, 1791, a Patriot from nearby La Pommeraye, Mathurin Gallard, started the action by buying a small farm for 4300 livres. (He was to return for another large purchase in November.) The next sale was the largest: a good-sized métairie went to a member of the substantial bourgeois Des-mazières family of Angers for 25,600 livres. These sales set the pattern: the rest of the buyers were mainly bourgeois from nearby cities and bourgs. There were no sales between November, 1791, and the counterrevolution.

Now we may shift to the District of Saumur. *Vaudelenay*, near the border of Poitou, was in the midst of the grain-growing plain. It contained a wide variety of ecclesiastical property, including farms and sizeable fields owned by the chapters of Montreuil-Bellay and Le Puy-Notre-Dame. The preliminary bidding there began, and quite vigorously, in September, 1790. The sales themselves started in March, 1791, with the purchase of all the land of the curé, for 19,000 livres, by a local notary, acting on behalf of a rentier from Argenton-l'Église. After that there was plenty of competition for the remaining properties, all of which were smaller, and most of which had belonged to monasteries, chapters, and priories. The purchasers came entirely from Vaudelenay (4 of 11) or the immediately adjoining communities. In addition to the bourgeois of Argenton and five buyers whose occupations remain unspecified, they included a government official, a notary, two bailiffs, a miller, and a laboureur.

The community of *Distré*, just to the south of Saumur, contained much richer ecclesiastical properties than Vaudelenay. The most impressive were two priories, each estimated to be worth more than 25,000 livres, and each selling for well over 50,000 livres. Most of the sales, however, were for under 1,000 livres. And even on these smaller sales, it was quite common for several buyers to combine their funds and efforts: there were 27 different buyers in 25 sales, even though Louis Archard (a cabinetmaker from Saumur) and Simon Mandin (a locksmith, also from Saumur) each took part in three or four of them. Of the 27, 6 or 7 were from Distré, and almost all the rest from within five kilometers of Distré. The minority whose occupations I have found include a merchant farmer, a carter, a laboureur, two coopers, two women, and a merchant potter, as well as the cabinetmaker and the locksmith. For the first time, we see a contingent of artisans. Whether the peasants were as few as this list makes it seem, however, is uncertain, because of the possibility that they are hiding among the many occupationally unlabeled buyers. In other respects, there was widespread and eager participation: the bidding was lively, and the auctioneers, who began their work at the end of January, 1791, had apparently gotten rid of everything by October.

Ambillou, finally, lies between Saumur and the Layon. It would not be outrageous to give the church properties there in 1791 a minimum value of 200,000 livres (compared with, e.g., 40,000 livres in Melay). Ecclesiastical revenues in the community were about 13,000 livres per year, and the curé was netting a comfortable 2,700 livres. Sixteen different ecclesiastical landlords were collecting rents in Ambillou, but the local chapter of La Grésille (whose control was the object of a running battle between the canons and the curé) had by far the largest share.

Ambillou was one of the rare communities of the District of Saumur where both the curé and the vicar refused to cooperate with the religious reforms of 1790–1791, and were replaced. This contretemps did not, however, spoil the sales. The preliminary bids, beginning in July, 1790, were thick and varied; among those proposing to buy the confiscated church lands were the former lord of Boisairault, the constitutional curé, a number of peasants, and some local bourgeois. Some of these men (including the lord and the curé) were successful in buying the properties they had originally bid for, but there were many new names among the final purchasers. Widespread participation and spirited competition marked the sales through most of the year 1791. The biggest buyers were local merchants, but the others included two priests, a notary, some artisans, and some small farmers. Eleven of the 24 purchasers were from Ambillou itself, and most of the rest were neighbors. In short, the sales at Ambillou were very much like the sales at Distré.

Detailed studies of the districts of Cholet, St. Florent, Angers, and Saumur will be more than welcome when they come. In the meantime, some provisional conclusions seem justified. Everywhere in southern Anjou the bourgeois were the principal beneficiaries of the sales of church property, but in the Mauges their predominance was overwhelming. The merchants, manufacturers, and professionals of the cities were especially active there. Some peasants took part in the early bidding and buying, but they soon withdrew from contention (or were maneuvered out). Over in the Saumurois, where a rich array of monastic property was available, more people, and a wider sample of the population, bid and bought parcels of various sizes. Of course, it is true that a number of eventual counterrevolutionaries like d'Elbée, Cesbron d'Argonne, Michelin, and Cady competed for the land available in 1791 (Port 1888: I, 108–111; Marion 1908: 90–92). Nevertheless, after the first flurry of participation, the acquisition of church properties came to be considered a mark of loyalty to the Revolution (cf. Chassin 1892: I, 149). "The Jacobins became buyers," said Jules Michelet, "and the buyers became Jacobins." Applied to the West, there is merit to the *mot*.

Applied to southern Anjou, Michelet's dictum implies that there were more Jacobins in Val-Saumurois than in the Mauges. True. I think the point may be made more broadly. To the extent that the major economic reforms of the early Revolution were in themselves sources of support for the new regime, they were calculated to be most effective in areas of widespread property ownership, commerce, bourgeois influence, and peasant independence. That is, their very nature destined them to attract more people to the Revolution in Val-Saumurois than in the Mauges. On the unlikely assumption of a peasantry with sufficient capital and the ability to dominate the auctions, one might argue that the sales of nationalized property *could* have changed things more in the Mauges, and *could* have helped produce peasants unwilling to strike out against the Revolution. But, as it actually worked out there, the effect of this reform was division, and the effects of the rest of the Revolutionary economic program . . . trivial.

Effects in the Two Complexes

Many historians have assumed that the way to explain the Vendée is to identify the attitude (or change of attitude) of the peasants toward the Revolution. And historians who have approached that task mainly with economic motives in mind have often concluded that the peasants "should have" supported the Revolution. Dubreuil ended his analysis with obvious disappointment:

The support that a government by consent needs is much more a matter of the hopes it arouses than of the benefits it gives. It is not rare for those whom it has most favored to turn against it when their interests are to consolidate their gains, rather to win new advantages. That is precisely what happened throughout the West of France, where, by the suppression of feudal dues, the peasants obtained all they wanted (1929–1930: I, 61).

Dubreuil was right to assert that it was not economic hardship that turned peasants against the Revolution. He was wrong to assume that the peasants of the counterrevolutionary West made significant economic gains through the reforms of the early Revolution. He neglected the probability that the short-run gains were significant mainly where peasant property and agricultural commerce already existed. He ignored, finally, the basic distinction between the peasants and the rest of the rural population.

The importance of this distinction makes it necessary to consider separately the states of the two complexes, agricultural and industrial, within the communities of southern Anjou. The survey of agriculture and industry to follow will move beyond the direct effects of Revolutionary reforms, and consider more generally the economic developments of 1789–1793.

Generally speaking, the grain growers of southern Anjou came through the first years of the Revolution without great pain, but the producers of wine began the Revolution in travail. Ernest Labrousse (1944) has shown the decline in wine trade at the end of the old regime. In Angers, the price of wine was, on the average, much lower from 1781 to 1789 than it had been in the previous decade — around two sous per *pinte* as compared with three sous in the earlier period (Hauser 1936: 283). On the other hand, prices were up near the old level again in 1788, and were not bad in 1789. In the years before the Revolution, grain prices rose much more than the price of wine. Peasants who sold wine but bought grain probably suffered most from these circumstances. The winegrowers of the Layon "saw the Estates General open without displeasure" (Wagret and Le Theule 1954: 178). Winegrowing areas in particular were hurt by the rising prices of staples because of their necessity of buying and their narrow dependence on the market. Like the textile centers, the wine centers, always overrun with day laborers, complained of high prices and unemployment (A.D. M-et-L 1 L 402). That much was chronic. The frigid winter of 1788–1789 had augmented the chronic complaints by killing a substantial part of the vines of Val-Saumurois (Port 1888: I, 17). The wine harvest for 1790 was so meager that the administration of Maine-et-Loire sought to collect the tithe, which they had inherited with the church properties, in cash (Gerbaux and Schmidt 1906: I, 36). At the end of the year, the officials of Varennes-sous-Montsoreau complained: "The area is not rich and hardly raises enough grain for its inhabitants. Its wealth, which used to consist of the production of wine, was partly destroyed by the winter of 1789 which, by freezing all the vines, deprived the landowners of their only resource" (A.N. D IV 40). Since the representatives of Val-Saumurois were still speaking of the catastrophe in 1791 (A.D. M-et-L 1 L 445), we may assume that it took the winegrowers some time to recover. No new crises, however, seem to have arisen after that first hard winter.

The grain harvest of 1788 was not good, but the following year there was grain in abundance (A.D. Indre-et-Loire C 99). 1790 was another good year: the curé of Neuvy called that year's crop "the best of a lifetime" (A.D. M-et-L 16 Q 101). Not until 1791 was there any trouble. Then, the districts of the Mauges reported that "mist" had half destroyed the staple, rye, although the other grains had survived the weather in better condition (A.D. M-et-L 1 L 455). Even this period of difficulty hardly deserves to be called a crisis. In sum, while the vintners had some reasons for grousing, the grain producers were undergoing nothing more than normal year-to-year fluctuations.

Considering the vivid reports of "famine" that have come down from the Revolution (e.g., Port 1888: I, 96–97), there is something mildly surprising about the conclusion that the grain supply was normal. Maybe grain production was normal *and* grain was in short supply. There are three related phenomena which help explain away the paradox: 1) the presence in the countryside of a large number of people too poor to buy much bread, but not too weak to demonstrate, 2) the frequent stopping of shipments of grain from farming areas by local residents, 3) the difficulties of cities in maintaining their supplies of grain in a time of uncertainty and fluctuating currency. The presence of the poor is such an important matter that I must reserve it for later discussion. The other two were very common occurrences in the France of the early Revolution.

Chassin (1892: I, 100–102) noticed the many incidents in which the rural population opposed the movement of grains out of their communities; he attributed the incidents, as many urbanites did in 1791 or 1792, to a counterrevolutionary plot. But in the Mauges, the clashes between villagers and carters, millers or farmers seeking to take grain out for sale, at Le May, Saint-Rémy-en-Mauges, or Melay, hardly seem to have been organized (A.D. M-et-L C 197, C 198, 1 L 204). Some were surely the products of heightened fears that the departure of grain would leave the folks at home without bread (Port 1888: I, 99).

The more shipments of grain were stopped, the more problems the cities had in feeding their own people. By 1791, any difficulties the cities had were compounded by the reluctance of rural grain growers to accept the new paper money, the *assignats;* from Beaupréau, for example, came the report that the métayers absolutely refused to take anything but hard money for their grain (A.D. M-et-L 1 L 364). Montreuil-Bellay, Saumur, Angers, all the cities of any size had difficulties maintaining the supply of grain. And most of them, at one time or another, had threatening demonstrations against "hoarders" and the high price of bread. Such demonstrations, as George Rudé (1959) has pointed out, were perfectly commonplace in eighteenth-century France. If Montreuil-Bellay was constantly nervous about hoarding, and the women of Saumur became violent over the price of grain (Charier 1913; Uzureau 1901), then, it hardly seems to mean much more than that these cities were sharing the unrest of most of France. Perhaps the grain stoppages on the one side and the grain riots on the other reflect intensified hostility between city and country. Neither one constitutes reliable evidence of crop failure, or even of difficulties in agricultural production.

Textile Troubles

It is in the industrial complex that we ought to look for extraordinary difficulties. Le Moy (1915: xvii) was clearly wrong to declare that "all the industries of Anjou were declining on the eve of 1789," and yet he may have spoken truly despite himself. For although the linen industry of the Mauges was reaching its peak just before the Revolution, it suffered a serious decline from 1789 to 1791. It is no news to historians of the region that the fabrique de Cholet went to ruin during the Revolution (see Gellusseau 1862: vol. II). All the more reason to be surprised that almost no one has recognized the turmoil in the industry before the foreign war of 1792 and the rebellion of 1793 are supposed to have ruined it, and that no one has spelled out the political significance of that turmoil.

The industry was booming in the fifteen years before the Revolution. The mayor of Cholet, in 1811, remembered the period 1775–1790 as "most important of all" for his city's manufacturing (A.D. M-et-L 67 M 5). The seneschal of Cholet referred to the "flourishing condition of our industry" in 1786 (A.D. Indre-et-Loire C 129). And 1787 may have been the best year the merchants of Cholet ever had. After 1787, however, things were not so bright. The statistical evidence available, I must admit, leaves something to be desired, partly because of the gaps in the reports, and partly because of the unknown quantity of production which escaped official attention. Perhaps its weaknesses are offset by the accumulating evidence that textile production elsewhere in the West went into crisis just before the Revolution (see Kaplow 1962: 131–146).

A table gives figures for the total value of goods inspected at the three bureaux de marque in the vicinity of Cholet from 1786 to 1790.

Table 21. Value of textile production, in livres, 1786–1790.

Year	Cholet	Vihiers	Maulèvrier
1786	2,812,631	87,222	50,868
1787	3,472,464	?	89,510
1788	3,412,415	149,880	98,808
1789	2,568,164	?	49,220
1790	1,226,500*	20,179*	39,390*

* Estimates based on the number of pieces.
Sources: A.D. M-et-L 1 L 546; A.D. Indre-et-Loire C 134–136; Dornic 1955.

The figures indicate a sharp contraction, but by no means a complete debacle, after 1788. Extrapolated for the entire year, the fragmentary figures for 1791 (the year the marque was abolished) suggest that production was at about the same level as in 1790. Considering the dependency of Cholet's textile production on foreign trade, it would be amazing if output turned out to be any higher during the war year of 1792. The statistical reports, then, indicate that the production of kerchiefs and cloth in the vicinity of Cholet was settling into a deep depression during the first four years of the Revolution.

The testimonies of those best qualified to know the state of the industry fortify this conclusion. In his year-end reports on the textile industry for 1786 and 1787, the Inspector General of the Generality of Tours, Huet de Vaudour, observed that Cholet's industry was gaining on the higher-priced products of Normandy and Béarn (A.D. Indre-et-Loire C 134). The report he filed early in 1789, however, contained a note of alarm:

The merchants of Cholet are complaining that their commerce is falling, and that they are losing their markets because of the ill effects of the commercial treaty with England. Their warehouses are full of textile merchandise, and they are unable to move them. Business is so bad that they do not dare to trust any merchant, whether from this kingdom or overseas. They have suffered bankruptcies and losses of more than 600,000 livres since last year, and as a result several of Cholet's houses have themselves failed and gone out of business. These unfortunate events have hurt the clothiers, who have also lost a great deal, and a number of them are crushed, ruined. The houses that failed used to put out a lot of work themselves, and so they supported and fed many workers and their families. Today, as a result, there are many poor souls without work and without resources (A.D. Indre-et-Loire C 135).

The Inspector General did not make it clear when the decline had started, but it could not have been much before the beginning of 1789. In any case, the decline became more serious as the pace of the Revolution itself quickened during 1789. Huet's report for the year as a whole stated:

This year production of all types of merchandise has considerably diminished, especially around last July, since when the decline has been more noticeable every week, both in regard to the amount produced and in regard to the difficulties the clothiers have in selling their goods, of which they now have an oversupply. The French, Spanish, and Anglo-American colonies are hardly buying from Cholet any more; within this kingdom, trade has been very moderate. People attribute the problem to the shortage of cash and the unhappy events of the times; since bread and every other necessity are very expensive, everyone is economizing (A.D. Indre-et-Loire C 134).

He went on to argue that the distribution of substandard goods under the Cholet trademark had played its part in the crisis. The essential point was made: the textile industry was in trouble.

The experts were not the only ones noticing the troubles. "All the artisans are out of work," reported Montfaucon in 1789 (A.D. M-et-L C 211). And at the beginning of 1790, the municipality of Trémentines was in fear and trembling at the danger their unemployed workers represented (A.D. M-et-L C 187). Later the same year, the supervisor of the office at Vihiers annotated his report for the "first semester of 1790" with the following remarks:

You can see by this account of the present state of the manufacturing and commerce of Vihiers how much they have fallen and continue to decline. This failure strikes the poorest class of people, the workers of the countryside, who are out of work and lack the resources to live and support their families (A.D. M-et-L 1 L 546).

A few days after, he followed up with a report on conversations with the municipal officers of Vihiers:

They observed that commerce was dead, that only ten to fifteen pieces of cloth per week, all for local consumption, were being produced. . . . Like me, they also expressed their sympathy for the poor, who are, so to speak, driven to begging by the sad state of our commerce (A.D. M-et-L 1 L 546).

There were three aspects to the situation, then: 1) a decline in commerce, 2) unemployment of textile workers, 3) mendicancy. It would be interesting to know how widely they were connected in southern Anjou.

For once, we are in luck. It was at the end of 1790 that the communal officers of Anjou had to prepare their statistical reports on the needy for the Comité de Mendicité of the National Assembly (A.D. M-et-L 1 L 402; see Bloch and Tuetey 1911). In the process, they were asked to comment on the reasons for mendicancy in their areas, and to give suggestions of means of reducing poverty. The replies from the District of Vihiers are, unhappily, missing from the archives. Among the other districts, Cholet reported 20.7 percent of its population as "needy," as against 18.4 percent for Angers, 15.8 percent for Saumur and 12.8 percent for St. Florent. On the whole, the textile-producing cantons cried poor more often than the rest: Chemillé claimed to have 33 percent of its population "needy," Cholet and St. Macaire 24 percent, Le May 23 percent. But the designation of "needy" is loose enough to permit a fair amount of padding. The descriptive responses may be more reliable than the statistics.

They reveal a sense of crisis in the linen country. The report from Chemillé said that "our sole profitable form of work was the manufacture of kerchiefs for Cholet, but that commerce fell off entirely two years ago, leaving more than two thousand workers out of work." And the municipal officers of Andrezé begged to observe that "Cholet's commerce of cloth and kerchiefs, which supported all the people of our bourgs, has fallen off; the greater part of them have been out of work for two years, and forced to beg in order to live, a fact which brings about many revolts in connection with the movement of grain." From Vezins: "The industry of this area, consisting of the manufacture of linen cloth, kerchiefs and *siamoises*, has fallen off through the competition of various other manufacturing centers and the small amount of sales in the colonies." In fact, every canton of the District of Cholet except Montfaucon and La Romagne (both of which complained of the "lack of commerce") explicitly described the decline in textile production. In the District of St. Florent, the cantons of St. Laurent, Beaupréau, and Montrevault did likewise, and all the other cantons significantly involved in weaving mentioned the "lack of commerce." Outside the two districts of the Mauges (always excepting the District of Vihiers, for which the information is not available), the only cantons complaining of faltering commerce as a source of poverty were Chalonnes (itself the supplier of flax to the textile industry) and Ponts-de-Cé. In other words, the correspondence between 1) reports of a commercial crisis and 2) the territory of rural manufacturing of linen was almost perfect.

The recognition that there was trouble in textiles brings some order out of the chaotic political agitation of 1790 and later. Port (1888: I, 96–98) saw the symptoms, but missed the malady. He properly reported that early in 1790 "at Trémentines, exasperation was at its height. A whole population of unemployed workers was wandering around the homes of the clothiers, merchants and well-off inhabitants, whose resources the crisis had exhausted." He noted the first steps taken to set up poor relief through work on the roads. But he attributed to the *peasants* the threat of an insurrection at Le May, under the motto, "No worse to die of gunshot than of hunger."

Port attributed all this malaise to the shortage of grain, darkly hinting at a plot either to carry off or to hoard the grain. In fact, almost every one of the ominous incidents of 1790 occurred in a center of weaving. As the inspector at Vihiers said of his own troubles with the weavers, "Often these poor fellows have no bread at home when they come to market, and the hard time they have selling their goods puts them in ill-humor and makes them reply angrily" (A.D. M-et-L 1 L 546).

The tension at Chemillé, whose municipality reported a third of the population "needy" in 1790, was acute. In August of that year, someone set up a gallows in the market place, a reminder to the municipal officers, accused of wanting to export grain (A.D. M-et-L 1 L 349). After their usual round of complaints against the country-men of the environs, those officers wrote, in January, 1791,

> It is not so much the enemies of the civic good we fear as a crowd of workers and weavers more than two hundred in number that we have supported as best we could with public works, and who are now about to lose their work and their bread. They are the cruelest enemies we have to fear because they may run wild and be driven to criminal excesses by the despair the lack of work occasions (A.D. M-et-L 1 L 349).

From that time on, the leaders of Chemillé were faced with rabid opposition among "the people." Furthermore, this opposition was regularly concerned with religious, as well as economic matters. Its leaders demanded the reopening of the churches of Notre Dame and St. Gilles; in October, 1791, they were said to be planning to force the doors of those churches. There were popular demonstra-tions, of a decidedly antirevolutionary tone, very likely involving the same people, during the cantonal elections of June, 1791. The city officials continued to write despairing letters, but also took more direct action by setting up cannon in the market place (A.D. M-et-L 1 L 349, 1 L 367; Mercerolle n.d.).

There is no easy way of knowing whether the workers who worried the municipal officers in Chemillé were the same ones who demon-strated against them in 1791. It seems highly likely. Elsewhere, there is no question at all that dissatisfied, unemployed workers joined and even led the hostility to the bourgeois administrators. In a small-scale uprising at Maulèvrier early in 1791, the unemployed workers who had been given jobs, à la WPA, on the local roads were the first to shout for the curé and against the bourgeois (A.D. M-et-L 1 L 357). Artisans and wives of artisans, who in any case were more likely to live in or near the bourg than were peasants, took regular part in the attacks on the prorevolutionary priests and their defenders. We shall see that the artisans of Cholet were among the first to demonstrate against conscription in 1793. From the beginning of the Revolution to 1793, this unrest and hostility formed a heavy threat to the bourgeois leaders of the cities and an even more immediate threat to their stalwart followers, the bourgeois of the commercial bourgs.

The textile crisis may help explain some of the concern over "beggars and brigands" in southern Anjou during the early Revolution. Even in more prosperous times, the complaints about "mendicants" had come in greatest volume from bourgs with many workers in the seasonal weaving industry: note the striking case of the twin towns of Villedieu-La Blouère, where all the many poor were reported to come from Villedieu, the commercial center (A.D. M-et-L C 191). At the same time, La Poitevinière declared that it had many poor folk *because* there were so many artisans dependent on Cholet's commerce (A.D. M-et-L C 191). And Roussay stated even more explicitly that its weavers were forced to beg in bad times (A.D. M-et-L C 192). These examples may be superfluous, since all the unhappy comments on the foundering of textile production already discussed were, precisely, answers to a question about the "causes of mendicancy."

That the industrial situation produced a large number of beggars is well established, but whether it produced the ill-identified roaming *brigands* commonly reported in southern Anjou is another question (A.N. F¹ᶜ III; A.D. M-et-L 1 L 566¹⁶; Duhamonay 1942: 101). It is likely that some of the "brigands" were smugglers left unemployed by the disappearance of the salt tax. But it is also likely that most of them were simply the unemployed, restless, wandering, in search of food, occasionally joining to stop a grain shipment or to demonstrate against the government.

The serious struggles of revolutionary and counterrevolutionary parties were at their most acute in Anjou in the territory of Cholet's textile industry. For conflict, the places to go in 1791 and 1792 were Cholet, Chemillé, Bégrolles, Gesté, Gonnord, Le May, Montfaucon,

Maulèvrier, Saint-Georges-du-Puy-de-la-Garde, La Tessoualle, Tilliers, Tourlandry, Trémentines: the bailiwicks of the weavers. St.
Florent, Champtoceaux, Montjean, and the other towns of the
Mauges outside the range of linen manufacturing were relatively
calm. The fact that the traditional accounts of the rebellion of 1793
begin with a riot in St. Florent in March, 1793, has confused our
understanding of the location of the counterrevolution. Even that
critical event involved a number of participants from outside the
city (the boys from Le Pin-en-Mauges said they had gone to "disarm
the district," A.D. M-et-L 1 L 1028). And most of the other initial
incidents of the counterrevolution took place much closer to Cholet.

In the Mauges, it is fairly clear, there was a connection between
the depression of Cholet's industry and the great unrest of 1790 and
later. That makes it all the more important to remark that the most
agitated sections of the departments of Vendée and Deux-Sèvres were
those involved in textile manufacturing. Dumouriez, surveying the
troubled areas of the West in August, 1791, noted in his journal that
"the very heart of fanaticism is at Châtillon and in the nearby parishes of the District of Montaigu" — that is, in exactly the sphere
of Cholet's influence (Chassin 1892: 27–28). The catalog of communes
in the fabrique de Cholet (A.D. M-et-L 1 L 546) is practically an
enumeration of the most worrisome localities of Vendée, Deux-Sèvres,
and Maine-et-Loire.

During the Year VII, long after the conflagration of 1793, but not
long before the final counterrevolutionary outbreak of 1799, the
deputy, Chapelain, of the Vendée recorded some penetrating comments on the political condition of his department. Among other
things, he remarked that:

The class of industrial workers is numerous in the formerly insurgent areas.
The fabriques are having a hard time recovering. . . . However if commerce
does not recover I fear that misery will empty some workshops and swell
the ranks of the brigands. These artisans are less interested in peace than the
farmers are; they have no grain in the ground, and no flocks to guarantee
their obedience to the law. While foodstuffs are priced low industrial workers
make a modest return, but if in winter grain becomes expensive because of
transportation difficulties, which can well happen, I fear that this class will
supply some recruits for the rebels (A.N.F[7] 3695[1]).

Dissatisfied weavers and areas where textile production was in difficulty, it appears, posed a serious political threat.

Political Consequences

I do not want to exaggerate the correspondence, or lull the reader into confidence that he now has the "cause" of the Vendée. In southern Anjou, several important centers of agitation — for example, Saint-Lambert-du-Lattay, Chanzeaux, Tigné, Saint-Sauveur-de-Landemont — appeared in 1791 in areas little affected by weaving. The coastal Vendée, around Challans, far outside the range of Cholet, was in the thick of counterrevolutionary activity very early. North of the Loire, in the Sarthe, there was, if anything, an *inverse* correlation between the presence of weavers and the extent of Chouannerie (Bois 1960b: 545–570). Furthermore, the centers of weaving were also important outposts of the Revolution; the paradox is only apparent, since (as I shall take great pains to show later on) the characteristic condition of the counterrevolutionary sections was not unanimous opposition to the Revolution, but bitter division between its vigorous supporters and their equally vigorous enemies. The new formula, "The weavers were hungry, *ergo* the Vendée revolted" would be no more useful than the old formula "The peasants were religious, *ergo* the Vendée rose." Neither one tells us how vague and various discontents were focused into extraordinarily drastic political acts.

My alert readers have no doubt noticed a possible inconsistency between these observations and the fact that industrial artisans played an important part in the Patriotic military organizations of the Revolution. The fact is that there were significant numbers of weavers among the Patriots, and significant numbers among their opponents. Therefore no simple interest theory will explain their political behavior. Two things seem to have happened. First, the weavers, always vulnerable and now in a precarious sort of idleness, were drawn into politics more than almost any other group in the population. They became activists. Second, they responded to the dominant local party. In the cities, many artisans were hostile to their bourgeois patrons, but many also followed their lead into active Patriotism. For them, military service may have had the additional benefit of respite from idleness, tedium, and economic hardship. In the country, where Patriotic activism entailed many risks and great isolation, the weavers tended to the opposition. It could also be that the textile crisis hurt the workers scattered through the countryside more than their better-organized brothers in the cities and large bourgs; but this is no more than a plausible hunch. In any case, the rural artisans added a venomous enmity for the bourgeois themselves to the political forces loose in the countryside. Their economic difficulties, that is, encouraged the artisans into political activism, but did not determine the side they took. If so, we may say that the textile crisis helped raise the level of conflict and agitation in the Mauges higher than everywhere else in the West, but it did not in itself create the counterrevolution.

One of the concomitants of the economic developments of the early Revolution was the emergence of several varieties of class conflict, and their channeling into political conflict. Neither rigid definitions of "class conflict" nor false assumptions of perfect unanimity are in order. What I mean to say is that conflicts of interest between groups significantly different from each other in terms of wealth and/or productive position appeared and became politically significant. The substance of the conflicts themselves was by no means necessarily economic.

In Val-Saumurois, where money and market position were important common denominators, a general division into rich and poor was not uncommon. We have already seen a few signs of such divisions in the organization of the National Guard at Saumur and Montreuil-Bellay, and in the disputes the redistribution of taxes occasioned in 1790. The wedge of the Loire valley between the Layon, Chalonnes, and Ponts-de-Cé is of particular interest, since it was one of the few sections of Val-Saumurois where a concerted antirevolutionary movement had a chance to develop. In contrast with the Mauges, Mozé, Rochefort, St. Aubin-de-Luigné, Vauchrétien, Chaudefonds, and the other four or five communities of that wedge were devoted to winegrowing and truck farming. They were very much in the market. Agricultural commerce meant a measure of prosperity for some residents but, as the city fathers of Saint-Aubin-de-Luigné remarked, "the great quantity of vines . . . attracts many poor people" (A.D. M-et-L 1 L 402). Even before the Revolution, the report from St. Aubin was that the richest citizens had "seized" the communal assembly (A.D. M-et-L C 192). And in both St. Aubin and Mozé, the political rivalry of a "radical" National Guard unit with a "moderate" municipality probably embodied the same division of rich and poor.

In a number of these communities, a minority of wealthy citizens was aligned against a majority, including the curé. A good example is Vauchrétien, a community sundered by the elections of 1790. The municipal officers prefaced their detailed account of the elections there with an indictment against a handful of the community's richest residents:

> The citizens we are referring to you today have always troubled our assemblies, always sought to contradict without reason, for the pleasure of contradicting; their wealth puffs them up and because the fortunes of many of the rest of us are mediocre, they despise us and at every moment repeat that we are nothing but trash; but our spirits are not cowed; we will not give in (A.D. M-et-L 1 L 349).

In particular, this small faction objected to the curé's designation as president of the electoral assembly; " 'We won't have him,' replied Toussaint François Serisier, in a rage, 'He's run this parish long enough!' " The municipal officers reported that they had admonished the *perturbateurs* by saying: "You've always troubled our assemblies, because you are the richest men of the parish, you want to run it, you won't ever be its masters; you'd do better to keep quiet." The minutes of the next meeting contained the following edifying dialogue between the curé and his parishioners:

> "Messieurs, this is the thirty-ninth year that I have had the honor to be at the head of this parish. Have I not always worked for its general welfare?"

> Everyone replied affirmatively.

> "Messieurs, do you know of my seeking to oppress any individuals?"

> Everyone replied negatively (A.D. M-et-L 1 L 349).

In Vauchrétien and in many of the other communities of this section, three elements came together: mutual distrust of rich and poor, alignment for and against the curé, a struggle for political control.

The coalescence of these elements was something the communities around Vauchrétien shared with the Mauges and the rest of the bocage. The peculiarity of the bocage was the frequency with which the division separated the bourgeois, narrowly defined — merchants, manufacturers, officials — from the rest of the community, rather than fracturing the community along the more general line between rich and poor. This was true in the depressed communities of the textile industry. Yet antibourgeois agitation was most explicit, not in the Mauges, but in the vicinity of Challans, in Vendée. There, the ill-organized insurgents of March and April, 1791, often entered the churches to drag out, smash, and burn the pews of the bourgeois, and openly said they intended to do as much to the owners of the pews. Jacques Rocquand of Saint-Christophe-du-Ligneron declared that "if they mistreated the bourgeois, it was because [the bourgeois] wanted to change religion" (Chassin 1892: I, 276). In reply to the suggestion of his interrogators that religion was no more than a pretext for an attack on the bourgeois, François Cautin, one of the ringleaders at Apremont, declared that "they intended to fight the *ci-devant* bourgeois because someone had told them that [the bourgeois] had fired on the peasants" (A.N. D xxix 14). Once again, the dispute over matters religious was inseparable from the political division or the conflict of class.

That leads to the general point. Economic development set many of the preconditions for the political orientations of the communities of southern Anjou, economic changes during the Revolution contributed new kinds of agitation and rivalry, economic divisions in the population took on political significance. But no model of *homo economicus* I am aware of can in itself account for the development of the counterrevolution of 1793. After all, economic dissatisfaction is well-nigh universal, poverty ubiquitous, class conflict common, but revolutions rare and counterrevolutions even more so. The questions remain: how did discontent become focused? How did economic and religious issues blend? How did they become matters of political concern? We might speculate on the meaning of the letter of the Procurator of Deux-Sèvres to the Minister of the Interior in September, 1791: "I urge you, Monsieur, to support the request we have made to the Minister of War to send us a cavalry regiment which could move as needed to our various districts and those of the department of the Vendée where fanaticism and the shortage of grain give us reason to fear insurrections that only force will hold back" (A.N. F⁷ 3690¹). Fanaticism and the shortage of grain! We already have an idea how to interpret that ambiguous "shortage of grain," but there is more to learn about "fanaticism" and about the link between the two terms. A full-scale inquiry into the religious changes of the Revolution is called for.

CHAPTER 11

Religion in Revolution

"Was the Vendean insurrection produced by plots and reactionary agitation against the established regime, or was it not the result of repeated vexations and increasingly tyrannical persecutions against the religious freedom of an entire people who, after trying by every legal means to obtain justice, finally grew tired of seeing its just demands trampled, and believed that the way to obtain justice from its executioners was to seize it by armed force?" That was the question of the Dom Chamard (1898: 7). I hope there is no reader who wonders what choice the good Dom made between the alternatives he posed. He was only one of the thousands of interpreters of the Vendée — right down to Sunday preachers of the present day — who have made of the great counterrevolution the defense of wronged religion by an outraged, upright people. The explanation is too simple. But so is the debunker's claim that religious belief had nothing to do with it. The fact is that religious belief, organization, and affiliation all became consuming concerns of political life in southern Anjou during the early Revolution. Disagreements over religious issues contributed heavily to both the formation and the conflict of the major parties. To the extent that the rebellion of 1793 can be said to have had articulated aims and ideology, they were cast primarily in religious terms. Can this be very surprising, considering that peasants everywhere have so rarely been familiar with any systematic view of the world, or any rhetoric, that was *not* religious? The most important task of the present chapter is to show how response to the religious reforms of the Revolution helped define the positions of the parties of revolutionaries and counterrevolutionaries — Patriots and Aristocrats — and committed an ever larger portion of the population to one party or the other.[1]

[1] Much of the material in this chapter is drawn from Tilly 1958: ch. 7, and Tilly 1959.

Ecclesiastical Politics and Political Ecclesiastics

Among the clergy, clear and irrevocable options for or against the Revolution took a long time to develop. While it is wrong to think of an abstract Public Opinion in southern Anjou as evolving from naïve enthusiasm for reform to massive enmity for the reformers, it is right to conceive of a substantial block of the lower clergy as veering from willing cooperation with the new regime to opinionated opposition to all its works and workers. From the beginning, priests played a significant political role.

There were many priests in southern Anjou, on both sides of the Layon, who saw the Revolution as a chance to right some wrongs of long standing, and even more who felt that some changes in the way France was governed would be timely. A number of curés and vicars (although theoretically barred from mixing in the affairs of the Third Estate) drafted their communities' Statements of Grievances in 1789. Some were articulate preachers of patriotism during the first year of the Revolution (see Port 1888: I, 102–107). The deputies of the clergy, Rabin, curé of Cholet, and Mesnard, curé of Martigné-Briand, were among the early migrants from the Assembly of the Clergy to the National Assembly. Numerous other priests became communal administrators, mayors, and even members of the departmental hierarchy. In short, the evidence available indicates no uniform or organized clerical resistance to the Revolution during its first year.[2]

In southern Anjou, the most "advanced" party of the clergy was formed by the monks. At Fontevrault, at Saumur, at the other

[2] For an intriguing historiographical question, the reader might consider how to sort out the evidence of a shift in sentiment among the clergy. He must somehow allow for the massive changes both in the system and in the personnel of provincial and local government in the second half of 1790, at precisely the time when the retreat of the clergy from the Revolution is supposed to have occurred. These changes meant that 1) a much more revolutionary administration than the Interim Commission, and one surely more sensitive to any suspicion of infidelity on the part of the clergy, stepped in; 2) a much more comprehensive and efficient governmental organization established sturdy lines of communication and representation from the newly elected communal officers right up to the National Assembly; it often meant the end of the curé's role as the principal reporter of local politics, and may have made it more difficult for those curés who were really not well disposed toward reform to substitute flowery phrases for revolutionary action; 3) the sheer volume of political reporting (as represented by the documents which survived to find a final resting place in the archives) swelled immensely; the contrast between series C (old regime) and series L (revolutionary regime) in the departmental archives shows this clearly. Any of these could help create an illusion of drastic change after the middle of 1790. Are the documents playing a joke on historians?

monastic centers, there were bursts of revolutionary enthusiasm. Later, many of the monks renounced their callings, married, joined the Republican administrations, and many others joined the Constitutional clergy, only to drift finally into civil life like their fellows. The position of the rest of the higher clergy, canons and other officials, was not so uniformly in the vanguard. On the whole, the canons were very likely the category most resistant to the Revolution (although even for this group I do not know how early outspoken opposition began; see Dubreuil 1929–1930: I, 66–67). The bishops of the West all eventually opted for emigration and against the Revolution. But in mid-1790, the Bishop of Angers, Couet du Viviers de Lorry, was ordering a *Te Deum* for the election of departmental administrators and enjoining parents to teach their children to honor God, Brother, and Nation (Couet 1790). In fact, the Bishop of Angers never did raise his voice very loudly against the ecclesiastical reforms, even if he rejected them personally.

While all parts of the clergy cooperated with the first steps of the Revolution, they were by no means all in agreement or harmony. The resentment of many years flamed in the 1789 assembly of the clergy in Anjou, pitting the parish priests against the rest. However, the curés of the Saumurois, rather than those of the Mauges, were the "radicals" of the province (see McManners 1960; Gallard 1960). The memoir of the abbé Chatisel of Soulaines complained that "the men who used to regard [the curés] as their fathers in the faith, who honored them as pastors, have risen against them; the regulars and the canons have conspired against the curés" (Proust n.d.: A, I, 24). That much was purest rhetoric; but the point became evident when the spokesman launched his bill of particulars against the comfortable monks, canons, and priors who were taking the tithe from the parish, while giving the local priest less than due honors and much less than a suitable wage. The parish priests hoped that the Estates General would settle some of these accounts. They underlined their message by electing the author of their memoir to the Estates, and by not electing any of the higher clergy. This was the clergy of the sénéchaussée of Anjou, who finally adopted a moderate Statement of Grievances. The assembly of the sénéchaussée of Saumur, which also avoided electing a member of the higher clergy, sent a vigorously reformist Statement of Grievances to Paris (Desmé de

Chavigny 1892: 9–10; Chassin 1882: 244–245; Gallard 1960: 122–124).

From the Estates General on, religious questions increasingly became political questions as well. One of the things that was revolutionary about the Revolution was that it made religious organization a matter of public policy. I am not thinking so much of the seizure of church property: while a drastic move, it was not much more revolutionary than Henry VIII's dispossession of English monasteries two and a half centuries earlier. Nor was the adoption of antithetical positions on religious questions by contending political factions entirely new, as the Wars of Religion amply illustrate. The novel idea of the Constituent Assembly was that the internal organization and practice of the Church, from top to bottom, ought to be legislated to conform to the new political regime. And the consequence of the new idea was that civil authorities had to oversee the reform of the Church at all levels. Result: religious reform became a fundamental political issue.

The first drastic step the Assembly took to define the place of the Church in the new regime was to seize its properties (Nov., 1789). The sale of these properties, beginning a year or so later, marked the beginning of two related developments: 1) the *public* alienation of a substantial part of the clergy of southern Anjou from the Revolution, 2) the clear definition of prorevolutionary and antirevolutionary parties in southern Anjou.

We have already seen that the sales of church properties were a commercial success throughout southern Anjou. We have also seen that they meant a greater transfer of property, and benefits spread more widely through the population, in Val-Saumurois than in the Mauges, where a smaller amount of property was practically monopolized. Finally, we have seen some [not entirely conclusive] evidence that the sales in the Mauges were the occasion of resentment on the part of some of the peasantry toward the bourgeois doing the buying. So the bourgeois were condemned for taking part in what they saw as an excellent means of serving the nation and themselves at the same time.

The fact that they considered their purchases a patriotic duty, and the fact that they benefited particularly from the sales hardly distinguishes the merchants of Cholet or Chemillé from the bourgeois of the rest of France. But they benefited more exclusively than elsewhere, more so than in Val-Saumurois. Furthermore, they did so in the face of growing opposition, in which the parish priests played an important part.

Even the appearance of religious resistance to the sales was not peculiar to the Mauges, since some spokesmen of the clergy everywhere were denouncing them as illegal and immoral (Lefebvre 1954: 230; Sagnac 1898: 168). The peculiarity was the vigor, unanimity, and effectiveness of the campaign. It is crucial to recognize that open clerical condemnation of the sales did not begin until *after* the initial application of the other religious reforms.

The Clergy's Choice

January, 1791, was a fateful month, for then the sales of church properties began through much of the Mauges, and the Civil Constitution of the Clergy was promulgated there as well. At the same time, parish priests began openly to preach opposition to the Revolutionary government's policies. An official of the District of St. Florent wrote on 29 January that "people are afraid that the oath for the clergy is going to cause trouble [with the sales of church property]; the country folk seem to be shaken by their curés" (A.D. M-et-L 2 Q 63). Around Maulèvrier, a few months later, several correspondents reported a "coalition" among the countrymen to oppose the sales, to resist the ousting of the priests who would not comply with the new laws, and to support the nobles (A.D. M-et-L 1 L 357).

The clergy of the Mauges rapidly became unanimous in their denunciation of purchasers of church properties. The *Journal des amis de la constitution* reported that the country priests had pronounced the buyers anathema. So long as people continued to come to them for confession, the curés held a weapon. The roving commissioners sent out by the department of Maine-et-Loire in mid-1791 reported that the commune of Chanteloup was disorganized, the municipality lacking necessary members, and that "difficulties in filling the offices resulted from the secret instructions given by the Refractory priests, threatening the buyers of the nationalized properties and the supporters of the Constitution with excommunication and refusal of absolution" (A.D. M-et-L 1 L 357 bis). The same report came from many another section of the Mauges. And as early as the middle of

February, the Directory of Maine-et-Loire, with characteristic bombast, described the situation in its territory:

Expiring fanaticism is broadcasting its screams. It was to be expected: property is rapidly leaving the hands of the old clergy; it no longer has its weapons. We hear nothing on every side but anathemas against those who sell and those who buy the properties; and Religion, if one believes the ecclesiastical party, will disappear with them. It is especially in the country that these scandalous prognostications find credence, and agitate ignorant, superstitious minds. They shout about impiety, about sacrilege: the law which calls for the oath of ecclesiastical officials, and their replacement if they do not take the oath, is incessantly presented to the people (especially from before the altar) as an abominable violation of the holy place, and it is not their fault if an avenging fire does not come out of the sanctuary to consume all the victims they, in their rage, have consigned to perdition (A.N. D xxix bis 21).

By this time, it is clear, the sale of church properties had become a burning political issue. By this time, it was correct to speak of an "ecclesiastical party" opposed to the supporters of the Revolution. By this time, the identification of Patriots, enforcers of religious changes, and purchasers of church properties in the Mauges was already established.

At the beginning of the uprising of 1793, the resistance to conscription in the Mauges, as elsewhere, often took the form of demands that the holders of church property be the first to serve their country. Unquestionably the ideas of Patriot, bourgeois, opponent of religion, and profiteer of the Revolution came to form a bitter amalgam. No doubt the exclusiveness with which the bourgeois and Patriots of city and countryside benefited from the sales (as opposed to the wider participation of all classes in Val-Saumurois) solidified the opposition to them. In this respect, the observations of Paul Bois on the disposition of ecclesiastical property in the Sarthe are a great contribution to our understanding of the counterrevolution. It is important to remark, however, that a substantial number of the buyers of 1791 and 1792 were not *outsiders*, but precisely the local merchants, notaries, and officials who had such a responsibility for translating the general reforms of the Revolution into changes in their rural communities. Otherwise, it would be hard to understand the frequency with which these rural Patriots were the ones called to account in 1793. Furthermore, from the beginning the condemnation of sales and sellers appeared as part of a more general denunciation of the religious reforms. As an overt public issue, the Civil Constitution of the Clergy was far more important.

The Civil Constitution

While the machinery for the sales of church property was rumbling into motion, its designers in Paris were assembling a new system for the operation of religion throughout France: the Civil Constitution of the Clergy. During the first year of the Revolution, a number of moves of the new lawmakers had shaken the old position of the Church: abolition of the tithe, curtailment of other fiscal privileges, the guarantee of religious freedom by the Declaration of the Rights of Man, the abolition of religious orders, and the confiscation of church lands. The clergy had already been reminded of their position in the new order by the requirement that they promulgate new laws at their Sunday Masses. But the first comprehensive attempt to define that position was the series of laws enacted in the spring and summer of 1790, the Civil Constitution (see de la Gorce 1909–1911: vol. I; Mathiez 1910; Latreille 1946–1950: vol. I).

The most important features of the laws were: 1) reorganization of the territorial divisions of the French church to correspond to the new civil divisions, 2) election of bishops and curés by the registered voters of the areas they were to serve, 3) fixed clerical salaries paid by the government, 4) great changes in the organization of church assemblies. The Constitution washed away the temporal power of the Pope in France, while cutting down the independence of the French ecclesiastical hierarchy. In effect, it made the Church a state agency, and the priests elected civil servants.

These sweeping changes in the national religious scene had their counterparts in the parish. The elections did not threaten the tenure of present curés; they would occur only as vacancies appeared. Nevertheless, they did put future appointments in the hands of the active citizens of the district. The new arrangements charged the local elected officials with the oversight of religious affairs. They reduced the curé, as the abbé Sicard (1927: II, 3) noted with disgust, to the position of a "mere wage earner."

The initiation of fixed salaries for parish priests took direct and immediate effect at the beginning of 1791. First of all, the salaries were generally below the accustomed net incomes of the curés of southern Anjou. Although they rid themselves of the necessity of overseeing lands and collecting rents, the curés of small parishes also lost half of the excess of their previous net incomes over 1,200 livres. This reduced Galpin of Melay from 2,500 to 1,850 livres, and Delacroix of St. Macaire from 3,400 to 2,300 (A.D. M-et-L 16 Q 86). Does this mean that simple self-interest turned the curés from the Revolution? If so, self-interest must have worked harder in the Mauges than in Val-Saumurois, for there were no great differences between the subregions in the amount of income change. Table 22

Table 22. Number of curés affected by income changes under the Civil Constitution.

District	Loss of 100 livres or more	Change of less than 100 livres	Gain of 100 livres or more	Total
Cholet	23	6	11	40
St. Florent	17	8	11	36
Vihiers	25	5	10	40
Saumur	24	5	16	45
Total	89	24	48	161

(compiled from A.D. M-et-L 16 Q 80–156) makes the point. A slightly larger proportion of the curés of the District of Saumur stood to gain by accepting the new regime, but this marginal difference is trivial compared with the massive differences in actual response.

These calculations probably underestimate somewhat the real advantages of the stated salaries, since the officials who reviewed the income declarations could not make allowances for payments to the vicar above the statutory minimum, or for the curé's private charity.

The latter may be a matter of some importance. The Civil Constitution took the responsibility for charitable works from the curé and gave it to the civil administration. The poor may have seen the responsibility for their welfare shifting to a much harder-nosed group than before, and the less poor may have seen that a municipality operating on a stringent budget would have a more difficult time providing for the indigent than the old curé had. In a time of widespread unemployment among textile artisans, this would be a serious matter. The report that Saint-Macaire-en-Mauges, an important outpost of Cholet's industry, sent to the Interim Commission just before the Revolution outlined (with some exaggeration) the nature of the problem in prosperous times: "The bourg contains about forty households forced to beg, and there are three other villages containing about 30 more households who beg . . . the aid that these families receive from M. le Curé and others being insufficient to keep them from begging" (A.D. M-et-L C 191). Considering the unrest that developed in St. Macaire in 1790 and 1791, it would not be surprising to learn that the decline of the textile industry had turned this white lie about the number of people on the dole into an honest truth.

In any case, the protests made against the new religious arrangements commonly stressed their deleterious effects on the poor. "What will become of the poor of our parishes," asked the citizens of La Plaine, "if somebody removes those who have so long nurtured them? We mean by that our curés" (A.N. D xxix bis 21). In replying to the 1790 questionnaire on causes and remedies of mendicancy — the context is significant — the spokesmen of the cantons of Saint-Laurent-de-la-Plaine and La Pommeraye proposed that the curés be allowed to keep their properties as means of "easing the plight of the poor" (A.D. M-et-L 1 L 402). The threatened loss of one of the bases of local charity may have been one more factor in the opposition to church property sales, as well as in the resistance to the Civil Constitution. Such a hypothesis would make some sense out of the themes that came up during the angry visit of the men of Saint-Aubin-de-Baubigné (both an active center of linen weaving and the seat of the famous counterrevolutionary Larochejacquelein family) to the District of Châtillon in January, 1791.

"Si tu ne payes pas notre curé, f. gueux," [they asked, in French too pungent to translate] et si tu ôtes tout á notre seigneur, de quoi nous fera-t-on travailler, et de quoi vivrons-nous? [After a futile attempt of the officials to reassure them, according to the report of those officials] ils continuerent, dirent que leur curé ne prêteroit pas le serment et qu'ils n'auroient plus de prêtre pour les confesser. Alors la rumeur s'augmenta; on parla de couper les administrateurs en deux et de leur arracher les *tripes pour les environner* autour de leurs bâtons, et l'on crioit: "qu'on ne s'attende pas à vendre les biens des curés" (A.N. F7 3690[1]).

Consider the issues that were balled together: the loss of the curé, the impoverishment of the lord, the end of charity, the sale of church properties.

Most of these changes, real or threatened, were just as imminent in many other parts of France as in the Mauges. The character of the local community in the Mauges made them particularly ominous there. The priest had dominated the *parish* and had held the strategic position in the internal operation of the *commune* as well. The new regime attacked his position in each. It limited his religious power by putting his salary in the hands of government officials with the power to discipline him for prolonged absence or other failings, by taking away his control over welfare activities and charities, by the very act of making him a governmental functionary. It curtailed his political power by forbidding him to be mayor, municipal, or district officer, by transferring most of his administrative functions to the newly formed, increasingly bourgeois municipality, by effectively undermining the vestry, by centralizing and strengthening the new administrative system. It even attacked his economic power by wiping out the rents, tithes, and offerings he had formerly collected. In all regards, that great independence of both civil and ecclesiastical hierarchy which had been such a support to his power in the local community was threatened by the Revolutionary changes. His losses were the gains of his most ambitious rivals, the most anticlerical part of the population, the bourgeoisie. The Civil Constitution of the Clergy, in short, was a direct threat to the power of the parish priest; it was the greatest threat where that power was the greatest.

One legislative move in particular made it possible for resistance to the Civil Constitution to crystallize: the oath prescribed for the salaried clergy. The civic oath was standard practice for all public servants in the new France of 1790. It is not surprising that it was made part of the installation of the newly elected religious officials. But the lawmakers, growing impatient and fearful with the lack of enthusiasm (and worse) that greeted the Civil Constitution, decided that all bishops, curés, and vicars then in office would have to take the oath or lose their posts (see Godechot 1951: 228). They asked for a showdown, and got a schism.

The oath in question was quite simple: "I swear to be faithful to the nation, the law and the king, and support with all my power the constitution decreed by the national assembly and accepted by the king." The wording hardly seems menacing. The sentiment is far from feverish. But the oath required the clergy to put themselves on public record in support of the Revolutionary government, its reforms, and above all, the Civil Constitution itself. In southern Anjou it signified alignment with the Patriots and continued enthusiasm for their goals. The curé was asked, simultaneously and publicly, to ratify the reforms which were undermining his position in the community and to acknowledge the new-found eminence of his rivals.

The Civil Constitution was officially promulgated in Maine-et-Loire early in January, 1791. It had already been attacked by most of France's bishops, and was denounced roundly again by most of those of the West. By the time the papal bull of 13 April arrived, labeling the Civil Constitution "heretical and schismatic," the opposition was long established.

The announcement of the new laws brought commotion to the bocage. On 24 January, sixty men from St. Aubin-de-Baubigné invaded the offices of the District of Châtillon-sur-Sèvre to protest the impending loss of their curé (A.N. F[7] 3690[1]). At Maulèvrier, later in the month, three days of disorders began with the declaration by the crowd that they would not let the city officials ask the curé to take the oath (A.D. M-et-L 1 L 357). In Le May, the combination of raucous demonstrations and direct threats convinced several of the local officials that it would be prudent to resign at once (A.D. M-et-L 1 L 364). The letter from La Plaine already cited, signed on 6 February "at the end of the High Mass," gives an idea of the way the countrymen understood the situation:

The municipal officers of the parish of La Plaine and all the other inhabitants of the parish have the honor to tell you that having learned that there was a decree requiring all curés and vicars of France to take an oath, under pain of losing their salary and being driven out of their cures to be replaced by others, not only our parish but all the neighboring ones have decided never to recognize any other curé or vicar but those who are now in our parishes or their legitimate successors, and that as for anyone who comes to us from elsewhere (who would doubtless have taken the oath) we will not allow him in our parishes (A.N. D xxix bis 21).

The issue is nicely simplified. There it is: The law condemns them to lose their curé and vicar and to receive an interloper. I cannot help suspecting that the villagers had just heard a sermon on the subject.

In many places, the new law could never be officially announced, since the old curé refused to read it to his congregation as he was

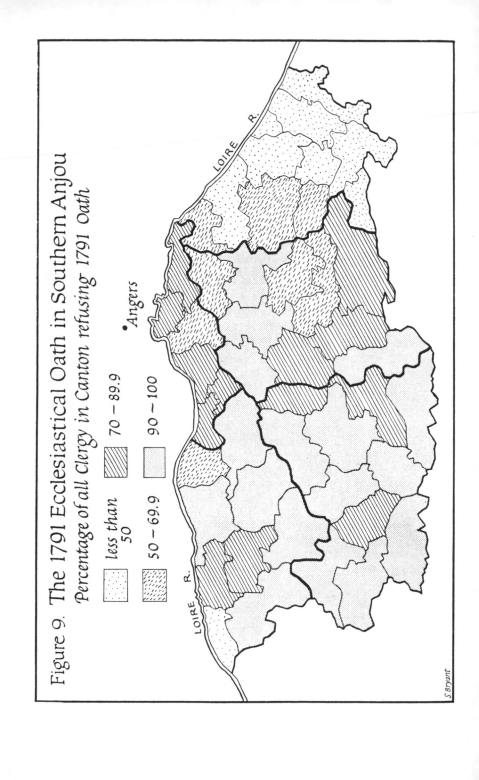

Figure 9. The 1791 Ecclesiastical Oath in Southern Anjou
Percentage of all Clergy in Canton refusing 1791 Oath

less than 50

70 – 89.9

50 – 69.9

90 – 100

LOIRE R.

LOIRE R.

• Angers

S. Bryant

supposed to, and demonstrators made it impossible for the Patriots of the commune to read it in public (see Walter 1953: 7 ff.). This, however, was nothing but a formality, since the contents of the law were widely known long before the official copies arrived.

Throughout southern Anjou, the priests had reached their decisions and had made them known by the end of January, 1791. From the beginning the Revolutionary administrations strove to convince the uncertain and staged ceremonious public initiations for those who came into the fold. All parties in the Mauges recognized that the oath aligned the priest with the Revolutionary party. So did the leaders of that party most of all (see Gruget 1902). It was the leaders of Val-Saumurois who were satisfied, then, and those of the Mauges who were disappointed, for the one place saw widespread acceptance of the oath, and other massive refusal.

The dimensions of acceptance and refusal of the oath in southern Anjou are clear from a study of the map by cantons.[3] It is drawn to emphasize the location of *refusals* to take the oath. They were few in the District of Saumur, more common in the Districts of Angers and Vihiers, and the overwhelming rule in most of the cantons of the Mauges. Even a crude definition of the subregional border, using the Layon as the dividing line, yields differences of this order: in the Mauges, 8 percent of the clergy took the oath; in the Layon area, 35 percent; in Val and Saumurois, 53 percent.

The differences appeared in each category, as the table of percentages taking the oath indicates. The statistics reflect not only the regional variations, but also the greater acceptance of the Revolutionary reforms by the monks, and the concerted opposition of the canons, so often noted in other contexts (Dubreuil 1929–1930: I, 65–66). If the line were redrawn to separate communities that joined the rebellion of 1793 from those that did not, the contrast would be even

---

[3] These figures describe first reactions to the requirement of the oath, with two qualifications: 1) Clergymen who retracted the oath within a day or two of taking it are scored as refusing it. 2) Those who initially took no position, but formally accepted or rejected the oath at some time in 1791, are classified in terms of that later decision. Sources: A.D. M-et-L, series L and Q; Queruau-Lamerie 1899; Gruget 1902; Uzureau 1915; Uzureau 1923; Uzureau 1925. See Tilly 1959: 183. Gallard's estimates for the District of Saumur as a whole at the end of May, 1791 (1960: 148) show a substantially higher proportion of each category of the clergy as "unsolicited" and therefore undecided, and a considerably higher proportion of those who *had* decided as accepting the oath. If those estimates are correct, the contrasts among the subregions were even greater than I have indicated.

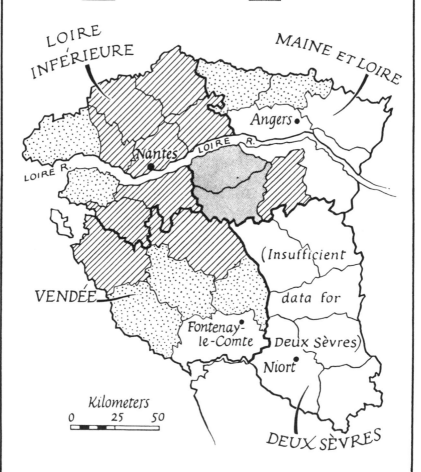

Figure 10. The 1791 Oath in the Area of the Rebellion

Percentage of all Clergy in District refusing the Oath

less than 50	70 – 89.9
50 – 69.9	90 – 100

LOIRE INFÉRIEURE

MAINE ET LOIRE

Angers

Nantes

LOIRE R.

LOIRE R.

(Insufficient

data for

VENDÉE

Fontenay-le-Comte

Deux Sèvres)

Niort

DEUX SÈVRES

Kilometers

0   25   50

S Bryant

Table 23. Percent of clergy taking the oath.

Area	Monks	Canons	Curés	Others	Total
Val-Saumurois	77	22	54	47	53
Layon	—	43	40	29	35
Mauges	12	5	10	7	8
Total	69	17	33	25	32
Number of cases	65	52	213	261	591

more striking. The range goes from only a single oath-taker in the communities of the Mauges adjoining Brittany and Poitou, to nearly unanimous taking of the oath in the communities along the Loire near Saumur, from complete acceptance of the oath at Fontevrault abbey to complete rejection at the Collège de Beaupréau.

The second map of the refusals shows that the correlation of counterrevolution and rejection of the oath operated on a larger scale than southern Anjou. The districts of Loire-Inférieure, Vendée, and Maine-et-Loire in which the most priests took the oath (which are blank or lightly stippled on the map) generally cooperated with the Revolution. On the whole, the more common the rejections of the oath, the more intensive the counterrevolutionary activity. The Mauges, the very hotbed of rebellion, had one of the highest rates of rejection in the West. There was the same striking correlation of refusal of the oath and resistance to the Revolution in the Sarthe (Bois 1960b: 597), and it seems to have appeared in Mayenne and in the departments of Normandy as well (Gaugain 1921: I, 222; Sévestre 1922: 185–191). Furthermore, considering the lapse of 160 years involved, what we have of the map of the oath in the West corresponds surprisingly well with the map of contemporary religious practice prepared by the Reverend Boulard (Le Bras 1955: I, 325). The distribution of the oath must represent more than a momentary accident.

We ought to pause for reflection on this remarkable correspondence. Port was deeply aware of the grave consequences of the clergy's decisions. But he found the geographic distribution of decisions of all things hardest to understand: "Who could describe the torments or the reasoning of these uncertain spirits . . . and who will explain why legality and independence, so surely justified for consciences on this side of the Layon, so easily became inexplicable error and rebellion for consciences on the other side?" (1888: I, 138). If the world

were only simple enough, we might be able to explain the correspondence of opposition to the Civil Constitution and participation in the
counterrevolution by saying that the rejection of the Civil Constitution by a region's clergy turned its people against the Revolution, or
that the decision of the priest simply reflected the already formed
attitude of the surrounding population toward the Revolution. I fear
the causal connections are not that elementary.[4] Unquestionably, the
curé's decision to refuse, plus the threat of his removal, forced a dramatic political choice on the other members of the community.
Equally unquestionably, the curé's decision was influenced by both
the local political climate and his relation to the community. To
speak of southern Anjou only, the curé tended to decide against the
Civil Constitution where his position under the old regime had been
dominant, where the bulk of his community's population was not
clearly under the influence of the leading Patriots, where those Patriots were already making the strongest bid to deplete his power.
His refusal was a blow against a new, rising, demanding elite. In a
grand French tradition, his noncompliance was a vote *against* —
against his loss of influence, against those who were striving to bring
it about. The effect was a formal rejection of the Revolution by most
of the clergy of the Mauges, and a formal acceptance of it by a
majority of those of Val and Saumurois.

The New Clergies

The application of the required oath in January, 1791, in effect
created two clergies, the "Constitutional" and the "Refractory,"
those who took the oath and those who refused it. The Refractories
had signified their resistance to the new religious order; they were
to be replaced by Constitutionals as soon as possible. The Constitutionals had thrown in their lots with the Revolution; they kept their
posts or received better ones. Most of them, indeed, had been its
active supporters long before. Martineau, Constitutional curé of
Les Gardes, was the son of a local Patriot leader; the same was true
of Thubert, of Melay.

---

[4] There is no apparent relation to loss or gain of income under the change of regime: among the
157 curés for whom the necessary information is available, 36% of those with 1790 incomes under
2000 livres took the oath, as against 32% of those netting 2000 or more. The tiny difference is
entirely the effect of the tendency of the better-heeled curés to reject the oath within the District
of Saumur; elsewhere, there was no such tendency. Compiled from A.D. M-et-L 16 Q 80–156.

There was, of course, a distinct shortage of Constitutionals in the Mauges. Among the 110 Constitutional curés for whom I have been able to collect the relevant information, the percentages of *replacements* who came from a previous post in the same district were: Saumur, 86; Angers, 19; Vihiers, 40; St. Florent, 27; Cholet, 22; total, 37. The figure for Angers is phony, since it refers only to the small section of the district below the Loire. Otherwise, it is clear that the replacements in Val-Saumurois tended to be from the region, while in the Mauges they were ordinarily outsiders. Add to this the fact that many more of the curés of Val-Saumurois, having taken the oath, simply stayed in place. Result: the reception of outsiders as state-imposed curés was almost entirely the problem of the Mauges.

The later careers of the Constitutionals were remarkably different from those of the Refractories. Many of them, like Brouard d'Argenté, Constitutional of Tigné, later renounced their vows and became public officials. Some, like Paterne of Vaudelenay, entered private life and married. A good number, like Levacher of Montrevault, soon joined the Refractories by formally withdrawing their oaths to support the Constitution. Most of the Refractories themselves disappeared sooner or later into hiding or into exile. Some took part in the counterrevolution. Many were reinstated under Napoleon. The choice between acceptance and rejection was the most crucial many of the clergy of southern Anjou had ever made.

It was a choice that was received and reported with foreboding by many local officials. In February, 1791, the mayor of Melay wrote:

It is with the greatest sadness that we forward this declaration of refusal, in fear that we may be deprived of the wise guidance of our zealous ministers. Although several weeks have passed since this refusal took place, we would hide it from you gladly if we could, when we consider that the same flock has been governed and led by the same pastor for thirty-eight years and that he has been assisted by such a worthy collaborator in the person of his vicar, [both of whom] teach us more by their examples than by their words. Sirs, do not be insensible to the emotion that affects us so deeply. Give us, please, the consolation that the same flock be governed by the same pastor and by his worthy collaborator (A.D. M-et-L 1 L 963).

They were not to have that consolation for long.

The administrators of Maine-et-Loire were soon aware of the problem on their hands. From the beginning of 1791, the Refractory clergy were the main topic discussed in the correspondence of the Department with the District of Cholet. "The coalition is already formed," wrote a departmental official in March, "among the office-holding ecclesiastics of your district . . . they are fortifying themselves with fantasies of counterrevolution" (A.D. M-et-L 1 L 202). The word *coalition* had already appeared in Angers' *Journal des amis de la constitution* two months before, and was to appear over and over again. It meant widespread unrest in the Mauges, and widespread resistance.

The first important uproar was at Maulèvrier.[5] The little city of Maulèvrier is near the border of Poitou, southeast of Cholet. A secondary center of the textile industry, it was plagued with unemployed workers in 1790. The city was the seat of a great absentee lord, the Count of Maulèvrier, and an important chtâeau. By the beginning of 1791, the lord had long since emigrated, putting his affairs in the hands of an overseer. Before his departure, the lord had a few spats with the municipal officers, and for a long time some rusty cannons at the château — symbols of aristocracy — had been a celebrated local cause. The leaders of the District of Cholet wanted them shipped to their city "for its defense," but nothing had come of it. There had been some minor scuffles over the shipment of grains in 1789. But it was at the announcement of the Civil Constitution of the Clergy that the first real disturbances occurred.

On 28 January, 1791, the unemployed workers who had been set to repairing the road to Vezins were in commotion. According to the city officials, "They said openly that they would try to keep the municipality from asking the curé to take the oath and they planned to meet for that purpose the following Sunday . . . most of the people were alarmed by the fear of losing their pastor; many said they would never let anyone replace him" (A.D. M-et-L 1 L 357). By the Sunday in question, apparently by coincidence, a formal request to hand over the famous cannon had arrived from the District of Cholet. This issue soon became confounded with the other. As the municipal council met, the citizens demonstrated against ceding the cannon, and then turned to the religious question: "Jean Devis, a weaver in this city, harangued the people, saying that they should

---

[5] Sources: A.D. M-et-L II F 1, 1 L 357; Port 1878: II, 619–623; Port 1888: I, 121–123; Uzureau 1924; Savary 1824: I, 32–33; Walter 1953: 8–9.

not listen to the municipal officers, since they were so happy to have gotten rid of the old judges and taken their places and that now they wanted to destroy religion" (A.D. M-et-L 1 L 357). Among his audience there was much talk of "defending religion and the good priests."

About the same time, to further complicate matters, it was rumored that the Count of Maulèvrier had written to his farmers, saying he was returning from emigration, that he wanted the cannons kept in place, and that he opposed the Civil Constitution oath.

On the 31st, there was a good deal of milling around, but no decisive action. But on 1 February, the news spread that the district was sending a force from Cholet to get the cannon. The news was false, but it was sufficient to encourage the sounding of the tocsin. Countrymen came to Maulèvrier in swarms from the surrounding communities, armed with pikes, scythes, staves, and clubs. Arrayed to defend their artillery, they met no enemy and eventually dispersed through the city, relieving a few patriots of their guns, shouting many threats against the district and the municipality, finally going back home. Not long after, the cannon disappeared into hiding, and the issue died down. Yet Maulèvrier was reported as a center of agitation, strongly divided, for long after that. Nearby, the communities of La Tessoualle, Tilliers, and St. Aubin-de-Baubigné all had their own similar but smaller flare-ups early in 1791 (A.D. M-et-L 1 L 356–358).

The analysis of Delaunay, the department's procurator, was straightforward:

The priests are doing all the harm; a most infernal coalition exists among them. They are abusing the ascendancy over the weak and the pusillanimous their places and characters give them. It is not the cannons that are causing the trouble. It is the abuse of the holy name of the Supreme Being in the interests of a faction (A.D. M-et-L 1 L 357).

A few days of altercation do not amount to a great crisis. The importance of the events at Maulèvrier is that they epitomize so much of the counterrevolutionary agitation of 1791 and later; the combination of hostility to the patriot administrators and support of the Refractory clergy, at this early date; the obvious reliance of a minority of Patriots on the support of their more powerful allies in Cholet; the participation of the artisans and the unemployed, apparently particularly hostile to the local bourgeois officials; the symbolic position of the absent lord as the defender of the old regime; the ready, armed response of the countryside to the tocsin. All of these will be met again, with a vengeance. And all of them are more characteristic of the Mauges than of any other section of Anjou.

In the face of this unrest and resistance, the departmental administrators had to perform four strenuous tasks: 1) recruitment of Constitutional clergy, 2) arrangement and administration of elections to vacated posts, 3) installation of the newly elected curés in their parishes, 4) support of those curés against the disaffected members of their parishes. Recruitment turned out to be almost entirely a matter of finding candidates outside the Mauges. Elections were made easier by the widespread abstention of all but the Patriots, due to scruples concerning the elections themselves and extensive rejection of the oath required of electors (A.D. M-et-L 1 L 364). But installation of the new curés was from the beginning a delicate and difficult operation. The Constitutional brought the new regime to the community, and did it by replacing the old curé. People were made inescapably aware of the conflict by their retiring curés. All had denounced the Civil Constitution and its attendant oath as intolerable, and all had accordingly denounced its supporters. Few, in fact, failed to label their replacements as heretics, schismatics, usurpers. The outgoing curé, Coulonnier, of Le May was only one of many who preached that the titles of the Constitutionals to their offices were invalid and their administration of the sacraments tainted (A.D. M-et-L 1 L 357). Young people were urged to marry before the Constitutional arrived, since his marriages would be worse than none at all. Preached against by his predecessor, his motives suspect, his allies already unpopular, his very coming a threat to his new community, the hapless Constitutional of the Mauges could hardly expect anything but trouble. The common labels for the two clergies in the Mauges reveal the flavor of popular feeling: *intrus* for the Constitutional and *bon prêtre* for the Refractory. It was the war of the Intruders and the Good Priests.

It did not take long for the Constitutionals to find out what was in store for them. Even before they set out for their new posts, some received threatening letters from their future parishioners (e.g., at Liré, A.D. M-et-L 1 L 364). But their first appearances were the real test. At Le May, the new arrival was hooted, cursed, threatened, chased, and finally stoned. After his departure, the inhabitants swore to fight any troops that might try to help him return. The candidate at Somloire got a drubbing. For many, this one visit was enough to persuade them to apply for jobs elsewhere.

The formal installations were no less harrowing for many new curés, but the frequent presence of troops reduced the danger of immediate violence. When the abbé Duret came to take office in Cerqueux-de-Maulèvrier, the crowd of 200 to 300 people gathered in the bourg refused to tell him who the municipal officers were, or where he could find them. After telling him to go back where he came from and threatening him and the official accompanying him with hard treatment, the crowd shrugged off a lecture on their duties: "We don't give a damn!" replied the scoundrel, saying, "You may be quite happy, you gentlemen, to do what you want while they're holding our king in jail in Paris; but it's you others instead that they ought to put there and even destroy" (A.D. M-et-L 1 L 364). From the beginning, hostility to the Intruder was inseparable from hostility to those — whether inside or outside the community — who were seeking to impose his services on the country parish.

The installation of the new curés was only the first phase. The administrators became deeply involved in the affairs of individual communities, defending the Constitutional and stirring up support for them. The Department sent messages, representatives and, on occasion, troops to show their support of the new clergy. The fact that attendance at the Masses of the Constitutional clergy was later taken as prima facie evidence of patriotism is simply one more example of the close identification of the Constitutionals with the new regime, in the eyes of both patriotic administrators and of ordinary citizens (see A.D. M-et-L 1 L 749, 1 L 1018, 1 L 1162). In fact, as investigators Gallois and Gensonné reported back to the National Assembly, Patriot became the ordinary term for anyone who attended the Constitutional Mass, and Aristocrat the ordinary term for anyone who did not (*Réimpression de l'Ancien Moniteur*, 12 Nov., 1791). In short, the religious issue immediately became political and split the entire population.

At the time when the Constitutionals were being introduced to their new jobs, power in many local governments was still in the balance between Patriots and non-Patriots. The new curés were able to count on the support of the Patriots, but in many communities that meant a handful of friends against a horde of enemies. Although few people shifted from one camp to the other once the lines were drawn, the composition of local governments changed considerably, however, and to the advantage of the Constitutionals. The change came with the mass resignations of the supporters of the Refractories: one report said two thirds of the municipalities of Maine-et-Loire had quit (de la Gorce 1909–1911: II, 355). Some of the resignations were strategic withdrawals by moderates and Patriots in the face of threats. Many were simple refusals by the leading citizens to have anything to do with the inauguration of the Intruder. A surprising number centered on the superficially trivial issue of the civic oath required of municipal officers, which became identified with the oath the Refractory had rejected. Over the course of 1791, as we shall see, reluctance to take public oaths without express exclusion of the Civil Constitution, was an important element in the withdrawal of Aristocrats from formal politics.

Where resignations did not decimate the community's government, the non-Patriot officials often chose to sabotage the Constitutional's efforts. The hard times of Coquille, the elected curé of Beaupréau, are among the best known because he described them in a witty and voluminous correspondence with the departmental leaders. He could not get the ornaments necessary for special services. He could not get servers for Mass; he could not even get his pay. Some time after he had arrived, Coquille wrote, "Holy Saturday and the three Easter holidays will give me the means of showing you that the municipality of Beaupréau is the most anti-Constitutional-curé that could exist in the French Empire" (A.D. M-et-L 1 L 364; cf. Port 1888: I, 416–421). He was wrong, of course. Nearby, other municipalities were even hiding the keys to the church or keeping the Constitutional from his parsonage.

Most of these activities were simply passive resistance; many even had a pretense of legality. But there were many cases where local officials obstructed the law consciously and directly. In Trémentines, New Year's Day, 1792, was a page from a comic opera. The curé's letter describes the affair:

Today the first of January, 1792, the undersigned, having departed to carry out his functions as curé, returned home at the end of Vespers, which were sung without difficulty, and went upstairs. His appearance at the window incited a call of *trut, truts* [short for *intrus*] from everyone in the square. At this shout he left and went down into his cellar. At that moment two pistol shots were fired at the windows of the salon, and it turned out that three panes were broken. His servant and the niece of Mr. Le Roy, the former mayor, who were in the salon fled more dead than alive. The writer went to the door leading to the court and addressing the populace asked who fired the pistol shots. They answered that no one knew. One of the company, a certain Olivier, said, "Ha, ha! You'll pay for the windows! You shot!" Taking one of these individuals by the arm, he took him to the parsonage. [That person] replied that he knew nothing about it and sneaked away. All these crimes were added to the insults and even mistreatments he has received since he became curé of Trémentines, which he has always hidden out of goodness of heart, notably a stone thrown at him last Thursday on the outskirts of Trémentines, as he left for Cholet, and the invective he received from the individuals Couet and Broua of Trémentines Wednesday evening at his garden gate. [These events] announce well enough the criminal intentions of all the inhabitants of this parish against him, and the small inclination of the Municipality to oppose them, wherefore he requests that to protect him now it please the administrators of Cholet to use their authority and to send an armed force with a commissioner to make this parish, now in revolt and absolutely enemies of the Constitution, return to good order (A.D. M-et-L 1 L 364).

This was not the end. The National Guards were sent in. The local Justice of the Peace held hearings on the case a few days later. The culprit admitted he had fired the pistol, but claimed he was firing "at a goose." Anyway, he said, the gun was hardly loaded. On that, the Justice dismissed the charges and required the curé to pay the costs of bringing the troops in unnecessarily (A.D. M-et-L 1 L 364, 1 L 472 bis).

In perspective, few of the disorders over the Constitutional clergy seem more serious than this. They were skirmishes, but not open warfare. By and large, local officials, even when decidedly partisan, wanted to keep the peace. Furthermore, the very presence of the Constitutional ordinarily meant that he had the support of at least a few powerful local Patriots, with influential allies in Cholet or Chemillé. The investigating team sent out by the Department in May, 1791, concluded that the policy of most non-Patriot municipalities toward the Constitutionals was: no resistance, but no cooperation either (A.D. M-et-L 1 L 357 bis).

A moderate policy put the local officials between the demands of the curé and the emotions of the people, for the public response to the new curé was, in general, immoderate. From the time he arrived, the parishioners alternated their relations with the Constitutional between avoidance and attack. The organized boycott was one kind of active avoidance. The curé would find that people were not only unwilling to talk to him, but also unwilling to work for him or sell him anything. Even where the organized boycott never developed, the isolation of the Constitutional — or, rather, his confinement to the small circle of the Patriots — was almost complete, his church almost empty.

The most common attacks took the traditional form of hoots, gibes, curses, shaken fists, tossed pebbles. Women and children were the players in this game. The men joined in the more serious business of threats and direct interference. It was standard practice to picket the Mass of the Constitutional, to raise a din outside, and toss refuse into the church. Someone in St. Quentin-en-Mauges smeared the church front with offal (A.D. M-et-L 1 L 364). Even the decorum of interments was disturbed. Gasnault, the Constitutional of La Séguinière, reported that his pallbearers had refused to enter the church, had trotted with the body from church steps to graveside, and had run from the cemetery to leave him at the mercy of a crowd of jeering boys (A.D. M-et-L 1 L 364). And in Saint-Lambert-du-Lattay the parishioners were not only burying their dead in the graveyard without warning or permission, but were stealing into the church to ring the bells for the ceremonies (A.D. M-et-L 1 L 364).

The next step from this wholesale interference in the curé's ministry was to public demonstrations and threats against him. They had already begun, as we have seen, with his arrival and installation, but they continued, gathering force on special occasions like elections and holidays. Poison penmen slipped crude warnings under the doors of their new pastors. The Constitutional, Besnard, of Saint-Aubin-de-Luigné, for example, enclosed in a letter to the Department two billets circulating among his parishioners. One was a rough cartoon of a figure with his neck in a noose, labeled: "Besnard is hanged, God would approve." The other read:

"You know that Besnard is not curé of Saint-Aubin-de-Luigné, there is only M. Boutiqui who is the only curé and so Besnard is nothing but an Intruder, a robber, a thief and schismatic and apostate and we, messieurs,

we who believe him will fall into error like him. New song to a pretty tune
on the subject of Besnard:
    True Christians, weep to see arrive among you
    A false pastor we must all belie
    Without power or acceptance from our true Bishop.
    Who gave him his place?
    An Intruder like himself" (A.D. M-et-L 1 L 364).
To accompany verbal violence, there were threats of physical violence. While the curé of Saint-Hilaire-du-Bois could only report that
his sexton had been told he would be killed if he did not leave town
in a fortnight, his counterpart in Tigné reported that his own life was
in danger, that he and his servants never went out unarmed.

But why linger over the matter? The long and short of it is that
the countrymen of the Mauges gave the Constitutionals the full,
time-honored treatment that rural communities reserve for unwelcome visitors. There was little the Constitutionals could do in response to the endless badgering they received. Some flooded the
higher echelons of the government with detailed complaints and
pleas for help; some wrote denunciations of the Refractories who
were stirring up trouble in their parishes; some even called for the
National Guard to "maintain order." But in general they were frus-
trated by the inability of the government, of even the Patriotic municipalities, to change the ways of the countrymen.

In all their attempts the new curés were handicapped by the fact
that there were a multitude of Refractories in the Mauges, but very
few Constitutionals. As a result, none had vicars to help them, and
many remained surrounded by communities with unreplaced Refractories instead of friendly Constitutionals until late in 1791. The shortage was so great that the Department took the expedient of closing
down a number of churches rapidly.

This redistribution of parishes stirred intense discontent. The standard procedure was to remove the sacred objects, take down the bells,
and formally close the church, turning over custody of parishioners
and sacred objects to a neighboring Constitutional. Each one of these
moves struck at the local loyalties of the people of the Mauges, and
each aroused an energetic protest. In La Fosse-de-Tigné, it took two
months to get together a large enough force to overcome the crowds
that were barring the removal of the bells and the ornaments (A.D.
M-et-L 1 L 360). In Landemont, Larevellière-Lépeaux himself thought

better of his first attempt to lead the closing down of the church of St. Sauveur, when he saw the size of the crowd that gathered and heard the tone of their remarks (A.D. M-et-L 1 L 976). This administrative move, the consolidation of parishes, did nothing to enhance the positions of the Constitutionals or the Patriots in the countryside, and left them encompassed by a crowd of displaced Refractories.

Refractory Religion

The Refractories themselves were displaced, but not idle. While the Constitutionals were intoning the Mass in empty churches, the Refractories were meeting large crowds. According to Chassin (1892: I, 183–184), the Bishop of La Rochelle had disseminated instructions for the continuation of the ministry by the Refractories after they were formally replaced; certainly many of them did carry it on. At first, parishioners simply went to a nearby church where the curé had not yet been replaced; either they went to the friendly priest's services or their curé held his own in the church. As the number of Constitutionals and the number of closed churches mounted, this became more difficult. Then a number of Refractories took to saying Mass in closed and abandoned churches and in private chapels. Even this became more difficult as the Patriots became more vigilant and the Constitutionals more vociferous. Although the use of churches and chapels continued up to the counterrevolution, more and more services were held in private homes, barns, open fields, wherever the Patriots were unlikely to find them, as time went on. These services were not as regular or as formal as those of the parish church had been, but they were followed with more enthusiasm, often by great crowds. Clandestine Masses gave religious life in the Mauges a flavor of conspiracy. Most people attended at one time or another. Most, then, were reached by the message of the displaced priests.

The underground activities of the Refractories built a phantom church in the shadow of the real one. Not only did they preach and say Mass, but also they continued to baptize, to hear confessions, to perform the usual range of priestly functions. To be sure, they left the burials to the Constitutionals and did very little marrying, but what religious services were given to most of the people of the Mauges were given by Refractory priests. Among a people for whom the weekly reunion at the parish church had been such a regular and significant ritual, this disruption of the usual order was a continuous reminder that they lived in disjointed times.

Baptisms in particular became a point of issue between the new priests and the old. People did not stop having children, and people of the Mauges had always been assiduous in bringing children to the priest soon after birth, but the Constitutionals were not baptizing any children. They rightly concluded that someone else was doing the baptizing. The midwives were doing a large share, for they had always baptized children whose survival was in doubt, and now the number of such children seemed to rise extraordinarily. But the local Refractories were also solemnizing births and teaching that it was a mortal sin to participate in a Constitutional baptism. Since birth records and parish records were one, this disorganized the official record-keeping as well as taking business from the Constitutional. One temporary solution was to call in the troops to "convert" the population. In June, 1791, a small band of troops, guided by a local Patriot, went from house to house in Saint-Georges-du-Puy-de-la-Garde, rounding up the new babies and their parents, and marching them off to the parish church for involuntary baptism (A.D. M-et-L 1 L 357 bis). The members of the National Guard became godfathers many times over on such expeditions. The method did not endear the Constitutionals or the National Guard to the countryside.

As religion went underground in the Mauges, public and private missionary activity grew. The missionaries of Saint-Laurent-sur-Sèvre, the Mulotins, had always preached on special occasions, but during Lent of 1791 they seemed to be everywhere. Their attacks on the Civil Constitution and its adherents raised bitter denunciations from the departmental and district officials. As the administrators of Maine-et-Loire later wrote to their colleagues in the Vendée:

What happened during their stay in our department? Two thirds of the municipalities resigned, the preliminary work on the property tax was stopped, the replacement of the nonjuring priests and the installation of the new functionaries [i.e., curés and vicars] became impossible. Fermentation grew, threats became violent, and there was reason to fear that blood would flow. We did not want to see your troubles of Challans repeated on our territory, and we have not forgotten our insurrections of Tilliers, St. Crespin, Maulèvrier, and Châtillon (A.N. F[7] 3695[7]).

As the Mulotins preached noncooperation with the Constitutionals, they distributed homemade circulars impugning the credentials of the Intruders, and telling how to fulfill religious obligations without resort to their services (see A.N. D xxix bis 39 for the originals of some of these tracts). This first flurry of Mulotin activity caught the Patriots unaware, although the missionaries, too, were soon driven underground.

One kind of public religious manifestation continued to grow regardless of what Patriots did: the pilgrimage. Like the mission, it was a custom of the old regime adapted to new circumstances. For centuries, the faithful of the Mauges had filed ceremoniously to special chapels, wayside crosses, and sacred places on appropriate days. In 1791, the number of faithful and the number of appropriate days began to grow wildly. By the end of the year, crowds of thousands were reported as assembling almost nightly in the most popular locales (A.D. M-et-L 1 L 364, 1 L 367).

Some of the assemblies reported were simply the secret Masses of the Refractories. The pilgrimage was, however, a different sort of thing. The participants from a given parish gathered there under a banner or a cross, trimmed with black crepe, tradition has it, if a Constitutional had already taken over the church. Together they walked across country to the sacred meeting place, following a leader in traditional hymns, often carrying lighted candles. Here is a scene the local Patriots of La Pommeraye came upon in November, 1791:

Two or three hundred people of all ages and both sexes were on their knees and had a wooden cross, around which and closest to which were three men carrying candles . . . and in the middle of them Jacques Gazeau, a carpenter living in the bourg of La Pommeraye, who chanted a psalm, *Miserere Mei Deus*, to which all the assembled people responded (A.D. M-et-L 1 L 364).

As the pilgrimages became more frequent, so did the organized expression of hostility to the new regime. In August, 1791, a special campaign of "prayer for the return of the Catholic religion" was marked by extraordinary meetings at Bellefontaine, St. Laurent, and Les Gardes (de la Gorce 1909–1911: II, 369–371). The leaders of the cities of the Mauges were particularly disturbed by the pilgrimages, because there was a large rallying point in the vicinity of each one of them, and a good deal of the rancor generated by the pilgrims was aimed at the cities and their National Guards. Chalonnes was worried about the gatherings at Saint-Laurent-de-la-Plaine, some five kilometers away, Cholet about those at Bégrolles, about ten kilometers away (A.D. M-et-L 1 L 368). Nor were these idle worries, as it became more and more obvious that the people who demonstrated against the Constitutional and interfered with local elections in the daytime were the same as those who went off on pilgrimages at night.

The well-known story of Saint-Laurent-de-la-Plaine summarizes most of what happened in the Mauges (see Guinhut 1909). There, the Chapel of Our Lady of Charity had long been an attraction to the devout. From June, 1791, the number of pilgrims began to swell, and the parish pattern to take shape. In July, the Jacobins of Chalonnes were denouncing St. Laurent as "infested with fanaticism" and singling out the assemblies at the chapel as threats to law and order. By this time, crowds of over a thousand persons were appearing there some nights. A few days after the National Guard had broken up the midnight gathering of 24 August, the District of St. Florent sent out a detachment to tear down the chapel. Very soon after, the Virgin that the pilgrims had been venerating was reported to be appearing in a nearby oak tree; the crowds swelled to thousands. The District started sending regular observers to the spot, and at this point they noted that the men were beginning to come armed. The number of spectators and the distance they came both increased continually. In November, 1791, detachments were coming to St. Laurent from Poitou and Brittany to see the Virgin in the tree . . . and to mutter threats at the Patriots. Larevellière-Lépeaux and his friends passed through a hostile crowd there in March, 1792, on a tour to convert the Mauges to Patriotism. What they saw there so inspired them that they returned in a few days to chop down the sacred oak. The maneuver was hardly successful, since the Virgin simply took to appearing in other nearby trees, and the crowds continued to come to St. Laurent, venting their feelings against the Patriots as they came.

Pilgrimages proliferated crazily after August, 1791. By the following April, according to an agitated local account, four to five thousand people were gathering regularly in Chanzeaux, ammunition was being distributed, and an armed guard for the Refractory was formed (A.D. M-et-L 1 L 365). One does not need to take the statistics literally to realize that these crowds, pilgrimages, and processions were beginning to take on the cast of rebellion.

These great movements did not take place without the collaboration of the Refractories. Many of them continued to preach the illegitimacy of the claims of the Constitutionals, and the obligation of the faithful to have nothing to do with them. Some added to the profusion of anti-Constitutional tracts circulating in the Mauges by late in 1791. Besides, the Refractories were giving the example of direct resistance to the new order themselves.

Before they were replaced, it was the standard practice of the Refractories to frustrate all the efforts of the Constitutionals who had already been installed in neighboring churches. They refused to honor the banns of their ecclesiastical neighbors. They did not report baptizing children from the Constitutionals' parishes. They refused confession and absolution to those who would not promise to stay away from the new clergy. This program is not surprising, not inconsistent with the view that the Constitutionals were sinful interlopers.

The resistance of the Refractories, however, was on a wider front than religion alone. It was aimed at the position of the whole body of supporters of the new regime, which meant the bourgeois administrators of the new regime, and the handful of Patriots in the country community. The Refractory clergy were commonly accused of impeding the collection of local taxes. While still in office, they often refused to read new Revolutionary decrees. Many citizens left or refused public positions on their account, if not on their instigation. In general, the Refractories preached and practiced subversion.

The most important single act of defiance to the Revolutionary government was hiding out in the countryside. The law and the decisions of the Directory of Maine-et-Loire varied, but before long it was illegal for Refractories to stay in their own parishes. Yet many stayed, even when they had been ordered deported. The curé of Neuvy practiced his ministry openly until 1792, when he went into hiding until the counterrevolution began (Uzureau 1923). Throughout the Mauges, that story was repeated. In fact, Refractories from less congenial areas flooded into the Mauges. Large gatherings of priests were reported in Bouzillé, and the tiny chapel of Sainte Foy became a "cathedral" for Refractories in 1791 (A.D. M-et-L 1 L 211, 1 L 365; Uzureau 1946; Conin n.d.).

From the time the oath to support the Constitution was enforced, the clergy of the Mauges were in an unbending stance of public opposition. From the point of view of the Patriots, their attitude was intolerable, not to mention illegal. Despite the pleas of various communities to maintain the Refractories who had not been replaced, and some abortive attempts to put the whole body of Refractories in the same legal category as Protestant ministers (featuring beguiling appeals to "freedom of religion"), there was little hope on the one side and no intention on the other of legalizing their position. So the clergy remained, scorning the law, soon proscribed, but always active.

Control of the Refractories

The attempts of the Revolutionary administrators to control the Refractories began with the imposition of the oath, early in 1791. Wherever refusals of the oath were concentrated in Maine-et-Loire, agitation was high. (Indeed, in all of Anjou, there was an impressive correlation among the incidence of refusals, the incidence of local political disturbances in 1791 and 1792, and the incidence of open participation in the counterrevolution in 1793; cf. the distribution of reports in A.D. M-et-L 1 L 364–368.) The spatial pattern of the counterrevolution was well set by the middle of 1791. Yet the Department had taken no direct steps to control the Refractories until May of that year. On the 13th, they sent out a pair of roving commissars — who were later to report the necessity of taking "prompt measures to forestall the immediate explosion threatening in the whole countryside" — to investigate the reasons for the troubles (A.D. M-et-L 1 L 357 bis). Before their investigators had returned, the Department practically outlawed the Refractories by making it possible to transport any ecclesiastic to Angers for surveillance on the complaint of a few citizens. In announcing the move, they made it clear that the Refractories had become their enemies: "These traitors to the fatherland, whose ruin they seem to have sworn, are intimidating municipalities and forcing them to resign; they are suggesting to impressionable persons that they attack the administrators and not respect their property, or the property of their associates" (Uzureau 1918: 267). In rapid succession came an unauthorized raid on the Mulotins and the unauthorized arrest of a prominent Refractory of Cholet. From that point on, the number of priests restricted to Angers rose steadily. By August, the National Guards of Angers, Chalonnes, and Cholet were in constant action against Refractories and their supporters.

It was about this time (16 July, 1791) that the National Assembly grew sufficiently concerned about the anxious reports arriving from the West to send out two representatives, Gallois and Gensonné, to make an investigation. Although they did not enter the Mauges, they discovered the same conditions in the adjacent areas of Vendée and Deux-Sèvres that the investigators of Maine-et-Loire had found in southern Anjou — division, bitterness, violence, and potential rebellion (*Moniteur*, 10 Nov., 1791). Gallois and Gensonné made rather moderate recommendations. But many other reports, less calm and conciliatory, reached the assemblies in Paris, to warn them of the volcanic situation in the West. Goupilleau, in August, described events in the southern part of Loire-Inférieure as "civil war" (Chassin 1892: II, 27). The Department of Deux-Sèvres, in September, used the familiar term "coalition" for the actions of the Refractories and their allies (Chassin 1892: II, 37–38). Dumouriez, then stationed in the Vendée, frequently mentioned "insurrection" in his correspondence with the Minister of War (Chassin 1892: II, *passim*). Delaunay, taking some liberties with the text of a letter from the Directory of Maine-et-Loire, told the assembly of troubles so serious that "if the National Assembly does not take prompt and severe action, incalculable misfortunes will result" (*Moniteur*, 7 Nov., 1791).

Despite such warnings, however, the National Assembly was generally more delicate in its dealings with the Refractories than the Patriots of the West would have liked. In September, for example, the national amnesty of political prisoners returned the Refractories who had been impounded in Angers to their parishes, and to their work against the Revolution. The urban Patriots and district administrators of the Mauges continued to importune the Department for sterner measures. The Department, in turn, appealed continually to the National Assembly, and in February, 1792 — disregarding the royal veto — applied the law of 29 November, interning the Refractories and seizing their property. The priests responded no more enthusiastically to this attempt to control them than to the last, and the disturbances in the Mauges continued.

In June, 1792, the National Guard took the initiative in actually imprisoning the priests who had come to Angers. By this time most of the Refractories of the Mauges, hunted, were in hiding. It was not long until the deportation of all Refractories, long sought by the Department, became law. In September, boatloads of priests began moving down the Loire, heading for Spain, Holland, and the rest of Europe, while other vessels carried priestly cargoes from Sables d'Olonne.

The mention of deportation raises an interesting question: who was left when the full-fledged counterrevolution began? It is possible to derive minimum estimates of the extent of absence through detention or deportation from E. Queruau-Lamerie's catalog of the clergy of Maine-et-Loire (1899). For the beginning of 1793, the proportions of all clergy listed who were gone from southern Anjou were, in percentages: from St. Florent, 25.2; Cholet, 29.8; Vihiers, 37.2; Angers, 47.6; Saumur, 11.2; total, 25.1. A minimum of a quarter of the priests of southern Anjou (and probably not too many more than that) were gone at the beginning of 1793. There were certainly enough still present to keep on causing trouble. Very few of the law-abiding priests of the Saumurois had been interned or exiled. Yet it was not the most troublesome areas that had the most absentees. What it seemed to take was a combination: a considerable number of Refractories *plus* a vigorous and effective group of local Patriots. So the Districts of Angers and Vihiers, where the parties of Patriots and Aristocrats were more evenly matched than they were deep in the Mauges, were able to rid themselves of many more of their non-conformist priests than the Districts of Cholet and St. Florent could. The conclusion overlaps the conclusions of the earlier discussion of emigration: where their defenders were strong enough, the Refractories apparently did not flee.

These findings throw some light on an old debate about the Vendée. Many ideologues have pictured the counterrevolution as nothing but the stronghearted defense of the "good priests" against the evil intentions of the Convention. Republican historians have often replied by deprecating the role of religion in the whole affair. Albert Soboul (1962: 246), following Georges Lefebvre, has pointed out that the Vendean peasants "did not move in 1792 to save their *good* priests from deportation." There are three observations to make: 1) The great majority of the curés of the counterrevolutionary sections of southern Anjou were not deported. 2) The internment and deportation of the priests did, in fact, excite a number of local disturbances, but they were not simultaneous and had little chance to coalesce into a major rebellion. 3) The choice between Refractories and Constitutionals was unquestionably the paramount public issue dividing the people of southern Anjou in 1791 and 1792. Religious questions *were* important; the "good priests" *did* matter. The mistake of the defenders of the Vendée has been to translate such a statement directly, all at once, into cause, motive, explanation, and justification of the counterrevolution (see Tilly 1963).

Subregional Contrasts

The religious troubles of 1791–1793 in southern Anjou mainly concerned the Mauges. The report from Val-Saumurois was largely negative. While difficulties with the Refractory clergy dominated the correspondence of the District of Cholet, they hardly appeared in the letters of the District of Saumur (A.D. M-et-L 1 L 206, 1 L 211). The departmental officers were perfectly aware of the contrast, when their procurator wrote to the District of Cholet that "your district contains the most anti-Constitutional priests of the department. They seem to reproduce themselves, like the Phoenix, from their own ashes" (A.D. M-et-L 1 L 206). The most important kinds of religious troubles were these: 1) resistance to the sale of church property, 2) rejection of the oath to support the Constitution, 3) attacks on the Constitutional clergy, 4) failure of local governments to support religious reforms, 5) adherence to Refractories, 6) illegal religious assemblies. Each of these became a many-thorned problem in the Mauges. None of them pricked the Patriots of Val-Saumurois seriously. In general, their Constitutionals got the support they needed (see Gallard 1960).

A cardinal fact, of course, is the relative lack of Refractories in Val and Saumurois. Outside the section near the Layon, only a handful of curés had to be replaced. The rest were staying in their own parishes. The Refractories, on the other hand, were easily isolated, surrounded, and replaced.

The contrast between the subregions of southern Anjou comes to this: in the Mauges, steadily mounting tension over religious matters from early in 1791, leading from crisis to crisis; in Val-Saumurois, few difficulties and no remarkable increase in dissension. In the Mauges, the steady growth of opposition; in Val-Saumurois, no successful resistance movement.

What troubles there were with priests and religion in Val-Saumurois were almost entirely crowded into the recalcitrant corner of Layon and Loire: Mozé, Saulgé-l'Hôpital, Saint-Aubin-de-Luigné,

Vauchrétien, Martigné, Juigné, Grézillé (see A.D. M-et-L 1 L 364–368). Even there the situation more often meant a struggle between matched, well-defined factions than the swallowing up of the Constitutional and a minority of his defenders in a crowd of enemies of the Constitution.

There is no reason to believe that this contrast of subregions was a simple matter of "morality" and "immorality," of the inherent goodness of the clergy on one side of a tiny river — whichever side the reader may prefer. There is every reason to believe that it is a matter of the differences in social organization I have already described at such great length.

I have presented these differences as a matter of community organization. Here the *parish*, the religious aspect of the community, is important. The varying religious histories of Mauges and Val-Saumurois after 1789 can be seen as processes initiated by the touching of importantly different forms of social organization by basically similar external influences. Rather superficially seen, the external influences were the acts of the new government affecting religious organization. There were several facts that made these attempted changes critical in the Mauges: 1) They came from outside the community — the most important were acts of legislators in Paris and administrators in Angers. 2) They were supported by the group that seemed to have gained most from the Revolution up to that point, who were monopolizing the purchases of church lands, and whose power was most likely to be enhanced by the further changes. 3) They were implemented, on the instigation of the local Patriots, by the bourgeois of the mercantile cities, with the assistance of their armed force, the National Guard. 4) They directly challenged the position of the priest in the community. 5) His response to the challenge threatened an immediate and visible rupture of the community. The crux is that the clergy of the Mauges were seriously challenged, but had the power to reply. No supporter of the Revolution within their communities had power enough to suppress them. On the other hand — and this is the point most histories of the Vendée have neglected — there were enough supporters of the Revolution in the countryside to keep the discussion of religion at the level of frenzy.

The Constitutional priest was the Intruder because he was allied with other menacing outsiders in attempting to change the old order. All at once, he personified the external origin of the religious changes, the source of those changes, the threat to the old curé, the victory of the local Patriots. Small wonder that when the rebels later captured a pair of Constitutionals from the vicinity of Cholet (Robin of Trémentines and La Crolle of Cholet), they told them that "they were the cause of all this trouble because they took the oath" (A.D. M-et-L 1 L 1030).

The other side of the coin is that the Refractory was looked upon as the defender of a way of life and, eventually, as a martyr. Support of the Good Priest became inseparable from a general rejection of the Revolution, its works, and its agents. As a result, many of the people arrested at the beginning of the counterrevolution said they guessed it was for being friendly toward the Refractories.

It was in this kind of setting that agitation over religious problems tightened its grip on the Mauges from 1791. It did not happen overnight. It was a steady process of party formation, the memberships of the parties well defined by the middle of 1791, but their enmities growing and their organizations developing up to the counterrevolution. The positions taken in 1791 were durable, lasting far beyond the insurrection of 1793; one could draw a map of the intensity of the insurrection from the illuminating *État politique du département de la Vendée sous le rapport de la tranquillité publique*, of the Year Seven (A.N. F[7] 3695[7]). And the positions taken not only marked off revolutionary and counterrevolutionary regions, but divisions within almost every community. It is this internal division that gives so much of the history of the counterrevolution its bitterness.

Of course, the discussion in this chapter has strayed beyond the nicely narrowed bounds of the parish, and nibbled at the neighborhood, the local economy, and the commune as well. That is because the public issues that racked southern Anjou were in such large measure connected with religious reforms and because, after all, whatever aspect of a community one begins with, the analysis inevitably draws in observations on the rest of its organization. But the religious problem by no means exhausts the problem of the origins of the Vendée. It is not yet at all clear how the parties were recruited or organized, what other griefs or rivalries may have contributed to the conflict in the Mauges, what form the struggle for power took, how the Vendée went from rumbling discontent to open insurrection. How did all this chaos become a political crisis?

CHAPTER 12

The Political Crisis

The turmoil of the early Revolution deeply affected the parish, the neighborhood, and the local economy of each community in southern Anjou. The focus of conflict and change, however, was the commune. Economic dissatisfactions, personal animosities, local rivalries, religious disagreements all flowed into a struggle for power.

I have attempted to show how economic and religious developments became relevant to politics during the early Revolution. It would not be useful to undertake a separate discussion of the neighborhood, because so much of it would consist of inferences from the more solid information available on the other aspects of community life. Kinship, friendship, and personal hostility undoubtedly played a significant part in the recruitment of local factions. But in the nature of the case there is no effective way to trace their independent general effects. The important things to recognize are that the Revolution did not impinge as directly on the neighborhood as on parish, economy, or commune, and that local affiliations and estrangements in themselves cannot explain the violent political disturbances with which we are concerned.

The Revolution's New Politics

Obviously, the Revolution did more than "impinge" on the commune; it often shook the commune profoundly. Both the profundity and the form of its local political effects, however, depended on the nature of the community. Jeffry Kaplow (1962), for example, has argued that the Revolution did not induce drastic political change or conflict in Elbeuf *because* the high commercial bourgeoisie was already in unchallenged control in the manufacturing city. Similarly, the arrival of the Revolution tended simply to confirm the preeminence of the bourgeoisie in the cities of southern Anjou and, to a lesser extent, in Val-Saumurois as a whole. It aroused the greatest conflict or resistance in the country, and in the Mauges. At the same time, largely because of the uneven effects of both its appeals and its benefits, the Revolution excited hostility between city and country as well as between those most involved in urban activities and the rest of the population.

Within the individual community, the Revolution commonly meant significant changes in the organization of power. The sheer formalization of political life hastened the differentiation of politics from other community activities and encouraged the appearance of political specialists. The attacks on the traditional bases of the elite positions of priest and noble opened opportunities to new elites who could effectively stand between the Revolutionary government and the commune. In particular, they gave the bourgeois of the Mauges a chance to expand their power. The numerous and drastic changes at all levels of French society from 1787 on, furthermore, helped make countrymen conscious of a connection between national politics and events within their own communities; they helped politicize local affairs.

In the Mauges, from 1791 to 1793, these transformations amounted to a political crisis.

The political crisis had a good deal in common with the religious crisis. It was visible a little earlier, perhaps, but it went through the same stages of local maneuverings, formation of distinct parties, and eventual withdrawal of the antirevolutionary mass from the official organization. The Revolutionary Church won possession of the buildings and titles of the old regime, but lost all religious authority. Something similar happened to the Revolutionary government in the Mauges. It erased the formal traces of the traditional government, but lost its political authority.

We have already examined in passing the Revolution's first rearrangement of the structure of local and regional government. It was, at least in principle, a rational, consistent, specialized, untraditional set of institutions (see Godechot 1951: 72–108). The blueprint for the revamped commune was ready by the end of 1789. It established a communal council composed, in all but the largest communes of southern Anjou, of a mayor, two other municipal officers, six "notables," and a nonvoting procurator (procureur de commune).

The mayor and municipal officers were to run the commune, subject to orders from district, department, and National Assembly; the procurator was vaguely expected to defend the interests of both nation and citizens; the notables were to be called into the council on extraordinary occasions.

The electorate was also redefined. In fact, it was trichotomized into passive citizens, first-degree active citizens, and second-degree active citizens. The first group could not vote. The second could vote but not hold office. The third could both vote and hold office. Before 1787, all heads of households had been able to participate in the communal assemblies. Then under the regime of the Interim Commissions stiff requirements for officeholding had been imposed. For the Estates General, most taxpayers 25 or older had been eligible to vote. The new rules were more restrictive than those for the Estates General, but more relaxed than the rules of 1787. The main feature identifying a first-degree active citizen in 1790 was his payment of the equivalent of three or more days' wages in taxes; the second-degree active citizen paid at least ten days' wages. The "days" were based on the local payment of a day laborer, which ranged from ten to eighteen sous daily in southern Anjou. The effect was to disfranchise the poor and the propertyless. Late in 1791, the criterion for second-degree citizenship in small communes was changed: the individual had to own property worth 100 days' work or to farm property worth 400 days' work. Finally, for the fall elections of 1792, the whole set of distinctions was eliminated and most men 25 or older made able to vote. Up to that time, the first-degree citizens had voted only for communal officers and for electors. The electors themselves had to be second-degree citizens. It was they who formed the periodic assemblies to elect district, departmental, and national officials.

The tedious details of the election law have an important meaning: up to the changes of 1792, total disfranchisement of the poor, partial disfranchisement of all but substantial citizens. By legal definition the active citizens did not include bankrupts, drifters, or servants, but by fiscal definition they also excluded many day laborers and artisans.

Such a conclusion is not self-evident. Bois (1960b: 223–245) has concluded that the restrictions hardly excluded any potential independent voters in the Sarthe. And his analysis is not only exceedingly careful but is also based on documentation far richer than that available for southern Anjou. Nevertheless, there is reason to think that a considerable proportion of potential voters of southern Anjou were kept from the polls by property requirements.

One reason for thinking so is that the ratio of the number of active citizens to the total population (that is, not just adult males, but men, women, and children) was considerably lower in southern Anjou than in the Sarthe. Whereas the figure ran around 15 percent in the Sarthe, among the nineteen communes of southern Anjou for which full voting lists from 1790–1791 are available (A.D. M-et-L 1 L 444), the ratio was 11.7 percent. A second reason is that in 1790 the districts of southern Anjou reported a substantial number of individuals paying less than three days' worth of taxes (A.D. M-et-L 1 L 402). Calculated as individuals per 100 households, the proportions were: Cholet 46.6 percent, St. Florent 28.4 percent, Angers 25.0 percent and Saumur 21.9 percent. All the males 25 and older in this group, who must have been the great majority of those named, were disfranchised. The third reason for believing that the number denied the vote was considerable is that with fair consistency the voting lists contain a smaller proportion of day laborers and weavers than do the comparable estimates of occupational distribution prepared for this study (see Appendix A).

These observations do not really resolve the question of disfranchisement. Most of the voting lists under consideration were prepared in 1791, when massive refusals to register may already have begun to take effect on the electorate. In any case, the evidence is all indirect; it would be better to base the conclusion on the direct comparison of population enumerations, tax rolls, and voting lists. Only tentatively, therefore, can we conclude that the electoral laws of 1790–1792 worked against the poor. Perhaps a quarter of the otherwise eligible voters of southern Anjou were excluded. A large share of those excluded were most likely day laborers and industrial artisans. On the other hand, very few of the large or medium farmers — who generally paid far more than the five or ten livre minimum in taxes on the land they leased — were barred from voting by this means test. The law seems to have worked mainly to keep wage earners from the polls and, a fortiori, from the electoral assemblies of second-degree citizens.

Not only the electorate was restricted. Public office outside the commune was also limited, although technically not so much as the electorate itself. For the Estates, all voters were eligible for election. The 1790 law made only citizens paying ten days' wages eligible for most offices and only citizens paying at least fifty livres, as well as having some property, eligible for the National Assembly. The 1791 change made all active citizens eligible (even though the actual voting outside the canton was still limited to second-degree citizens), and the 1792 reform, in abolishing the active-passive citizen distinction, also made most men, regardless of wealth, eligible for offices.

The election laws put stringent limits on the number and kind of men who might hold departmental positions; in practice, inevitably, the choice was even more limited. Just as every representative Maine-et-Loire sent to Paris was a bourgeois, so were practically all members of the departmental council and all departmental procurators (Bodinier 1888; Uzureau 1902). Furthermore, these departmental officers were generally the most distinguished and wealthiest of the bourgeois of their own milieux, and these milieux were most often the larger cities of Maine-et-Loire. In short, they were most commonly outstanding members of the substantial urban bourgeoisie.

At the time of the Estates, all ten of Anjou's Third Estate representatives were of this urban bourgeois circle, already experienced in administration, ambitious, interested in reform, jealous of the nobles. This group was the nucleus of a body of administrators who almost immediately took over the department and kept the significant offices within their grasp. With many exchanges of position but few important changes, they occupied the high-level departmental posts throughout the early years of the Revolution.

On the *district* level, there may have been a little more turnover, but there was just as great a concentration of membership in the bourgeoisie. The electors for these offices were the same as those for departmental and national posts; here, again, they chose from their own number, and rather consistently chose the wealthy. Except for one priest elected in 1790, and one famous renegade noble, the ranks of the District of Cholet were solidly bourgeois from 1790 to 1793. In Cholet, the officials were drawn especially from among the merchants and notaries; the District of Saumur, on the other hand, leaned more heavily to lawyers and administrators (Uzureau 1945, 1947).

The composition of district and departmental administrations was a crucial fact in the political history of Maine-et-Loire. In one respect, the officials were old hands: most of them had held administrative positions, many in local branches of the royal government. In another, they were new men: they now filled posts the likes of which had always been noble property, responsible no longer to the Court but to the all-important body of bourgeois in Paris. This bourgeoisie, then, with its long-standing struggle against both nobles and clergy, with its enlightenment and education, with its recent acquisition of power, was charged with guiding Revolutionary change in Maine-et-Loire. This meant, for the department, administering the Civil Constitution, apportioning taxes, eventually raising troops, and keeping order. For the district, it meant especially conducting the sales of church properties, getting taxes collected, keeping Patriots in public office, and subduing uncooperative communes.

The *cantonal* elections did not directly form any administrative bodies, but they produced the electors who did that job and who selected the district and departmental officers. They are especially interesting because they involved enough people, and were close enough to the local level, to convey some of the substance of day-to-day politics.

Most cantons contained four or five communes; they were small enough units to give full expression to local solidarity, or local rivalry. Although the higher assemblies witnessed plenty of maneuvering and electioneering, it was in the cantons and individual communes that factions formed early and fought bitterly. While the elections of 1790 went off without great commotion, the elections of 1791 and 1792 were often occasions of anger and disruption. In Chemillé's elections of June, 1791, for example, the bickering between the Patriots (based in the city) and their opponents (coming mainly from the surrounding countryside) went on for two full days, with threats of mayhem from each side (A.D. M-et-L 1 L 321). Ineligible voters from St. Sauveur forced their way into the electoral assembly at Landemont, and the National Guard of Chaudefonds ejected the unacceptable voters from Saint-Aubin-de-Luigné who had come to the cantonal elections (A.D. M-et-L 1 L 349).

A similar sort of exclusion occurred at La Chapelle-Sainte-

Radegonde in Vendée. A large group of residents of Le Bois-de-Cené stormed the electoral assembly in La Chapelle. Many of them were ineligible to vote because they paid too little in taxes and because they were not signed up for the National Guard. The group attacked and disarmed the line troops sent to keep order in the assembly. The interrogation of Jean Poupet, a day laborer of Bois-de-Cené, went as follows:

Asked if he and other residents of aforesaid parish did not decide to go to the assembly.
Replied that many people had told him that everyone had to go, but that he had no intentions in going.
Asked if there was not some trouble at the door of the Chapel of Ste. Radegonde.
Said yes.
Asked what caused the trouble.
Said the trouble was caused by the fact that they had not called out all the citizens of the parish, not even the well-to-do ones, and they would not let them into the chapel where the assembly was to be held (A.D. Vendée L 1726).

In fact, they were kept out because they were already known to be enemies of the Patriots. Disputes over the religious reorganization and antibourgeois violence had kept the vicinity of La Chapelle-Sainte-Radegonde stirred up since the end of 1790 (see Chassin 1892: I, 215 ff.).

Some of the issues involved in these last cases were characteristic of the political maneuvering of 1791 and 1792. The citizens from St. Sauveur and those from Bois-de-Cené were considered ineligible, among other reasons, because they had not signed up for the National Guard. That was a common failing in the Mauges. The unacceptable voters from Saint-Aubin-de-Luigné had refused to take the standard civic oath without explicit reservations on matters of religion. The oath became a burning issue (see de la Gorce 1909–1911: II, 386). In form, it was nothing but a simple statement of allegiance to the nation, but it was widely thought to be equivalent to the fateful oath of the clergy. The electoral body of the canton of Jallais disqualified itself during the 1791 proceedings by refusing to take the oath; later, its leaders complained that "insidious maneuvers convinced them that by taking the required oath before naming their electors they renounced their religion, [so] most of them refused it"

(A.D. M-et-L 1 L 323). At Jallais' cantonal elections of the following year, the issue came up again and led all but a small number of Patriots to withdraw from the assembly (A.D. M-et-L 1 L 324). The attempt of the Aristocrats to avoid the oath was the main point of contention during the 1792 elections of the canton of Le May (A.D. M-et-L 1 L 324). There and elsewhere, the Patriots sought to use the Aristocrats' refusal of the oath to disqualify them from voting. Where the counterrevolutionaries were in the clear control, as at Clisson in 1792 (A.D. Loire-Atlantique L 166), a common counterstratagem was to "assume" that everyone present had already taken the oath. On the whole, however, the effects of the dual requirements — oath and National Guard registration — was to discourage the active citizens least likely to vote for good Patriots.

It is of some interest to see whom these cantonal elections elected. From a wide variety of sources (esp. A.D. M-et-L 1 L 321–324 and Uzureau 1903, 1915, 1930, 1945, 1947), I have assembled lists of the communal representatives to the Estates General and of the electors chosen by the cantonal assemblies, with occupational identifications for as many as possible. By scouring voting lists, population enumerations, parish registers, and a number of other sources, it was possible to identify about 80 percent of the persons on the lists. Table 24 presents the occupational distribution of those who were identified for each year and district. The communal representatives and cantonal electors were reasonably representative of the local political activists of southern Anjou. For the later years, the lists for many places read like rosters of the outstanding Patriots. The table therefore has information to offer on three problems: 1) the identities of those most active in formal politics in southern Anjou, 2) changes in political participation, 3) differences among the districts.

The outstanding fact about the political activists is how many of them were bourgeois. At every time in every district, the bourgeois (who comprised less than a tenth of the total population) had more than half the places; at times they had over three quarters of them. The only other group that ever had a substantial number of representatives were the large farmers, and they did not last long. In the District of Cholet, with its numerous merchants and manufacturers, the commercial bourgeois predominated, but in the other districts the lawyers, doctors, notaries, and officials outweighed them.

The changes from 1789 to 1793 are equally interesting. As a matter

Table 24. Occupational distribution of cantonal representatives, 1789–1792.

	Percent of representatives identified															
District	Cholet				St. Florent				Vihiers				Saumur			
Year	1789	1790	1791	1792	1789	1790	1791	1792	1789	1790	1791	1792	1789	1790	1791	1792
Noble	—	1.6	3.6	1.7	—	1.7	0	0	—	0	0	0	—	0	0	0
Priest	—	6.4	1.8	5.0	—	13.3	3.4	14.6	—	2.0	2.0	5.3	—	0	4.4	5.6
Large farmer	39.2	14.3	3.6	8.3	31.0	18.3	8.6	0	11.3	4.1	5.9	13.2	23.3	11.4	1.5	7.7
Other peasant	0	0	0	5.0	0	0	0	0	3.8	2.0	1.9	0	4.6	0	0	1.9
Commercial bourgeois*	32.4	44.5	44.7	50.0	21.4	13.3	24.1	9.8	41.5	34.7	35.3	34.2	32.6	25.0	33.8	26.9
Other bourgeois	19.6	25.4	35.7	28.3	31.0	40.0	43.1	43.9	29.3	36.7	43.1	39.4	24.0	56.8	53.0	48.1
Industrial artisan	2.0	4.8	3.6	0	1.2	6.7	5.2	7.3	5.7	2.0	2.0	0	2.3	2.3	2.9	1.9
Other artisan	2.9	1.6	5.3	1.7	7.1	3.3	12.0	19.5	4.6	12.3	9.8	7.9	6.2	2.3	2.9	3.9
Other	3.9	1.4	1.7	0	8.3	3.4	3.6	4.9	3.8	6.2	0	0	7.0	2.2	1.5	4.0
Total identified	102	63	56	60	84	60	58	41	106	49	51	38	129	44	68	52
Total unidentified	13	7	7	9	21	14	8	25	12	15	8	19	22	45	32	46

* Including innkeepers.

of principle, we ought to disregard any minor percentage differences, based as they are on small numbers and incomplete identifications. That restriction still leaves us with some important findings. Nobles and priests were ineligible to represent their communes in 1789. After then, the nobles were virtually absent from formal politics. The role of the priests (all of whom were Constitutionals in 1791 and 1792), in contrast, generally increased. The artisans, who never controlled a large number of offices, remained relatively constant.

The most important changes were in the positions of peasants and bourgeois. The peasants, who were prominent among the communal representatives to the Estates General, declined sharply in numbers in 1790, and again in 1791, only to recover some of their places in 1792. That the peasants should have lost ground through withdrawal and exclusion is not surprising, but their partial return in 1792 is harder to explain. It may be related to the relaxation of the requirements for voting that year. In any case, as the peasants receded from public office, the bourgeois acceded to it. The bourgeois were greatly overrepresented in public office from the beginning, and their share actually increased as the Revolution proceeded, even if they did suffer setbacks in 1792.

The differences among the districts are not so clear or so consistent. It may be safe to say that 1) in Val-Saumurois as a whole, the bourgeois achieved their control over public offices earlier in the Revolution than they did in the Mauges and 2) the loss of peasant representation was more remarkable in the Mauges than in Val-Saumurois. By 1792, close to three quarters of the electors of southern Anjou, and a higher proportion of the public officials, were bourgeois. Only the District of St. Florent, where Constitutional priests and artisans contributed an unusual number of electors, was an exception. Even there, the bourgeois were the masters of the Revolutionary government.

Their mastery was much less certain in the communes, particularly in the Mauges. When we reach the level of the individual community, moreover, we begin to realize that the roughly valid equation, bourgeois = Patriot, is not perfectly accurate. It is true that the Patriotic forces were headed by the bourgeoisie, and that the bulk of the rural Patriots were bourgeois. But it is also true that a small number of bourgeois were counterrevolutionary activists, and that another group played the part of "moderates" as long as they could. The principal facts which make it reasonable to keep on talking about party divisions within the community in terms of social class are the frequency with which the local Patriots were spearheaded by rural merchants and officials, the rarity of peasants and nobles in their midst, and the regularity with which their active opposition grouped substantial peasants, parish priests, and a segment of the local artisans.

In the Commune

While departments, districts, and cantons were fresh inventions, the communes were age-old institutions, refurbished. The first sets of officials for the Revolutionary communes were elected early in 1790. The active citizens voted, and the second-degree active citizens were supposed to be elected. The fact is that this rule was often disregarded, due largely to the sheer lack of second-degree citizens in country communes. In the Mauges, there was a general shortage of qualified and available personnel. Few enough of the active citizens could write more than their names; only a third of those on the voting lists analyzed earlier could even do that (A.D. M-et-L 1 L 444). Almost none were experienced at record-keeping and interpretation of technical government edicts. Furthermore, the peasant substantial enough to be an active citizen was running a farm that gave him little leisure or energy to transcribe laws, attend meetings, and deliberate over local taxes. All the active citizens at Yzernay, for example, were said to be like the secretary: "As a laboureur running a farm, he had to boss his workers and spend all his time on his own business" (A.D. M-et-L C 187). The artisans who were qualified to hold office were in a similar position. This left the bourgeois, the noble, and the priest.

Everywhere, from the beginning, the bourgeois sought and received communal offices, although they were generally most successful where there was the most commercial activity. Almost nowhere in the Mauges did the nobles appear in the (somewhat degrading) communal offices, particularly after 1790. But in many places the priests appeared as mayors and procurators, and throughout the countryside they were members of the communal councils of 1790. The retiring members of the old District of Beaupréau doubted that anyone else was available for the technical work of the communes (A.D. M-et-L C 186).

This was the state of affairs in 1790. The communal councils, however, were not as stable in composition as those of district and department. By 1791, priests had disappeared from public office. By 1792, wherever there was an effective party of Patriots, the non-Patriots had also virtually disappeared. Where there were bourgeois, they took more and more control; where there were Patriots, they came more and more to have the communal offices to themselves.

This change in membership was by no means imperceptible, gradual, or tranquil. It was the resultant of bitter conflicts, constant maneuvering, and the eventual turbulent withdrawal of many non-Patriots. The Patriots won earlier in the cities, but even there they faced the same struggle for position in the commune.

There were, as we have seen, some factional fights in 1790 and some premonitions of the later electoral struggles, but open contention between parties did not become the rule in local elections until 1791. The first regular communal elections after the religious troubles broke out were held in November, 1791. They were full of fireworks. The disgruntled Aristocrats of Saint-Sauveur-de-Landemont, allied with the Refractory curé, sought to repeat an earlier success at the cantonal elections by breaking up the communal elections controlled by the Patriots of Landemont (A.D. M-et-L 1 L 204). The same legalistic points that were so much mooted in the cantonal assemblies, registration for the National Guard and acceptance of the civic oath, were matters of heated argument in the communes. In La Plaine, a large crowd heard a tailor and an innkeeper deliver inflammatory speeches against the "democrats," then angrily surrounded the house of the mayor, who had refused to let them sign up for the Guard at the last minute before the elections. The crowd conducted its own illegal election and chose the innkeeper mayor. But the District refused to accept an election in such bad form (A.D. M-et-L 1 L 349). At Mozé, the outnumbered Patriots sought to have a representative of the department at their elections in order to force the taking of the oath, and thus rule out their opposition. This was, they said, the only way to foil a plot to elect only Aristocrats. Indeed, after their request had been ignored, a certain Bâtard, "connu pour son incivisme," was elected (A.D. M-et-L 1 L 349). At La Poitevinière, where Patriotism was practically unknown, the municipal officers reported frankly that they had been unwilling to administer the oath. The explanation was simple:

> If we had asked for the oath prescribed by law we could not have found a single citizen in the parish who would have been willing to take it without restriction; not in order to avoid the law, to which all the citizens of La Poitevinière profess to conform, but in order to avoid the disturbance which would grow out of the permanent annulment of the municipality, we proceeded to the new nominations (A.D. M-et-L 1 L 204).

The new oath of Liberty and Equality, at the end of 1792, again brought agitation, division, and the resignation of municipalities (Port 1888: II, 38–39). As in the case of the earlier decisions of the clergy, the requirement of a public oath forced even the temporizers to declare where they stood, and thus served to hasten the bifurcation of the population into opposing parties. It crystallized the conflict.

The installation of the Constitutional priests also forced people to commit themselves on local politics. Once they were on the scene, the Constitutionals religiously took part in local elections. Elections thereupon became occasions for demonstrating against the religious reforms as well as complaining against the local Patriots. At La Pommeraye, by November, 1791, frequent and massive nocturnal processions were demonstrating the depth of local feeling against the new regime. When the communal elections came along that month, disorder broke out. An unruly crowd of citizens hooted the Constitutional, and protested his presence at the assembly. The chief hooters, according to the community's Patriots, were the same people who were leading the processions (A.D. M-et-L 1 L 349, 1 L 364). By that time, the religious and political questions were inseparable. The choice a person made on one determined his choice on the other.

One can see the troubled context of the communal elections at Le May. Le May's bourg was an important center of the textile industry, and the home of a good number of weavers, merchants, and manufacturers. Among them, there was a determined group of Patriots. However, there were also plenty of energetic Aristocrats at Le May. The textile crisis had hit the big community hard, and many of the workers were already muttering threats early in 1790 (A.D. M-et-L C 187). When the mayor, Lebreton, sought to read the decree announcing the Civil Constitution of the Clergy at the beginning of 1791, he was greeted with jeers and stones. In the commotion of the next few days, half his municipal officers resigned, and he began receiving threats on his life (Port 1888: I, 119–120). Roving investigators from the department soon heard the local Patriots, mainly bourgeois and artisans, complain that the Refractory priests were stirring up the people of Le May. Their curé, the abbé Coulonnier, was openly preaching against the religious reforms and reformers (A.D. M-et-L 1 L 357). By the middle of the year, according to another group of traveling investigators, the entire community was split between the two unequal camps, with the supporters of the curé on one side and the Patriots on the other (A.D. M-et-L 1 L 357 bis). Over the summer, pilgrimages to Bellefontaine abbey, not four kilometers from Le May's bourg, became incredibly popular; a full 12,000 people were said to have gone there the week of 20 August (A.D. M-et-L 1 L 367). When the time came for the year-end elections, it was mainly the Patriots of the National Guard versus a crushing majority of Aristocrats. Renou, one of the patriotic handful, gave his impressions of the electoral assembly:

Patriots cannot regard that assembly but as a sectarian mob of violators of the civil law, whom one heard repeating from every side of the hall, "No oath! No oath! No civic register and no National Guard! Yes, we'll bear arms for the defense of the king and the law well enough without that," and of course they were referring to the old regime and religion, for this was the way they swore: "I swear to be faithful to the law, to the law and the king." That was the oath of the president, who was like a little catechumen, and could not be made to pronounce the name of the Nation, which they all hold in horror! Such is the wisdom and prudence of our unworthy opponents. You will see in this new so-called municipality those who resigned from the previous one six months ago or so. And you will see here all the features of complete aristocracy or anarchy (A.D. M-et-L 1 L 203).

The Aristocratic majority succeeded not only in voting without taking the dreaded oath but also in electing their own candidates. The Patriots claimed that the minutes of the meeting had been altered (probably by the curé, they said) in order to make it seem that everything had been in order.

This was a short-run victory for the Aristocrats, but it returned the municipal officers who had resigned earlier to their problems. If the voters of Le May and the rest of the Mauges had to commit themselves, so did the men who were eligible for public office. More and more, they had to choose among three alternatives: 1) faithfully execute the laws of the Revolution, and incur the wrath of many local people, 2) subvert or resist the law, and incur the wrath of the region's Patriots and higher-level officials, 3) stay out of office, or get out of it. They had less and less chance to compromise. A number of municipal officers solved their problems by resigning during 1791. Many other potential officers avoided the electoral assemblies and refused to run. At first, the Department of Maine-et-Loire attributed its difficulties in staffing municipalities to the peasants' lack of competence and fear of responsibility (A.N. F^{1c} III M-et-L). If they really thought so, they were soon disabused, as commune after commune reported the abdication of its officers. As the Directory of the department of Vendée declared in its report of October, 1791:

It is generally in order not to install the pastor elected by the people . . . it is in order not to be obliged to pronounce among their fellow citizens, often equally hot-headed in the means they use to express or argue their opinions, it is in order to have nothing to do with the quarrels so improperly called religious . . . that peaceful but weak citizens avoid municipal offices and lay down the honorable burden of public trust (Chassin 1892: II, 120).

And Coquille, the vigorous Constitutional curé, had to defend his election as a municipal officer at the end of 1792 on the grounds that there were so few voters signed up no other candidates were available (A.N.F.^{1c} III M-et-L 10). Everyone but the Patriotic nucleus had withdrawn.

Not that withdrawal was universal. There were places, like Melay or La Poitevinière, where the Aristocrats remained in office, blocking the work of the Revolution. There were others, like Tigné and Saint-Lambert-du-Lattay, where formal control seesawed between the parties. But the net effect of the many hesitations and departures was increasing domination of the public offices by the Patriots.

The greater the concentration of the bourgeois, in general, the earlier was the shift to Patriotic control of the commune. The extreme case was the cities, in many of which the change never had to occur at all. In Cholet, the bourgeois were already beginning to exclude the peasants from city offices in 1788, and simply accelerated the process with the Revolution. In Chemillé, the bourgeois held the honored places from the beginning.

This shift in control of the formal organization of the commune is the outstanding fact visible in the study of successive local elections in the Mauges. I do not want to exaggerate the regularity, irreversibility, or simultaneity of the change. Nevertheless, it occurred, and most of the important shifts occurred during the year 1791, also the pivotal year for religious changes. Overt support of the Constitutional clergy, moreover, was the most outstanding single issue in these changes. It was present in the mass resignations of communal officers and in the wrangles over the civic oath. But the parties were not formed by this issue alone. They were already forming in 1790 in the efforts of bourgeois factions to wrest control of communes from the curés. In any case, support of the Constitutional was by no means a random matter, but tended to follow the long-standing division between bourgeois and priests-peasants-nobles. The introduction of the Constitutional was a point of mobilization of interests — religious certainly, but political and economic as well — that divided the bourgeois from the rest of the commune. For the first time, the bourgeois had the advantage of the support of government outside the commune. Even the extension of the right to vote in 1792 did not seriously affect their standing, for an increasing number of Aristocrats failed to exercise that right.

Our review of the Revolutionary elections in the Mauges serves two purposes: 1) to indicate the trends in composition of the various levels of government, 2) to illuminate the issues and conflicts that agitated those elections. The higher the level, it appears, the earlier the shift, but in department, district, canton, and commune the personnel were increasingly bourgeois, and increasingly Patriotic, as the early years of the Revolution went on. The higher the level, furthermore, the more uniform the personnel from the beginning, and the less the appearance of party struggles. In the communes themselves developed the bitterest conflicts over the issues that aligned the parties.

For present purposes, the commune and the rest of the administrative apparatus can be treated separately as "inside" and "outside." The district, department, and National Assembly formed a political environment for the communes of southern Anjou, one which was increasingly Revolutionary and eventually Republican, and was always ahead of the communes of the Mauges in this regard. The communes of Val-Saumurois followed much more closely on the heels of national politics. In the Mauges, the "inside," the commune, was constantly dealing with an "outside" that applied pressure for Revolutionary changes.

Divisions by Class

Within the commune, class divisions were important. Artisans, clergy, nobles, peasants, and bourgeois were relatively distinct groups with fairly individual political histories.

Information on the political activity of *artisans* in the Mauges is hard to find. A significant number of them were disfranchised. Very few were officeholders. Many of them, however, led the anti-Patriot demonstrations that accompanied local elections. Others filled the ranks of the National Guard and the battalions of volunteers. Apparently the artisans were more sharply split than the other classes. Whichever side they took, the artisans probably furnished more than their share of political activists.

The *clergy* had occupied an elite position in the commune as well as in the parish. The Revolution, as we have seen at great length, challenged that elite position. The Civil Constitution simply barred parish priests from administrative public offices. Refractories were automatically barred from representative positions as well. This meant that after January, 1791, it was legally impossible for the priests of the Mauges to hold any political offices. As a direct result, the curés who had commonly occupied communal posts in 1789 and 1790 disappeared completely from them in 1791. Then grew a phantom church, an organized attempt to subvert the work of the formal government. The curés kept their places in this government, while losing them in the other.

The study of election minutes and returns hardly gives a hint of the part the *nobles* were playing. They, too, had held elite positions in the commune, especially as advocates before the high officers of the royal government. The disappearance of those high noble officers and the emergence of a government devoted to striking down the nobility wiped out the capacity of the lord to stand between inside and outside, between commune and Court.

Legally, the nobles could have sought offices in their own communes or even outside, as they did so successfully during the nineteenth century. In fact, they did not. Some lords of the Vendée, according to Chassin (1892: I, 119–120), connived to "seize the offices that would conserve their former influence," but there is hardly any evidence of such activity in the Mauges. The political prominence of d'Elbée (whose claims to noble rank were, in any case, disputed by the gatekeepers of Anjou's nobility) at Beaupréau was wholly exceptional. A number of nobles did become commandants of their National Guards, but left long before the Guards became executors of patriotic policy. The events of 1789 and 1790, which abolished all the legal privileges of the nobles, all their special rights to public office, all their priority in the military services, forced the nobles to compete with commoners for what special places remained; most did not care to compete. When the requirement of a civic oath was added, most of the nobles left whatever offices they still held (see Gabory 1925: I, 191 ff.). It is true that a number of the greater nobles, many of whom the counterrevolution made famous, were with the king's Constitutional Guard until its dissolution in mid-1792, and stayed with him until even later. But far more simply retired from public life altogether.

For many who retired, escape to their châteaux was only a prelude to escape from France. The nobles of Maine-et-Loire emigrated early and in good numbers (Greer 1951). For them, emigration had two virtues: it took them from an intolerable situation, and it put them in the direct service of the counterrevolutionary cause. As the official chronicler of the noble house of Gibot put it:

The Civil Constitution of the Clergy and the requirement of the ecclesiastical oath had brought about troubles which were precursors of the Vendean insurrection which was to break out two years later. Seditious movements at Maulèvrier and Tilliers had been reported in January, 1791. People were announcing that an explosion was imminent in other parishes, notably at Montfaucon and St. Germain. By then, Luc-René de Gibot no longer felt safe. The hour of emigration had sounded for him (Duhamonay 1942: 97).

Many nobles of the Mauges were beyond the borders during most of the troubles which led up to the insurrection. They could have no direct part in the affairs that shook so many communes.

Even those that stayed behind mixed little in village politics. In the many reports of disorders in the Mauges, only their absence makes the nobles conspicuous. This does not mean they were rigidly inactive. Châteaux like Bouzillé-Melay were favorite rallying-places for the Refractory clergy (A.D. M-et-L 1 L 364). Nobles like Béri-tault de Salboeuf or de la Haye des Hommes undoubtedly organized counterrevolutionary cabals and dreamed rich dreams of rebellion (A.D. M-et-L 1 L 353). Unquestionably the Marquis de la Rouairie was working in Brittany to assemble an armed conspiracy against the Revolution (see Goodwin 1957). Very likely the counterrevolution-ary communication lines of the Baron de la Lézardière reached from his château, La Proustière, into the Mauges (see Dubreuil 1929–1930: I, 122–123). The real question is whether these maneuvers had much to do either with the ubiquitous political agitation of 1791 and 1792 or with the rebellion of 1793.

So far, no scholar has been able to trace the connection. Not for lack of trying. The gigantic noble plot that created the counter-revolution existed mainly in the mind of Célestin Port. There were many pipe dreams, no plot. *Both* sides talked a lot about counter-revolution before 1793. There were even preparations: Stofflet, the military chief of Maulèvrier and vicinity, is said to have accumulated ammunition for months before the insurrection. Two Patriots who escaped from Saint-Pierre-de-Chemillé at the rebellion, Geneteau and Sochard, declared that "one could see the preparations for this move-ment of the brigands long before. . . . They [the brigands] had even told them several times that all the Patriots would be slaughtered the 14th of March" (A.D. M-et-L 1 L 1018). Certainly an intriguing statement, but not one that shows any general coordination of the movement, even by the local nobles. To put it more generally: so far as the commune was concerned, the part played by the nobles of the Mauges in the organization of the counterrevolutionary party was negligible.

For the *peasants*, the same cannot be said. They were in the thick of it. From the beginning of the Revolution they resisted and resented the efforts of the bourgeois to gain control of the commune. The complaint of trouble with the *gens de la campagne*, the country folk, re-echoed regularly through the reports of the bourgeois administra-tors. Some of the peasantry was kept from voting by the laws of 1790 and 1791, and the richest farmers were sometimes found on the bourgeois side, but in general election disputes aligned those peasants who were active at all with the counterrevolution. As hostility for the Patriots sharpened and the incompatibility of communal offices with support for the Refractory clergy grew, more and more peasants withdrew from any formal participation in the commune.

The gap left by the departing peasants was most often filled by the bourgeois. They had sprung happily into political action at the beginning of the Revolution. The new form of government was well suited to enhance their power in the commune, at the particular expense of the curé. The law gave them advantages both as voters and as candidates for office. Ideologically, the reforms of the government outside were more congenial to them than to any other class in the commune. The administrators they had to deal with were men of their own kind. For these reasons, they were the most likely of the class to receive outside support for their actions within the commune, and the most likely to take action within the commune which would receive outside support. They used this advantage not only to take office themselves but also to accelerate the withdrawal of their competitors.

Modes of Party Conflict

Politics, of course, is a matter enveloping far more than elections and public office. The contention of parties in southern Anjou extended far beyond the occasional electoral assemblies. Party membership actually crystallized around the religious issue, or more specifically around the support of the Constitutional and Refractory clergies. The rivalry of parties absorbed and fed on the rivalry of bourg versus hinterland, or of adjacent bourgs; such parochial jealousies heightened the hostility between Patriots and Aristocrats at Landemont and St. Sauveur, at Les Gardes and Saint-Georges-du-Puy-de-la-Garde, at Villedieu and La Blouère, at Beaupréau and Saint-Martin-de-Beaupréau (see Tilly 1961, 1962). Likewise, the ancient mutual suspicion of city and country nourished the enmity between the Patriots of Cholet, Chemillé, Maulèvrier, Montaigu, or Bressuire and the restless rural population. The party division also drew sustenance from the discontent of the textile industry's unemployed. The important thing is that the contest between Aristocrats and Patriots activated all these old tensions and more, and concentrated them all on a single point: Which party would prevail? The two parties moved further and further apart, and their members became ever more clearly identified.

The Patriots had their identifying marks ready-made for them in the wealth of Revolutionary symbols that accumulated after 1789: cockades, songs, publications, slogans, liberty trees. Hampered by the absence of a cheering populace, the country Patriots still followed the rituals of Revolutionary France with sermons, speeches, and celebrations. To a smaller extent, they showed their zeal by forming Revolutionary clubs on the models of the Jacobins and the Cordeliers. That was mostly an urban pursuit, for only cities like Cholet, Montjean, and Chalonnes offered the place, security, and numbers to make club organization feasible. The National Guards were likewise most effectively organized in the cities, but where the rural Patriots could, they had their own. They did in Les Gardes, Vezins, St. Macaire, La Tessoualle, for example, all centers with fair numbers of Patriots. There were many small but stalwart units of the Guard in Val-Saumurois.

The National Guard was a patriotic creature that sometimes ran away from its creators. Quite commonly in southern Anjou, the supporters of the Revolution were divided between the moderates of the communal council and the activists of the National Guard. Beginning around the middle of 1791, various units of Anjou's Guard — notably those of Angers, Chalonnes, and Cholet — made a series of unauthorized raids on suspected centers of Aristocracy, much to the embarrassment of the communes, districts, and departments involved. The Guard of Cholet caused an interdepartmental incident by bringing back "two fat Mulotins and one very fat bundle of inflammatory writings" from the house of the missionary order in Saint-Laurent-sur-Sèvre, Vendée (A.D. M-et-L 1 L 366). In another case, after the District gave them a public scolding for their indiscretions, the Guards of Vihiers sulkily declared they would not serve any longer. "It's the Guard's job to make the law," they were saying, "not to be run by it" (Port 1888: I, 228–229). Thirty-two Patriots of Mozé wrote in September, 1791, to complain that the municipality had formed its own National Guard, with its own man as colonel, and was now trying to abolish *their* unit (A.D. M-et-L 1 L 566[16]). And in July, 1792, the communal officers of Gonnord confessed that they wondered whether their Guard ought to assemble with arms "because of the danger to other citizens" (A.D. M-et-L 1 L 566[16]). The Guards were often eager to arrest, to purge, to strike down those who would not display the sure signs of Patriotism. That created a tactical conflict among the adherents of the Revolution. But it also gave them a very important means of control.

The very characteristics that contributed to the Patriots' control of local offices — those which made them supporters and beneficiaries of Revolutionary law — multiplied their problems as administrators. In all of their principal tasks, collecting taxes, supervising public works, regulating religious affairs, maintaining order, the Patriots as public officers had to deal with a recalcitrant, hostile population. This reduced their chances of effecting their orders without force. The Patriots reduced those chances further by following a policy of energetic devotion to the Revolution, rather than compromise. In terms of such problems as dealing with Refractories and other "enemies of the Revolution," one of the curious traits of Revolutionary politics in Maine-et-Loire was that the districts were more intransigent than the department, and the Patriotic communal officers more intransigent than the district. Curious, but not inexplicable. The district's officers were dealing more closely with their enemies than were the department's, and the communal officers could never escape them. To compound the confusion, the uncompromising communal officers had the least authority of all with the people they had to deal with, and the least possibility of backing up their directives with force. They did, however, use force when it was available, in the form of the National Guard and the few regular troops stationed in the Mauges. At the end of 1792, the Directory of the District of Cholet made it clear that the function of the local Guard was "to keep the bad ones in line and in respect for the law" (A.D. M-et-L 1 L 567). The usual result of their intervention was temporary conformity, followed by even greater troubles when the troops moved on.

About the only other instruments of persuasion the Patriots had at their disposal was the occasional Revolutionary commissar or orator they sent out. He rarely had much success. The best known of these emissaries was Larevellière-Lépeaux, who made several tours of the Mauges. And his most interesting missions were those he made with his *Club Ambulant des Mauges* in April, 1792. He and his companions, in full Patriotic regalia, stormed through the middle of swarming, inhospitable masses of counterrevolutionary pilgrims, and went on to preach the Revolutionary doctrine at Beaupréau (Larevellière-Lépeaux 1895: I, 93–104; Port 1888: I, 322–331). Later, they moved to Chemillé, and "converted" the city, at least for the day. Nowhere did the effects of such moral preaching last very long. It may even have made those who were already in opposition more resistant than before.

I have emphasized the increasing control of the governmental machinery in southern Anjou by the Patriots. For the Mauges, another element must be added: increasing control, decreasing authority. The ability of the Patriots to do their jobs as officers of commune or district dissolved in the hostility and passive resistance of the rest of the population. They bemoaned their isolation and ineffectiveness, but could do nothing about it. They divined the signs correctly, crying "counterrevolution" long before it came.

The correspondence of these Patriotic coteries of the countryside with their allies in the district and department is full of a sense of encirclement. From Tigné came the complaint that "the dominant party is Aristocrat, militantly opposed to the five or six Patriots" (A.D. M-et-L 1 L 360). At Bégrolles there were eleven who called themselves Patriots, in a population of a thousand (A.D. M-et-L 1 L 361). "We ask you, gentlemen," wrote the minority at Saint-Lambert-du-Lattay, "can 12 Patriots stand up to 800 Aristocrats?" (A.D. M-et-L 1 L 349).

Throughout the countryside the Patriots felt enmity rampant and doom impending. They did not hesitate to talk of insurrection, rebellion, counterrevolution. The area around Montfaucon was already a "seedbed of insurrection" in May, 1791 (A.D. M-et-L 1 L 357 bis). At the same time, there were fears of an "immediate and menacing explosion in the countryside" (A.D. M-et-L 1 L 357 bis). By July, the department had received the message so well that its representative wrote, "It appears that they have not abandoned their plans of counterrevolution and that they are working on the sentiments of the people of your district" (A.D. M-et-L 1 L 202). The Patriots heard the war drums' long crescendo. There was little they could do about it, and they surely did very little but stop their ears.

The necessary counterpart of the encirclement of the country Patriots in the Mauges was the surrounding of the cities. It was they that had first generated Revolutionary enthusiasm and they that kept it alive. Within their walls there was plenty of discord, even counterrevolutionary agitation, but almost everywhere the Patriots stayed in unquestioned control.

Among their most important emissaries into the country were their National Guards, who were by that token their most unpopular exports. The Guard of Chalonnes was ever attentive to protect the rights of country Patriots: "But all its promenades across the Mauges resulted in the alienation from Chalonnes of everyone who normally did business there, and we later paid dearly for the terrors our National Guards had inspired, for the Vendeans felt a deep hatred for our city" (Forestier 1900: 12).

The Guard of Cholet also acted. By the middle of 1792, its ministrations to the counterrevolutionary countryside were meeting violent resistance. Lieutenant Boisard, the military handyman of the Mauges, had to report in June, 1792:

On Sunday, the 24th of the present month, five national guards of this city [Cholet] having appeared in the bourg of Puy-Saint-Bonnet, about forty individuals from that parish and the adjoining ones immediately attacked and pursued them. Having caught up with them about a half quarter of a league from the bourg, they overcame them with sticks and stones. Two of the guards had sabers; people took them away, and used them to attack the guards. The peasants did not abandon them until they saw two of them unconscious and bathed in blood. Two others, grievously wounded, were forced to kneel and plead for their lives; furthermore, they were forced to abjure the Patriotic party. The criminals grabbed the national cockade and trampled it, saying that they would slaughter as many Patriots as they could find (Port 1888: I, 437).

Since Puy-Saint-Bonnet was a textile-producing suburb of Cholet, it is quite possible that Lieutenant Boisard's "peasants" were actually weavers. In any case, the attack on the men from Cholet is simply one more instance of rural resistance to the exportation of the Revolution from the cities.

The uneasy relations of city and country in the Mauges, of long standing, had only grown after 1789. The typical fracases with the National Guards and the stopping of grain shipments to the cities are only two of many examples of constant mutual irritation. Chalonnes, again, provides one of the best testimonies:

On the fourth of July 1791, while passing through the bourg of St. Lezin, I stopped at the place of M. Prévost, blacksmith and innkeeper in St. Lezin, where I found four or five young men, weavers, drinking there, who were talking about the aristocracy, and I asked the innkeeper for a mug of wine and asked him to drink with me. In the time it took to drink the mug one of these young men kept saying that if he knew a democrat he would stick a knife through his belly . . . after I had talked with the innkeeper a while he asked me "Aren't you afraid? We're five or six parishes against you at Chalonnes." I answered no that I hadn't heard about it but that when ten thousand men of their parishes came a hundred men of the National Guard of Chalonnes would push them back handily, and at that moment one of those young men came to the table where I was drinking with his knife in his hand saying that if he knew a democrat he would stick his knife in his belly, and then I told that lad to go away, that I had nothing to do with him and at that moment his friends led him away to play at bowls and right away I grabbed my horse to leave, telling the innkeeper not to let anyone say things like that (A.D. M-et-L 1 L 365).

This might be nothing but the wine at St. Lezin, if it were not for the fact that the incident was repeated around every city in the Mauges, in quickening cadence, up to the counterrevolution.

I have not discussed the internal organization of the Patriotic party because so little information is available concerning it. In each commune that had any articulate Patriots at all there were a few individuals who kept the Patriots together, led their planning, and prodded the uncertain. These individuals were ordinarily the liaison with the Patriots of neighboring communes and the higher-ranking leaders of the Mauges. The entrenched positions of the urban Patriots gave them a good deal of influence with their country counterparts. The party in Chemillé, for example, gave moral and military support to their allies in the surrounding communes, Saint-Georges-du-Puy-de-la-Garde, Melay, Saint-Lezin-d'Aubance, La Chapelle-Rousselin, while those allies continued to look to them for guidance. Beyond these general characteristics, the organization of the Patriots in the Mauges is hard to piece together.

The same may be said for the Aristocrats. Within each commune it appears that the individuals who held public offices at the beginning of the Revolution but later withdrew were the usual opposition leaders. This includes the curé himself. Likewise, these local leaders were in communication with each other, but whether there were any nuclei corresponding to the cities in the Patriotic network remains a good question. In neither case is it accurate to speak of a highly coordinated organization, rationally assembled.

The lack of tight organization did not mean a lack of party identification for the non-Patriots any more than for the Patriots. First of all, that "prudent neutrality" into which most people are said to have fled elsewhere (Lefebvre 1924: 778) was impossible in the Mauges. Moderates were squeezed between the factions. The sheer inevitability of a choice between attendance and nonattendance at the services of the Constitutional in a country where church attendance had been close to universal forced the waverers to place themselves in one camp or the other. This decision made, the immoderates of each camp pressed for further proofs of faith from those on their side of the line. Counterrevolutionary proofs took the form of attendance at clandestine religious ceremonies, refusal to cooperate with Revolutionary authorities, assiduous avoidance of all the paraphernalia of Patriotism.

One sign of developing communication among the local Aristocratic parties is the "conspiracy of La Poitevinière" (A.D. M-et-L 1 L 353).

At the beginning of May, 1792, the municipality of Chemillé wrote to the department that an ominous meeting had taken place in the bourg of La Poitevinière a few days before, probably coupled to the return from Paris of the Chevalier de Salboeuf, a noble of Saint-Pierre-de-Chemillé. Another meeting, they said, was planned for 7 May.

The meeting actually took place 8 May, at Courbet's café in La Poitevinière. The district, forewarned, sent a detachment of troops to break it up. They arrived in time to find a table set for a banquet, and found about twenty distinguished citizens, including a number of officers of communes still in the hands of Aristocrats. About a dozen had escaped, and a number of latecomers turned away in time to avoid arrest. The party present were taken for questioning, but maintained that they had met by chance, had no idea of the purpose of the gathering. Several of the Patriots of La Poitevinière questioned, however, claimed that three objectives had been announced: 1) to prepare a demand for the expulsion of the Constitutional clergy and the return of the Refractories; 2) to destroy the Revolutionary clubs; 3) to lay plans for a counterrevolution in the event of failure. Furthermore, the testimony indicated that at the first meeting, the Refractory of Le Pin-en-Mauges had been commissioned to prepare a manifesto, which was to be approved on the 8th of May, and that de Salboeuf had indeed been behind the scenes, although the inn-keeper, Courbet, had done the organizing. At the very minimum, the participants were planning a public appeal against the new religious regime; they may have been contemplating the massive use of force. The episode of La Poitevinière reveals a certain amount of cohesion, determination, and common purpose among the anti-Patriots of the Mauges by the middle of 1792.

Despite the growing unanimity of the counterrevolutionary party, the facts that made control of the governmental machinery easier for the Patriots correspondingly made it more difficult for the non-Patriots. As the conflict deepened, non-Patriots in public office had to disregard or even sabotage more and more of the orders that came from higher echelons. When the Constitutional complained to the district about the treatment he was getting, the officers of the commune had to subvert the investigation that often followed (see A.D. M-et-L 1 L 364–367). This kind of action was feasible in a unanimous community, but increasingly difficult with a vocal patriotic clique on hand.

The demands of both sides — Patriots in commune, district and department versus non-Patriots in commune — for the cooperation of communal officers grew more insistent. As the need of the government for funds grew, the agreement not to pay taxes spread. Administrators were scored by their superiors for failure to collect taxes, by their fellow citizens for any attempts they made to collect them. More trivial, but just as acute, were the conflicting pressures to observe and not to observe national holidays or display Revolutionary symbols. The problem of administering the laws governing the clergy was paramount. Communal councils, we have seen, resigned en masse to avoid installing the Constitutional. Since the Refractories were becoming the department's main worry and the laws concerning them stiffening regularly, the pressures from above to control their activities increased as the determination below to defend them hardened. For those communal officers with Constitutional curés on their hands, another dilemma: how to preserve law and order without appearing to side with the Intruder. All officers of country communes were caught in some form of this conflict. The Patriots generally resolved it by identifying themselves with the Revolutionary authorities; the few moderates stayed in turmoil;

the non-Patriots resisted as long as they could, then left their places.

The alliance of the Patriotic minorities with outsiders was important in itself. The Patriots alienated their friends by the very means they used to strengthen their own positions in the commune. Most significant of all was their calling in of National Guards and regular troops to settle local squabbles and quell their enemies. It was serious enough that the National Guard of La Tessoualle should call for arms from outside to "make safe our brave citizens, who are acting with all possible zeal to maintain good order and the Constitution" (A.D. M-et-L 1 L 566[16]). It was even more critical that the Patriots of Tigné felt impelled to call in troops from outside three or four times in 1791 and 1792 (Sausseau 1900–1901). Troops came in to install Constitutional curés, guard electoral assemblies, break up processions, arrest Refractories, interrogate suspects, or simply to impress the populace. In August, 1791 alone there were soldiers dispatched to Chanzeaux, Beaulieu, Joué, Étiau, Gonnord, Denée, Rochefort, Saint-Aubin-de-Luigné, Sainte-Foy, Saint-Lambert-du-Lattay, Chemillé, Bégrolles, Le May, Jallais, and many other places (A.D. M-et-L 1 L 202). No doubt such forceful interventions reinforced the solidarity of the country Patriots and their friends in the Revolutionary administration. They also reinforced the reputation of the local Patriots as allies of the outsiders, the meddlers, the city-dwellers. The short-run gains of the Patriots led to long-run exacerbation of their struggle with the Aristocrats.

It is this set of circumstances that leads me to speak of a "political crisis" in southern Anjou. Two energetic, angry, unequal parties formed in the countryside. In Val-Saumurois the Aristocrats were generally an ineffectual minority, but in the Mauges they were commonly a powerful majority. A large bloc of the population of the Mauges was alienated from the laws, the personnel, and the available offices of the Revolutionary government. This bloc formed a concerted opposition to the attempts of that government's representatives in the commune to do their jobs. The government lost its local authority, and its means of enforcing its decisions.

Some Local Cases

So far, my account of political developments has been general and far from chronological. A careful recapitulation of events in one canton of the Mauges will help put the political changes in their context of time and place.[1] The city of Chemillé had some 1700 inhabitants at the beginning of the Revolution. There were roughly 4800 more people in the rural communes adjoining Chemillé — Saint-Pierre-de-Chemillé, Saint-Georges-du-Puy-de-la-Garde, and Melay. The city and some of the surrounding bourgs were secondary centers of the textile industry. The bourg of St. Pierre was the most active commercially; in St. Georges the center of industry and trade was in the settlement called Les Gardes; Melay was the most rural of all, with some weaving in the bourg, but very few merchants and an estimated 60 percent of the adult males peasants.

The differences in the activities of the inhabitants of Chemillé, St. Pierre, and St. Georges appear in the occupations of the active citizens of these communes in 1791 (Table 25; A.D. M-et-L 1 L 444).

Table 25. Occupational distribution of active citizens in the canton of Chemillé.

Category	Chemillé	St. Pierre	St. Georges
Bourgeois			
a) merchants and clothiers	40	14	11
b) other	17	3	0
Artisan	71	33	28
Peasant	46	134	87
Priest	3	1	0
Other	17	16	3
Unidentified	0	1	1
Total	194	202	130

Clearly, Chemillé's population was more "urban" than the rest. The city's commercial and industrial activity encouraged mobility, contact with the outside, and at least a modicum of education. Chemillé had the characteristics of other trading cities of the Vendée, while its hinterland remained separate and agricultural.

During the Revolution, Chemillé was the pivot of Patriotic activity in its canton, and the source of guidance and encouragement for the small, beleaguered Patriotic parties in the neighboring communes. The leading Patriots of Chemillé were bourgeois like the notaries, Thubert and Prévost, and the merchant, Briaudeau; they were active and dominant from the beginning of the Revolution. Thubert, for

[1] The following account comes with few changes from Tilly 1961.

example, was not only a deputy to the provincial Estates in 1789, the occupant of posts in the municipal government, and later the holder of such offices as member of the departmental Directory, but also a strong influence on the form and tone of the Statements of Grievances of at least half a dozen communes near Chemillé (Le Moy 1915: II, 32–82).

These merchants and notaries of the city, with their few allies in the rest of the canton, rapidly formed a near-monopoly of Revolutionary offices. The deputies of Chemillé, St. Pierre, St. Georges, and Melay to the Estates General were 8 bourgeois (3 merchants plus 5 notaries and officials), 5 peasants, and a miller. The cantonal electors of 1790, from the same communes, were 3 merchants, a notary, and 3 peasants. By 1791, they were 4 merchants, 2 other bourgeois, a hatter, and an innkeeper. In 1792, it was 4 merchants, 2 other bourgeois, the same innkeeper, and Chemillé's Constitutional curé. In the course of these years, the peasants disappeared and the bourgeois became even more prominent. The pattern appeared with more variations in the communal offices. In Melay, the most unanimously counterrevolutionary of the four communes — and the one with the fewest bourgeois — it never occurred.

This acquisition of the available offices does not mean that the bourgeois Patriots extended their control without opposition, even within the city of Chemillé. As we have seen, the strangulation of kerchief and cloth production in the city after 1789 cut off the work of the textile artisans, and prepared them to curse the merchants and manufacturers for their hard time. Local officials reported in 1790 that "the only remunerative work was the manufacture of kerchiefs for Cholet, but that commerce fell off entirely two years ago, leaving more than two thousand workers unemployed" (A.D. M-et-L 1 L 402). And at the beginning of January, 1791, the municipal officers of Chemillé stated that they feared "criminal excesses" by the unemployed (A.D. M-et-L 1 L 349). They had already witnessed violent demonstrations in the preceding months, and later in the year they were faced with a popular movement in opposition to their closing down of two churches, a popular movement which very likely attracted the same group of the poor and unemployed, and gave them a splendid opportunity to rail against the regime of the bourgeois. Yet the Patriots handled these threats as masters of the city. In the hinterland, on the other hand, they simply tried to keep up the faith of their colleagues in the bourgs and to still the most strident voices of rebellion.

Most of the dealings of the Patriots of Chemillé with the people of the countryside demonstrate the isolation of the two groups from each other and their orientation to conflicting ends. Of course, the Patriots had outspoken allies in the country — a few in the bourg of St. Pierre and an energetic group at Les Gardes. The Patriots of city and country were much more aware of their common purpose and their need to stay in communication than were their counterrevolutionary opponents. Their troubles began when they tried to bring the Revolution to the countryside.

First of all, the local bourgeois were the greatest purchasers of church properties in the canton, while hardly a peasant even bid on them. Prominent on the lists of buyers for the canton were Briaudeau, Prévost, Paumard, Dailleux, Martineau — stalwarts of the canton's Patriotic party (A.D. M-et-L 12 Q 280–281). In addition to buying church properties, the Patriots of Chemillé reached out into the countryside in an unsuccessful series of attempts to keep the work of the Revolution going. They strove to assure the collection of taxes. They recruited and encouraged the Constitutional clergy; Thubert and Martineau alike arranged for their sons to serve as curés; Prévost and Thubert persuaded the Constitutional of Le May to return for a second try at winning the affections of his parishioners, after the parishioners stoned him on his first appearance in town (A.D. M-et-L 1 L 353). They reported to the department on uncooperative communal officers and suspicious events. They were the ones who gave word to the department of the conspiratorial meetings at La Poitevinière. Furthermore, the National Guard of Chemillé, as well as other troops stationed in the city from time to time, often went out into the country in response to the pleas of the bedeviled rural Patriots. The armed force of Chemillé, however, was insufficient to keep the country in peace and Revolutionary order; the frequency with which the Patriots of Chemillé called on district and department to send in troops measured both the depth of their anxiety and the magnitude of their problem.

The Patriots devoted special attention to the control of the most obvious opponents of the regime: the nobles and the clergy. Although the three prominent noble families of the canton — De la Béraudière, Béritault de Salboeuf, and De la Sorinière — all received close inspection more than once during 1791 and 1792, they did not present the major problem, the more so since most of them emigrated in 1792. The Refractory clergy attracted the most worried attention. At the end of June, 1791, the Patriots complained, "The country is infested with Refractory priests and other Aristocrats. . . . We are barely 1 against 30 — We need some weapons, some ammunition, some orders to use them, since on every side we already see our enemies rejoicing at whatever harms the public good" (A.N. F^{19} 445).

The leaders of Chemillé had more than the usual interest in the situation in nearby Melay, where young Thubert, the son of one of their most prominent Patriots, was the Constitutional curé. Melay did not treat its new pastor kindly. Thubert's parishioners hooted him, stoned him, kicked him, manhandled his servant, left unattended corpses on the church steps for burial, drummed on the doors of his house and his church "at all hours of day or night." Thubert gave the old sexton a key to the church so he could wind the village clock. "He excuses that person for missing Mass," Thubert sadly reported, "but it is intolerable for him to have insulted his curé from the bell-tower and to have thrown stones down into his yard at him" (A.D. M-et-L 1 L 364). At the same time, the citizens of Melay were taking all their religious affairs to the Refractory curé and vicar, officially replaced by Thubert, who remained in the bourg. On Thubert's instigation, troops came in from Chemillé at least twice during the five or six months he actually resided in Melay.

Through all his troubles, young Thubert had the firm support of the Patriots of Chemillé, but not of the people of Melay, who avoided and hindered him as much as possible. When Thubert formally complained about his situation early in 1792, the municipality just as formally filed a rebuttal, claiming that the new curé himself was the troublemaker.

His long and dolorous account of conditions in Melay showed the gap that separated the city-bred Patriotic priest from his parishioners. He begged the department to observe that "his parish is nothing but country in the fullest sense of the term, filled with peasant plowmen, with a village composed of twenty or thirty households for a bourg, inhabited by a few weavers, smiths and day laborers, of whom

the larger part only subsist through 'the alms of their curé" (A.D.
M-et-L 1 L 364). His meaning was plain: it would have been un-
reasonable to expect anything but ill will from such a parish.

The situation in Melay was exceptional in only one regard: the
absence of even a handful of outspoken Patriots. In the other communities of Chemillé's vicinity, where there were small bands of
Patriots, most of them connected with the textile industry, the same
pattern appeared: identification and alliance of the Constitutional
with the Patriots, hostility of the vast majority of the population
to both curé and Patriots, continuing local intervention by the leaders
of Chemillé on behalf of the Constitutional and his supporters.

The records of Chemillé's cantonal elections of June, 1791, bear
the imprint of the struggle that marked local politics in the Vendée
from the promulgation of the Civil Constitution to the outbreak of
the counterrevolution (A.D. M-et-L 1 L 321). On the nineteenth of
June, the voters from the city of Chemillé, plus a few allies from the
other communes of the canton, had already finished the preliminaries
and rushed through the choice of officers for the electoral assembly
itself when the first detachment of country people, a group from
Melay, arrived. "Twenty or thirty voters from Chemillé had started
the meeting," says the protest from Melay, "and were hurrying to
finish it promptly, but their eagerness died down at the arrival of
the other voters, they hardly did anything the rest of the day."
Hardly anything, that is, but argue. Immediately a dispute arose
over the hour for which the meeting had been called. This took
until lunchtime. After lunch, the Chemillé group sought to disqualify the country voters by protesting the form of the registers in
which people had signed up for the National Guard. Then they
challenged the qualifications of many of those present, on the basis
of age or taxes paid. Next came a heated discussion of the civic oath,
during which the countrymen tried to insert qualifying clauses (ex-
empting the Civil Constitution, most likely) in the oath they took.
Such a commotion developed that the line troops and members of the
National Guard standing by were asked to quiet things down; they
did so with gusto. Two or three of the demonstrators were arrested,
then rushed off to Angers. By then, it was time to adjourn. The
business begun when the men from Melay arrived in the morning,
the election of tellers, had not yet been completed

The end of the meeting was not the end of the day's disturbances in Chemillé. A noisy crowd gathered in the town that evening, shouting against the local Patriots. A farmer was applauded for declaring that he preferred the old regime, because the new one had done away with "freedom of religion." The same night the chief of a large band seen near Chemillé was captured wearing a white cockade — a symbol of counterrevolution.

The next day, according to their report, the rural contingent arrived early, but went out to eat when they found no one in the church. When they returned, business had begun, and the previous day's recriminations were repeated. Then began another hour or so of accusations, threats, and chaos; once again the troops stepped in, and finally the votes for tellers were counted. The next step was to choose the electors themselves, but it was noon again. That afternoon, the qualifications of all rural voters (except those of the original Patriotic band) were again challenged on one basis or another so effectively that they retired, albeit vociferously, to the back of the church. After they had failed to have their protest officially registered, the countrymen finally left the scene, with the strong encouragement of the city folk. Then the business of the electoral assembly proceeded smoothly.

The official record distinguishes consciously and clearly between the country voters and the urbanites, and leaves no doubt of Chemillé's view on the matter: The others were the tools of nobles and priests. The rural view of the affair appears in the conclusion of St. Georges' report:

Gentlemen, you know from this account that the citizens of country communes are not free in the primary assemblies of the canton of Chemillé, since they spent two days without being admitted to vote, since when they asked for the execution of the law the others mistreated them, sometimes forcing them to remain in the assembly (when natural necessity made them go out, the others had them taken to the door by the soldiers, who were instructed to hold them by the coat), sometimes telling them to leave because no one had need of them, sometimes accusing them of a plot, without proving it when asked to do so (A.D. M-et-L 1 L 321).

The attitude of their opponents was confirmed by the comment the officers of the District of Cholet·appended to the report:

Having examined the request of the municipality of St. Georges, and the endorsement of the Department, the administrators of the District of Cholet

. . . knowing the dispositions of the greater part of the citizens of St. Georges, think that their plan was to name electors who would have followed their principles, and that there is therefore no reason to consider their complaint (A.D. M-et-L 1 L 321).

Evidently, "their principles" were not those of the Revolution. The district greatly preferred to support the Patriots of Chemillé and their few confreres from St. Georges. And in the elections of the following year, it was almost they alone who appeared at the cantonal assembly (A.D. M-et-L 1 L 324).

As the Revolution moved on, the Patriotic colony of Chemillé grew more isolated from the indigenes it was supposed to govern, and lost some of its missionaries to the countryside, although it never ceased its round of Patriotic fêtes, liberty tree plantings, and ceremonial oaths. By the end of 1791, its members were quite aware of the alienation of the surrounding communes and even of the possibility of armed rebellion. In November they reported that "the parishes of St. Pierre and Melay, which are in our canton, and of Jallais, the seat of the adjoining canton, want to fall on Chemillé to crush the municipality and the Patriots, who are in small number here" (A.D. M-et-L 1 L 349).

The analysis was accurate, and it took only fifteen months to prove it. On 13 March, 1793, a contingent of young men from St. Pierre, Melay, and St. Georges, who had gathered in the same kind of haphazard protest against conscription that was occurring everywhere else in the Vendée, joined the band which had first taken over Jallais, and was to overrun Chemillé the same day. The "battle" of Chemillé was one of the first successes of the great counterrevolution. The invaders captured the Patriotic notaries, Thubert and Prévost, and held them as hostages. They were to be killed in three days if the citizens of Melay who had been imprisoned almost a year before for their treatment of Thubert's son, the Constitutional curé, were not released. A daring midnight razzia by troops from Angers snatched the prisoners from rebel hands. Even if the prey escaped, the demands of Melay's forces and their choice of hostages show how much the Revolution they were fighting was for them embodied in the Patriots of Chemillé and in their attempts to control and manipulate the affairs of Melay.

In fact, we may state the case more generally: throughout the

Vendée, the first attacks the rebels made in March, 1793, were against the cities and large bourgs which had been Patriotic centers, against the local leaders of the Patriots, against the very enemies with whom the country people had been doing less violent battle for more than two years. The daughter of a prominent merchant-Patriot of St. Pierre, whose home the rebels had taken over, stated that "their plan was to massacre all the Patriots," and that the rebels "had announced they were going to make everyone who had deviated from the old laws do penance for it" (A.D. M-et-L 1 L 1018). The most immediate penance the Patriots thus singled out had to do was to suffer the pillaging of their personal property, since most of the men themselves fled to the safety of larger cities than Chemillé when the counterrevolutionary forces came near.

The events at Chemillé during the early Revolution display both the urban-bourgeois character of Revolutionary activity and the uneasy relationship of city, bourg, and country. It is convenient and desirable to take one further step into the country, in order to show how the enmity between Patriots and Aristocrats racked the internal lives of rural communes. The records of Saint-Georges-du-Puy-de-la-Garde provide bountiful information on this subject, as do those of each of the other communes of the canton of Chemillé.

St. Georges is just to the south of Chemillé. At the Revolution it had two poles, the bourg, properly speaking, at St. Georges itself, and Les Gardes, a concentration of textile workers and merchants about a nearly depopulated Augustine monastery. I shall refer to the bourg as St. Georges, to the other center as Les Gardes, to the commune as a whole by its full, sesquipedalian name, Saint-Georges-du-Puy-de-la-Garde. St. Georges was an old center for the rural population, while the weaving at Les Gardes was an eighteenth-century growth, an offshoot of Chemillé's industrial prosperity. The outstanding citizens of Les Gardes, all bourgeois, stayed in close contact with the bourgeois of Chemillé, who were their business associates as well as their friends. In 1789 this influence was strong enough to allow Thubert of Chemillé to play a decisive part in the preparation of the local Statement of Grievances.

There is no significant record of troubles in 1790. The monastery was closed down without much difficulty, the property seized. During the year, the people of Les Gardes seem to have formed the plan of establishing themselves as a legally separate commune. At this time, the farmers of St. Georges and the bourgeois of Les Gardes were rivals, but fairly peaceful ones. At any rate, the richer peasants were well entrenched in the communal offices. Early in 1791, the municipality of Saint-Georges-du-Puy-de-la-Garde consisted of fifteen peasants (métayers and bordiers), two clothiers, and one weaver. The substantial merchants of Les Gardes were left out.

There were signs of the struggle to come. The most prominent leaders of the two parties were already visible: Hilaire of St. Georges, a well-to-do peasant, part-time clothier, and mayor in 1790; Martineau of Les Gardes, an important textile merchant, spokesman of a large family of bourgeois Patriots, closely allied with the merchant families of Chemillé and St. Pierre.

The real troubles between the parties began with the Civil Constitution. The curé and the vicar both refused the required oath, and by April, 1791, M. Martineau had arranged the election of his son as Constitutional curé. The entire municipality resigned, giving three reasons: 1) Almost all the laws they had to administer were against the will of their fellow citizens. 2) The seat of the commune was to be moved to Les Gardes (while they were mostly inhabitants of St. Georges). 3) They wanted nothing to do with the election of the curé. Despite this, they kept nominal possession of their offices for quite a while. At about the same time, the leading citizens of Les Gardes complained to the district that the old curé, at the end of his tenure, was running a regular boycott of the Patriotic workers of Les Gardes, keeping them out of work to force them to keep attending his services. "The municipality," they commented, "as Aristocrat as its curé, who was its adviser, refused to fulfill its function and has announced its resignation" (A.D. M-et-L 1 L 365).

After the installation of young Martineau as curé, apparently without help from the old communal officers, complaints about the Refractories of the vicinity and about the Aristocratic faction flowed steadily from Les Gardes. It was not long before the new Constitutional called in the troops to strengthen his position. As a result, May, 1791, was one of the most turbulent months of the community's history.

The troops were composed of a few regulars and a company of the National Guard of Cholet. They began their work on 15 May by threatening Jean Picherit with "three bullets in the belly" if he did not attend the services of the Reverend Martineau. The next day, the soldiers beat up Jacques Bureau, apparently because he was loitering outside the church during the Constitutional's Mass. They grabbed and threatened Jacques Legeay, a former monk pointed out by the Martineau family as preaching sedition, and gave his brother their favorite threat: three bullets in the belly. Two days later, M. Martineau took the troops on a tour of the houses where children had recently been born. The little band of missionaries spent the day collecting babies, parents, and witnesses at sword's point, taking them off to the parish church for the appropriate ceremonies.

The same day the baptisms were going on, an election was held at St. Georges. The municipality was simply reelected, without the inconvenient formality of civic oaths for the voters. But when the department sent its agents to investigate — and presumably to assure the execution of the oath — on 22 May, the officers simply resigned once again.

The departmental agents interviewed a number of citizens and tried to get to the root of the troubles. The men from St. Georges simply blamed the "many intemperate actions" of the Martineau family (A.D. M-et-L 1 L 357 bis). But M. Briaudeau of Chemillé, in his comments on local affairs, blamed the mayor's attempt to shelter the Refractory clergy, to disorganize the National Guard, and to hamper the enterprises of Les Gardes in every way (A.D. M-et-L 1 L 365). In the light of all this, the conclusion of the agents was rather mild: "We are convinced that there are two parties in this parish, that of the old curé, generally followed by the residents of St. Georges, and that of the new curé, supported by the residents of Les Gardes" (A.D. M-et-L 1 L 357 bis). They offered no solution, and the troubles went on.

Complaints against the Refractories redoubled, but the leaders of St. Georges, somehow back in office, denied all the charges and refused to act. The National Guard of Les Gardes took the initiative in June, 1791, searched the house of M. Le Goust at St. Georges, discovering an altar prepared and a number of people gathered as if for a religious service, but they did not find the former vicar, Barbotin, who was surely not far away. It was at this time that

M. Martineau reported that "Aristocratic clubs" were forming at St. Georges, with subversive intentions.

At this stage of the Revolution, the most obvious issue separating the two parties of Saint-Georges-du-Puy-de-la-Garde was the Civil Constitution, or, in more personal terms, the division of allegiance between the two young priests, the deposed vicar and the imposed curé. The rival priests carried on a bitter correspondence, each claiming the other was illegitimately practicing his profession. Barbotin wrote to Martineau:

M. le curé of I don't know where, you have enjoined me by your letter to leave the parish of St. Georges, whose curé you claim to be in spite of me, within three days. M. l'abbé of I don't know where, I have no orders to receive from you, but from MM. the administrators of the Department of Maine-et-Loire, with whom I hope to find greater indulgence, justice, politeness, uprightness, and honesty. I am not a lawbreaker, and I say so on the authority of the Bishop of Autun. Since the National Assembly has decreed the liberty of religious opinion and the freedom to practice any sort of religion, I choose my own way and leave everyone else the liberty to choose his (A.D. M-et-L 1 L 970).

But Barbotin was too optimistic concerning the indulgence of district and department toward Refractories. Their police measures forced him into hiding later in 1791, somewhere in the vicinity of St. Georges; he did not return to public view until 1793, when he appeared as one of the notorious soldier-priests of the counterrevolutionary armies.

June, 1791, was also the time of the cantonal elections at Chemillé, the elections already described which pitted St. Georges and the other country communes against Chemillé and the Martineau group from Les Gardes. Here the latter party won out, and began to win more often in the local political arena. With the assistance of their National Guard and that of Chemillé, the Patriots of Les Gardes were able to check their enemies at St. Georges, although never to enlist their cooperation in Revolutionary endeavors. Despite the passionate but unheeded protests of the St. Georges group, they were able to transfer the parish church to Les Gardes, and to strip the old church of all its goods.

By the end of 1791, the Patriots had taken over the communal offices, to hold them to the time of the counterrevolution. Young Martineau became mayor as well as curé, and was able to recruit four volunteers to fight for the nation, as well as a small but active National Guard. The control of the Patriots was strong enough that none of the commune's Aristocrats appeared at the cantonal elections of 1792. Yet that control was largely limited to the formal politics of the commune. The opponents of the Revolution withdrew from politics, but they did not cease their resistance to Patriotic attempts to institute religious and economic changes.

Bickering continued and bitterness increased. An undated letter (probably from mid-1792) from the National Guard of Les Gardes reads: "Just as they do to us, we raise our arms to curse the blasphemies of our neighbors, St. Georges, Tourlandry, Trémentines, and Melay, sworn enemies of the Constitution" (A.D. M-et-L 1 L 567).

The cursers and the cursed were soon to do battle. In the days just before the counterrevolution began, the band of young men from St. Georges, St. Pierre, and Melay who had assembled to protest conscription milled about not far from Les Gardes. The Patriots of Les Gardes, in a foolhardy gesture, sent their National Guard to the defense of Cholet, only to be overrun themselves shortly thereafter.

The Martineau family and their allies were the first targets of the local rebels, led by the former mayor, Hilaire. According to the mayor-curé:

They were especially out to get my family. Prices had been put on our heads. Returning through a thousand dangers to die at my post, I saw five hundred tigers make up to twenty-seven visits in a day, to avenge, they said, the outrages to religion that my father, my family, and I had committed. "The Martineaux and the Briaudeaux of Chemillé have overturned the Catholic faith. We want their heads!" the wild men shouted in the streets, as they continuously searched for us in the bourg and in the fields for a half league around (A.D. M-et-L 1 L 1018).

The curé's father and his cousin, when found, were killed outright. He himself was tied before a cannon, as if to be blown to bits, and then released — for he was still a priest — on condition that he sign a statement promising the reopening of the church of St. Georges, at his family's expense. The first moves of the rebels of Saint-Georges-du-Puy-de-la-Garde were to redress the grievances which had separated them from the Patriots for the previous two years.

And who were these rebels? "In our commune," replied Martineau, "all the métayers are guilty, except for two" (A.D. M-et-L 1 L 1018). He forgot to mention a number of weavers and a couple of clothiers. Their chiefs were the same Hilaire, Pineau, Bernard, and Barbotin who had been the leaders of the party, composed mainly of peasants, based at St. Georges (A.D. M-et-L 1 L 1018). In fact, the rebels were, for the most part, the same group who had been opposing the Patriots of Les Gardes for the previous two years.

The case of the canton of Chemillé has been worth examining at length. It demonstrates how deeply the party divisions penetrated the countryside, how long and bitterly the factions fought before the counterrevolution, how close a connection there was between the political crisis of 1791–1792 and the first actions of the counter-revolution. All the important events in the Vendée between 1790 and the outbreak of the counterrevolution found the two parties opposed to each other, and almost all of them involved attempts of the Patriots to enforce the laws of the Revolution. The installation of a Constitutional, the closing down of supernumerary churches, the policing of religious pilgrimages, the organization of local troops of the National Guard, the holding of local elections, the recruitment of soldiers for the national army all brought them into violent disagreement. Precisely in the districts where incidents of these kinds were most common in 1791 and 1792 — the districts of Montaigu, Challans, Clisson, Machecoul, St. Florent, Cholet, Châtillon — the counterrevolution took hold first and with greatest force. That is hardly surprising: the counterrevolution was simply the last and most disastrous clash of the series.

In Val-Saumurois, as in the other sections of the West which stayed in the Revolutionary camp, the political report is largely negative. There were few unusual happenings, few disturbances, few open conflicts. Some of the same kinds of rivalries that tore communes in the Mauges strained them in the other subregions, but they were usually cases of Patriots competing with Patriots. There were non-Patriot factions and supporters of the Refractories, to be sure, but they were almost never in control of their communes, and never in the majority. The party which became the Patriots continued a control of the machinery of government it had long exercised, dealing with the opposition as pests rather than as an engulfing plague. Although there were plenty of avid Patriots and some militant Aristocrats, there was also a mass in between. The sharp division of the entire population into two parties and the transfer of political control which marked communal life in the Mauges did not appear in the rest of southern Anjou. It is good to bear this in mind when labeling one section Revolutionary and the other counterrevolutionary.

CHAPTER 13

Counterrevolution

No one who has an interest in the Vendée should have any trouble finding a dependable account of the history of the region between March and December, 1793, for that was the period of the Great War (see Clémenceau 1909; Dubreuil 1929–1930; Gabory 1925; Godechot 1961; de la Gorce 1909–1911: vol. II; de Malleray 1924; Paret 1961; Port 1888). The events of the war are more dramatic, more stirring, and more the matter of traditional history, than the events that preceded it. This study neglects the heroes of 1793 to attend to the ordinary men of 1792 and before, because the counter-revolution only makes sense in the light of what went before it.

The parties formed long before they fought in 1793, and they formed along class lines. Bourgeois Patriots faced the opposition of most of the rest of the population. Support of the Constitutional or Refractory priest was the obvious point of choice, but a variety of conflicts led to the basic political division. The party of Patriots assumed most of the formal political positions, but lost authority and met increasing resistance to their attempts to enforce the Revolutionary law. Their attempt to enforce the conscription law of 1793 was a continuation of this process, which resulted in their complete loss of authority and in forcible resistance. All this happened in a multitude of places at about the same time, on an essentially local, decentralized basis. There was little coordination of the efforts of the Aristocrats during the formative years or the opening weeks of the war. Eventually, a fairly compact body of leaders formed, who developed a haphazard military organization. That organization, aside from its highest echelon, was a temporary and changing coalition of a number of small but similar local bands brought together for short military actions, concerned first of all with conditions in their own communities. The purpose of this chapter is to rivet these generalities to the girders of all the previous analysis.

Anticipations

Fixing on the events of 1793 can blind us to the frequency of counterrevolutionary outbreaks in the Vendée during the preceding years. The District of Challans, after all, had a series of near-rebellions — complete with the massing of countrymen, threats, beatings, and the smashing of the church pews of Patriots — beginning as early as the end of 1790 (Chassin 1892: I, 220–296). We are already well aware of the acute disturbances at Maulèvrier, Tilliers, Châtillon, and elsewhere at the beginning of 1791. In 1792, there were minor insurrections near Sables-d'Olonne, near La Roche-sur-Yon, and on the Ile d'Yeu, not to mention in Maine and Brittany. At the same time, the nocturnal religious assemblies were swelling and growing more ominous; three or four thousand people were reported to be gathering regularly around St. Crespin in August (A.D. M-et-L 1 L 364). The most serious event of all was the uprising around Bressuire and Châtillon in August, 1792 (see A.D. M-et-L 1 L 368[3]; A.N. F[7] 3690[1] Deux-Sèvres; Port 1888: II, 3–25). That rebellion is little remembered because it fell to pieces rapidly, but it is very much a part of the development of the counterrevolution. It was the first time that the conflict between the two parties led to pitched battles and plentiful bloodshed.

The scene was outside the Mauges, just to the south, but the people of the Mauges were very much embroiled. The turbulent history of the District of Châtillon from 1790 to 1792 had been very much like that of the District of Cholet. In the middle of 1792, the government had begun a campaign against the Aristocrats, had started to enforce the internment of Refractories and had announced a new recruitment law, with a new crackdown on those who did not sign up for the National Guard. At the same time, the municipality of the small city of Bressuire had split, forcing out the non-Patriot mayor. Finally, a number of nobles of the district had recently returned from Paris.

On Sunday, the 19th of August, 1792, a crowd gathered at Moncoutant, protesting the National Guard registration scheduled for that day, then protesting the actions of the Patriots in general. "A bas les cocardes nationales!" they shouted, and then chanted "Vive le Roi, Vive la Noblesse!" (A.N. F⁷ 3690¹). The crowd ransacked the house of a departmental official, then dispersed. Two days later, another mob formed, armed with a few guns and a great many improvised weapons, and started moving toward Châtillon, drinking and looting on the way. From a few hundred, their numbers multiplied. Volunteers rushed in from the southern Mauges and elsewhere. After camping overnight, they set out for Châtillon the next morning, the 22d, now led by the ex-mayor and several local nobles.

Châtillon gave no resistance to the swarm of disorderly rebels, although troops from Cholet were on their way to save the city. Amid the usual shouting, drinking, and pillage of Patriotic households, the crowd's only concerted act was to pile up all the district's papers for a bonfire. Not long before the troops from Cholet arrived in mid-morning, the invaders had straggled onto the road to Bressuire. From Châtillon, the Blues — for that was how all Revolutionary troops were then dubbed, regardless of the colors of their uniforms — used a small cannon to fire on the last of the rebels, and killed two. That started a skirmish, in which a few Patriots were killed and a number of Aristocrats captured.

By evening, the horde, now some 5,000 to 6,000 strong, reached Bressuire, a walled city reinforced by National Guards from all around. Their attempt to take the city was easily repelled, and they disappeared into the countryside. But the next day they tried again with no more success, losing a few more lives. Once again dispersed for the night, they flocked together on the 24th, the following day, for a pitched battle with the National Guards near Bressuire. The insurgents were trampled. That was the end of the rebellion. Altogether, several hundred lost their lives in the few days' battles and in the numerous raids of the Guard into the countryside. About ten Patriots were killed.

Immediately, arrests, investigations, and executions began. Yet after a few days of terror, the authorities became remarkably clement. Most of the suspects were released, a few imprisoned, only a handful executed. Throughout the West, however, action against the Refractories — capture and deportation — took on new vigor. The Department of Deux-Sèvres, having learned that many of the corpses were loaded with religious objects, and having heard from prisoners that the weapons had been blessed before the battles, was prepared to blame the priests for the rebellion. Furthermore, the officials of Maine-et-Loire started a drive to disarm the Aristocrats. The National Guard Units of Chalonnes and elsewhere toured the Mauges, sequestering what weapons they could find in La Jumellière, Neuvy-La Plaine, La Poitevinière, and a number of other centers of counter, revolutionary agitation.

The rebellion of Châtillon aborted, yet signaled things to come. The inchoate army, the noble leaders, the ransacking of Patriotic households, the bonfire of the district's papers, the ebb and flow of rebel forces all reappeared in the first stages of the great counter-revolution half a year later (see Gabory 1925: I, 104). Furthermore, the rebellion apparently set off a variety of secondary explosions in the rest of the bocage, like the armed attack on a Revolutionary courier near Coron, on the 26th of August. And the rebellious area itself stayed in commotion. In December, the rumor was going around the fairs and markets of the District of Châtillon that another, better-organized, insurrection would come just before Christmas. Similar rumors probably flitted from place to place throughout the bocage over the next few months.

There were more minor uprisings early in 1793, most of them directly connected with the increasingly strenuous efforts of the departments to raise troops for the defense of France. In February came disturbances in Saint-Jean-des-Monts, near Fontenay, and at Landeronde. At the very beginning of March fighting broke out over recruitment at Beaulieu and elsewhere in the Vendée. During the same period, there were a number of clashes between countrymen and the forces of the Republic north of the Loire, in Maine and Brittany. In other words, violence was erupting continually in the counter-revolutionary sections of the West from the time of the attacks on Châtillon and Bressuire to the time of the great rebellion. The eruptions came more frequently as the recruitment of new soldiers intensified.

Conscription and its Aftermath

The wars of 1793 began with resistance to military service. For that reason, many writers have not only postulated an extraordinary aversion to conscription among the "peasants" of the Vendée, but also offered revulsion against conscription as cause and motive of the counterrevolution. Thus Michelet (1879: VI, 388): "However fanatical they were, it was not fanaticism that was decisive: it was self-interest, the refusal to sacrifice. *Throne and altar*, agreed; *God and our Good Priests*, yes, but in order not to go to the front." How Michelet or his successors could know this is a mystery. Certainly the often cited Statements of Grievances (as we have seen in Chapter 9) do not bear up the notion that the people of the Mauges were exceptionally hostile to military service.

Until 1793, the new fighting men were volunteers from among the National Guard. Then it became necessary to draft soldiers throughout the country, 300,000 of them, since France had gone to war with most of the European powers. In a population of 25,000,000, this levy did not have the impact of the universal conscription decreed later in the year.

From all of southern Anjou, about three thousand men were to be called. That meant 82 from Cholet, 19 from Melay, 18 from Les Gardes, 50 from Le May, 18 from Andrezé, 26 from Trémentines, 43 from Jallais, only 8 from little Cossé (A.D. M-et-L 1 L 551). Only the single or widowed men, 20 to 40 years of age, were eligible, public officials in general were exempt, and the National Guard was "mobilized in place." But even with these exclusions, the proportion of the eligibles to be drafted was small.

It is not quite right to say that these men were to be *drafted*, since each commune could decide among three methods: 1) filling the quota with volunteers, 2) choosing the soldiers in popular elections, 3) drawing lots. Small matter. Everyone in southern Anjou knew from the beginning that it would be a question of drawing lots.

Why did conscription excite more violent resistance in the Vendée than elsewhere? There were riots, brawls, and demonstrations in many places, but they did not lead to open counterrevolution. The extra factor in the Vendée was the rapid absorption of the narrow grievance of conscription by the broad conflict of parties.

The first point of conflict was the exemptions. The law exempted public officials. Public officials, ergo Patriots. The National Guard, likewise Patriots, were "mobilized in place," and so stayed home. Nothing could be more of a goad to the rest of the people. The Patriots, of course, had a good argument: if they went, there would be no one left to run the government. From Cholet came this dispatch:

> The young people, infected with fanaticism, have fled. Workers have abandoned their shops, the sons and hired hands of our farmers their work in the fields. The heads of families alone have stayed home. As a result, recruitment could not work here without taking merchants and manufacturers. Even then their number would be less than our quota. But these citizens are the only ones who have always behaved well and on whom we can depend. If they have to leave, who will defend our country, in which the enemies of the Nation have never stopped breathing the spirit of rebellion and resistance to the law? You know that Cholet, surrounded by fanatical, counterrevolutionary communes, has been alone in maintaining the Revolution here (A.D. M-et-L 1 L 757, 7 March, 1793).

The departure of these Revolutionary stalwarts would have given the Aristocrats who stayed behind the greatest pleasure. In fact, it was widely rumored that if elections took place, the Aristocratic majority was prepared to designate none but Patriots. The exemption of the numerous officeholders among the Patriots was a stinging insult to their enemies.

As serving the Revolution in communal offices had repelled so many countrymen before, serving it in the army repelled the young men of the Mauges now. No doubt the abstract question of the service of good cause or bad meant something, but it appeared most often as a question of the victory or defeat of the local Patriots. Along the Layon, a gang of young men "went to Coquin's inn to drink, and the idea there was that if they let recruitment go on the Patriots would have the upper hand and the Aristocrats would be sunk (*foutu*), and if they took thirty-five today they would take as many more a month from now" (A.D. M-et-L 1 L 1018: Tigné). They decided not to let the Patriots have the upper hand. Just north of the Loire, at Ligné, a "crowd of men armed with great staves" broke up the preparation of the list of individuals eligible for the draft and declared "that they knew no other law than that of their King, and that if they had to draw to serve the King they were ready to do it, and if they had to make war they were ready to do it that very day" (A.D. Loire-Atlantique L 1504). They followed up their lofty declaration by disarming the local Patriots and pillaging their property.

Another link between conscription and the long-standing conflict of parties was the demand, apparently not so common in southern Anjou as in the Sarthe (Bois 1960b: 640–641), that the buyers of church properties go first. The rebels at Beaulieu offered this challenge: "That they did not plan to draw, but that they would all go on condition that all the other citizens of the parish who had bought national properties and other citizens of the parish would go with them, which response we, the municipal officers, took for a refusal" (A.D. M-et-L 1 L 1018). There were similar ultimata from the vicinity of Vihiers (Port 1888: II, 76–77). Such declarations were inseparable in tone and meaning from the more frequent demands that the Patriots be the first to be drafted.

There had been unpopular governmental moves, of course, long before the levy of 300,000 men. In general, they had been applied piecemeal, depending on the vicissitudes of local affairs. Even the internment and deportation of the clergy had been only partial and episodic. As a result, the resistance to these moves had been sporadic. Conscription was the first attempt of the new regime to enforce a radical, unpopular measure in all of southern Anjou simultaneously. The multitude of party fragments were able to coalesce. From the beginning, the real issue was which party would win out.

In Val-Saumurois, nothing like this conflict developed. Conscription went smoothly, almost without incident (A.D. M-et-L 1 L 206 bis).

The conscription decree of 24 February, 1793, reached most of the Mauges on 2 March. Over the following fortnight, place after place in the Vendée moved from deep agitation to open rebellion. Sunday, 3 March, the young men of Cholet, 500 to 600 strong, gathered and grumbled their discontent with the new law, but nothing serious happened. That night, posters mysteriously appeared on walls in Beaupréau: WOE TO THOSE WHO ANNOUNCE CONSCRIPTION! The next day, the workers of Cholet (apparently drawn mainly from the textile industry, and perhaps including the unemployed) were joined by some of the neighboring countrymen. After the usual drinking and discussion, the crowd grew even surlier than the day before. A cabinetmaker proposed a mass oath to refuse conscription. The National Guard commandant and five men, arriving to calm the mob's temper, were grabbed, manhandled, disarmed, two of them slashed and stabbed. They called for help; more troops came. The reinforcements fired on the crowd, killing three outright and wounding several more gravely. That dispersed the demonstrators, but put them on the road to Le May. There, a group ransacked the houses of the Constitutional and the justice of the peace, took all weapons from the Patriots, and killed one who resisted.

By the next day, the southern Mauges were scintillating with rebellion. The disarming of Patriots went on apace in all the surrounding bourgs, but Cholet still attracted the most attention and the most vituperation. It was reported that the pack of rebels now concentrated in Le May had framed three major demands: 1) release of the prisoners taken at Cholet the day before, 2) no drawing, 3) surrender of the district's arms. They threatened to attack the district at Cholet. Still, nothing happened that day or the next (6 March) but the lumbering of the insurgents from bourg to bourg around Cholet, seizing weapons from the Patriots as they went. A crowd of countrymen murdered the Constitutional curé of Château-Thébault, near Clisson, on the 7th. That was Thursday. No crowds, no threats, no manifestoes appeared for another three days. But with the new weekend, agitation returned, as never before.

The 12th of March was the day scheduled for the recruitment of troops in most of the Mauges. On Sunday, the 10th, and Monday, the 11th, the mobs which had dissipated the week before formed anew, with refreshed determination. This time, however, much more than the immediate vicinity of Cholet was involved. "Seditious gatherings" were sighted near the Loire, in mid-Mauges, on the Layon, near Brittany — not to mention in the rest of the Vendée and north of the Loire. Generally, the young men from several adjacent communities gathered, milled around, drank, brandished their weapons, and muttered their unwillingness to be drafted. The terrified communal officers of Gonnord reported that a troop of 700 to 800 men from the surrounding area was threatening to take their lives. On Sunday, someone shot the department's representative in the shoulder after he had officially announced the draft law in Saint-Sauveur-de-Landemont. Another representative was threatened at Neuvy and St. Christine, but escaped unscathed.

If it were necessary to assign an exact starting date to the great counterrevolution of 1793, Monday, 11 March, would be the logical one. The rebellious gatherings in the central Mauges simply grew more menacing that day. But in the nearest section of Brittany a mass of invaders entered Machecoul and slaughtered its Constitutional. Another mass attacked Bourgneuf, on the coast of Vendée, and small bands raided the Patriots in the vicinity of Montaigu.

Along the Loire clouds of rebels billowed into Landemont and Liré as well as into Varades, just across the river from St. Florent. Lest we think of the "invaders" as foreign hordes, however, and forget how many of them were angry local people, perhaps we should study the testimony from Liré:

Monday, the 11th of March, Jacques Coueffard, Jean Jouin, carpenter, Ethienne Vincent, carter, René Bigeard senior, all residents of Liré, conferred with their sons and their workers at the place of Augustin Javelet, innkeeper in the bourg, on how to block recruitment and work a counterrevolution. That same day, they went to Bouzillé and brought back twenty-five young men, and had the tocsin sounded to call the Aristocrats. Coueffard senior sent emissaries to La Boissière to find out what was happening there, and these people, returning, said they had seen the good Aristocrats assembled and that the patriots were *foutus*. At that news, Coueffard said, "Good, my children, we'll get those buggers!" Tuesday, the sons of Coueffard, the aforesaid Vincent and his workers, the sons of Bigeard and of Jean Marteau, tailor in the bourg, Francois Thuitins, cooper, and Verrous junior, encouraged by fathers Coueffard and Bigeard, went to attack St. Florent (A.D. Loire-Atlantique L 1504).

That attack on St. Florent, the seat of the district, is the traditional starting point of histories of the rebellion in the Mauges.

Early Tuesday morning, the 12th, detachments like the one from Liré, perhaps two thousand strong, converged on St. Florent from all parts of the district. There were few more than a hundred armed Patriots at St. Florent. Three spokesmen for the invaders presented the alternatives: 1) cancel the drawing and give up all weapons or 2) fight. Before any negotiations were possible, someone shot one of the city's officers; that forced the decision. In a brief affray, half riot, half battle, four rebels were killed, but the Patriots were routed. Then came the celebration — bonfires of official papers, emptying of the district's till, raids on the houses of Patriots, abundant wine-bibbing.

The same day, that scene was being played elsewhere — on the same scale outside the Mauges, in miniature at Chanzeaux, La Romagne, Gesté, Cossé. The counterrevolution had begun. Yet we should avoid the common illusion that everything began at the same instant. We have already observed a series of false starts stretching from the end of August, 1792. Scuffles, murders, raids, or demonstrations in one part of the Vendée or another marked the calendar for almost every day from the 3d of March on. While rebels trampled Machecoul on the 11th, and others sacked St. Florent on the 12th, there was silence around Châtillon, and no more than buzzing from the Layon. Along that little river, even the characteristic preliminary incidents — the gathering of Aristocrats in the bourg, the drinking, threats, and disarming of Patriots — did not occur widely until the 13th.

Then, as one of the participants testified:

The day of the drawing in the commune of St. George Chambelaison [*sic*] there were about one hundred thirty other boys like him who were from the parishes of Martigné Briand, Tigny, Cernuson, or Trémond at St. Georges to tell the boys of the parish of St. Georges who were then assembled to draw for recruitment in the army, that their intention was not to draw in their parish, that they wanted to form a battalion with the citizens Aurioux and Duquesne who are commandants of the National Guard of Martigné at their head and if Aurioux and Duquesne refused to march at their head they would not go (A.D. M-et-L 1 L 1018).

The challenge to Aurioux and Duquesne was nothing but a pretext, for after breaking up the assembly at St. Georges:

They went to the bourg of Tigné and to the inn of the citizen Coquin, where they stayed to drink and there they all said that if the boys of the other communes did not want to furnish their contingent for recruitment in the army they would join them and we wouldn't have them except by force. Asked if they had stayed at the inn a long time he said they stayed there at least three hours, and during that time they kept repeating that they would not furnish their contingent (A.D. M-et-L 1 L 1018).

It was several more days before the area broke into open rebellion.

The same day, nearer the center of the Mauges, the first actions that could be called military took place. A force which assembled in La Poitevinière and gained recruits all along its way headed for Jallais, complete with a handful of leaders, artisans and innkeepers, on horseback. Perhaps 800 of them pressed into Jallais without harm and overwhelmed the tiny National Guard. This netted them their first field piece, baptized the *Missionaire*.

The other actions of the day were mostly like this one, for there were few Patriotic defenders left anywhere in the heart of the Mauges. Vezins was taken, and Beaupréau. The horde which had seized Jallais, swollen to several thousand, overran Chemillé. The total deaths by counterrevolution in the Mauges that day were probably under fifty.

On the 13th, the first important leaders of the counterrevolution appeared. Stofflet, the gamekeeper of Maulèvrier, a retired soldier, had taken Vezins. Perdriau, old soldier and tobacconist, and Cathelineau, innkeeper-carter, were among those on horseback at La Poitevinière. By sundown, several rebel bands had sought out nobles as their chiefs, among them Bonchamp and d'Elbée. Still, it does not appear that any unit fought under noble leadership for another two days.

On the 14th, the combined forces of most of the eastern Mauges fell on Cholet. It was still a matter of overwhelming a handful of regulars and a number of National Guards. The counterrevolutionary "army" was no doubt motley and ill-disciplined, but it was 10,000 strong and under the command of a professional soldier, Stofflet. The Revolutionary force of 400 melted quickly in the heat of battle. In the name of the Christian Army, Stofflet took over the city and began to track down the Patriots. The total dead and wounded for the day may have been 300.

By the end of the 14th, almost all the Mauges were in the hands of the rebels. All but the fringe cities had been taken. The Layon was still feverish but *hors de combat*. The next few days erased the remaining cities and established the Layon as a military frontier. On the 15th, the rebels occupied Montjean. On the 16th, Vihiers fell, after the first pitched battle of the counterrevolutionary soldiers with regular troops of the Republic.

By the 19th of March, the administrators of Maine-et-Loire had to dispatch a worried report to the Minister of War. They had been able to calm the area north of the Loire, but

Our affairs on the left bank of the Loire are in much worse shape. The districts of St. Florent, Cholet, and Vihiers pillaged, ravaged, and burned, more than five hundred Patriots slaughtered in these different cities. Two formidable columns of rebels led by experienced men are marching en masse on Saumur and Angers. The little army we put into the field tried in vain to battle that enormous mass. It was forced to retreat rapidly to Ponts-de-Cé in order not to be cut off (A.N. M 669).

Three days later, Chalonnes capitulated without a battle to a great force led by Stofflet, d'Elbée, and Bonchamp. By then, the counterrevolution was a force to be feared.

The Coalescence of Local Rebellions

What appalled administrators of the West had witnessed during the first three weeks of March was the coalescence of a number of separate counterrevolutionary movements into one great rebellion. The initial outbreaks shared an interesting combination of common themes and deep localism. The localism stands out in the earnestness with which each little group of rebels sought to even the score with its own particular set of Patriotic enemies, the immediate appearance of demands for the redress of entirely local grievances, and the apparent lack of any plans beyond righting the balance in the community, or handful of communities, from which the band of rebels came. The common properties begin with the fact that most of the local bands formed initially in ill-organized demonstrations against conscription. Young, unattached men predominated in the earliest outbreaks. They were the ones who were subject to the draft, and this alone may account for the large proportion of hired hands, day laborers, and artisans in the first demonstrations against conscription. But these were also the "boys" who could generally be counted on for action instead of talk. And they included the very individuals who had suffered most from the price rises and economic pressures of the early Revolution. They were the men who were readiest to lash out at the Patriots.

Around the nuclei of young men formed increasingly well-defined local rebel bands. During the week between the first riots in Cholet and the first invasion of St. Florent, whatever leadership and organization appeared among the rebels was shadowy indeed. During the months to follow, on paper at least, a system of squads, companies, and the like emerged. Not only were there captains and lieutenants, but there were "parish companies" as well. On the whole, the highest offices — those of the generals and their staffs — were the last to be invented and distributed.

Although there were no uniforms, no standard equipment, and no unit symbols, there were some signs of membership. Many rebels wore small cloth sacred hearts, white cockades, and rosaries. Young André Fauvin reported that the troop which took him away snatched his tricolor cockade and gave him a white one (A.D. M-et-L 1 L 1027). In the account of a pair of refugees from Saint-Pierre-de-

Chemillé appear all the signs of emerging membership, leadership, and consciousness of the cause:

Wednesday, 13 March, toward 5 P.M., a large number of men in a band, armed with guns, hooks, forks, scythes, etc., all wearing white cockades and decorated with small, square, cloth medals, on which are embroidered different shapes, such as crosses, little hearts pierced with pikes, and other signs of that kind, appeared in the bourg of St. Pierre. All these fellows shouted, "Long live the King and our Good Priests! We want our King, our priests and the old regime!" And they wanted to kill off all the Patriots, especially the present witnesses. All that troop, which was of a frightening size, cast itself at the Patriots, who were assembled to resist their attempt, killed many, made many of them prisoners, and dispersed the rest (A.D. M-et-L 1 L 1018).

The two refugees, a weaver and a drover, then named the chiefs, all of whom had troubled the community's Patriots for many months before. In St. Pierre and elsewhere, on this second day of open insurrection, a conscious organization and an identification with the cause were emerging, but were still blurred and changeable.

With surprising regularity, the first action the local rebels took against the Patriots was their systematic disarmament. Resisting conscription and disarming the Patriots were but two sides of the same coin. It may well be that memories of the Patriots' widespread attempts to disarm the Aristocrats after the rebellion of Châtillon and Bressuire were still burning bright. At Joué and Gonnord, some witnesses stated that the boys had gotten together to take the Patriots' weapons, while others said they gathered to resist conscription. Both were right. The process was quite regular: The raiders visited each Patriot's house in the bourg in turn, demanded all the weapons and powder, then ransacked the house for good measure. Some houses were searched many times during the first few days of turbulence. From the number of times this process was mentioned in the accounts of the early insurrection, it is not hard to believe that these tours were a major source of rebel arms.

Augustin Ardré, judge in the District of St. Florent, was seized by the rebels of La Poitevinière (A.D. M-et-L 1 L 1028). From his house they took a gun, a bayonet, a pistol, some powder and, finally, him. As a result, he heard their first deliberations and reported that "their plan was to go disarm the National Guard and municipality of Jallais." There, the detachment from Le Pin-en-Mauges apologized for their small number, explaining that many of their men had gone to "disarm the District of St. Florent." That bit of disarmament, of course, was the start of the open counterrevolution in the Mauges. The process of relieving the Patriots of their weapons had gone on for some days before the rebels began taking the owners of the weapons as well. At about that point, the rebels began to couple attacks on local Patriots with raids on their winecellars, and joyous bonfires of their official papers.

While most communities of the Mauges first witnessed their own midget rebellions, sooner or later the men in arms joined the larger forces that attacked the cities and fought the troops sent in by the Republic. The boys of St. Lambert filed off, to return a few weeks later in the midst of the great rebel army. The contingents from La Poitevinière and Le Pin-en-Mauges became the core of the mass striking Jallais and then Chemillé. It is probably safe to say that within the first week of counterrevolution almost every local force formed in the Mauges was incorporated in a larger confederation. Most likely, ranks and rosters suddenly became better defined at exactly this point. Even after the so-called armies formed, however, the clusters of fighting men from individual communities remained the basic units, and the troops called together for any particular action usually scattered and made their way home soon after the fighting was over — far too soon to make any occupation of alien territory practicable.

The common properties of the first bursts of counterrevolution in southern Anjou support the view that the rebellion was an intensified continuation of the conflict of the previous two years. As great a grievance as conscription was, it was immediately assimilated to the party struggle. The two sides simply continued their wrangling, and then came to blows. Yet the outbreak could not have been part of a precise and comprehensive plan. The first flashes were almost aimless. The first targets were quite local. The highest level was the last to form. The impressive similarities among the multitude of local histories are mainly the result of the basic similarities in the social situations of the multitude of communities in the Mauges.

The way the rebellion spread confirms this view. Within the Mauges it was like batter dropped in a pan: first many small spots, but soon one big spot. Because of the persistent myth that the

Vendée rose as a man, in an instant, I must stress again how long it took for the whole region to join the rebellion. Even within the small compass of the Mauges, there was a significant lag from one section to another. While Patriots and Aristocrats were killing and maiming each other at Cholet and Le May on the 4th of March, the towns near the Loire were still at peace. Rebels took over Drain, Liré, and Landemont on the 11th, but no rebels came to the bourg of Saint-Pierre-de-Chemillé until the 13th. The Patriots of Trémont, Cerqueux-de-Maulèvrier, Vezins, and Montilliers were still able to send troops to the defense of Vihiers on the 15th and 16th, after the capture of Cholet. The Patriots of Gonnord were still at home later than that. So much for the simultaneity of the counterrevolution.

On the other hand, ten days or so after the fatal demonstration at St. Florent, the borders of the rebel area were already set where they were to stay until the Republicans finally chased their enemies from home. The map of this territory is quite familiar: it is about the same as the map of the disturbances of 3 to 12 March and, more important, essentially the same as the map of struggles over Constitutionals and Refractories in 1791. It was where resistance had so long been forming that the counterrevolution took immediate hold.

Except for the narrow strip between the Mauges and the Loire, Val and Saumurois were unmistakably different. There were no warning rumbles with the news of conscription, no explosions when it was enforced. The first news from the Vendée, in fact, aroused not enthusiasm, but fear. The people of the Saumurois did not join the rebels; their National Guards sprang forward to fight them. Within the District of Vihiers, Beaulieu, Rablay, La Salle-de-Vihiers, La Plaine, Vihiers, Cerqueux-sous-Passavant, Cléré, Nueil-sous-Passavant, Montilliers, Trémont, Concourson, Martigné, Saint-Georges-Châtelaison, Chavagnes, Saulgé-l'Hôpital, Notre-Dame d'Alençon, Luigné, Brigné, Faveraye, Faye, and Thouarcé — that is, mainly the communities of the Saumurois — sent troops against the counterrevolution, while of these only Beaulieu, La Salle, La Plaine, and Montilliers had significant counterrevolutionary movements. The line between revolutionary and counterrevolutionary areas was remarkably sharp.

The cities, as might be expected, did not display as much of the basic contrast between subregions. Although their defenses could hardly be called heroic, Chemillé, Cholet, and Vihiers had to be attacked before the rebels took control of them. Nor did they stay with the counterrevolution when evacuated, as they were periodically. At the same time, the cities that were still free mixed the greatest enthusiasm with the greatest anxiety; one might call the mixture hysteria. Angers, Saumur, Montreuil-Bellay eagerly supplied citizen-soldiers to put down the "brigands." A crowd in Saumur massacred some citizens of Vihiers arrested for proposing the surrender of the city, just as a crowd in Vihiers had slaughtered citizens of Tigné. Fear of treason gripped Montreuil-Bellay. All of Anjou's cities prepared to defend themselves; many sent frenzied requests for troops to each other, to the department, and to the National Assembly. Their worries were justified, for it was at the cities that the great surges of rebel strength were directed.

One of the impressive things about these violent events of 1793 is their continuity with the events of the previous years. I have just discussed the geographic continuity between the counterrevolution and its antecedents. In addition to that superficial sort of coincidence, there was profound continuity in the conflict of parties in southern Anjou. Essentially the same groups fought in 1793 as in 1791 and 1792. The issues were not much different. The seismic struggle of 1793 was an intensified form of the local tremors of the two years before. All this is particularly true of the first outbursts. In Saint-Pierre-de-Chemillé, Saint-Georges-du-Puy-de-la-Garde, Saint-Macaire-en-Mauges, Saint-Lambert-du-Lattay, Landemont, and just about every other place for which adequate information is available, the first rebel attackers turn out to be the same individuals who had pestered the Patriots most persistently in previous years, and their targets the same local leaders they had tried to hinder, their demands not much different from before.

Who Were the Antagonists?

Despite this general assurance of continuity, we do not know as much as we ought to about the persons marked by the rebels as their enemies. We know, of course, that they fell into the general category, "Patriots." But it would be useful to learn exactly where they fit into rural community structure, how many were buyers of church properties, how many had held office or belonged to the National

Guard and, for that matter, just how large a proportion of the rural population they were. For southern Anjou, the lists of refugees from the rebellion and the fascinating Lists of Good Patriots (A.D. M-et-L 1 L 1157–1159, 1 L 1310 bis), which I have not used fully because of the immense identification job their analysis requires, probably contain many of the answers to these questions. At St. Macaire, for example, the lists name 81 refugees (including women) and 25 Good Patriots (men only), with a great deal of overlap between the lists. The lists include a substantial sample of the community's merchants and clothiers, almost all the municipal officers of 1791 and 1792, almost all the local buyers of church property, and numerous individuals from the most prominent families of Patriots (Mondain, Dupé, Gilbert, Daviaud, etc.), but also many people I have not been able to place at all. Although there are some peasants and artisans on the lists from elsewhere, the bourgeois seem to have occupied an exceptional position. Among the bourgeois, the merchants were especially noticeable. Of the 20 bourgeois identified as Good Patriots at La Tessoualle (A.D. M-et-L 1 L 1159), 9 were clothiers, 10 merchants, and only one was a doctor. If it turned out that the mercantile bourgeois were the outstanding enemies of the counterrevolution, while the professionals and administrators were more often sympathetic to it, the tendency would be consistent with all the preceding analysis. Just because such a finding would be so convenient, however, it would be well to reserve judgment until someone has been able to enumerate the Patriots of March, 1793, more carefully than I have.

Are we on firmer ground when it comes to identifying the rebels? Who fought in the Vendée is apparently so obvious to most of its historians that they do not ask the question. Yet no one really knows. The names of the leaders, of course, are inescapable anywhere in the West; the lives of its antiquarians are cluttered with them. It is even generally agreed that a great many rustics, plus some nobles and priests, marched in the rebel armies. Beyond this, there is not much accord.

During the counterrevolution and immediately after it a great many contradictory observations on the identities of the rebels appeared. One of the earliest dispatches to the National Assembly spoke of the "fanatics, Refractory priests and emigrant nobles, of which the enemy is composed" (Aulard 1889–1897: II, 499). The estimate of the following week expanded to "almost the entire countryside, marching in battle order" (Aulard 1889–1897: II, 468). The simple terms *fanatics* and *brigands* served to identify the enemy for most purposes, but the greater the success of the counterrevolution, the readier were the correspondents to believe that everyone in all the West was its willing servant.

The early historians of the Vendée, especially the Republican eyewitnesses, generally treated the counterrevolution as a mass movement of the countryside. Savary spoke of the peasants specifically, but most of his contemporaries implied or stated that only a few isolated cities offered any support to the Revolution anywhere in the Vendée (Savary 1824; Choudieu 1889; Lequinio Year Three; Bénaben Year Three; Berthre de Bourniseaux 1819, etc.).

As the counterrevolution has slipped into the past, its analysts have become more sophisticated. They have stumbled over facts pointing inescapably to the existence of a Patriotic nucleus in the Vendée, and thus have been forced to abandon the simple view of the Vendée as a whole against France as a whole. However, even recent historians have been content to distinguish priests, nobles, and "peasants" among the rebels, and leave the problem at that. This means that the participation of artisans, of different segments of the bourgeoisie, and of various types of peasants has never been explored.

I know of only one attempt to identify the enemies of the Revolution in the West quantitatively. Donald Greer (1935, 1951) developed statistical measures of the incidence of the Terror and the Emigration. Who was executed during the Terror (and therefore during the counterrevolution) should be a rough index of who was seen as working against the Revolution. Greer gives figures for both the

Table 26. Executions in the Vendée, during the Terror.

Category	Vendée region as a whole	Department of Maine-et-Loire
Nobles	2%	2.5%
Clergy	2	3.2
Peasants	48	43.3
"Middle class"	6	7.6
"Working class"	41	43.4

department of Maine-et-Loire and for the Vendée region as a whole (1935: 100–101, Appendix). The departmental figures have the defect of including not only Angers but all the department north of the Loire; however, they are not impossible to use. The percentages deserve some confidence, because most of the executions were made under the law of March, 1793, directly instigated by the Vendée, which prescribed military trials and immediate execution for rebels caught bearing arms or counterrevolutionary insignia. The Department of Loire-Inférieure, through the patriotic vengeance meted out at Nantes, led all of France in executions; over half of all the nation's executions took place in the West (Greer 1935: 38–40). Loire-Inférieure had 3548 of them, Maine-et-Loire 1886, Vendée 1616. So the figures above are not based on a trivial number of cases.

Greer's figures must look a trifle peculiar to anyone who has depended on traditional accounts of the Vendée. The proportions of priests and nobles are quite low (although both are higher than their estimated proportion in the general population). The proportion of "Working Class" individuals, roughly equivalent to the category "Artisans and Others" used in this study, is very high. If the executions accurately represent the participants in the counterrevolution, in other words, they indicate rather slighter involvement of nobles, and much heavier involvement of nonpeasants, than the usual histories would lead one to believe. Such a conclusion, of course, is quite consistent with what we now know about the development of party conflict before the outbreak of the 1793 rebellion.

There are, unfortunately, good reasons for wondering whether the recipients of the death penalty *do* represent the whole population of counterrevolutionaries. Perhaps the most evident reasons are the inclusion of a number of people, especially in the cities, who never had a real connection with the rebellion, and the greater likelihood that certain kinds of participants in the rebellion would be captured and executed. We need to check the implications of Greer's figures.

What we need is a census of the rebellion. Does one exist? Of course not. But there are two sets of sources which give an idea of what a census might show: 1) the interrogations of prisoners and refugees from the area of the counterrevolution; their questioners ordinarily asked them to name the rebels they knew; 2) the rosters of local counterrevolutionary military units.[1] From such sources, I have assembled a file of just over 3,000 rebels, about 2,100 from the interrogations and 900 from the rosters. However, over 900 of the original 3,000 found their way into the file through service on counterrevolutionary committees, communication with the enemy, sympathy with the rebels, and other nonmilitary offenses. Furthermore, even after careful combing of other sources (voting lists, parish registers, and the like), there were another 800-odd whose social status it was impossible to discover. The list of occupationally identified persons reported to have borne arms against the Republic thereby shrank to 1,176 men: 804 from the interrogations, and 372 from the rebel rosters, after eliminating the overlap between the two sources.

Altogether, from 60,000 to 120,000 men probably took part in the counterrevolution of 1793 (Dehergne 1939: 333–334). My best guess is that in southern Anjou from 15,000 to 20,000 men were under arms at one time or another during the year. If it were a random sample, therefore, the list of 1,100-plus names would be large enough to yield some moderately reliable conclusions as to the composition of the whole fighting force.

Of course, it is not a random sample. The informants may well have compounded selective memories with selective testimonies. The loss of 44 percent of the sample through inability to learn their occupations, by every indication I have been able to squeeze from the data, serves to exaggerate the proportion of prominent and high-ranking individuals among the rebels. The informants themselves were by no means randomly selected. The people they named were heavily concentrated along the Layon and to the northeast of the Mauges; the cantons of Chemillé, Saint-Lambert-du-Lattay, and Saint-Laurent-de-la-Plaine alone account for more than a third of the names in the file. This is not because the most rebels came from those cantons, but because the Republicans had the greatest opportunity to interrogate their people.

With all these qualifications, the compilation still offers some valuable information. Let us begin with the rebels named in interrogations of refugees and prisoners. By percentage, the 804 persons were

---

[1] Sources: A.D. M-et-L 1 L 750, 835 bis, 840 bis, 1018, 1027, 1028, 1029, 1038, 1094, 1125 bis, 9 L 84, 9 L 86, 15 Q 272–273. The bulk of the names from the interrogations are neatly listed in registers prepared by the Republicans.

distributed as follows: noble, 2.1; priest, 0.2; hired hand, 11.3; other peasant, 29.8; commercial bourgeois, 6.2; other bourgeois, 5.5; industrial artisan, 13.8; other, 31.0. The percentages are similar to Greer's figures for executions, but here the priests and peasants are lower, the bourgeois higher. The largest groups by far were the artisans and the peasants, which is no great surprise. But all classes except the clergy contributed a significant number of counterrevolutionary soldiers.

If we were to take this as an accurate representation of all the rebels, and the estimates of occupational distribution presented in Chapter 4 as precise, we would probably have to conclude that the artisans had more than their share of rebels, the peasants were underrepresented, and the bourgeois were slightly over strength. Maybe so. It would certainly be a delightfully novel conclusion. However, I think it fair to say that the eighteenth-century documents from the West tended to omit occupational designations for peasants much more often than for other classes. If such a tendency were operating here, it would leave a disproportionate number of peasants in the "unidentified" file. Very likely the refugees from the bourgs of the Mauges also began by reporting the rebels they knew best, that is, the artisans and bourgeois who shared the bourgs with them. These biases would inflate the artisans and bourgeois (and the nobles?) at the expense of the peasants. Maybe we should look a little further before rendering a final judgment on the composition of the rebels.

The rebel rosters open another avenue. These documents have titles like List of the Soldiers of the Catholic and Royal Army (as at La Jumellière, A.D. M-et-L 1 L 840 bis), and ordinarily include a substantial number of men from a single community. In three cases, we can compare a roster with a detailed estimate of occupational distribution for the same community. The three cases appear in Table 27. Even these three comparisons deserve inspection *cum grano salis*, since they are based on incomplete identification of the persons on the rosters, and since there may have been some individuals from the communities (especially nobles) who served at a higher level than the "parish company." They do offer two conclusions about rebel organization at the level of the rural community which are probably worthy of confidence: 1) Almost all the local soldiers were peasants or artisans. 2) The bourgeois were significantly underrepre-

Table 27. Comparisons of rebel rosters with estimates of occupational distribution.

Category	La Poitevinière		La Chapelle-du-Genêt		Saint-Laurent-de-la-Plaine	
	Adult males	Roster	Adult males	Roster	Adult males	Roster*
Noble	0.2	0	0.2	0	0.4	0
Priest	1.3	0	3.1	0	1.5	0
Peasant	59.5	79.7	48.9	46.4	63.8	75.8
Bourgeois	5.7	0	5.2	3.6	4.0	3.3
Artisan and other	33.3	20.3	42.6	50.0	30.3	20.9
Number of rebels identified		59		56		91
Number not identified		87		13		22

* This one is not actually a roster, but the list reconstructed by Guinhut (1909).

sented. The people named in rosters from individual communities differ significantly from the people named in interrogations. Many more of them are ordinary workers.

Now it may be useful to put the results from all the rosters (including four others besides those just discussed) together with the results from the Revolutionary sources and to give the totals for both sets of sources. Table 28 presents the data. The table shows, first of all,

Table 28. Occupational distribution of men named as bearing arms, by type of source.

Category	Percent of individuals with occupational identification		
	Interrogations	Rosters	Total
Noble	2.1	0.0	1.4
Priest	0.2	0.0	0.2
Hired hand	11.3	9.4	10.7
Other peasant	29.8	54.0	37.5
Commercial bourgeois	6.2	0.8	4.5
Other bourgeois	5.5	0.8	4.0
Industrial artisan	13.8	14.5	14.0
Other	31.0	20.4	27.6
Number identified	804	372	1176
Number not identified	459	471	930

the remarkable differences in the pictures of the counterrevolutionary forces given by the two kinds of sources. The rosters include no nobles or priests, and almost no bourgeois. They show a much higher proportion of peasants than the interrogations do, and a somewhat lower proportion of nonindustrial artisans. I suspect that the rosters represent their universe (all members of local companies)

more accurately than the interrogations represent theirs (all participants in the rebellion). In the absence of any independent means of
testing hunches about the relative merits of the sources, however,
we have little choice but to take the combined totals as the best
available description of the men who bore arms in the rebellion. Just
under one-half peasant, just over two-fifths artisan, the rebels were
apparently not far from a cross section of the rural population.

Table 29 indicates how the composition of the rebels varied from

Table 29. Occupational distribution of men named as bearing arms, by district.

Category	Percent of individuals with occupational identification					
	St. Florent	Cholet	Vihiers	Angers	Saumur	Outside
Noble	0.7	0.4	0.3	8.2	—	6.4
Priest	0.5	0.0	0.0	0.0	—	0.0
Hired hand	9.6	6.5	18.0	4.1	—	8.1
Other peasant	42.8	30.0	34.3	55.1	—	36.3
Commercial bourgeois	4.0	7.6	3.5	6.1	—	2.4
Other bourgeois	6.6	2.3	1.6	2.0	—	4.0
Industrial artisan	12.9	25.9	9.0	2.0	—	10.5
Other	22.3	27.4	33.3	22.4	—	32.3
Number identified	425	263	312	49	0	124
Number not identified	278	286	331	16	0	20

one district to another. Most of the variations of any size correspond
to differences in the distribution of the general population. But the
very large proportion of industrial artisans, and of artisans in general, in the District of Cholet is worth noticing. It is probably another reflection of the industrial crisis in that area. Aside from this,
the district totals agree fairly well in making 40–50 percent of the
rebels peasants, another 40–50 percent artisans, 5–10 percent bourgeois, and a tiny proportion priests and nobles.

Bearing arms was not the only way people could serve the counterrevolution. Even the rudimentary logistics of the rebels called for
some military supplies, and even their rudimentary intelligence procedures called for some spying. Many noncombatants provided food,
clothing, powder and arms, and some provided estimates of the
enemy's strength and information on his movements. Others took no
active part in the counterrevolution, but incriminated themselves, in
the eyes of the Republicans, by their "uncivic attitudes" or their
"counterrevolutionary sentiments."

In addition to these fairly unambiguous ways of aiding the rebellion, a number of people served on the local committees set up by the rebels to keep order, raise supplies, and take the place of the old government. While the most ardent Republicans of a community usually fled the rebellion if they could, they often left behind a few distinguished citizens who had been relatively moderate or politically inactive. These citizens frequently served on the local committees. Their service is by no means a sure sign that they were sympathetic with the counterrevolution. Under military occupation, there was little else they could do. Some of the most prominent citizens of Chalonnes, although admittedly not the most zealous of its Patriots, were on its counterrevolutionary committee (Uzureau 1941). Throughout the District of Vihiers former communal officers were forced into the counterrevolutionary committees (A.D. M-et-L 9 L 86). Despite their lack of commitment to the cause, they were often the only people with the time, the skills, and the experience for the jobs.

Table 30 presents some information on who involved themselves

Table 30. Occupational distributions of different types of participants in the counterrevolution.

Category	Percent of individuals with occupational identification						
	Bore arms	Officer	Service to rebels	General sentiments	Committee member	Other	Total
Noble	0.6	12.4	3.2	2.3	0.7	17.6	1.8
Priest	0.2	0.0	28.0	4.2	0.7	5.9	2.9
Peasant	50.2	23.6	40.8	47.7	31.2	29.4	46.1
Bourgeois	7.3	24.7	13.6	10.3	39.0	17.6	11.8
Artisan and other	41.8	39.3	14.4	35.3	28.4	29.4	37.5
Number identified	1087	89	125	262	141	17	1721
Number not identified	884	46	92	182	202	61	1309

with the counterrevolution in these various capacities. In addition, it offers a crude classification of those who bore arms: Among the warriors appeared the distinction between ordinary soldiers and "chiefs," "commanders," "leaders," as well as the more formal designations of sergeant, lieutenant, captain, and general. This table treats anyone with any such title as an officer.

About two thirds of the persons incriminated by the documents under analysis had joined the armed forces of the counterrevolution.

The officers included much higher proportions of nobles and bourgeois than the ordinary soldiers did. The peasants (according to tabulations not shown here) were much more common among the sergeants and corporals than at any higher ranks, and were much more likely to serve as simple soldiers than were the members of any other class. Artisans, on the other hand, were quite common among the chiefs of local bands. Despite the many democratic, even anarchic, features of the counterrevolutionary armies, in short, the positions of leadership eluded the peasantry, and the highest positions went mainly to individuals who already had wealth, influence, and prestige (cf. Paret 1961: 30–31).

The situation was not so much different when it came to civilian collaboration with the rebellion. The individuals who gave specific services to the rebels were largely priests (who preached, but rarely bore arms) and peasants. The group cited simply for their counter-revolutionary sentiments form a rough cross section of the population. But the local bourgeois occupied a very large share of the places on counterrevolutionary committees. The evidence from the District of Vihiers, where the lists of rebels often include indications of public offices the individuals named had held, suggests that men who had earlier been municipal officers quite regularly joined (or were drafted by) their local committees (A.D. M-et-L 9 L 84–86). Perhaps the individuals who left office during the party struggles of 1791 and 1792 were particularly good candidates for the committees, but this is no more than a speculation. In any case, there was a good deal of carry-over from the old regime in the distribution of honors and responsibilities during the counterrevolution.

No one should take these statistical findings, based on partial identification of a partial sample, as definitive. They are an improvement over the guesses and impressions which have studded most accounts of the Vendée, but they unquestionably call for both completion and criticism. Incomplete or not, they do lead to a few fairly solid conclusions, some positive, some negative. The findings expose the inaccuracy of the label, "peasant" rebellion. Rural artisans, by no means simply peasants slightly modified, took a large part in the counterrevolution. Other classes were involved as well. They were involved at different levels, however, so that the armed forces in individual communities were much closer to purely peasant and artisan than were the higher reaches of the rebel organization. There are at least suggestions that artisans were often local activists (since they held a large share of the intermediate ranks) and that the bourgeois were significantly underrepresented in the rebellion.

The question of representation, however, brings up the negative side of the findings. Participation in the counterrevolution cut boldly across class lines. Therefore, no simple scheme of class alignment can account adequately for the division of forces in 1793. For that reason, we should give severe scrutiny to any attempts to explain the counterrevolution in terms of the problems, attitudes, or actions of a single class, be it peasant, noble, clergy, bourgeois, or some other one.

Such a caveat, of course, strikes the present study as well as others. The considerable number of bourgeois named in the interrogations raises some question about the Revolutionary propensities of that class. At least some of them joined the counterrevolution. The findings from the interrogations, however, contradict the information both in the communal rosters and in the community case histories I have been able to reconstruct. Hence it still seems best to conclude, tentatively, that the solid bourgeois nucleus stayed with the Revolution, and that few bourgeois — especially, few merchants and manufacturers — opposed it actively. The important thing is not to overstate the case. There were some bourgeois (like Cady, the physician of Saint-Laurent-de-la-Plaine or Body, the seneschal of Maulèvrier) who plunged wholeheartedly into counterrevolution. There were others (like Boutillier de Saint-André, the seneschal of Mortagne, or Fleury, the rentier of Chalonnes) who were dragged halfheartedly into it. Yet by far the strongest support of the Revolution in southern Anjou before 1793 came from the bourgeois, and it was the bourgeois, by and large, who held out against the counterrevolution.

This statement may be made more general. The parties that fought in 1793 were essentially the parties that emerged in 1791. The Patriots, basically bourgeois, stood against the Aristocrats, composed of peasants, clergy, nobles, with a substantial part of the rural artisans. No Patriotic parties fought for long in 1793. The odds in the Mauges were so great that they could only fly or capitulate. The troops of the Republic had to do the fighting against the armies of the counterrevolution.

The Warriors and Their Warfare

The armies of the counterrevolution, as many commentators have pointed out, hardly deserved to be called armies. Their sources of recruitment condemned them to a very low level of organization. There are many skills, norms, and items of knowledge the sustained pursuit of war demands which are not common among peasant peoples. Traditional rural life does not prepare men for disciplined mass maneuvers, for time-table routine, or for a radical separation of work from family; life in an industrial society, for example, does. Since these and other equally alien features are necessary in an effective army of any size, it is extremely difficult to recruit and train an army of peasants and rural artisans.

The counterrevolutionary "army" of the Mauges mirrored the social organization of the countryside. It was an unstable federation of local units, themselves shifting in membership from one expedition to the next. Its organization consisted mainly of an irregular network of communications connecting local leaders with a small, relatively constant group of chiefs. The local troops defended their own territories and joined together when called for short but massive engagements with the enemy. As the Revolutionary official Joseph Clémenceau, who was captured by the Vendeans, described it:

> The generals could never form the Vendeans into a permanent army or keep them under arms; it was never possible to make them remain to guard the cities they took; nor could anyone make them camp or subject them to military discipline. Accustomed to an active life, they could not stand the idleness of the camp. They went to battle eagerly, but were no less prompt to return home; they often fought with courage, but they were never soldiers (1909: 8).

Their combination of endless skirmishes and occasional large-scale attacks was an extraordinary kind of warfare. It gave the Vendeans a considerable advantage in holding their own territory, but seriously hampered the efforts of their commanders to develop a strategy. Their basic localism formed the rebels into units that were an effective means of defending their territory and tending to their private affairs at the same time, but that localism also kept them from consolidating their victories over the Republic.

The units of the rebel army were almost purely local parish companies, as they called them. When they heard the tocsin, the soldiers put down their everyday tools and picked up their arquebuses, muskets, scythes, staves, and the rest of their makeshift weapons, gathered in the bourg to march off "as in a procession" (A.D. M-et-L 1 L 1030). As Savary described it:

The army was not at all permanent; it only formed on the chiefs' convocation. These orders were transmitted rapidly by couriers designated in each commune, and always ready to leave. The peasants gathered at the sound of the tocsin, the parish commandant gave the orders to them, the number of men needed, the day and the place of the rendezvous, and the time the expedition would last, which was hardly ever more than four or five days. The group formed, the priests officiated, built up enthusiasm with their preaching, distributed indulgences and absolutions, and then the expedition got under way. When the appointed time had run out, the peasant felt free to go home, regardless of what was happening, and soon there was no army left (1824: I, 24).

The fighting force, it appears, was more like a home guard than an army.

The local organization of the rebels appeared almost at the beginning of the conflict. It consisted simply of a community infantry company with an elected captain (or commandant) and a few elected lieutenants. All able-bodied men were supposed to serve, but the wealthy could buy exemption. When the generals needed a certain number of men for an action, they apportioned the number among the communities in their areas, and each commandant filled his quota. Nobles were not ordinarily members of these companies, but artisans and peasants were. As I have said, the information now available indicates that peasants led the local bands rarely, while innkeepers, blacksmiths, employees of nobles, and even weavers were captains and lieutenants fairly often.

These local units operated more or less autonomously, under no direct discipline, with only local enthusiasm and the diligence of their captains to keep them going to battle. Later in the counterrevolution, some attempts were made to organize true military units, but they were far from successful.

Under the new skin of the rebellion moved the bones of the old regime's institutions. The apportionment of a quota of armed men from the top down, so that first an area was assigned its number, and then the number was subdivided among the communities of the area, mimicked the methods by which taxes had always been collected and the perennial procedures for military conscription. The counterrevolutionary committees of notables resembled the communal councils of 1787. And the traditional integrity of the rural community persisted in the local units with their elected officers and temporary troops.

The way these temporary soldiers fought dismayed their Republican enemies; it was the same trouble the British regulars had in the American Revolution. The rebels refused to march in order. Instead, they hid behind trees and houses, fired from thickets, and crept up on their enemies without warning. These tactics suited the bocage; they were so strange they baffled and infuriated the enemy. "Some atrocities have been committed in villages as our troops have passed through," wrote Augis, one of the National Assembly's many representatives on the scene. "The enemy shot at them from the windows of the houses in the place called Les Échaubrognes" (Aulard 1889–1897: III, 290). Although all this is part and parcel of modern war, to eighteenth-century military men it was a shocking and unthinkable way to fight. Sometimes, however, the rebels had to draw up in order, to meet the Republicans in a plain, or to attack a city. Then, as a rule, their disorganization and guerrilla tactics told against them.

By winning battles, the Vendean inevitably took prisoners. There were a few blood baths, mostly in the first rush of counterrevolution. Then someone invented the savage technique of marching the prisoners, bound two by two, before the rebel army, so they would be first into the fire of their friends. This was first tried in the original attack on Chemillé. It was a method soon abandoned. In fact, the Vendean troops became renowned not for their cruelty, but for their leniency to prisoners. The best-remembered actions of the generals Bonchamp and Lescure alike were the protection of prisoners. The armies in which the men of the Mauges fought had the best reputations. Two factors helped transform the rebels from furor to gentleness toward their prisoners: the insistence of their generals and the increasing difficulty of handling the swarms of prisoners that fell into their hands. The eventual solution was to shave the captives' heads, extract from them oaths not to fight any more, and send them packing. Needless to say, the Revolutionary generals did not consider such oaths binding.

Their softness with prisoners was no sign of general flabbiness. Even in full-scale battles the enthusiasm of the Vendeans impressed their enemies, indeed appalled them. They were said to fight like madmen, like fanatics, like men heedless of death. This was true of the fervent nucleus, at least. It was also said that many others stood by until the battle was won, and then joined in.

The rebels began with few and motley arms. One of the astonishing sights of 1793 was the advance of an army bearing ancient firearms, farm tools of all kinds, improvised pikes and simple clubs, dragging a few old field pieces. Of their firearms, many of the original weapons came from the châteaux of the Mauges, and many more came from the raids on patriotic homes and headquarters in early March. After that, the soldiers took their guns from the enemy. Despite innumerable accusations, no one has yet unearthed any evidence that the weapons used by the Vendeans came from England, the Emigration, or elsewhere.

This warfare and these warriors stunned the Republicans during the first months of the counterrevolution. Clémenceau recorded the whole effect as he had seen it:

What made the Vendeans fearsome in the beginning was their way of making war. They fought without order, in squads or crowds, often as individual snipers, hiding behind hedgerows, spreading out, then rallying, in a way that astonished their enemies, who were entirely unprepared for these maneuvers; they were seen to run up to cannons and steal them from under the eyes of the gunners, who hardly expected such audacity. They marched to combat, which they called *aller au feu*, when they were called by their parish commandants, chiefs taken from their ranks and named by them, centurions, so to speak, who had more of their confidence than did the generals chance had given them; in battle, as at the doors of their churches on Sunday, they were surrounded by the acquaintances, their kinfolk and their friends; they did not separate except when they had to fly in retreat. After the action, whether victors or vanquished, they went back home, took care of their usual tasks, in fields or shops, always ready to fight (1909: 7–8).

Although far from centralized, the movements of the local companies were not entirely random. The units combined into loosely formed armies, at whose heads were the famous leaders of the counterrevolution. During the successful days of the rebellion there were four armies: of Poitou, of Anjou, of the Center, and of the Marsh. The first two recruited men from the Mauges; the center of gravity of the army of Poitou was Châtillon; the pivot of the army of Anjou was near Beaupréau.

The nobles who fought in the Vendée were for the most part officers of these armies, rather than of the local companies. They were joined in the high ranks by a few commoners, but the former professional soldiers dominated more and more of the top posts as time went on and organization progressed. They were uniformly men of the region, few of them from great families. Their service as high-ranking leaders, but not as chiefs of local troops, was quite consistent with the positions they had long held in the Mauges, as powerful, distant figures who mixed little in strictly local affairs.

At times, the chiefs of the armies planned their actions jointly. More often, jealousy, cross-purposes, rivalries stifled their cooperation. The one formal organization that claimed a kind of authority over all the Vendée was the Council established at Châtillon early in June, 1793. The locale is significant, for it was best supported by the army of Poitou (whose headquarters were at Châtillon) and completely rejected by the armies of the Center and the Marsh. The Council was actually double: an ecclesiastical body and a civil one. The ecclesiastical council was the rather ineffective tool of de Folleville, a peculiar individual who successfully passed himself off as the bishop of Agra, *in partibus infidelium*, and of the abbé Bernier, an able, ambitious man who later became bishop of Orléans. The civil council made some attempts to impose fiscal and legal order on the counterrevolution, but was itself shaken by the rivalry between the same de Folleville and Bernier, not to mention numerous others.

In theory, at least, the civil council stood over the councils and committees set up in the captured cities and bourgs. The effectiveness of these committees varied enormously, and their communication with the civil council was not very great. The fact that they were generally set up just in time for the departure of the rebels from a briefly occupied city drained most of their strength. Local organization was at its best in gathering supplies for the war; that was true particularly within the rebellious area, rather than in the places the rebels occupied. It was not a genius for organization that made the

Vendeans successful. What organization existed was decentralized and cumbersome. The spirited participation of individual communities kept the fight going.

Putting Down the Rebellion

This decentralized rebellion threatened the very existence of a government already preoccupied with external wars and internal dissension. Thomas Carlyle, with his usual verve, described the first news of the Vendée:

In the early days of March, the Nantes post-bags do not arrive; there arrive only instead of them Conjecture, Apprehension, bodeful wind of Rumor. The bodefulest proves true. Those fanatic peoples of La Vendée will no longer keep under; their fire of insurrection, heretofore dissipated with difficulty, blazes out anew, after the King's Death, as a wide conflagration; not riot, but civil war. Your Cathelineaus, your Stofflets, Charettes, are other men than was thought: behold how their Peasants, in mere russet and hodden, with their rude arms, rude array, with their fanatic Gaelic frenzy and wild-yelling battle-cry of *God and the King*, dash at us like a dark whirlwind; and blow the best-disciplined Nationals we can get into panic and *sauve-qui-peut*. Field after field is theirs; one sees not where it will end (n.d.; XVI, 140).

The tidings of the first riots at Cholet were put aside in a rush of other business in Paris. When the rebellion cut off communications with Nantes, it stirred some attention. When, on the 18th and 19th of March, pleas began to arrive from the departments of the West, it drew anguish and agitation. The debates began, troops were assigned, agents dispatched, the law of 19 March — death within a day for rebels caught armed — passed, the incident forgotten. The Vendée rose when the struggle of Gironde and Mountain was forming and then breaking into the open; this struggle drew far more attention than the counterrevolution.

After a brief period of confidence, the agents of the National Assembly began to falter and then to despair, for they could not put down the rebels, and they could not get more aid from Paris. After Saumur fell, Coustard cried from Nantes: "We shall perish, and we shall perish soon, if we do not receive help at once" (Aulard 1889–1897: IV, 583). Later in the summer, official and unofficial reports flowed from the war theater, but excited more mutual accusations and party conflict than direct and decisive action. For months, the

National Assembly did not appreciate the magnitude of the counter-revolution.

For what was happening, explanations had to be found; they, too, flowed abundantly. The Vendeans were "fanatics" who did not know what they were doing. They were the tools of priests and émigrés. They were the hirelings of the British. The war was the result of a long-planned, cleverly executed plot. The self-styled patriots of the West, with their allies in Paris, were accomplices in counterrevolution. When the troops thrown against the rebels did not succeed, it was treason, by generals and agents of the Assembly alike. Choudieu drove that accusation to its extreme: "As for me, I declare that it is either the generals or the representatives of the people, and, to speak more frankly, I shall say that I think it is both the generals and the representatives of the people" (Aulard 1889–1897: VII, 401).

In truth, there was very little treason, and a great deal of bungling. To begin with the soldiers who faced the Vendeans in the first months of the counterrevolution were untrained, undisciplined, and unprepared for the kind of war they had to fight. There were few regulars in the West in March, 1793 (de Malleray 1924: 9 ff.). The first troops sent in were National Guards and fresh volunteers. The war in the North, and then the independent insurrections at Lyon, Toulon, and elsewhere diverted regular forces from the Vendée. The citizen-soldiers were in numbers great enough, but when they did not desert, they panicked.

Even the seasoned soldiers who came to fight the Vendée did not do their jobs well. They were handicapped by the variable and contradictory actions of their generals, who were harassed by the variable and contradictory actions of the agents of the National Assembly (see de Malleray 1924: 16). The agents themselves countermanded the war plans sent from Paris, accused each other of bungling and treason, hounded and hamstrung the generals, and then took to protecting their favorite military men and trying to get rid of the rest. The combination of lost battles and negative reports from the agents cost such generals as Quétineau, Berruyer, and Biron their jobs and even their lives. The result of the process was that the generals were chosen rather for their patriotism and personality than for their military ability. Barère's diagnosis of the stumbling attempts to put down the Vendée was "too many representatives, too many generals, too much division of opinion, too much division of forces, too much indiscipline in success, too many false reports, too much avidity, too much love of money and desire for a long war among a large part of the chiefs and administrators" (Walter 1953: 225). Were the victories of the Vendeans therefore only sleight-of-hand? Not at all. By June there were over 30,000 Republican troops in the West, part of them veterans. The rebels held them at bay. Even the elite troops were smashed by the Vendeans at various times between June and October. General Turreau reported:

A way of fighting until then unknown, . . . inviolable attachment to their party, unlimited confidence in their chiefs, such fidelity to their promises that it could take the place of discipline, indomitable courage, strong enough to meet the test of all sorts of dangers, fatigues and privations; that is what makes the Vendeans fearsome enemies, and ought to put them into history in the front rank of warrior peoples (1924: 19).

Even Turreau could not put them down permanently. In the long run, it took a Napoleon to pacify the country, six years after the counterrevolution began.

In a country where the rebels were so many and their opponents so few, civil control was almost as great a problem as military control. The old administrators had fled to Angers or Nantes. Few of them wanted to return to the interior before they were sure it was quite safe. At the same time, the central government was no longer sure who were the dependable Patriots in the West. So the Revolutionary committees and the agents of the National Assembly made the law (Sirich 1943: 47–50).

Along the borders of the Vendée, the law that was made was full of repression and suspicion. The search for traitors quickened. Near Angers, 84-year-old Mlle. Chardon was imprisoned because "her religious opinions were open to too much question" (A.D. M-et-L 1 L 1033). In Angers, Saumur, Fontenay, Niort, La Rochelle, and Nantes, the guillotine was readied. The National Assembly's agents forwarded the task, but with their usual inconsistency and bickering. Their policies varied; they established and disestablished local governments at whim; they fought with each other over how to maintain order.

Carrier, the executioner of Nantes, deserves mention only because he was the most bloodthirsty of all the agents. The day after he arrived at Nantes, he wrote: "I ought to warn you that there are people in the prisons of Nantes arrested as champions of the Vendée. Instead of amusing myself by putting them through the formalities of a trial, I shall send them to their place of residence to have them shot" (Aulard 1889–1897: VII, 288). Not long after, the idea that made him famous came to him: "Another kind of event seems to have diminished the number of priests; ninety of those we call Refractories were closed up in a boat on the Loire. I have just learned, and the news is quite certain, that they have all perished in the river" (Aulard 1889–1897: VIII, 505). It was by such means that Loire-Inférieure won its distinction: the department of all France with the greatest number of executions under the Terror (Greer 1935: 38).

These measures controlled the borders, and the military moves eventually quelled the rebellion in the interior. By the 21st of October, the triumphant Bourbotte, Turreau, Choudieu, and Francastel were able to write from Angers, "The National Convention wanted the Vendée finished before the end of October, and we can say today that the Vendée exists no more" (Aulard 1889–1897: VII, 549). The boast was premature, for the rebels were to pass two months of hegira north of the Loire, and to strike out again in 1794, 1795, 1796, and 1799. Yet the great counterrevolution was over. The Vendeans never again threatened to destroy the revolution.

Final Thoughts

Here my task ends. The task: to place the Vendée in sociological perspective. That really amounts to two somewhat separate undertakings, the one being the analysis of the social situation of part of the West in the light of some broad conceptions of urbanization and community organization, the other being the use of that analysis to help identify the conditions and processes which led to the political disturbances of 1791–1793. Both undertakings have turned out to be enormously complicated. Despite the endless outpouring of volumes about the Vendée, many of the basic, even obvious, questions remain practically unexplored: the relations of nobles, peasants, and manorial officials under the old regime; transfers of property during the eighteenth century; the prerevolutionary political position of the bourgeoisie; the nature of local political maneuvering in 1789 and

1790; the conditions and effects of the sales of church property in 1791 and 1792. I suppose that such lacunae are not surprising, considering how recently Georges Lefebvre and his heirs have directed the attention of historians to the independent importance of the rural Revolution, and to the richness of the materials available for its study. If it does nothing else, the present study fully confirms Lefebvre on both counts. Inferences from the political evolution of the entire nation, from the crises of Paris, by means of unrecognizably simplified models of "the peasantry," have often supplied the substance of analyses of the response to the Revolution in provincial France; they are no substitute for an understanding of rural society's actual operation. And the archives still hold uncounted riches for those explorers who come to them with patience, well-formed questions, and a concern with the social setting of political upheaval.

This does not mean that we have learned nothing except that it is hard to learn anything. Far from it. The sociological questions, formulations, and methods which have guided this historical inquiry have proved exceedingly useful. First of all, the general conceptions of urbanization and of its relationship to community organization, drawn from contemporary studies, help identify economically and accurately the significant differences among the areas and groups of southern Anjou which varied in their response to the Revolution. The most urbanized sectors of the West gave the most uniform support to the Revolution. The intensest conflicts arose at the junctions of rural and urban life. And, most concretely, the struggle of city and country informed the whole development of the counterrevolution.

Second, the systematic comparisons to which sociological questions almost unavoidably lead an investigator illuminate the distinctive features of the counterrevolutionary subregions, classes, and parties. They have produced, for example, some new and interesting observations on the Statements of Grievances of 1789, on the residence of the nobility, on the revenues of the clergy, on the occupational composition of rural communities, on the incidence of emigration. Even more importantly, the systematic comparisons have confirmed the deep continuity of behavior within rural communities under the old regime, response to the early Revolution, and participation or nonparticipation in the counterrevolution of 1793. And they have stimulated a corollary observation: the contrast between the relatively businesslike peacefulness, from 1789 to 1793, of the sections that stayed with the Revolution, and the division of the population, the formation of parties, the incessant agitation, the aggravation of conflict in the section that produced a counterrevolution.

Third, a sociological perspective aids in redefining the traditional historical questions. The time-honored debate which opposes the argument that the Vendée's rebellion was "spontaneous" to the idea that it was "incited," for example, turns out to pose two false alternatives. The great desire of almost all historians of the Vendée to assess the motives of "the peasantry" now appears to have led them to neglect the crucial distinctions among artisans, farmers, and other types of peasants, and to have simplified unforgivably the question of motivation. Because of this, the depression of the textile industry of the Mauges after 1789 has completely escaped historical attention. The much-vexed question of whether "the peasants" were content or malcontent with the old regime and with the noble landlords now seems not only hopelessly imprecise but also futile, unless set in some kind of comparative framework. Finally, "What turned the people of the Mauges against the Revolution?" still seems worth asking, but with the very important provisos that no single factor, policy, motive, or group can be the answer; that one must ask *which* people turned, how much, and how; that firm answers can only come from systematic tests of proposed explanations in areas which did *not* turn against the Revolution.

Enough! To review where a sociological understanding of the problem has been useful would be to begin this book again . . . and that is an enterprise I, for one, do not care to consider. Suffice it to say that the commonplace procedures of sociology can often aid immensely in unsnarling historical problems, just as a great deal of the knowledge perfectly familiar to working historians can only be ignored by the sociologist to his peril.

These thoughts suggest some more general methodological observations for historians and sociologists which one might draw from this study of the Vendée. Very often, historians combine great sophistication in their reconstruction of events with great crudeness in their assessments of the motives and structures of the principal groups involved in those events. Certainly this has been true of analyses of the Revolution in provincial France. The everyday questions of the sociologist — What is the social composition of the group under discussion? What are the arrangements of power within and among groups? What important changes is this society undergoing? How did the social movement form? Why did it gain supporters in area A and not area B, in class X and not in class Y? — have at the very least the virtues of helping the investigator to criticize his own formulations and of leading him to new sources of information. Such questions suggest useful comparisons in other terms than repeated sequences of events. They could, in the long run, produce a systematic, comparative understanding of the ramifications of drastic political change through the many sectors of a complex society.

Contemporary sociologists, on the other hand, have generally eschewed historical materials, or treated them only with the hugest of abstractions. It is true that the historical investigator cannot produce his own data in the way that the user of questionnaires or of social experiments can, and that he often begins with the mixed blessing of already knowing how things came out. But against these disadvantages (which, in fact, a great many varieties of contemporary social research share) weigh the unmeasured richness of historical data, and their great relevance for testing of the sociologist's cherished propositions. Sociologists have cut themselves off from a rich inheritance by forgetting the obvious: that all history is past social behavior, that all archives are brimming with news on how men used to act, and how they are acting still.

Appendixes

List of Writings Cited

Index

APPENDIX A

Procedure for Estimating
Occupational Distribution

Full enumerations of the population, with at least a majority of the occupations specified, were in the archives for thirteen communities: Vezins, Saint-Laurent-de-la-Plaine, Trémont, La Poitevinière, Blaison, Grézillé, Ambillou, Rou, Courchamps, Brossay, Saint-Pierre-des-Verchers, Antoigné, Varrains, (Guinhut 1909, A.D. M-et-L 2 L 49, 6 L 19, 7 L 97, 7 L 98). These were all from the period of the early Revolution. There were voting lists from 1790 to 1791 for twenty-four communities (A.D. M-et-L 1 L 444). Andrews (1935: 164–165) had used parish registers for 1780–1790 to estimate the occupational distributions of adult males in twenty communities of the Mauges: Beausse, St. Florent, Bouzillé, Champtoceaux, Saint-Laurent-des-Autels, La Poitevinière, La Chapelle-du-Genêt, Le Pin-en-Mauges, Montrevault, Le Puiset-Doré, La Chapelle-Rousselin, Neuvy, Saint-Georges-du-Puy-de-la-Garde, Chaudefonds, La Salle-de-Vihiers, Saint-Macaire-en-Mauges, La Romagne, Nuaillé, Le Voide, Montigné. I augmented these sources with parish registers for 1780–1784 from the following twenty-three places: Chaudefonds, Chanzeaux, Notre-Dame-de-Chalonnes, Soulaines, Vauchrétien, Saint-Lambert-du-Lattay, Beaulieu, Trémont, La Chapelle-sous-Doué, La Chapelle-Saint-Florent, Vezins, La Poitevinière, La Chapelle-du-Genêt, La Romagne, Saint-Pierre-de-Cholet, La Pommeraye, Gesté, Saint-Pierre-de-Chemillé, Saint-Jacques-de-Montfaucon, Saint-Jean-de-Montfaucon, Le May, La Tessoualle, Chanteloup (A.D. M-et-L, series B).

The problem was to derive estimates of occupational distribution, according to a standard set of categories, for the cantons in which these places were located in 1790. The sources gave a fair amount of information on occupations. Generally speaking, occupational designations appeared for at least 75 percent of the men named in a parish register, over 90 percent of those in a complete enumeration, and almost everyone in a voting list.

For the full enumerations and the voting lists, the procedure was to tally all occupations on a detailed checklist, and then to combine them into occupational classes according to the listing presented in Appendix B. The parish registers, which record baptisms, marriages, and burials, presented a different kind of problem. After some experimentation, the best procedure seemed to be to tally the occupations of the fathers of all newborn children. That procedure assumes that all occupational groups had equal fertility, an assumption which is patently incorrect, and yet probably not so incorrect as to vitiate comparisons made on the basis of parish registers from the same region. The procedure also requires that the estimates for nobles and priests come from some other source, since even the resident nobles so often had their children baptized in elegant ceremonies in the city, and since the priests had no acknowledged children among those baptized. The estimates for nobles came from the list of resident nobles prepared for the analysis reported in Chapter 4 (from A.D. M-et-L C 192, IV C 3). The enumeration of priests came from a theoretically complete list of all clergy of southern Anjou (taken mainly from Queruau-Lamerie 1899, but supplemented by a variety of other sources). The numbers of nobles and priests were converted into percentages of the number of households in the canton in 1790 (per A.D. M-et-L 1 L 402), and the remaining percentages calculated on the basis of the distribution of births in the parish registers among the occupational groups. For example, if priests and nobles together made up 2 percent of the cantonal population, and 50 percent of the births in the parish registers were to the wives of peasants, then the final estimate for peasants was 50 percent $\times$ (100 percent $-$ 2 percent) $=$ 49 percent. Where there were several parish registers from a single canton, the cantonal estimate was based on a weighted average of all the registers.

Then came the question of the equivalence of the various sources of estimates: the parish registers, Andrews' analysis of other registers, the voting lists, and the complete enumerations. There was enough overlap among the sources that a number of communities appeared in two of them, and one — La Poitevinière — appeared in three. So it was possible to compare the estimates derived from the various sources for four categories: 1) peasant, 2) bourgeois, 3) artisan, 4) other. Andrews' figures and those derived from my analysis of parish registers came very close to each other, as they should have, considering that both sources and methods were essentially the same. The correspondence between the parish registers and the complete enumerations was much less satisfactory, with discrepancies of more than 5 percent on five of sixteen comparisons in four communities. There were no communities for which both complete enumerations and voting lists existed; a comparison of the voting lists with the parish registers and with Andrews' figures disclosed a very poor relationship: discrepancies over 5 percent on sixteen of thirty-two comparisons. Unfortunately, there was too little regularity in the discrepancies to permit the introduction of a constant correction to the figures from any of the sources. I finally decided to drop the voting lists and use Andrews' calculations, the parish register results, and the complete enumerations.

The deportation or internment of the clergy and the emigration of the nobles almost certainly reduced the number of members of those two classes named in the complete enumerations. Because of the inherent features of the parish registers, Andrews' statistics also underestimate the clergy and (most likely) the nobility. So it seemed best to correct the estimates derived from the complete enumerations and from Andrews by using the compilations of nobles and priests already set up as a supplement to the parish register analysis. All three sources therefore ended up being used in a similar way to estimate bourgeois, peasants, artisans, and other (as well as finer sub-divisions of those classes), while the compilations supplied the estimates for nobles and priests.

It is by no means certain that this method gives an accurate statistical picture of any individual community. It probably produces moderately reliable information on *variations* in occupational distribution from one place to another. That is the purpose for which it was used in this study. Considering the substantial discrepancies among the different sources, it very likely would have been better to have taken many more parish registers — perhaps one randomly selected community per canton — and to have abandoned the attempt to combine results from diverse types of documents.

APPENDIX **B**

Occupational Classification Scheme

1. *Noble*

2. *Priest*

    A. *Secular:* chanoine, chapelain, curé, prêtre habitué, prieur-curé, vicaire
    B. *Regular:* moine, any order

3. *Peasant*

    A. *Large farmer:* bien-tenant, cultivateur, laboureur, métayer
    B. *Small Farmer:* bordager, bordier, closier
    C. *Winegrower:* vigneron
    D. *Hired Hand:* domestique, journalier, toucheur de bœufs
    E. *Other:* bêcheur, laboureur à bras, ménager, traiteur de bestiaux

4. *Bourgeois*

    A. *Administrative:* arpenteur, caissier de mines, commis, controlleur des actes, écrivain, gabelou, geomètre, huissier, inspecteur des laines, intendant, juge, officier seigneurial, procureur fiscal, receveur des enregistrements, receveur des fermes, régisseur, sénéchal, sergent.
    B. *Professional:* architecte, avocat, avoué, bâtonnier, chirurgien, ingénieur, maître d'école, médecin, médecin vétérinaire, notaire, praticien, précepteur, tabellion
    C. *Commercial:* droguiste, entrepreneur, fabricant, fermier, marchand (all varieties), mercier, négociant
    D. *Other:* bourgeois, propriétaire, rentier, "sieur" (with no other designation), "vivant de son bien"

5. *Artisan*

    A. *Industrial:* armurier, bagier, blanchisseur, camelotier, cardeur, carreyeur, chamoiseur, chaufournier, chapeletier, compagnon, corroyeur, drapier, fabricant de chaux, faiseur de balloy, fendeur, filassier, fileur, filtoupier, flanellier, foulonnier, gantier, graveur, imprimeur, imprimeur en toile, mineur, orfèvre, ourdisseur, ouvrier, paulmier, peignier, salpétrier, serger, tanneur, teinturier, tisserand, tixier, verglasier

B. *Agricultural Service:* affranchisseur, cerclier, maréchal, maréchal ferrant, maréchal taillandier, sellier, taillandier, tonnellier

C. *General Service:* boissellier, boîtier, boucher, boulanger, bourrelier, bûcheron, cendrier, chaisier, chandellier, chapellier, charbonnier, charcutier, charpentier, chaudronnier, cirier, cloutier, cordier, cordonnier, couvreur, épicier, épinglier, faiteur, ferblantier, fournier, harsounier, maçon, menuisier, paveur, pelletier, penacier, perruquier, poêlier, potier, sabotier, scieur de bois, scieur de long, serrurier, tabletier, tailleur, tailleur d'habits, tailleur de pierre, toupier, tourneur, tuilier, vaissellier, vitrier.

6. *Innkeeper:* aubergiste, cabaretier, hôte

7. *Miller:* meunier

8. *Other:* batellier, cavalier, charger, charon, colporteur, concierge, cuisinier, écolier, étudiant, garde-chasse, garde-messier, gendarme, jardinier, marinier, mendiant, messager, mineur, musicien, organiste, pêcheur, philosophe, postillon, sacristain, servante, soldat, voiturier, volontaire

NOTE: The exact combination of the classifications above used varies slightly from table to table. Where "weaver" appears as a separate category, it includes *tisserand* and *tixier*. Where innkeeper is not treated as a separate category, it is combined with bourgeois. "Artisan and other" means artisans, millers, and others. There are some doubtful classifications in the scheme (e.g., *gabelou, mercier, camelotier*), but on the whole they bear on extremely rare cases.

APPENDIX C

Textile Production in the Mauges

The only practical sources for a continuous quantitative account of textile production are the annual or semiannual reports of the bureaux de marque established at Cholet, Vihiers, and Maulèvrier at various times during the eighteenth century for the inspection and stamping of yard goods and kerchiefs destined for sale outside the immediate area. I have found such reports for most of the years from 1752 to 1790 in A.D. M-et-L 1 L 546, A.D. Indre-et-Loire C 114, 134, 135, and 136 and A.N. F^{12} 564, 650, and 1427. They surely do not include all the cloth produced in these areas. Some was marked at La Tessoualle (an office whose operation was farmed out, and which did not therefore produce any detailed reports), and some was not marked at all. Substandard goods and cloth made for local consumption generally escaped the mark, but were sold anyway (see A.N. F^{12} 1428). Nevertheless, the mark probably touched the great bulk of the goods openly traded, the ratio between marked and unmarked goods was probably fairly constant, and the records of the bureaux were probably moderately accurate, so that the production figures are a reliable guide to annual fluctuations in textile output.

In preparing the curves presented in Chapter 7, I used some conservative estimating procedures to fill gaps in the records. For 1760 and 1774, only one semester's report was in the archives. In these cases, I used the average ratios between the two semesters for the periods 1753–1759 and 1771–1773 respectively to estimate production for the missing semesters. For the years 1775–1782, the number of pieces marked was reported, but not the total value of those pieces; there I estimated total value at the rate of 35 livres per 20-yard bolt and 21 livres per dozen kerchiefs, on the basis of the relatively fixed value of these items throughout the rest of the period. The table offered here includes no estimates, but presents the figures actually reported in the documents consulted.

Table 31. Cloth marked at bureaux de marque of southern Anjou, 1752–1790.

	Vihiers			Maulèvrier			Cholet		
Year	Pieces of cloth	Dozens of kerchiefs	Total value (livres)	Pieces of cloth	Dozens of kerchiefs	Total value (livres)	Pieces of cloth	Dozens of kerchiefs	Total value (livres)
1752*	1562	1484	47123				9742	34326	1152956
1753	3527	1405	126980				23979	68971	2396756
1754	3957	1615	148282				24225	62710	2449566
1755	3395	1383	127867				21759	58768	2229795
1756	3683	937	115274				19406	44123	1572563
1757	4206	1838	145205				17070	58328	1838209
1758	3784	636	106606				17425	43710	1460237
1759	2976	505	94710				17840	45636	1487872
1760**	1480	641	49489				8510	30668	886708
1771	4357.5	5183	249119				13533	41942	1248478
1772	3033.5	3221	162821				13302	53944	1615995
1773	3769	2141	184512				20445	42438	1596746
1774**	1933.5	873	80462				12349	11686	709638
1775							20096	34298	
1776							12291	40508	
1777							18300	81698	
1778							17982	64373	
1779							18852	44967	
1780							2534	69702	
1781	1500	1519		1208	10179		13259	94040	
1782				792	9971		14089	125975	
1783	1174	2329		Bureau closed from			29287	113080	2969794
1784	2117	1148		August 1782 through			30746	92691	2605892
1785	2171	4043	137934	December 1785			24745	109886	2437395
1786	1459	1966	87222	1136	101	50868	20789	115946	2812631
1787				1867	268	89510	14892	139027	3472464
1788	1995	3001	149880	2060	382	98808	15412	134677	3412415
1789				1426	91	49220	16272	105030	2568164
1790	161	808		1212	20				

* Second semester only.
** First semester only.

List of Writings Cited

(Note: this list includes only writings actually cited in the text and is, therefore, neither a catalogue of all the works consulted nor a comprehensive bibliography of the subject. It does not include archival sources, which are identified in the text as used.)

Andrews, R. H. *Les Paysans des Mauges au XVIIIᵉ siècle.* Tours: Arrault, 1935.

Ardouin-Dumazet, ———. *Voyage en France*, 16th series: *De Vendée en Beauce.* Paris and Nancy, 1898.

Arnault, Charles. "Questions vendéennes," *Société de sciences, lettres et beaux-arts de Cholet et de sa région*, (1945–1946–1947, single issue), 121–157.

Aulard, Alphonse. *The French Revolution* (Bernard Miall, tr.), vols. I and II. New York: Scribner's, 1910.

——— ed. *Recueil des actes du comité de salut publique*, vols. II–X. Paris, 1889–1897.

Babeau, Albert. *Le Village sous l'ancien régime.* Paris, 1878.

Baguénier-Desormeaux, H. *Les Origines et les responsabilités de l'insurrection vendéenne.* Fontenay-le-Comte: Lussaud, 1916.

Baudrillart, H. *Les Populations agricoles de la France.* Paris, 1888.

Beauchamp, Alphonse de. *Histoire de la guerre de la Vendée*, 2nd ed., 4 vols. Paris, 1820.

Bellugou, Henri. *La Gabelle dans le Bas-Anjou.* Angers: Siraudeau, 1953.

Bénaben, ———. *Considérations générales sur la guerre de Vendée.* [n.p.], an III.

Berthre de Bourniseaux, P. V. J. *Histoire des guerres de la Vendée et des Chouans*, 3 vols. Paris, 1819.

Blackwell, Gordon W. "Theoretical Framework for Sociological Research in Community Organization," *Social Forces*, XXXIII (1954), 57–64.

Bloch, C. and A. Tuetey. *Procès-verbaux du comité de mendicité de la Constituante.* Paris: Imprimerie Nationale, 1911.

Bloch, Marc. *Les Caractères originaux de l'histoire rurale française*, new ed. Paris: Colin, 1952.

——— *Les Caractères originaux de l'histoire rurale française.* Supplément établi d'après les travaux de l'auteur par Robert Dauvergne. Paris: Colin, 1956.

——— Review of R. H. Andrews, *Les Paysans des Mauges*, *Annales d'histoire économique et sociale*, IX (July 1937), 393–396.

Bodinier, Guillaume. *Les Élections et les représentants de Maine-et-Loire depuis 1789.* Angers, 1888.

Bois, Paul. *Cahier de doléances du tiers état de la sénéchaussée de Château-du-Loir pour les États Généraux de 1789.* Gap: Imprimerie Louis-Jean, 1960a.

——— "Dans l'Ouest, politique et enseignement primaire," *Annales: économies, sociétés, civilisations*, IX (July–September 1954), 356–367.

——— *Paysans de l'Ouest.* Le Mans: Imprimerie M. Vilaire, 1960b.

———— "Réflexions sur les survivances de la Révolution dans l'Ouest," *Annales historiques de la Révolution française*, XXXIII (April–June 1961), 177–186.

Boissonade, P. *Histoire de Poitou*. Paris: Boivin, 1915.

Bonnemère, Eugène. *La Vendée en 1793*. Paris, 1866.

Bonniveau, L. "Manufacture de Cholet en 1751," *Bulletin de la société de sciences, lettres et beaux-arts de Cholet*, 1923, 96–97.

Bouchard, M. A. *L'Influence économique et sociale des voies de communication dans le département de Maine-et-Loire*. Angers, 1884.

Boutillier de Saint-André, Marin-Jacques-Narcisse. *Une Famille vendéenne pendant la grande guerre* (Eugène Bossard, ed.). Paris, 1896.

Brinton, Crane. *A Decade of Revolution*. The Rise of Modern Europe series, New York: Harper, 1934.

Brunhes, Jean and Pierre Deffontaines. *Géographie humaine de la France*, II. Paris: Plon-Nourrit, 1926.

Carlyle, Thomas. *The French Revolution*. New York: Caldwell [n.d.].

Carré de Busserolle, J.-X. *Inventaire de la noblesse d'Anjou et du Saumurois en 1789*. Montsoreau, 1890.

Carte des postes de France divisée en ses 83 départements. Paris, 1791.

Cavaillès, Henri. *La Route française*. Paris: Colin, 1946.

Cavoleau, J.-A. *Statistique ou description générale du département de la Vendée* (A.-D. de la Fontenelle de Vaudoré, ed.). Fontenay-le-Comte, 1844.

Chamard, François. *Les Origines et les responsabilités de l'insurrection vendéenne*. Paris, 1898.

Charier, Camille. *Montreuil-Bellay à travers les âges*. Saumur: Charier, 1913.

Chassin, Ch.-L. *La Préparation de la guerre de Vendée*. 3 vols. Paris, 1892.

Châtelain, Abel. "Évolution des densités de population en Anjou (1806–1936)," *Revue de géographie de Lyon*, XXXI (1956), 43–60.

Chevalier, Louis. *Classes laborieuses et classes dangereuses*. Paris: Plon, 1958.

Chiva, I. *Rural Communities*, Paris: UNESCO Reports and Papers in the Social Sciences, no. 10, 1959.

Chollet, N. *Chalonnes à travers les âges*. Angers: Imprimerie Centrale, 1952.

Choudieu, Pierre-René. *Notes sur la guerre de Vendée* (E. Quereau-Lamerie, ed.). Vannes, 1889.

Cingari, Gaetano. *Giacobini e Sanfedisti in Calabria nel 1799*. Messina: D'Anna, 1957.

Clémenceau, Joseph. *Histoire de la guerre de la Vendée (1793–1815)* (F. Uzureau, ed.). Paris: Nouvelle Librairie Nationale, 1909.

Conin, René. "Recherches historiques sur St. Lambert-du-Lattay, Beaulieu et Ste. Foy," unpub. ms, Archives of the Bishopric of Angers [n.d.].

Couet de Viviers de Lorry, Michel-François. *Mandement de monseigneur l'évêque d'Angers*. Paris, 1790.

Davis, Kingsley and Hilda Hertz Golden. "Urbanization and the Development of Pre-Industrial Areas," *Economic Development and Cultural Change*, III (October 1954), 6–26.

Dehergne, Joseph. *Les Vendéens* (1793). Shanghai: Imprimerie de T'ou-Sè-Wè, 1939.

Demangeon, Albert. *France économique et humaine*, vol. VI of Géographie universelle (P. Vidal de la Blache and L. Gallois, ed.). Paris: Colin, 1946.

Denecheau, Joseph. "La Vente des biens nationaux dans le district de Vihiers," unpub. Mémoire pour le Diplôme d'Études Supérieures d'Histoire, Université de Poitiers, 1955.

Déniau, Felix. *Précis historique de la paroisse de St. Macaire en Mauges*. Cholet: Gaultier, 1908.

Desmé de Chavigny, O. *Histoire de Saumur pendant la Révolution*. Vannes, 1892.

Dion, Roger. *Essai sur la formation du paysage rural français*. Tours: Arrault, 1934.

——— *Histoire de la vigne et du vin en France des origines au XIXe siècle*. Paris: privately printed, 1959.

——— *Le Val de Loire*. Tours: Arrault, 1934.

Dogan, Mattei and Jacques Narbonne. "L'Absentionnisme électoral en France," *Revue française de science politique*, IV (January–March 1954), 5–26.

Dornic, François. *L'Industrie textile dans le Maine et ses débouchés internationaux*. Le Mans: Éditions Pierre-Belon, 1955.

Dorsey, Deborah Worthington. "An Economic Interpretation of the Cahiers of Anjou," unpub. honors thesis Radcliffe College, 1960.

Dubreuil, Léon. *Histoire des insurrections de l'Ouest*, 2 vols. Paris, 1929–1930.

——— *La Vente des biens nationaux dans le département des Côtes-du-Nord*. Paris: Champion, 1912.

Duhamonay, Georges. *Trois Anciens Fiefs seigneuriaux en Anjou et leurs seigneurs*. Rennes: Lascher, 1942.

Dumas, F. *La Généralité de Tours au XVIIIe siècle*. Paris, 1894.

Duncan, Otis Dudley. "Community Size and the Rural-Urban Continuum," in *Cities and Society* (Paul K. Hatt and Albert J. Reiss, Jr., ed.). Glencoe, Ill.: The Free Press, 1957.

Dupeux, Georges. "Le Problème des abstentions dans le département de Loir-et-Cher au début de la troisième république," *Revue française de science politique*, II (January–March 1952), 71–86.

Dupin, Claude-F.-E. *Mémoire sur la statistique du département des Deux-Sèvres*. Niort, 1801–1802.

Eisenstadt, S. N. "The Place of Elites and Primary Groups in the Absorption of New Immigrants in Israel," *American Journal of Sociology*, 57 (1951), 222–231.

Faucheux, Marcel. *Un Ancien Droit ecclésiastique perçu en Bas-Poitou: le boisselage*. La Roche-sur-Yon: Potier, 1953.

——— "La Vendée," in *Les Élections de 1869* (Louis Girard, ed.), Bibliothèque de la Révolution de 1848, vol. XXI. Paris: Marcel Rivière, 1960.

Feldman, Arnold. "The Interpenetration of Firm and Society," in *Economic*

Development and its Social Implications (Georges Balandier, ed.). Paris: Presses Universitaires de France, 1962.

Forestier, M. *Histoire de la commune de Chalonnes-sur-Loire pendant la Révolution et la guerre de Vendée.* Angers: Germain & Grassin, 1900.

Forster, Robert. "The Provincial Noble: A Reappraisal," *American Historical Review*, LXVIII (April 1963), 681–691.

Furet, Pierre. *Cholet, Étude de géographie historique.* Cholet: Farré et Freulon, 1950.

Gabory, Émile. *La Révolution et la Vendée*, 3 vols. Paris: Perrin, 1925.

Gallard, Louis. "Le Clergé saumurois de 1789 à 1795," unpub. Mémoire pour le Diplôme d'Études Supérieures, Université de Poitiers, 1960.

Garaud, M. "Le Régime agraire et les paysans de Gâtine au XVIIIᵉ siècle," *Bulletin de la société des antiquaires de l'Ouest*, II, 4ᵉs. (1954), 637–664.

———— *La Révolution et la propriété foncière.* Paris: Sirey, 1959.

Gaugain, F. *Histoire de la Révolution dans la Mayenne.* Laval: Chailland, 1919.

Geertz, Clifford. "The Javanese Kijaji: the Changing Role of a Cultural Broker," *Comparative Studies in Society and History*, II (January 1960), 228–249.

Gellusseau, M. Auguste-Amaury. *Histoire de Cholet et de son industrie.* Paris, Angers, Nantes, and Cholet, 1862.

Gerbaux, Fernand and Charles Schmidt. *Procès-verbaux des comités d'agriculture et de commerce de la Constituante et de la convention.* Paris: Imprimerie Nationale, 1906.

Gerth, Hans and C. Wright Mills, ed. *From Max Weber: Essays in Sociology.* New York: Oxford University Press, 1946.

Godechot, Jacques. *La Contre-révolution.* Paris: Presses Universitaires de France, 1961.

———— *Les Institutions de la France sous la Révolution et l'empire.* Paris: Presses Universitaires de France, 1951.

Goguel, François. *Géographie des élections françaises de 1870 à 1951.* Cahiers de la Fondation Nationale des Sciences Politiques, 27. Paris: Colin, 1951.

Goodwin, A. "Counter-Revolution in Brittany; the Royalist Conspiracy of the Marquis de la Rouérie, 1791–1793," *Bulletin of the John Ryland's Library*, 39 (1957), 326–355.

Gouldner, Alvin. "Cosmopolitans and Locals: Toward an Analysis of Latent Social Roles," *Administrative Science Quarterly*, II (December 1957), 281–306; II (March 1958), 444–480.

Greer, Donald. *The Incidence of the Emigration during the French Revolution.* Cambridge, Mass.: Harvard University Press, 1951.

———— *The Incidence of the Terror during the French Revolution.* Cambridge, Mass.: Harvard University Press, 1935.

Greer, Scott. *The Emerging City.* New York: The Free Press of Glencoe, 1962.

Grille, Fr. *La Vendée en 1793*, 3 vols. Paris, 1851-1852.

Gross, Feliks. *The Seizure of Political Power.* New York: Philosophical Library, 1958.

Gross, Neal. "Cultural variables in rural communities," *American Journal of Sociology*, LIII (1948), 344–350.

Gruget, S. "Histoire de la constitution civile du clergé en Anjou," *Anjou historique* (F. Uzureau, ed.), II (1902), 151–161, 223–242, 337–353.

Guérin, Daniel. *La Lutte des classes sous la première république: bourgeois et "bras nus" (1793–1797)*, 3rd ed., vol. I. Paris: Gallimard, 1946.

Guinhut, A. *Notice historique sur Saint-Laurent-de-la-Plaine*, Angers: Siraudeau, 1909.

Hauser, Henri. *Recherches et documents sur l'histoire des prix en France de 1500 à 1800*. Paris: Les Presses Modernes, 1936.

Hawley, Amos. *Human Ecology*. New York: Ronald, 1950.

Heberle, Rudolph. "The Application of Fundamental Concepts in Rural Community Studies," *Rural Sociology*, VI (September 1941), 203–215.

———— *Social Movements*. New York: Appleton-Century-Crofts, 1951.

Hill, Mozell C. and Albert N. Whiting. "Some Theoretical and Methodological Problems in Community Studies," *Social Forces*, XXIX (December 1950), 117–124.

Hiller, E. T. "The Community as a Social Group," *American Sociological Review*, VI (April 1941), 189–202.

Hillery, George A., Jr. "Definitions of Community: Areas of Agreement," *Rural Sociology*, XX (June 1955), 111–123.

Hobsbawm, E. J. *Primitive Rebels*. Manchester, Eng.: Manchester University Press, 1959.

Homans, George C. *English Villagers of the Thirteenth Century*. Cambridge, Mass.: Harvard University Press, 1941.

Hoselitz, Bert F. *Sociological Aspects of Economic Growth*. Glencoe, Ill.: The Free Press, 1960.

Hughes, Everett C. "The Making of a Physician," *Human Organization*, XIV (Winter 1955), 21–25.

Hunter, Floyd. *Community Power Structure*. Chapel Hill: University of North Carolina Press, 1953.

Jaurès, Jean. *Histoire socialiste de la Révolution française*, 8 vols. Paris: Librairie de l'Humanité, 1922–1924.

Jeanneau, Benoît. "Les Élections législatives de novembre 1958 en Maine-et-Loire," *Revue française de science politique*, X (September 1960), 562–607.

Jeanvrot, Victor. *Monseigneur d'Agra*. Paris, 1894.

Kaplow, Jeffry. "The Social Structure of Elbeuf (Seine-Maritime) During the Revolutionary Period, 1770–1815," unpub. diss. Princeton University, 1962.

Kautsky, Karl. *La Lutte des classes en France en 1789* (Edouard Berth, tr.). Paris, 1901.

Kerr, Clark and Abraham Siegel. "The Interindustry Propensity to Strike — An International Comparison," in *Industrial Conflict* (Arthur Kornhauser, et al., ed.). New York: McGraw-Hill, 1954.

Kornhauser, William. *The Politics of Mass Society*. Glencoe, Ill.: The Free Press, 1959.

—— "Social Bases of Political Rebellion," unpub. paper delivered at Princeton University, 1961.

Kroeber, Alfred. *Anthropology*. New York: Harcourt, Brace, 1948.

Labrousse, Ernest. *La Crise de l'économie française à la fin de l'ancien régime et au début de la Révolution*, vol. I. Paris: Presses Universitaires de France, 1944.

La Gorce, Pierre de. *Histoire religieuse de la Révolution française*, vols. I–III. Paris: Plon, 1909–1911.

Lancelot, Alain and Jean Ranger. "Les Abstentions au référendum du 28 septembre 1958: Note sur une carte par cantons," *Revue française de science politique*, XI (March 1961), 138–142.

Larevellière-Lépeaux, L. M. *Mémoires de Larevellière-Lépeaux*. Paris, 1895.

La Rochejaquelein, —— de. *Mémoires de Madame la Marquise de la Rochejaquelein écrits par elle-même, rédigés par M. le Baron de Barante*. Bordeaux, 1815.

La Roque, Louis de and Édouard de Barthélemy. *Catalogue des gentilshommes d'Anjou et pays Saumurois qui ont pris part ou envoyé leurs procurations aux assemblées de la noblesse pour l'élection des deputés aux États-Généraux de 1789*. Paris, 1864.

La Sicotière, L. de. *Étude historique et critique sur l'ouvrage de M. Port, la Vendée angevine*. Angers, 1889.

Latreille, André. *L'Église catholique et la Révolution française*, 2 vols. Paris: Hachette, 1946–1950.

Le Bras, Gabriel. *Études de sociologie religieuse*, I and II. Paris: Presses Universitaires de France, 1955–1956.

Leclerc-Thouin, O. *L'Agriculture de l'Ouest de la France*. Paris, 1843.

Lefebvre, Georges. *The Coming of the French Revolution* (R. R. Palmer, tr. and ed.). Princeton: Princeton University Press, 1947.

—— *Études sur la Révolution française*. Paris: Presses Universitaires de France, 1954.

—— *La Grande Peur de 1789*. Paris: Colin, 1932.

—— *Les Paysans du Nord pendant la Révolution française*. Lille: Robbe, 1924.

—— *Questions agraires au temps de la terreur*, 2nd ed. La Roche-sur-Yon: Potier, 1952.

—— *La Révolution française*, Peuples et Civilisations, XIII. Paris: Presses Universitaires de France, 1951.

Lefebvre, Henri. "Problèmes de sociologie rurale: la communauté paysanne," *Cahiers internationaux de sociologie*, VI (1949), 78.

Le Lannou, Maurice. *Géographie de la Bretagne*, 2 vols. Rennes: Plihon, 1950.

Le Moy, A. *Cahiers de doléances des corporations de la ville d'Angers et des paroisses de la sénéchaussée particulière d'Angers pour les États Généraux de 1789*, 2 vols. Angers: Burdin, 1915.

Lequinio, ——. *Guerre de la Vendée et des Chouans*. Paris, an III.

Le Theule, Joël. "Le vignoble du Layon, étude de géographie humaine et économique," unpub. thesis for the diploma in geography, Caen [1950].

Lipset, Seymour Martin, Martin A. Trow, and James S. Coleman. *Union Democracy*. Glencoe, Ill.: The Free Press, 1956.

Lockroy, Édouard, ed. *Une mission en Vendée*. Paris, 1893.

Long, Norton. "The Metropolitan Community as an Ecology of Games," *American Journal of Sociology*, LXIV (November 1958), 251–261.

Loomis, Charles P. and J. Allen Beegle. *Rural Social Systems*. Englewood Cliffs, N.J.: Prentice-Hall, 1950.

Lucas de la Championnière, ———. *Mémoires sur la guerre de Vendée (1793–1796)* (Pierre Suzanne, ed.). Paris: Plon-Nourrit, 1904.

McManners, John. *French Ecclesiastical Society Under the Ancien Régime*. Manchester, Eng.: Manchester University Press, 1960.

Maisonneuve, P. *L'Anjou, ses vignes et ses vins*. Angers, 1925.

Malleray, Henri de. *Les Cinq Vendées*. Angers: Siraudeau, and Paris: Plon-Nourrit, 1924.

Marboeuf, L. "L'Administration des voies publiques en Anjou à la fin du dix-huitième siècle," unpub. ms departmental archives of Maine-et-Loire, 1954.

Marchegay, Paul. *Archives d'Anjou*, 2 vols. Angers, 1853.

Marczewski, Jan. "Some Aspects of the Economic Growth of France, 1660–1958," *Economic Development and Cultural Change*, IX (April 1961), 369–386.

Marion, Marcel. *La Vente des biens nationaux pendant la Révolution*. Paris: Champion, 1908.

Marx, Karl and Friedrich Engels. *The German Ideology* (R. Pascal, ed.). New York: International Publishers, 1947.

Mathiez, A. *La Révolution et l'église*. Paris: Colin, 1910.

——— *La Révolution française*, 3 vols. Collection Armand Colin, nos. 17, 52, 93 (vols. I and II, 11th ed.; vol. III, 10th ed.). Paris: Colin, 1951–1954.

Meadows, Paul. "The City, Technology, and History," *Social Forces*, XXXVI (December 1957), 141–147.

Menil, Georges de. "Saint-Lambert-du-Lattay, a Village on the Border of the *Vendée Militaire*, 1789–1793," unpub. honors thesis Harvard College, 1962.

Mercerolle, J. "Notes pouvant servir à l'histoire de Chemillé: guerres de Vendée," vol. I, unpub. ms communicated by the author [n.d.].

Merle, Louis. *La Métairie et l'évolution agraire de la Gâtine poitevine de la fin du moyen âge à la Révolution*. Paris: S.E.V.P.E.N., 1958.

Merton, Robert K. *Social Theory and Social Structure*, rev. ed. Glencoe, Ill.: The Free Press, 1957.

Meyer, Jean. "Le Commerce négrier nantais (1774–1792)," *Annales: économies, sociétés, civilisations*, 15 (January–February 1960), 120–129.

Meynier, André. *Les paysages agraires*. Paris: Colin, 1958.

Michelet, Jules. *Histoire de la Révolution française*. Paris, 1879.

Millet, P.-A. *État actuel de l'agriculture dans le département de Maine-et-Loire*. Angers, 1856.

Miner, Horace. "The Folk-Urban Continuum," *American Sociological Review*, XVII (1952), 529–537.

Mogey, John M. *Rural Life in Northern Ireland*. London: Oxford University Press, 1947.

Mols, Roger. *Introduction à la démographie historique des villes d'Europe du XIVe au XVIIIe siècle*. Louvain: Publications Universitaires, 1955.

Momoro, A. F. *Rapport sur l'état politique de la Vendée*. Paris, an II.

Mumford, Lewis. *The City in History*. New York: Harcourt, Brace and World, Inc., 1961.

Murphey, Rhoads. "The City as a Center of Change: Western Europe and China," *Annals of the Association of American Geographers*, XLIV (December 1954), 349–362.

Musset, René. *Le Bas-Maine*. Paris: Colin, 1917.

Paret, Peter. *Internal War and Pacification, The Vendée, 1789–1796*. Princeton: Center of International Studies, 1961.

Parsons, Talcott. *The Social System*. London: Tavistock Publications, 1952.

——— *Structure and Process in Modern Societies*. Glencoe, Ill.: The Free Press, 1960.

Pitt-Rivers, Julian. "Social Class in a French Village," *Anthropological Quarterly*, XXXIII (January 1960), 1–13.

Poirier de Beauvais, Bertrand. *Mémoires inédits de Bertrand Poirier de Beauvais* (first pub. 1798). Paris, 1893.

Poirier, Louis. "Bocage et plaine dans le Sud de l'Anjou," *Annales de géographie*, XLIII (1934), 22–31.

Port, Célestin. *Dictionnaire historique, géographique et biographique de Maine-et-Loire*, 3 vols. Paris and Angers, 1878.

——— *La Vendée angevine*, 2 vols. Paris, 1888.

Proust, Antonin, *Archives de l'Ouest*. Paris: Librairie Internationale [n.d.].

Queruau-Lamerie, E. *Le Clergé du département de Maine-et-Loire pendant la Révolution*. Angers, 1899.

Raimbault, Louis. "Extrait d'un manuscrit format in 4° relié en chagrin noir doré sur tranche, au dos duquel est le titre *Chronique de Saint Lambert du Lattai, Sainte Foi et Beaulieu*," unpub. ms departmental archives of Maine-et-Loire [n.d.].

Raveau, Paul. *Essai sur la situation économique et l'état social en Poitou au XVIe siècle*. Paris: Rivière, 1931.

Réau de la Gaignonnière, Jean de. *La Commission intermédiare de l'assemblée provinciale d'Anjou*. Angers: Siraudeau, 1911.

Redfield, Robert. *The Folk Culture of Yucatan*. Chicago: University of Chicago Press, 1941.

——— "The Folk Society," *American Journal of Sociology*, LII (1947), 293–308.

——— *Peasant Society and Culture*. Chicago: University of Chicago Press, 1956.

——— and Milton B. Singer, "The Cultural Role of Cities," *Economic Development and Cultural Change*, 3 (October 1954), 53–73.

Rees, Alwyn D. *Life in a Welsh Countryside*. Cardiff: University of Wales Press, 1950.

Reinhard, Marcel. *Histoire de la population mondiale.* Paris: Éditions Domat-Montchrestien, 1949.

Reiss, Albert J., Jr. "The Sociological Study of Communities," *Rural Sociology*, XXIV (June 1959), 118–130.

Richard, J.-E. and P.-R. Choudieu. *Rapport sur la guerre de la Vendée présenté à la convention nationale.* Paris, 1793.

R[omain], ——— de. *Récit de quelques faits concernant la guerre de la Vendée relatifs seulement aux habitans [sic] de l'Anjou.* Paris [n.d.].

Roupnel, Gaston. *La Ville et la campagne au XVIIe siècle.* Paris: Colin, 1955.

Rudé, George. *The Crowd in the French Revolution.* Oxford: Oxford University Press, 1959.

Sagnac, Philippe. "Les Cahiers de 1789 et leur valeur," *Revue d'histoire moderne et contemporaine*, VIII (1906–1907), 329–349.

——— *La Législation civile de la Révolution française.* Paris, 1898.

Sanders, Irwin T. *Balkan Village.* Lexington: University of Kentucky Press, 1949.

——— *The Community.* New York: Ronald, 1958.

Sausseau, Paul. *Tigné*, 8 brochures. Angers: Hudon, 1900–1901.

[Savary, J.-J.-M.]. "Un Officier supérieur des armées de la république," *Guerres des Vendéens et des Chouans contre la republique française*, vol. I. Collection des mémoires relatifs à la Révolution française, no. XVIII. Paris, 1824.

Sée, Henri. "Le commerce des toiles du Bas-Maine," *Mémoires et documents pour servir à l'histoire du commerce et de l'industrie en France* (Julien Hayem, ed.), 10e s., 1–79. Paris: Hachette, 1926.

——— "L'Économie rurale de l'Anjou dans la première moitié du XIXe siècle," *Revue d'histoire économique et sociale*, XV (1927), 104–122.

——— *Histoire économique de la France*, 2 vols. Paris: Colin, 1948–1951.

Seebohm, Frederic. *The English Village Community.* London, 1896.

Seignobos, Charles. *Études de politique et d'histoire.* Paris: Presses Universitaires de France, 1934.

Sévestre, E. *L'acceptation de la constitution civile du clergé en Normandie.* Paris: Picard, 1922.

Sicard, A. *Le Clergé de France pendant la Révolution*, vol. II. Paris: Lecoffre, 1927.

Siegfried, André. "Le Régime et la division de la propriété dans le Maine et l'Anjou," *Annales du musée social* (1911), 195–215.

——— *Tableau politique de la France de l'Ouest sous la Troisième République.* Paris: Colin, 1913.

——— "En Vendée," *Le Figaro*, 17 July, 1950, 1, 7.

Sirich, John Black. *The Revolutionary Committees in the Departments of France, 1793–1794.* Cambridge, Mass.: Harvard University Press, 1943.

Sjoberg, Gideon. "The Preindustrial City," *American Journal of Sociology*, LX (March 1955), 438–445.

——— "'Folk' and 'Feudal' Societies," *American Journal of Sociology*, LVIII (November 1952), 231–239.

Soboul, Albert. "La Communauté rurale (XVIIIe et XIXe siècles): problèmes de base," *Revue de synthèse* (July–September 1957) 283–307.

——— *Précis d'histoire de la Révolution française*. Paris: Éditions Sociales, 1962.

Spal, Jules. "Étude sur les assemblées des communautés d'habitants en Anjou," *Bulletin de la société des sciences, lettres, et beaux-arts de Cholet et de l'arrondissement* (1886), 223–246.

——— "Monographie de la commune de Saint-Macaire-en-Mauges," *Bulletin de la société des sciences, lettres et beaux-arts de Cholet et de l'arrondissement* (1887), 305–335.

Steward, Julian et al. *The People of Puerto Rico*. Urbana: University of Illinois Press, 1956.

Sutton, Francis X. "Representation and the Nature of Political Systems," *Comparative Studies in Society and History*, II (October 1959), 1–10.

Sutton, Willis A. and Jiri Kolaja. "The Concept of Community," *Rural Sociology*, XXV (June 1960), 177–203.

Sykes, Gresham M. "The Differential Distribution of Community Knowledge," *Social Forces*, XXIX (May 1951), 376–382.

Taine, Hippolyte Adolphe. *The Ancient Regime* (John Durand, tr.). New York, 1876.

Tanguy, Jean. *Le Commerce du port de Nantes au milieu du XVIe siècle*. Paris: Colin, 1956.

Tilly, Charles. "The Analysis of a Counter-Revolution," *History and Theory*, III (no. 1, 1963), 30–58.

——— "Civil Constitution and Counter-Revolution in Southern Anjou," *French Historical Studies*, I (no. 2, 1959), 172–199.

——— "Local Conflicts in the Vendée before the Rebellion of 1793," *French Historical Studies*, II (Fall 1961), 209–231.

——— "Rivalités de bourgs et conflits de partis dans les Mauges de 1789 à 1793," *Revue du Bas-Poitou et des provinces de l'Ouest*, LXXIII (July–August 1962), 268–280.

——— "The Social Background of the Rebellion of 1793 in Southern Anjou," unpub. diss. Harvard University, 1958.

Tocqueville, Alexis de. *The Old Regime and the French Revolution* (Stuart Gilbert, tr.), Anchor Books. New York: Doubleday, 1955.

Trocmé, Etienne and Marcel Delafosse. *Le Commerce rochelais de la fin du XVe siècle au début du XVIIe*. Paris: Colin, 1952.

Turreau, Louis Marie. *Mémoires pour servir à l'histoire de la guerre de la Vendée*. Paris: Baudouin, 1924.

Uzureau, F. "Abbayes, prieurés, et couvents d'hommes en Anjou (1768)," *Anjou historique*, III (1903), 168–172.

——— "Les Administrateurs du district de Saumur (1790–95)," *Anjou historique*, XLVII (1947), 109–111.

——— "L'Application de la constitution civile du clergé dans le district de Vihiers," *Anjou historique*, XV (1915), 484–515.

——— "Le Canton de Nueil-sous-Passavant (1792–1801)," *Anjou historique*, XLVI (1946), 119–121.

——— "Le Clergé de Neuvy-en-Mauges pendant la Révolution," *Anjou historique*, XXIII (1923), 228–233.

——— "La Constitution civile du clergé dans le district de Saint-Florent-le-Vieil," *Anjou historique*, XXV (1925), 226–229.

——— "Le District de Cholet (1790–95)," *Anjou historique*, XLV (1945), 166–168.

——— "Les Élections des administrateurs du district de Cholet (1790)," *Anjou historique*, XXX (1930), 87–90.

——— "Les Administrateurs du département de Maine-et-Loire (1790–93)," *Anjou historique*, II (1902), 547–552.

——— "La Municipalité de St. Martin de Beaupréau (1787–92)," *Anjou historique*, XXXI (1931), 22–29.

——— "Physionomie morale, intellectuelle et politique du département de Maine-et-Loire en 1834," *Anjou historique*, XIX (1919), 81–96.

——— "Pourquoi Beaupréau et Saint-Florent demandaient le tribunal du district (1790)," *Anjou historique*, XVIII (1918), 215–221.

——— "Pourquoi Beaupréau voulait avoir un tribunal (1790)," *Anjou historique*, XXXIII (1933), 206–212.

——— "Pourquoi Cholet voulait être chef-lieu de district (1790)," *Anjou historique*, XXXIV (1934), 91–94.

——— "Pourquoi Montrevault voulait avoir un tribunal (1790)," *Anjou historique*, XL (1940), 159–162.

——— "La Subdélégation de Cholet en 1768," *Anjou historique*, XLI (1941), 141–149.

——— *Tableau de la province d'Anjou (1762–66)*, Angers: Siraudeau, 1901.

——— "Troubles à Maulèvrier (1791)," *Anjou historique*, XXIV (1924), 232–235.

Vidal de la Blache, Paul. *Tableau de la géographie de la France*, vol. 1, p. I of *Histoire de France* (Ernest Lavisse, ed.). Paris: Hachette, 1903.

——— *Principles of Human Geography* (Emmanuel de Martonne, ed., Millicent Todd Bingham, tr.). New York: Holt, 1926.

Vidich, Arthur J. and Joseph Bensman. *Small Town in Mass Society*. Princeton: Princeton University Press, 1958.

Wagret, Paul and Joël le Theule. "Le Vin du 'Layon' " [in] "Deux monographies du vignoble français," *Annales: économies, sociétés, civilisations*, IX (1954), 165–188.

Wagret, Paul, Jacques Boussard, Jacques Levron, and Simone Maillard-Bourdillon. *Visages de l'Anjou*. Paris: Éditions des Horizons de France, 1951.

Walter, Gérard. *La Guerre de Vendée*. Paris: Plon, 1953.

Weber, Max. *The City* (Don Martindale and Gertrude Neuwirth, tr. and ed.). Glencoe, Ill.: The Free Press, 1958.

Wirth, Louis. "Urbanism as a Way of Life," *American Journal of Sociology*, XLIV (July 1938), 1–24.

Wolf, Eric R. "Aspects of Group Relations in a Complex Society: Mexico," *American Anthropologist*, LVIII (December 1956), 1065–1078.

———— "Closed Corporate Peasant Communities in Mesoamerica and Central Java," *Southwestern Journal of Anthropology*, XIII (Spring 1957), 1–18.

———— "Types of Latin American Peasantry: A Preliminary Discussion," *American Anthropologist*, LVII (1955), 452–471.

Wylie, Laurence. "As Chanzeaux Sees the French Crisis," *New York Times Magazine*, September 14, 1958, 26–27, 40, 44, 46.

———— "Revolution in Western France," *The French Review*, XXXII (May 1959), 539–546.

———— *Village in the Vaucluse*. Cambridge, Mass.: Harvard University Press, 1957.

Index

Active Citizens: occupations of, 91; ratio to total population, 266; of Chemillé, 291

Agriculture: winegrowing, 31–32, 40–41, 116, 126, 213–214; grain production, 32, 114–115; cattle raising, 32–33, 53–54, 55, 114–115; textile crops, 33–34, 116, 118, 126; contrast of Mauges and Val-Saumurois, 115, 118–119; during Revolution, 213–215

Ambillou, 211

Andegaviana, 8

Andrews, R. H., 54, 73–74, 109, 114, 115, 116, 120, 121, 125, 126, 127, 148, 346–347

Andrezé, 219

Angers, 4, 26, 30, 34, 35, 36, 42, 57, 70, 171, 187, 210, 213, 215, 283, 315, 320, 338

Angers, District of, 41–42, 79; marriage patterns in, 89–90; clergy of, 105, 239, 259; Grievances in, 178, 182, 184; enlistments in, 189; poverty in, 218; disfranchised voters, 266; counterrevolutionaries of, 327

Anjou, 27; northern, 14; southern, 14; changed to Maine-et-Loire, 170

Anjou historique, 8

Anticlericalism, 101

Apremont, 226

Ardouin-Dumazet, M., 83

"Aristocrats," party of counterrevolution, *see* Parties

Army, counterrevolutionary, 4, 5, 316, 325–329, 331–336

Arnault, C., 111

Artisans, 66–70 *passim*, 346; economic position of, 71, 144; relation to other classes, 71, 98, 140; marriage patterns, 90–91, 92, 96–98; location of, 137–138; as recruits in Revolutionary army, 190–191; political activity of, 219–224 *passim*, 279; participants in counterrevolution, 326–330

Assembly, local: 150–153; of notables after 1787, 151; attendance at, 151–152; importance of, 163; and Grievances, 177. *See also* Communal council

Aubigné, L. F. d', 128

Aulard, A., 6, 198, 322, 333, 336, 337, 339

Avranches, 5

Babeau, A., 151

Baguénier-Desormeaux, H., 8, 176

Barante, G. de, 126

Barbotin, L., 300–301, 303

Barère, B., 6, 337–338

Barthélemy, É. de, 75n

Bas-Maine, 31, 35

Baudrillart, H., 36, 73n

Béarn, 217

Beauchamp, A. de, 8

Beaulieu, 290, 311, 319

Beaulieu (Vendée), 308

Beaupréau, 4, 42, 49, 51, 56, 132, 137, 170, 171, 176, 187, 188, 215, 219, 248, 282, 284, 311, 314, 335; Collège de, 241; District of, 273

Beegle, J. A., 58

Bégrolles, 56, 221, 255, 285, 290

Bellefontaine abbey, 254, 276

Bellugou, H., 166

Bénaben, agent of National Assembly, 322

Bensman, J., 58, 149

Béritault (family), 52, 70

Béritault de Salboeuf, Chevalier, 281, 288–289, 294

Bernier, É., 335

Berthre de Bourniseaux, P. V. J., 322

Blackwell, G., 58

Bloch, C., 78, 218

Bloch, M., 84n, 127

Bocage: described, 28, 83; cities of, 29; cattle raising in, 32–33; textile industry in, 35–36; in southern Anjou, 39; origin of, 84–85n; community layout in, 85, 87–88. *See also* Mauges

Bodinier, G., 267

Bois, P., 7, 26, 32, 54, 73n, 75n, 78, 88, 101, 104, 133, 143, 156, 178, 203, 223, 241, 265, 310

Boisairault, 211

Boisard, Lieutenant, 286

Bonchamp, C.-M.-A. de, 4, 176, 315, 333

Bonnemère, E., 8–9

Bonniveau, L., 132, 137n

Bordage, 72n

Bordeaux, 50, 51

Bouchard, M. A., 141
Boulard, abbé, 241
Bourg, 85; role of, 55–56; percentage of population in, 87
Bourgeois and bourgeoisie: general position, 25–26, 155–156, 346; in Cholet, 52; economic position and activity, 54–55, 70, 121–122; marriages, 90–91, 92, 96–98; relations with other classes, 111, 131–132, 140, 143–145, 157–158, 225–226, 281–282; position within community, 154, 173, 236, 264; political position and activity, 155–156, 267–268, 270–272, 277, 282; in Revolution, 161; and local assemblies, 163; and franc-fief, 166; and sale of church property, 176, 205, 207, 211–212, 293; enlistments in Revolutionary armies, 190–191; participation in counterrevolution, 330
Bourgneuf, 312
Boutillier de Saint-André, M.-J.-N., 122
Bouzillé, 188, 256, 313
Bouzillé-Melay, 280
Bressuire, 2, 30, 282, 306
Brest, 26, 27
Briaudeau, T., 208–209, 291, 293, 300
Brigné, 319
Brissac, 42, 46, 47, 187
Brittany, 5, 14, 27
Brunhes, J., 30
Bureau de marque, 51, 133, 350–351

Cady, S.-J., 212
Cahiers de doleances, see Grievances
Calabria, 122
Carlyle, T., 336
Carré de Busserolle, J.-X., 75n
Carrier, J.-B., 338–339
Cathelineau, J., 315
Cavaillès, H., 25
Cavoleau, J.-A., 33, 139
Cernusson, 314
Cerqueux-de-Maulèvrier, 202, 247, 319
Cerqueux-sous-Passavant, 319
Cesbron d'Argonne, a counterrevolutionary chief, 212
Challans, 4, 223, 226, 253; District of, 303, 306
Chalonnes, 42, 45–46, 51, 118, 139, 171, 176, 190, 219, 254, 255, 283, 286–287, 315
Chamard, F., 227
Champtoceaux, 222
Chanteloup, 202, 231
Chantonnay, 30
Chanzeaux, 4, 102, 223, 255, 290, 313
Chapelain, deputy of Vendée, 222

Charier, C., 176, 215
Charity, 234–235
Chassin, Ch.-L., 103, 165, 168, 172, 176, 189, 212, 215, 222, 226, 230, 252, 258, 269, 277, 280, 306
Château-du-Loir, 34
Château-Thébault, 312
Châtelain, A., 86n, 102
Châtillon, 2, 222, 253, 306, 314, 335
Châtillon, District of, 303; insurrection in, 306–308
Chatisel, P.-J., 229
Chaudefonds, 224, 268
Chavagnes, 319
Chemillé, 4, 42, 47, 48, 49, 51, 52–53, 54, 55, 68, 70, 73, 79, 109, 132, 137, 151, 155, 165, 187, 188, 189, 190, 191, 202, 208, 218, 219, 220, 211, 268, 277, 282, 285, 287, 288, 290, 314, 318, 320, 324, 333; events of Revolution in, 291–298
Chevalier, L., 23n
Chiva, I., 58
Cholet, 4, 5, 30, 33, 42, 47, 49, 55, 56–57, 66–67, 79, 109, 141, 152, 166, 176, 178, 187, 188, 189, 190, 194, 202, 206, 208, 209, 255, 257, 277, 282, 283, 286, 309, 311, 312, 315, 319, 320; textile industry of, 50–52, 132–139, 216–222
Cholet, District of, 41–42, 44–45, 78–79, 202, 267, 270, 284, 296, 303; population characteristics, 68, 69, 86; marriage patterns in, 89–90; clergy of, 105, 108, 244, 259, 260; economy of, 115, 137–138, 150; Grievances in, 178, 180, 182, 184; enlistments in, 189–190; church property sales in, 206, 207; poverty in, 218, 219; disfranchised voters, 266; counterrevolutionaries of, 327
Chollet, N., 46, 176
Chouannerie, 5–6, 27–28, 203, 223
Choudieu, P. R., 322, 337
Church: property sales, 2, 169, 175–176, 203–212, 230–231; ecclesiastical establishments, 30, 40–42, 108–109, 184; closing down and consolidating of, 173–174, 251–252; changes in Revolution, 197, 233, 261–262. See also Religion
Cingari, G., 122
Cities: problems of definition, 42–43; of Mauges, 42–48 passim, 48–53; of Val-Saumurois, 42–48 passim
Civil Constitution of the Clergy, 167, 231, 233–242; economic effects of, 233–234, 242n; oath, 236–237, 239, 241–242, 299; correlation of rejection and counterrevolution, 257, 319. See also Clergy

Class(es): in southern Anjou, 66–73, 79; dualism of structure, 79–80, 96, 99; and marriage patterns, 90–91; and nativity, 91; conflict, 157–158, 224, 225, 226; of church property buyers, 207, 211–212; of counterrevolutionaries, 322–329

Clémenceau, J., 305, 331, 334

Cléré, 319

Clergy, 346; economic position of, 199–200; response to Revolution, 204, 228–231, 261–262; pro-Revolutionary position of monks, 228–229; conflict within, 229–230; and church property sales, 231–232
  Constitutional, 242–243, 246–252, 253, 256, 261–262, 275, 289; support of a political issue, 278
  Parish, 2; property of, 70–71; described, 100–101; relations with peasants, 144; effects of Revolution on, 201, 236
  Refractory, 232, 242–246, 248, 252–262, 281, 289, 294; deportation of, 258–259; in Val-Saumurois, 260–261. See also Curé(s)

Clericalism, 101

Clisson, 4, 171, 270; District of, 303

Colbert, C., 149

Colbert de Maulèvrier, E.-V.-C.-R., 207, 244, 245

Coleman, J. S., 86

Commerce and trade: expansion of, 30–31; of manufactured goods, 31, 135; of agricultural products, 31–32; in Mauges, 49

Communal council, 264–265, 273–275

Commune: defined, 82; Revolutionary changes in, 172–173

Community, see Rural community

Concourson, 319

Conin, R., 256

Conscription, 308–314; resistance to, 4, 232; as explanation of counterrevolution, 8; in Grievances, 180–181

Coquille, Constitutional curé, 248, 277

Coron, 202, 308

Cossé, 105, 309, 313

Côtes-du-Nord, 27

Couet du Viviers de Lorry, M. F., 229

Coulonnier, E., 246, 276

Counterrevolution: accounts of, 2–6, 312–320; stages of, 4; later uprisings, 6; literary treatments of, 6; significance to Revolution, 6; traditional explanations of, 6–9; sociological view, 9–13; inadequacies of explanations, 13; geographical area of, 27, 137, 297–298; in Chemillé, 297; in St. Georges-du-Puy-de-la-Garde, 302–303; participants, 321–330; committees, 328, 329, 335–336; tactics, 333;

council at Châtillon, 335; suppression of, 336–339

Courbet, innkeeper at La Poitevinière, 288–289

Courchamps, 194

Coustard, agent of National Assembly, 336

Cuba, 23

Curé(s): position within community, 101, 103–104, 110, 197; birthplaces of, 104–105; income and economic position, 105–108, 204, 233–234; relations with other classes, 110–111; political activity of, 152–153, 155, 172–173; "radicals" from Saumurois, 229; agent for charity, 234. See also Clergy

Davis, K., 24

Deffontaines, P., 30

Dehergne, J., 324

Delafosse, M., 36

Delaunay, P.-M., 245, 258

Demangeon, A., 29, 124

Denecheau, J., 74, 102, 204, 206, 207

Denée, 290

Desmé de Chavigny, O., 229–230

Deux-Sèvres, Department of, 2, 27, 171, 226, 258, 307–308; unrest in textile areas, 222

Dijon, 55

Dion, R., 30, 32, 46, 50, 51, 73n, 84n, 116, 137, 141

Distré, 143, 210–211

Districts: formation of, 171; elections in, 267–268; of southern Anjou, see those of Angers; Cholet; St. Florent; Saumur; Vihiers

Dogan, M., 86

Dornic, F., 133, 216

Dorsey, D. W., 167, 178

Doué, 42, 45, 46

Drain, 319

Dubreuil, L., 8, 175, 176, 186, 205, 212–213, 229, 239, 281, 305

Duhamonay, G., 76, 221, 280

Dumas, F., 133

Dumouriez, C.-F., 222

Duncan, O. D., 44, 59

Dupeux, G., 86

Dupin, C.-F.-E., 30, 139

Economy: agriculture, 31–34; industry, 35–36; as system of social relationships, 82; industrial and agricultural complexes, 96, 98, 99, 113–114, 132–133; effect of Revolution on, 212–215. See also Agriculture; Commerce and trade; Textile industry and commerce

Egypt, 23

Eisenstadt, S. N., 60

Elbée, M.-J.-L. d', 4, 176, 212, 280, 315

Elbeuf, 263

Elections, Revolutionary: requirements for voting and office, 265–267; refusals to register, 266; cantonal, 268, 270–272, 295; communal council, 273–276; significance of, 278–279

Elite: role in rural community, 60–61, 80–81; differentiation of, 64–65, 141–142, 173; clergy and conflict in, 101, 112; and Grievances, 177; Revolutionary change in, 196, 279

Émigrés and emigration, 5–6, 192–195

Engels, F., 21, 61

England, 24

Enlistments: in Revolutionary army, 189–192; occupations of recruits, 190–191

Estates General, 2, 104, 164, 229; effect of calling, 167; voting for, 265

Étiau, 290

Fabrique de Cholet, 133, 139, 216, 222

Faucheux, M., 101, 156, 199, 200

Faveraye, 319

Faye, 166, 319

Feldman, A., 63

"Feudal reaction," 21, 127, 129, 130, 143

"Feudist," 127–128

"Folk-urban continuum," 59–60

Folleville, J.-L. G. de, 335

Fontenay-le-Comte, 31, 36, 338

Fontevrault, 45, 47, 228; abbey of, 241

Forestier, M., 286

Forster, R., 77, 129

Fragmentation-pervasion, 63

Franc-fief: defined, 165; in Grievances, 180

Furet, P., 51, 132

Gabory, É., 109, 175, 176, 186, 280, 305, 308

Gallard, L., 105n, 229, 230, 239, 260

Gallois, J.-A., 247, 258

Garaud, M., 73n, 122, 139, 200

Garonne River, valley of, 37

Gaugain, F., 241

Geertz, C., 60

Gellusseau, M., 216

Gensonné, A., 247, 258

Gerbaux, F., 214

Gerth, H., 18, 62, 112

Gesté, 221, 313

Gibot (family), 76, 280

Girondins, 37

Godechot, J., 200, 236, 264, 305

Goguel, F., 157

Gonnord, 173, 221, 283, 290, 312, 317, 319

Goodwin, A., 281

Gouldner, A., 59

Goupilleau, deputy, 258

Government:
    Local: syndic, 150–151, 152, 163; assembly, 150–153; informal, 153; communal council, 264–265, 273–275
    National, 147–148; centralization of, 17–18, 21–22; Intendant, 51, 148; subdelegate, 52, 148; lack of contact with communities of, 148–149
    Revolutionary: reorganization of administration, 170–172; civic oath, 248, 269, 274, 275

Granville, 5

Great Fear, 168–169

Greece, 24

Greer, D., 37, 280, 322–323, 339

Greer, S., 60, 86

Grézillé, 66–67, 261

Grievances (cahiers de doléances), 164–167; composition of assemblies which approved, 177; "influenced," 178; "original," 178; complaints about government in, 180–181; complaints about nobles in, 181–183; concerning clergy, 183–185; general significance of, 185–186; priests' role in drafting, 228; of assembly of clergy of Anjou, 229–230; influenced by Thubert, 292; on conscription, 309

Grille, F., 190

Gross, N., 59

Gruget, S., 239

Guérin, D., 161

Guinhut, A., 150, 255

Haiti, 23

Hauser, H., 213

Hawley, A., 58

Heberle, R., 58

Hilaire, F., 299, 302, 303

Hill, M., 58

Hiller, E. T., 58

Hillery, G. A., 58

Hobsbawm, E. J., 158

Homans, G., 84n

Hoselitz, B., 19, 24

Huet de Vaudour, Inspector General of the Generality of Tours, 217–218

Hughes, E. C., 59

Hundred Days, 6

Hungary, 24

Hunter, F., 60

Ile d'Yeu, 306

Ile-et-Vilaine, Department of, 27

Industrialization, 10
Interim Commission(s), 162–163, 170
Intermarriage Index, 94–96

Jallais, 269–270, 290, 297, 309, 314, 317, 318
Jeanneau, B., 156
Jeanvrot, V., 9
Joué, 173, 290, 317
Juigné, 261

Kaplow, J., 216, 263
Kautsky, K., 153
Kerr, C., 61
Kolaja, J., 58
Kornhauser, W., 61, 86, 154
Kroeber, A., 19

La Blouère, 282
La Boissière, 313
Labrousse, E., 21, 116, 213
La Chapelle-du-Genêt, 326
La Chapelle-Rousselin, 165, 287
La Chapelle-Sainte-Radegonde, 268–269
La Crilloire, 202
La Flèche, 5, 31, 34
La Fosse-de-Tigné, 174, 251
La Gorce, P. de, 233, 248, 254, 269, 305
La Grésille, chapter of, 211
La Jumellière, 70, 308
La Lézardière, Baron de, 281
La Mothe-Saint-Heraye, 136
Lancelot, A., 102, 156
Land: ownership and control, 54, 74–75, 119–
    121, 144; exchange of, 73–74; use, 114
Landemont, 251–252, 268, 274, 282, 313, 319,
    320
Landeronde, 308
La Plaine, 235, 237, 274, 308, 319
La Poitevinière, 275, 277, 308, 314, 315, 318,
    326; conspiracy of, 288–289
La Pommeraye, 66–67, 209, 235, 254, 275
Larevellière-Lépeaux, L. M., 163, 165, 174,
    251–252, 255, 284–285
La Roche-Bernard, 4
La Rochejaquelein (Larochejacquelein): Mme
    de, 126; family, 235
La Rochelle, 26, 27, 30, 32, 35, 51, 338
La Roche-sur-Yon, 4, 306
La Romagne, 219, 313
La Roque, L. de, 75n
La Rouairie, Marquis de, 281
La Salle-de-Vihiers, 165, 319
La Séguinière, 152, 250

La Sicotière, L. de, 175
La Tessoualle, 87, 188, 202, 222, 245, 283, 290,
    321
Latreille, A., 233
Laval, 5, 34
Layon River, valley of, 39, 46; bridge between
    Mauges and Saumurois, 40–41; land owner-
    ship in, 74–75; religious practice in, 102; re-
    fusal of oath in, 239
Le Bois-de-Cené, 269
Le Bras, G., 101–102, 241
Leclerc-Thouin, O., 73n, 123, 125
Lefebvre, G., 120, 142, 168, 200, 203, 231, 259,
    288, 340
Lefebvre, H., 58
Legeay, Jacques, 300
Le Jaunais, treaty of, 5
Le Lannou, M., 84n
Le Longeron, 166
Le Loroux-Bottereau, 171
Le Mans, 5, 26, 28, 34
Le May, 56, 105, 109, 137, 155, 186, 190, 215,
    218, 219, 221, 237, 246–247, 270, 275–276,
    290, 309, 311, 312, 319
Le Moy, A., 126, 164, 165, 166, 177–178, 215,
    292
Le Petit Foüy, métairie, 83–84
Le Pin-en-Mauges, 165, 222, 317, 318
Le Puy-Notre-Dame, 109, 172, 187, 194
Le Puy-Saint-Bonnet, 286
Lequinio, agent of National Assembly, 7, 322
Le Ronceray, convent of, 109
Lescure, counterrevolutionary chief, 333
Les Gardes, 109, 188, 190, 242, 254, 282, 283,
    293, 309; events of Revolution in, 298–303
    passim. See also St. Georges-du-Puy-de-la-
    Garde
Le Theule, J., 40, 102, 116, 213
Le Voide, 165
Ligné, 308
Lipset, S. M., 86
Liré, 246, 313, 319
Livre, value of, 25n
Lockroy, É., 8
Loire-Inférieure, Department of, 27, 258, 339;
    refusal of oath in, 241; Terror in, 323
Loire River, valley of, 28, 31–32, 34, 39, 141.
    See also Val-Saumurois
Loir River, valley of, 28
Loménie de Brienne, É. de, 162
Loomis, C. P., 58
Lorient, 27
Lucas de la Championnière, M., 8
Luçon, 30, 31
Luigné, 319

Machecoul, 4, 312, 314; District of, 303
McManners, J., 229
Maine, 5, 14, 27, 135
Maine-et-Loire, Department of, 27, 258, 308; districts of, 41–42; formation of, 170–171; enlistments, 189; and Civil Constitution, 237, 241, 246, 247, 249, 253, 257; and political reorganization of Revolution, 277; Terror in, 323
Maisonneuve, P., 116
Malleray, H. de, 305, 337
Marboeuf, L., 141
Marchegay, P., 150
Marczewski, J., 21, 22
Marion, M., 203, 212
Market: expansion of in eighteenth century, 17–18, 21; and urban-rural contacts, 55, 62–63; involvement and marriage, 92–93; insulation from in Mauges, 125–126
Marriage: patterns of, compared, 88–90; local endogamy, 89–90; measure of exogamy of, 91–93; class endogamy, 93–94; Intermarriage Index used in measuring patterns of, 94–96; and residential pattern, 98
Martigné, 261, 319
Martineau (family) of St. Georges-du-Puy-de-la-Garde, 242, 293, 299–303
Marx, K., 21, 61, 80, 161, 199, 203
Mathiez, A., 6, 20, 233
Mauges: described, 39; cities of, 42–53 *passim;* economy of, 48–49, 79, 114–115, 131, 149–150; conflicts among groups, 53–57, 130–132, 143, 157–158; land ownership and exchange in, 54–55, 74–75, 119–120, 123–124, 201; community patterns, 65, 83, 87, 114–115, 140–141; classes and roles in, 66–67, 71–72, 80–81, 211–212; post-Revolutionary politics, 102, 154–155; church and religion in, 102–103, 108–109, 239, 243; political organization, 150, 151–153, 272–273; response to Revolution, 156, 175, 177–186, 188–189, 193–194, 202, 222
Maulèvrier, 42, 49, 178, 216, 220, 222, 231, 237, 244–245, 253, 280, 282, 306
Mayenne, 5, 27
Melay, 105, 165, 208, 209, 215, 242, 243, 277, 287, 291, 292, 294, 295, 297, 302, 308
Mendicity, Committee on, 78, 218
Menil, G. de, 109, 177
Mercerolle, J., 220
Merle, L., 72n, 73n, 77, 78, 84n, 122, 123, 125n, 126, 127–128
Merton, R. K., 59
Métairie, 72n; example of, 83–84; origin of,

84–85n; described, 121, 123; lease of, 123–124; cash surplus of tenant, 126
Meyer, J., 30, 135
Meynier, A., 84n
Michelet, J., 212, 309
Millet, P.-A., 116, 125
Mills, C. W., 18, 62, 112
Miner, H., 59
Mogev, J. M., 84n
Mols, R., 23, 24n
Moncoutant, 306
Montaigu, 4, 30, 282, 312; District of, 222, 303
Montfaucon, 42, 49, 78, 218, 219, 221, 285
Montfort, G. de, 103
Montiersneuf, abbey of, 109
Montilliers, 71, 319
Montjean, 39, 42, 47, 206, 222, 283, 315
Montreuil-Bellay, 30, 42, 46, 51, 79, 132, 149–150, 171, 176, 187, 194, 206, 215, 224, 320; District of, 163
Montrevault, 42, 47, 49, 78, 132, 171, 190, 219, 243
Mortagne-sur-Sèvre, 4
Mozé, 78, 224, 260, 274, 283
MRP (political party), 156
Mulotins, 253–254, 257, 283
Mumford, L., 17, 18, 44
Murphey, R., 19
Musset, R., 35, 119, 135, 136

Nantes, 4, 26, 27, 30, 32, 36, 50, 51, 133, 338
Narbonne, J., 86
National Assembly: attempts to deal with situation in West, 247, 258, 333, 336, 337; eligibility requirements, 267
National Guard, 254, 255, 258, 261–262, 283–284, 286, 290, 293, 309; formation of, 187–189; support of Constitutionals, 249, 253; and Refractories, 257; registration, 269–270, 274; in Les Gardes, 299–300
Neighborhood: as system of social relationships, 82; physical layout of, 83–88
Neuvy, 209–210, 214, 256, 308, 312
Newspapers and pamphlets, patriotic, 167
Niort, 31, 35, 36, 171, 338
Noble(s), 346; land ownership and control by, 69–70, 75–77, 119–120; absentee, 76–77; marriage patterns of, 90n; relations with other classes, 110–111, 126–127, 130–131, 144; fief described, 121–124; political role, 149, 153, 154; mentioned in Grievances, 181–183; in Revolution, 196–197; in counter-revolution, 326–330
Normandy, 5, 14, 27, 33, 217

Notre-Dame d'Alençon, 319
Nuaillé, 165
Nueil-sous-Passavant, 171, 319

Oath, civic, 248, 269, 275
Occupations in southern Anjou: 66–72, 91; and marriage patterns, 90–91; estimates of distribution, 345–347; classification of, 348–349
Overurbanization, 24

Paret, P., 305, 329
Paris, 18, 33, 37, 208; concentration of urban population in, 23; predominance of, 24, 159–160
Parish: as system of social relationships, 82; defined, 100; organization of, 100–103; change in Revolution, 261–262
Park, R. E., 83
Parsons, T., 82n
Parthenay, 30, 33, 171
Parties: "Aristocrats," 227, 247 270, 274–277 passim, 287–290; "Patriots," 227, 232, 237, 239, 242, 245, 247–248, 258, 270, 274–277 passim, 283–287, 317, 320–321; division into, 232, 245–246, 247, 256–257, 261–262, 268, 270, 272–273, 274–279, 282–283, 289–290, 305–306; conflict in counterrevolution, 318, 320
Passavant, 171
"Patriots," party of counterrevolution, see Parties
Peasants, 346; opposition to Revolution of, 7, 168; society of, 19; relationship with other classes of, 71, 98, 130–132, 143; kinds of, in southern Anjou, 71–72; wealth of, 72–73; marriage patterns of, 90–91, 92; political activity of, 271–272, 281–282; participants in counterrevolution, 326–330
Pitt-Rivers, J., 59
Poirier, L., 84
Poirier de Beauvais, B., 8
Poitiers, 30, 36
Poitou, 27, 33
Political lag, 20–21
Ponts-de-Cé, 42, 46, 194, 219
Population: urban, 22–23, 24; density, by district, 86
Port, C., 56, 77–78, 127, 140, 160, 163, 168, 170, 175, 176, 181, 186, 198, 202, 212, 214, 215, 219–220, 228, 241, 244n, 248, 275, 276, 281, 283, 285, 286, 305, 306, 311
Poverty, in southern Anjou, 77–79, 218–221, 234–235

Prévost, J.-C., 25, 291, 293, 297
Proust, A., 229
Provincial: assemblies, 2, 152, 162; Estates, 122; administration, 148, 170–172

Querau-Lamerie, E., 105n, 239, 259, 346

Rablay, 166, 319
Raimbault, L., 109, 169, 188
Ranger, J., 102, 156
Raveau, P., 36
Réau de la Gaignonnière, J. de, 162
Redfield, R., 19, 59, 60
Rees, A. D., 84n
Reinhard, M., 21, 23n, 24, 26
Reiss, A. J., Jr., 58
Religion: and counterrevolution, 8–9, 101–102; issue of baptisms, 253; growth of pilgrimages, 254–255. See also Church; Clergy
Rennes, 26
Rents: typical, of métairie, 123–124; changes in, 125, 128–130
Revolution, French, of 1789: effects in West, 13, 160–161, 167–168, 195–198, 263–279; current theory of, 20; religious reforms, 197, 233, 261–262; Terror, 322, 323; economic changes, 200–202, 213–215
Rhône River, valley of, 37
Roads and communications, 25, 30, 62–63, 140–141
Rochefort-sur-Loire, 177, 208, 224, 290
Romain, M. de, 8
Rougé, Comte de, 50
Roupnel, G., 55
Roussay, 221
Royalism, 7–8, 154–155
Rudé, G., 215
Rural community: organization, 11; units of, 53, 55–56; defined, 58; classes in, 58, 66–73; elite roles in, 59–60; "folk-urban continuum," 59–60; urbanization and, 61–64

Sables d'Olonne, 27, 306
Sagnac, P., 166, 200, 231
St. Aubin-de-Baubigné, 235, 237, 245
St. Aubin-de-Luigné, 194, 224, 250–251, 260, 268, 290
St. Brieuc, 28
St. Christophe-du-Ligneron, 226
St. Crespin, 253, 306
Ste. Christine, 312
Ste. Foy, 256, 290
St. Florent, District of, 41–42, 44, 79, 231, 255, 272, 303, 317; population characteristics, 68–

69, 86; marriage patterns in, 89–90; clergy of, 105, 108, 259; economy of, 115, 218, 219; Grievances in, 178, 182, 184; enlistments in, 190; church property sales in, 206–207; disfranchised voters, 266; counterrevolutionaries of, 327

St. Florent-le-Vieil, 4, 39, 42, 47, 49, 55, 171, 178, 188, 190, 207, 222, 313, 314, 315; abbey of, 46, 54, 108

St. Georges-Châtelaison, 314, 319

St. Georges-des-Sept-Voies, 194

St. Georges-du-Puy-de-la-Garde, 55, 83, 165, 222, 253, 282, 287, 291, 292, 296–297, 320; events of Revolution in, 298–303

St. Hilaire-du-Bois, 165, 251

St. Jean-des-Monts, 308

St. Lambert-du-Lattay, 109, 168, 177, 188, 223, 250, 277, 285, 290, 317, 320, 324

St. Laurent-de-la-Plaine, 139, 219, 235, 254–255, 324, 326

St. Laurent-des-Autels, 87

St. Laurent-sur-Sèvre, 103, 283

St. Léger, 56, 202

St. Lezin d'Aubance, 165, 286–287

St. Macaire-en-Mauges, 105, 106, 155, 165, 188, 209, 218, 234–235, 283, 320, 321

St. Maixent, 171

St. Malo, 26, 27, 28, 31, 35

St. Martin-de-Beaupréau, 282

St. Pierre-de-Chemillé, 208, 281, 291, 292, 293, 297, 298, 316–317, 319, 320

St. Pierre-de-Cholet, 66–67

St. Quentin-en-Mauges, 85, 250

St. Rémy-en-Mauges, 215

St. Sauveur-de-Landemont, 223, 252, 268, 274, 282, 312

Sanders, I. T., 58, 60

Sarthe, Department of, 27, 32, 54, 203, 265–266, 310; weavers and Chouannerie in, 223

Saulgé-l'Hôpital, 260, 319

Saumur, 4, 32, 34, 42, 46, 47, 57, 132, 156, 171, 187, 190, 194, 206, 210, 215, 224, 228, 315, 320, 338

Saumur, District of, 41–42, 44–47, 79, 267–268; population density, 86; marriage patterns in, 89–90; clergy of, 105, 108, 238, 260; enlistments in, 190; church property sales in, 206, 210–211; poverty in, 218; disfranchised voters, 266

Saumurois: described, 39. See also Val-Saumurois

Sausseau, P., 290

Savary, J.-J.-M., 8, 102, 244n, 322, 332

Savenay, 5

Schmidt, C., 214

Sée, H., 21, 73n, 120, 125, 200, 201

Seebohm, F., 84n

Seignobos, C., 6

Sévestre, E., 241

Sèvre Niortaise River, valley of, 28

Sicard, A., 233

Siegel, A., 61

Siegfried, A., 40, 73, 73n, 86, 101, 110, 112, 119, 154, 155, 156

Singer, M., 19

Sirich, J. B., 338

Sjoberg, G., 19

Slave trade, 30, 50, 133

Smith, A., 17

Soboul, A., 58, 200, 259

Spal, J., 150, 151

Steward, J., 64

Stofflet, J.-N., 4, 281, 315

Sutton, F. X., 60, 153

Sutton, W. A., 58

Sykes, G., 59

Taine, H., 161

Tanguy, J., 36

Taxes: and urbanization, 62–63; protests against, 166, 169–170, 179–180

Tenant farm, see Métairie

Textile industry and commerce, 35–36, 49, 132–140; source of raw material, 33–34, 116, 118, 126; domestic system in, 51, 136–137; urban-rural contact in, 55; production figures of, 133–135, 350–351; organization of, 139–140; decline in, 215–222, 292

Third Estate, in provincial assemblies, 162

Thouarcé, 73, 149, 166, 194, 319

Thouars, 30, 171

Thubert, notary of Chemillé, 165, 208, 291–292, 297, 298

Thubert, Constitutional curé of Melay, 242, 294

Tiffauges, 4

Tigné, 223. 243, 251, 277, 285, 290, 308, 314

Tilliers, 105, 222, 245, 253, 280, 306

Tilly, C., 7, 124–125n, 126, 157, 170, 175, 227, 239, 260, 282, 291

Tithes, 105–108 passim

Tocqueville, A. de, 22, 24, 159, 160

Tourlandry, 222, 302

Tours, 30, 36; Generality of, 34

Trémentines, 218, 219, 222, 248–249, 302, 309

Trémont, 314, 319

Trocmé, E., 36

Trow, M. A., 86

Tuetey, A., 78, 218

Turreau, L. M., 338

United States, 24
Urbanization: defined and discussed, 10–12,
16–17; in rural areas, 18, 62–63, 63–65; uneven permeation of society, 18–20, 57; "percent urban" population, 44–45; effects of on
elite, 64–65, 112; political results of, 146–
147; economic effects of, 199
Urban-rural contact, 53–57, 61–62, 158, 203,
264
Uzureau, F., 8, 40, 46, 49, 52, 56, 103, 115, 126,
132, 171, 215, 239, 244n, 256, 257, 267, 268,
270, 328

Val: described, 39. *See also* Val-Saumurois
Val-Saumurois: economy of, 31–34, 40–41, 45–
47, 114, 115–116, 126, 131–132, 137, 139,
213–214; described, 39; cities of, 42–48
passim, 57; community patterns, 65, 83, 85–
87, 140–141; classes and roles in, 66–67, 71–
72, 80–81, 154, 211–212; land ownership in,
73, 74–75, 120; poverty in, 79; conflicts
among groups, 130–132, 143, 224; politics
in, 150, 151–153, 156, 172, 272–273; Grievances, 170, 177–180, 183; response to Revolution, 188, 201, 239, 260–261, 283, 303–304,
311; counterrevolution in, 224–225
Varades, 313
Varennes-sous-Montsoreau, 214
Vauchrétien, 111, 224, 225, 261
Vaudelenay, 210, 243
Vendée, Department of, 27, 176, 223, 258; enlistments, 189; response to Revolution, 222,
241, 262, 277; Terror in, 323
Vendée counterrevolution, *see* Counterrevolution

Vezins, 165, 188, 189, 194, 208, 219, 283, 314,
319
Vidal de la Blache, P., 83, 86, 87
Vidich, A., 58, 149
Vihiers, 4, 42, 49, 132, 133, 165, 188, 216, 218,
220, 283, 311, 315, 319, 320
Vihiers, District of, 41–42, 44, 319, 328; land
ownership in, 74–75; population density of,
86; marriage patterns in, 89–90; religion and
clergy in, 102, 105, 108, 239, 259; Grievances
in, 178, 182, 184, 239; enlistments in, 190;
church property sales in, 206, 207; counterrevolutionaries of, 327
Village, 53; dwellers, 70, 86–87; in Val-
Saumurois, 85–86
Villedieu-la Blouère, 55, 221, 282
Volney, C. de, 164

Wagret, P., 40, 85, 116, 213
Walsh de Serrant, Count, 164, 178, 181–183
Walter, G., 6, 239, 244n, 338
Warner, L., 99
Weber, M., 44, 62, 80, 112
West, French: geography of, 26–29; cities of,
29–30; monasteries in, 30; agriculture in,
31–34; rural industry in, 35–36; contrasts
in, 36–37
White Terror of 1795, 37
Whiting, A., 58
Winegrowing, *see* Agriculture
Wirth, L., 44, 58
Wolf, E., 19, 58, 59, 60, 62
Wylie, Laurence, 102, 157

Yzernay, 273

DATE DUE

WITHDRAWN

DEMCO 38-296